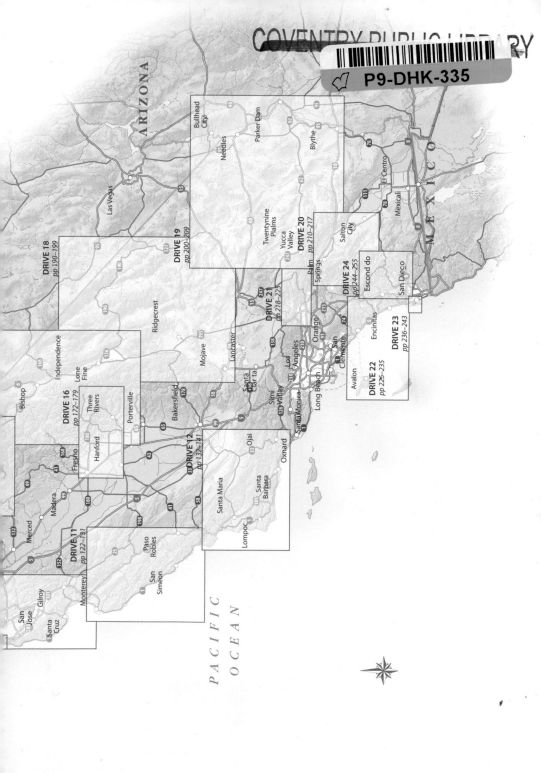

ARIZONA

MEXICO

PACIFIC OCEAN

Las Vegas

Bullhead City

Needles

Parker Dam

Blythe

El Centro

Mexicali

San Diego

Escondido

Encinitas

San Clemente

Orange

Los Angeles

Long Beach

Santa Monica

Avalon

Salton City

Palm Springs

Twentynine Palms

Yucca Valley

Ridgecrest

Mojave

Lancaster

Santa Clarita

Simi Valley

Ojai

Oxnard

Santa Barbara

Lompoc

Santa Maria

Independence

Lone Pine

Bishop

Three Rivers

Porterville

Bakersfield

Hanford

Fresno

Madera

Merced

Gilroy

San Jose

Santa Cruz

Monterey

Paso Robles

San Simeon

EYEWITNESS TRAVEL

BACK ROADS
CALIFORNIA

EYEWITNESS TRAVEL

BACK ROADS
CALIFORNIA

CONTRIBUTORS:

CHRISTOPHER P. BAKER, LEE FOSTER

LONDON, NEW YORK,
MELBOURNE, MUNICH AND DELHI
www.dk.com

MANAGING EDITOR
MadhuMadhavi Singh

EDITORIAL MANAGER
Sheeba Bhatnagar

DESIGN MANAGER Mathew Kurien

PROJECT EDITOR Divya Chowfin

PROJECT DESIGNER Namrata
Adhwaryu

DESIGNER Rupanki Arora Kaushik

PICTURE RESEARCH MANAGER
Taiyaba Khatoon

PICTURE RESEARCHERS Lokesh Bisht,
Nikhil Verma

SENIOR DTP DESIGNER
Azeem Siddiqui

SENIOR CARTOGRAHIC MANAGER
Uma Bhattacharya

CARTOGRAPHER
Subhashree Bharati

ILLUSTRATOR
Arun Pottirayil

Printed and bound by South China
Printing Co. Ltd., China

12 13 14 15 10 9 8 7 6 5 4 3 2 1

First published in Great Britain in 2013 by Dorling
Kindersley Limited, 80 Strand, London
WC2R 0RL, A Penguin Company

**Copyright 2013 © Dorling
Kindersley Limited, London**

A CIP catalogue record is available from the
Library of Congress.

ISBN 978 0 7566 7494 6

Front cover: Highway 1 along the Pacific
coastline, Big Sur

MIX
Paper from
responsible sources
FSC™ C018179
www.fsc.org

CONTENTS

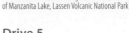

Above Lassen Peak towering over the forested shores
of Manzanita Lake, Lassen Volcanic National Park

Below "Jumping cholla" cacti in the Cholla Cactus
Garden, Joshua Tree National Park

Below The landmark single-arch Bixby Bridge
along the Big Sur coast

Above Tractor ride through the vineyards at Benziger Winery in Glen Ellen, Sonoma County

Above Waves gently lapping the sands at the scenic La Jolla Cove, La Jolla

Below The massive General Sherman Tree in the Giant Forest, Sequoia National Park

Below Gingerbread trimmed Firehouse Number 1 Museum, Nevada City

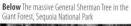

Title page Highway through Death Valley National Park
Half-title page A typical country house in Navarro

About this Book

The 24 drives in this book capture the fantastic diversity of California, from the snow-capped mountains and fog-shrouded redwood forests of the north to the deserts and sun-baked beaches of the south. The dramatic scenery changes with regularity, while the urban settings range from the sleepy 19th-century Gold Rush-era towns of the Sierra foothills to vibrant cities such as Los Angeles and San Francisco. With its superb highway system, California is tailormade for driving tours, whether it is a sojourn through the vineyards of Napa Valley from San Francisco, exploring the Mojave Desert when the spring wildflowers bloom, touring along the dramatic Mendocino coastline, or navigating the twisty mountain roads of Yosemite National Park. These drives do not shun the region's lesser-known regions, but introduce you to some of the most spectacular hidden corners of the state, allowing visitors to explore facets of California that many never experience.

Getting Started

The front section of the guide provides all the practical information needed to plan and enjoy a driving holiday in California. It includes an overview of when to go and how to get there, advice on hiring a vehicle and details of any documentation required. In-depth motoring advice ranges from driving rules to road conditions, from buying fuel to breakdown or accident procedures – the background knowledge that makes a driving trip stress-free. There is also information on money, communications, opening hours, health and safety, as well as advice on accommodation and dining options, to ensure that you experience the very best of California's hospitality.

The Drives

The main section of the guide is divided into 24 scenic drives, ranging in duration from one to five days. All the tours can be undertaken in a standard vehicle, and no special driving skills are required, although a few tours include side-trips along sections of unpaved road where a 4WD vehicle is recommended. The drives encompass every region of the state, from Southern California's rugged Mojave Desert to Northern California's Redwood Empire, and from the alpine spectacle of the Sierra Nevada to the beaches and craggy cliffs of the Pacific Coast.

Each drive begins with a list of highlights and a mapped itinerary. There is advice on the best time of year to do the drive, road conditions, market days, and major festival dates. The tour pages contain descriptions of each stop on the route, linked by clear driving instructions. Side panels highlight information on the most authentic places to stay and eat. Tinted boxes feature background information and interesting anecdotes that relate to the specific drive. Each drive features at least one mapped town or countryside walking tour or hike, designed to take a maximum of three hours at a gentle pace, with stops along the way. The tours are flexible: some can be linked to create a longer driving holiday; or can be experienced as segments and dipped into as day trips.

Using the Sheet Map

A pull-out road map of the region is supplied at the back of the guide. This map contains all the information you need to drive around California and navigate between the different tours. All motorways, major roads, ferry ports, and airports are clearly identified. A comprehensive index will allow you to locate sights quickly and easily, and a handy distance chart will enable you to gauge the distances between the major cities. All these features make the pull-out map a great addition to the individual drive-itinerary maps within the book.

Top left Sprawling vineyard in Anderson Valley **Top right** Windswept South Beach, Point Reyes National Seashore **Center left** Lush pastures near Etna **Center right** Picnic tables at Armstrong Redwoods State Natural Reserve **Bottom left** Colored cliffs in Rock Canyon State Park **Bottom right** Scotty's Castle in Death Valley

Above Driving on a winding road through Owens Valley

Introducing California

With a kaleidoscopic array of terrains, including over 1,200 miles (1,930 km) of coastline, and elevations that range from 282 ft (86 m) below sea level to 14,505 ft (4,421 m) atop the highest peak in Continental USA, California is a region of superlatives. The coast highway unfurls past surfing beaches, leaps the headlands of Big Sur, and sidles beneath towering redwood trees often shrouded in fog. Inland, the wine regions and Gold Rush-era towns lend themselves to a lazy pace. The wild Shasta-Cascade region is a realm of crystal-clear streams and volcanic peaks, while the glacier-carved canyons of Yosemite and Sequoia National Parks are breathtaking in their majestic grandeur. In addition to a myriad of natural wonders, there are cosmopolitan cities full of excellent restaurants and world-class museums. Away from the well-maintained major highways, California's countryside is laced with scenic back roads waiting to be discovered.

When to Go

Each of the drives suggests the best time of year to make the trip, whether it is because the scenery is at its most spectacular or the weather is at its best. With a huge span of latitudes and elevations, climates vary markedly across the state, with many extremes. The southern deserts invite exploration in winter and, especially, in spring, when wildflowers bloom; summer months are brutally hot. Winter also offers skiing in the Sierra Nevada and Shasta-Cascade region. Most of California basks in sunshine during summer – thick fogs, however, can shroud the northern and central coast in July and August, when beach-crazy Southern Californians work on their tans. Early summer snowmelt feeds the waterfalls of Yosemite National Park, and white-water rafting is at its best; by late-summer the cascades can even dry up. Fall is the best time to experience fall colors (September to November, depending on the region), especially in the wine regions and mountain foothills, when vines and trees turn gold and crimson.

In July and August, San Francisco may be cold when shrouded in morning fog, which can extend up and down the coast, while the southeast deserts, especially Death Valley, can be extremely hot. In winter, even Southern California's mountain roads can be icy and snowbound, and tire chains may be required. Many high-elevation roads can be closed for weeks or even months on end – the High Sierra passes, such as the Tioga Road through Yosemite National Park, usually remain closed Nov–May (or longer), depending on snow levels.

Festivals and Events

California hosts a plethora of fairs, concerts, sporting events, festivals, and special events including folk festivals and agricultural fairs. Art and music festivals fill the annual calendar – in any month, a major event is hosted somewhere within the state, while December is synonymous with Christmas celebrations. The state owes much of its cultural appeal to a dynamic ethnic mix – source for a rich trove of festivals, often linked to the cultural heritage of the host town or region.

Public Holidays
New Year's Day (Jan 1)
Martin Luther King Jr.'s Birthday (3rd Mon in Jan)
Presidents' Day (3rd Mon in Feb)
George Washington's Birthday (Feb 22)
Memorial Day (May 31)
Independence Day (Jul 4)
Labor Day (1st Mon in Sep)
Columbus Day (2nd Mon in Oct)
Veterans Day (Nov 11)
Thanksgiving Day (4th Thu in Nov)
Christmas Day (Dec 25)

Times to Avoid

Summer weather may be the best overall, but accommodations can be booked up well in advance in popular places, as many US and international visitors vacation then.

Left Scenic Coast Highway 1, near Elk **Right** Folk dancing during Danish Days festival, Solvang

Getting to California

A popular destination, California is well connected to the rest of the world. The three largest cities – Los Angeles, San Diego, and San Francisco – have major international airports, and several other cities receive flights from abroad. If flying in from Europe or across the Pacific, be prepared to endure jet lag for the first couple of days in the US, for which reason it may be wise to wait a day or two before renting a car. California is connected to neighboring states by interstate highways and there are domestic flights to most major cities. Car rental services are well-established at the major airports, and in every city throughout the state.

Above Greyhound, North America's most popular intercity bus service

Arriving by Air

Traveling to California by air and then renting a pre-booked car is certainly the best option for visitors from overseas. Flights to the US can be expensive, especially in mid-summer, which is the peak season, and around holidays, such as Thanksgiving and Christmas. It is also cheaper to travel on weekdays rather than on weekends. Off-peak or "shoulder" season fares are much more reasonable. For those who can fly at short notice and are flexible about which airport they arrive at, it is a good idea to check with online discount travel agencies, as major airlines often release unsold seats at the last minute.

Dozens of international airlines serve California, including **United Airlines**, which uses San Francisco as a major hub, and flies to the major airports from leading cities in Europe, Asia, Australasia, and South America. **American Airlines** and **Delta Airlines** also operate daily flights from London, Paris, and other major cities on all four continents.

Other key operators with direct flights from the United Kingdom are **British Airways** and **Virgin Atlantic**. Most of the big European airlines fly to California from major continental cities, such as Amsterdam, Berlin, Madrid, Paris, and Rome. These include **Air France**, **Alitalia**, **KLM**, and **Lufthansa**. Many flights from Europe are routed via Miami, New York, or other major US gateways. There are also a number of smaller carriers, many of them charters, that often offer cheaper fares than the large scheduled airlines.

From Australia and New Zealand, **Qantas** and **Air New Zealand** fly nonstop to San Francisco and Los Angeles, and major Asian carriers such as **Japan Air Lines**, **Cathay Pacific**, **Singapore Airlines**, and **Thai Airways** have flights from key Asian gateways. **South African Airways** flies to New York from Johannesburg. Most flights from Asia, Australasia, and South Africa last around 14 hours. Consider a stopover in Hawaii (if crossing the Pacific) or New York (from South Africa). Also consider

arranging flights so that they account for international time differences. Try and stay awake during the day and sleep at nighttime so that your body can sync with the local time as soon as possible.

Domestic flights to and within California are frequent, and it is fairly easy to add a domestic connection to your flight plans. For example, it only takes one hour to fly between Los Angeles and San Francisco. Within California, **Southwest Airlines** offers good fares and services to all major cities. Before making any bookings, it is best to check what the luggage allowance is, as it can be lower on domestic flights and excess baggage fees may apply. Also check to see if international and domestic flights use different terminals, and make sure you have enough time for connections, especially if you have to clear immigration and customs lines for check-in. Security processing can also take a considerably long time. Visitors are given immigration and customs declarations to fill out

SAN FRANCISCO INTERNATIONAL

before they arrive in California. Check the **US Customs and Border Protection** website for prohibited and restricted items, especially if carrying food. Food items constitute a potential biological hazard to California's agricultural industry, and fresh fruit and vegetables are among banned items. Customs officials routinely use sniffer dogs around the baggage halls. Always fill out the customs form truthfully, and declare anything you are uncertain about rather than risk a problem. Remember to discard uneaten travel snacks before landing.

California Airports
California's most important airports are **Los Angeles International Airport** (also called Tom Bradley Airport) and **San Francisco International Airport**, from where connecting flights can be made to other California cities. If coming from outside the US, visitors are most likely to arrive at one of these major airports. **Oakland International Airport**, **San Jose International Airport**, both **Ontario International Airport** and **John Wayne International Airport**, near Los Angeles, and **San Diego International Airport**, also receive international flights, while **Palm Springs International Airport** handles flights from Canada and Mexico. Most other airports handle only domestic flights.

All the main airports have information booths that help with any enquiries. Visitors will also find car rental kiosks, currency exchange facilities, and shuttle bus services at the airports.

Arriving by Rail
Long-distance trains operated by **Amtrak**, America's national railway company, connect California to cities throughout the US. The "California Zephyr" connects Chicago and Denver to San Francisco; the "Southwest Chief" operates from Chicago to Los Angeles via Albuquerque, while the "Texas Eagle" links Chicago and Los Angeles via St. Louis and Dallas; the "Coast Starlight" runs between Seattle and Los Angeles via San Francisco; and the "Sunset Limited" links New Orleans and Los Angeles via San Antonio. Amtrak Thruway buses provide connections to more than 90 destinations throughout the state.

Arriving by Bus
Greyhound, North America's largest intercity bus company, serves California from every neighboring state and across the US. Within California, it has stations in more than 100 cities and towns. Costs are usually much cheaper than flying, and modern air-conditioned buses are comfortable, with reclining seats and even Wi-Fi. Most long-distance journeys from out of state include night travel. For example, a journey from New York takes at least three days and may involve changing buses. Be aware that many bus stations are in unsavory parts of cities, and the buses are often overbooked. However, traveling by bus offers the chance to see many parts of the country that visitors would otherwise miss if flying.

Below far left San Francisco International Airport **Below left** Checking in at San Francisco International Airport **Below** Amtrak at San Diego

Practical Information

An important tourist destination, California is well-equipped to cater for international visitors. Most towns have visitor information centers that offer guidance on activities, attractions, accommodations, and restaurants. Public services operate smoothly and the highway system is extensive and well-maintained. The health system is excellent, the communication networks are world-class, and all banks have conveniently located ATMs. California has superb accommodations across the budget spectrum, and dining options from around the globe.

Above Sign for Del Mar Vitamin Center pharmacy at San Clemente

Passports and Visas

All visitors to the US are required to have a passport valid for at least six months beyond the intended duration of their stay. All visitors other than citizens of Canada and Bermuda need a pre-arranged visa to enter the country; tourists need a B-2 visa, although citizens of the UK and most European countries, Australia, New Zealand, and some Asian countries, are eligible for the Visa Waiver Program; waivers can be obtained online for a fee via the **Electronic System for Travel Authorization** (ESTA) website as late as the date of departure. Tourist visas are valid for six months, although immigration officials have the discretion to determine the maximum length of your stay and will write this into your passport upon arrival. No paperwork is required for entry with ESTA – the visa waiver is stored electronically.

Travel Insurance

All travelers are strongly advised to purchase travel insurance that covers a broad range of emergencies. It is especially important to have

adequate medical coverage, as health services can be very expensive in California. Note that dental emergencies are usually not covered under standard travel insurance, so make sure that your insurance policy covers this. Visitors not covered by these arrangements can face hefty bills for medical treatment.

Most travel insurance policies will cover for loss or theft of luggage and other property as well as personal accident and repatriation in case of a serious medical condition. Delayed or cancelled flights are generally covered, as are the expenses incurred in such cases. Policies also cover lost luggage, allowing you to replace missing items (such as clothes and toiletries) immediately. Note that if you wish to undertake activities and sports considered dangerous by the insurer, this will usually require a different insurance policy or an extra premium to the normal policy.

Read the terms and conditions carefully because coverage, excess amounts, exclusions, and deductibles vary widely. Also check to see what kind of cover, if any, is offered under

your home insurance policy. Some credit card companies also offer limited travel insurance benefits if you use your card to book your trip or to hire a rental car.

Health and Safety

California poses no serious health hazards for travelers and no vaccinations are required before entering the country. California's medical services are generally world-class, and most hospitals and clinics are private and fee-based. In addition, almost every city also has public facilities serving low-income and uninsured patients, but where emergency rooms are often crowded, waiting times can be very long. Hotels can call a doctor to visit your hotel room if needed. Dial 911 for ambulance assistance.

Pharmacies are found in all urban centers, as well as in large supermarkets. These sell a wide range of over-the-counter medicines, although the brand names of familiar items may be different, and some medicines sold over the counter at home may be available only by prescription in the US. Visitors who

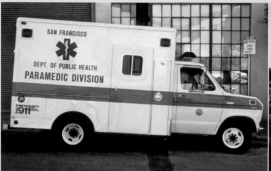

Above A public ambulance **Above right** Warning sign at the Carpinteria State Beach

need prescribed medication should ensure that they carry enough to cover their stay.

Hikers should watch out for rattlesnakes; give them a wide berth. In mountain zones, mountain lions and black bears are common; never leave food lying around.

Personal Security

Although California is relatively safe, most major cities have some dangerous neighborhoods – check with hotel staff about which parts of town should be avoided. As with any country, vigilance in urban zones is needed against pickpockets and petty thieves. Leave passports, jewelry, and expensive items in the hotel safe and keep valuables such as cameras concealed or worn across the chest when walking around. Avoid poorly lit areas and parks at night. Taxis are generally safe, but caution may be needed if using public transport at night. In the event of a serious problem, such as loss of a passport, visitors should approach their **consulate**. Many nations, including the UK, have consulates in Los Angeles and San

Francisco, and can help travelers obtain a new passport, get legal advice, and even provide emergency funds if needed.

Disabled Travelers

California law requires that every public building is accessible to those with disabilities and also has special toilets and other facilities. In addition, hotels, restaurants, most tourist sites, plus cinemas, theaters, and event arenas have wheelchair access, and many state and national parks have trails designed for wheelchairs. Most urban buses, plus trains and inner-city subways, are also equipped to handle wheelchairs. Sidewalks are fitted with ramps, many pedestrian crosswalks have audio signals for the visually impaired, while bank ATMs are fitted with instructions in braille. Disabled people also receive privileges in parking lots. The **Society for Accessible Travel & Hospitality** (SATH) is an excellent resource.

Below far left Warning sign, Big Morongo Canyon Preserve **Below left** Taxi in San Diego's Gaslamp District **Below** Café in Little Italy with wheelchair access, San Diego

DIRECTORY

CONSULATES
Australian Consulate
2029 Century Park E,
Century City,
Los Angeles; 310 229 2300;
www.losangeles.consulate.gov.au

British Consulate
11766 Wilshire Blvd, Suite 1200,
Los Angeles; 310 481 0031;
http://ukinusa.fco.gov.uk

Canadian Consulate
550 S Hope St, Los Angeles;
213 346 2700;
www.canadainternational.gc.ca

Irish Consulate
100 Pine St, Suite 3350,
San Francisco; 415 392 4214;
www.consulateofireland
sanfrancisco.org

South African Consulate
6300 Wilshire Blvd, Suite 600, Los
Angeles; 323 651 0902;
www.link2southafrica.com

VISAS
Electronic System for Travel
Authorization (ESTA)
https://esta.cbp.dhs.gov/

HEALTH
Police, Fire, and Ambulance
911

DISABLED TRAVELERS
Society for Accessible Travel &
Hospitality (SATH)
www.sath.org

Communications

California has well-developed postal and telecommunications services. The state has 25 three-digit area codes followed by a seven-digit local number. Districts covered by multiple area codes require that you dial 1 plus the area code even when calling within the district.

Public telephones are ubiquitous in urban areas, and can usually be found outside major stores and at petrol stations in rural areas. Most accept coins, phonecards, and payment by credit card. Prepaid phonecards issued by major phone service carriers can be purchased at stores and petrol stations. The cost of a local call within the same area code is usually a minimum of 50 cents, and direct calls usually cost less than those made through an operator. Note that hotels charge premium rates for calls.

Check with your domestic network provider if your cellphone will work in the US. A GSM cell may work in most cities, but coverage in rural areas is weak. Consider buying a prepaid SIM card while in California, but these are not as widely available. Of the US carriers, **AT&T** and **T-Mobile** use GSM while **Sprint** and **Verizon** use CDMA. AT&T and Verizon have much stronger coverage than T-Mobile, especially in rural areas. Some CDMA phones now also support GSM networks for international use. If you need to rent a phone while in California, airtime can be expensive.

Internet services are widespread. Most motels and hotels now provide Wi-Fi (and/or broadband cable) in guest rooms, or at least in public lounges; some charge a fee. Airports, bus stations, and many other public facilities are also Wi-Fi enabled, as are many state and national parks, cafés, and restaurants. In urban areas, you will rarely be far from an Internet café.

The US government-run postal service is efficient. All domestic mail is first class and will usually arrive within 1 to 5 days. International airmail will take 4–10 days to Australasia, Canada, or Europe, depending on destination. Priority mail promises faster delivery, and Express Mail promises next-day delivery for domestic mail and within 72 hours to many international destinations.

Banking and Currency

The currency in California is the US dollar ($), which breaks down into 100 cents. It can be difficult to change $50 and $100 denomination notes, especially in rural areas, so change these at banks if needed. Taxi drivers especially need to know in advance if you want to pay with a large denomination note to ensure that they have change.

ATMs are found at virtually every bank and shopping mall, and at many other outlets. MasterCard and Visa credit cards are accepted almost everywhere, and many places also accept American Express, Discovery, and Diners cards. It is a good idea to inform your bank of your travel plans, as they may restrict the use of your credit or debit card for security reasons. Also ask about any bank charges that may be incurred if you use your bank card to withdraw cash abroad; and check whether your debit card will work while in the US. You will need your Personal Identification Number (PIN) to use a

Above American dollar notes and coins of various denominations

debit card; the cost of purchases is debited directly from your account and you will often be asked if you wish to take out extra cash at the point of purchase. This can be handy in remote areas where banks and ATMs may be scarce. Bureaux de change can be found in international airports, but are otherwise few and far between. Many banks will exchange foreign currency for a fee.

Visitor Information

The **California Travel & Tourism Commission** is the state's tourism body, and operates 20 California Welcome Centers strategically located throughout the state. These are well-stocked with brochures, guidebooks, and maps, and offer useful information for state-wide touring. In addition, each major city and region has its own tourism authority, most of which operate visitor information bureaus focused on regional activities and sightseeing. The offices located in smaller towns – often staffed by volunteers – are a wealth of local information, including on road and weather conditions, excursions, and guided tours. Many tourist bureaus

Above Bank of America building in Palm Springs **Above right** Public telephone outside a shop in Fiddletown, Shenandoah Valley

distribute or sell privilege cards or passes for discount access to museums and other attractions.

Smoking
California has banned smoking inside restaurants, bars, offices, federal and public buildings, and on public transport. Smoking is sometimes permitted at outside tables in bars and restaurants. Many hotels also ban smoking, while others permit smoking only in rooms on designated floors.

Opening Hours
The opening hours of shops, offices, and other businesses depend to a great extent on the size of the town. In larger cities and towns, the usual opening hours for shops and businesses are 9am–5pm Mon–Fri and 9am–noon Sat. Supermarkets and many shops often have longer opening hours. Many supermarkets remain open until 10pm, and a few stay open around the clock. Banks are generally open 9am–6pm Mon–Fri and 9am–4pm Sat, although banks in rural areas have more restricted hours. Museums typically open 10am–5pm, but hours can vary widely. Most museums also close on

a particular day, often Monday, so check opening hours before arranging a visit. In recent years, many state parks have closed until future notice due to California's budget crisis.

Electricity
The electrical system in the United States is a standard 110–120 volts AC (alternating current). To operate 220-volt appliances, you will require a voltage converter and an adapter plug with two flat parallel prongs to fit US outlets.

Time
California uses Pacific Standard Time (PST), which is behind Greenwich Mean Time (GMT) by eight hours. Most of the US, including California, begins Daylight Saving Time on the second Sunday in March, when the clocks move forward one hour. It reverts to Standard Time on the first Sunday in November.

Below far left Kohm Yah-Mah-Nee Visitor Center, Lassen Volcanic National Park **Below left** Welcome sign, Laws Railroad Museum & Historical Site **Below** Post office, Pioneer Town **Below right** Sign with opening hours for one of the Shenandoah Valley wineries

Driving in California

Driving is the best way to explore California. The road conditions are excellent, including an extensive freeway system stretching the length and breadth of the state, plus paved roads that reach almost every corner of California. Easy access plus stunning scenery combine to provide a wealth of incredible drives, from gorgeous coastal roads along craggy headlands and through fishing towns to near-deserted back country roads through the rugged Mojave Desert. Driving in California is easy, but to make the most of your trip, it is best to know the basics of driving in the state before setting off.

Above Sign denoting the starting point of a Scenic Route

Insurance and Breakdown Coverage

If traveling in your own vehicle, make sure that your insurance is valid in California. While few auto insurance policies abroad will cover you when driving in California, most policies issued within the US will. Check if the auto insurance on your personal vehicle covers you in the event of an accident while driving a rental car. Sometimes the credit card used to rent a vehicle offers coverage, so check this too, along with any exclusions – in certain circumstances, coverage might not apply or may be limited. If your auto insurance or credit card definitely applies, you can decline the collision damage waiver (CDW), which costs $8–15 per day and covers the cost of damages to the rental car if you are involved in an accident.

Rental companies usually require written proof of liability insurance covering injury to third persons or their property. Valid auto insurance policies provide liability insurance if you injure someone in an accident. Rental companies usually have an arrangement with a breakdown service and will supply a toll-free number to ring for assistance. The **California State Automobile Association** and **Auto Club of Southern California** are excellent resources, and membership with them offers privileges, such as breakdown assistance.

What to Take

Drivers must have a valid driver's license in their possession while driving in California, along with the registration and insurance policy for the vehicle. Foreign driver's licenses are accepted, as are International Driving Permits issued in your home country. However, check with the car rental company in advance, especially if your national driver's license is in a language other than English. National motoring services such as the UK's **Automobile Association** (AA) and **Royal Automobile Club** (RAC) issue International Driving Permits. Global Positioning System (GPS) units can usually be hired from the car rental companies and cost about $12 a day.

The companies also provide warning triangles plus tools for changing a tire. California law requires that children under 6 years or 50 lbs (23 kg) ride in a child seat in the back seat. All rental companies provide these seats.

Road Systems

California has a network of multi-lane freeways (motorways), designated by blue-and-red shields bearing the freeway number. The prefix "I" indicates that a freeway is an "Interstate" that connects California to a neighboring state. Besides the freeways, there are well-maintained "California State Highways" (denoted by an inverted green shield and the prefix "SR," for State Route). Many roads are designated as "County Routes" (denoted by the prefix "S"), "Scenic Routes" (denoted by light blue signs with a flower symbol) or "Historical Routes" (denoted by brown signs). A few recommended sites in this guide are reached by unpaved country roads, but these are usually well-graded and can be driven easily in a family sedan.

Above Driving through Mendocino County **Above right** Death Valley Gateway sign

Speed Limits and Fines

The maximum speed limit on most California highways is 65 mph (105 kph); you may drive 70 mph (113 kph) where posted. Unless otherwise posted, the maximum speed limit is 55 mph (89 kph) on two-lane undivided highways and for vehicles towing trailers. The speed limit in business and residential districts is 25 mph (40 kph), unless otherwise posted. Other speed limit signs are posted based on local conditions. School and construction zones usually have reduced speed zones. The **California Highway Patrol** (CHP) and local police use radar guns to catch speeders, and mobile speed cameras are positioned at strategic locations. Fines can also be incurred for tailgating and parking in prohibited areas. Car rental companies will bill you for any ticket that is sent to them, along with an administrative fee.

Do not drink and drive; drink-driving laws are strictly enforced and mandatory arrest applies to anyone found driving at or above the blood-alcohol level of 0.08 percent (0.04 for commercial vehicles). If you are involved in an accident while over the drink-driving limit, your vehicle insurance will be invalidated.

Rules of the Road

Driving is on the right in California and seat belts must be worn at all times by anyone in a moving vehicle. It is also illegal to use a cell phone while driving, although Bluetooth headsets are allowed. Overtaking to either left or right of another vehicle is usually allowed unless signs indicate otherwise. Drivers must always give way to emergency vehicles; you are required to pull over to the side of the road to let them pass. Unless posted otherwise, you may turn right after stopping at a stop sign or red light; similarly, you may turn left onto a one-way street at a T-junction. Californians are easy-going drivers, and aggressive overtaking is not a norm. On mountain roads, whenever five or more vehicles are behind, slow-moving vehicles are required to pull over when safely possible to permit vehicles behind to overtake. It is a good idea to always maintain a three-second distance behind the vehicle in front of you.

Distances are indicated in miles. Most road signs are internationally understood. Download the free California Driver Handbook from the **California Department of Motor Vehicles** website.

DIRECTORY

INSURANCE AND BREAKDOWN COVERAGE
Auto Club of Southern California
www.calif.aaa.com

California State Automobile Association
www.csaa.com

WHAT TO TAKE
Automobile Association
www.theaa.com

Royal Automobile Club
www.royalautomobileclub.co.uk

SPEED LIMITS AND FINES
California Highway Patrol (CHP)
www.chp.ca.gov

RULES OF THE ROAD
California Department of Motor Vehicles
www. dmv.ca.gov/pubs/pubs.htm

Below far left Driving through scenic Marin County **Below left** Entering Sequoia National Park **Below center** Road name sign **Below** Highway snaking through the Sonoma Coast

Road Conditions

Most roads in California are well surfaced and all are well marked. However, many roads and freeways show signs of wear and tear. The well-established network of freeways allows visitors to travel large distances within a few hours, although the full journey between the Mexican and Oregon borders requires at least 20 hours behind the wheel. Allow sufficient time if you plan on covering long distances.

Traffic conditions vary markedly. Although the inner cities are well signposted, the traffic can be quite challenging for novices. Drivers may be more aggressive than on quieter roads of smaller towns and rural areas. Time your arrival in a major metropolis to avoid the peak rush hour traffic times of 7–9:30am and 4:30–7pm. Most freeways have a "carpool lane", designated with a diamond symbol, which can be used by cars with more than one passenger during rush hours. Traffic reports are broadcast on city radio stations, and highway signs often indicate where to tune in to stations dedicated to local road conditions. When driving in cities, study and memorize a map and the highway numbers beforehand so you are not distracted by multiple signposts and destinations. If you get lost, pull over safely to the side of the road (however, on freeways, stopping is not permitted except for emergencies) and look at the map or ask for directions.

The **California Department of Transport** (Caltrans), the state agency in charge of highway maintenance, provides regular updates on road conditions throughout the state on its website. It is particularly important to check mountain routes in winter, as highways are often closed at short notice due to snow storms. Many routes in this guide include mountain drives along narrow, winding, single-lane highways. Be cautious about overtaking slow-moving vehicles – be patient, as there are almost always sections of broader highway that have overtaking lanes. Mountain roads are also often subject to rock-falls. Deer on the road are the cause of many accidents, so keep your speed down.

Taking a Break

Distances in California can be deceiving and it may take much longer to reach a destination than it appears when studying a map. If you feel tired, pull over and take a break. There are many signposted rest areas along freeways and major roads where you can park the car, stretch your legs, and consult a map. A short stop can go a long way to defeat drowsiness – the cause of many accidents, especially on freeways. Such rest stops usually also have clean toilets. Freeways also have service stations at regular intervals, where you can fuel up with gas as well as coffee and snacks.

The scenic landscape can sometimes be a distraction to drivers, so it is best to stop and admire the views. Parks and areas with nature trails also make good places to take in some fresh air while enjoying California's beauty. Most drivers are less alert at night, especially after midnight, and if planning on driving at night, take more frequent rest stops. If driving through the desert in summer, drink plenty of water, as dehydration often causes drowsiness.

Breakdown and Accident Procedures

If you have a problem on a freeway, you can use one of the telephones located along the highway to call for help. In case of a breakdown or accident, move the car safely off the road, turn on the hazard lights, and put out a warning triangle about 20 yards (18 m) behind the vehicle. Car rental companies normally supply a number to call in case of an emergency or problem with the vehicle. Many freeways are patrolled by Caltrans tow trucks, which provide a free emergency tow.

In case of an accident that involves another vehicle, you will need to exchange the insurance details, name, address, and car registration information with the other parties involved. In case of a serious accident, the police will quickly respond to a call. Circumstances can be confusing at the time of an accident, so do not admit fault, accept liability, or give money to any party. If possible, take down details and contact information

Above Warning to drivers to look out for elk at Prairie Creek Redwoods State Park

Above Taking a break to admire the landscape on the 17-Mile Scenic Drive **Above right** One of the many Visitor Information offices across California

from any independent witnesses. It is also wise to take photographs of any damage to the vehicle, as well as the scene of the accident. If someone is injured, call 911 to summon an ambulance. It is illegal to leave the scene of an accident causing serious damage, injury, or death; a driver who leaves the scene of such an accident will be subject to criminal charges for "felony hit and run." For insurance purposes, report any accident involving vehicle damage to the police and to your car hire company.

Parking

As with most cities, the bigger and busier the city, the harder it is to find a parking space in the city center. Parking restrictions are well sign-posted. Street parking in city centers is usually metered and often limited to one or two hours during business hours. It is a good idea to have plenty of loose change for the meters. In fee-based public parking lots, a parking ticket machine is usually within 50 yards (45 m) of your parking place; display the ticket on the dashboard of your vehicle. If you wish to park for longer periods of time, there are usually multi-story car parks in close proximity; you pay for the number of hours you park, and it is

usually possible to pay by credit card. Some cities have zones which are well signed where parking is only permitted outside peak traffic hours. Many towns designate a day for street cleaning, when no parking is allowed between specified hours; your vehicle will be towed or cited for a fine if you park here during these times. If towed, you will need to contact the local traffic authority or the police to find out where the vehicle pound is and retrieve your car – but only after paying a hefty fine plus towing and storage fees. If your car is towed at night, you may not be able to retrieve it until the next day.

Maps

It is helpful to have a detailed map with you when driving around California. Free tourist maps are available at visitor centers but they are seldom adequate for city driving or for back roads. It is a good idea to buy an up-to-date map of the local area, as well as a detailed **Thomas Bros.** California road atlas. Most service stations sell these. Keep in mind that all major car hire companies now also rent Global Positioning System (GPS) units with their cars, which take away a lot of the stress from navigating in unknown areas.

Below far left Hiking on the Pacific Crest Trail, off Highway 96 **Below left** Well-paved road to Death Valley **Below center** Metered parking, Sausalito **Below** Sign with map, Muir Beach **Below right** Street parking in San Francisco

Buying Gas

California has a good network of gas or service stations selling lead-free gas and diesel. A few gas stations also sell biofuels. Fuel in California is relatively cheap by European standards, and prices can vary widely between companies. In more remote areas, the price can be 50 cents more per gallon than in urban areas. On smaller roads and more remote areas, such as the deserts of the southeast, distances between service stations are sometimes considerable, so make sure that you have enough fuel when traveling through such areas. Almost all fuel stations are self-service; you will pay much more at full-service pumps.

Caravans, Campervans, and Mobile Homes

There are hundreds of well-maintained commercial campsites across the state for caravans and motorhomes; many have swimming pools, shops, and kids' playgrounds. The largest entity is **KOA**, with 35 campsites throughout California. Most national parks, and many state parks, also have campsites, which vary from those equipped with electrical hook-ups plus showers and toilets to basic sites that offer little more than a fire pit. Many are open year-round, while others open seasonally, usually Apr–Oct. California has a great tradition of towing a sedan or 4WD behind a motorhome – the former is used to explore an area, while the parked motorhome serves as a base. Caravans and RVs are subject to the same rules of the road as other vehicles, although additional speed limits often apply for vehicles towing trailers.

Transporting Bicycles, Roof Racks, and Trailers

Bicycle carriers, roof racks, and caravans must be securely attached to the car. You can either fix the bicycle behind the vehicle or on top of the car using special bicycle racks. If using a roof rack, ensure that the weight of the items is evenly distributed. In the case of trailers, make sure that the items inside are properly secured so that nothing moves around in case of sharp braking or defensive driving action.

Motorcycles

California is an excellent destination for motorcycle touring, and all the drives in this guide are also ideal for a motorcycle trip. You can rent many kinds of motorcycles, from a classic Harley-Davidson street bike to the BMW 1200GS adventure tourer, capable of handling rugged off-road conditions. **Eaglerider** rents both Harley-Davidsons and BMWs.

It is mandatory to wear a helmet at all times in California. You should also take additional precautions, including wearing proper riding gear.

Driving with Children

Drivers are legally required to ensure that kids wear seat belts. For kids under 6 years old or 50 pounds (23 kg), an approved child seat must be secured in the back seat. All car rental companies make these available, but remember to request any necessary child seats in advance when making your car hire booking. Smoking in a vehicle with minors (those under 18) present will incur a fine. California has ample sandy beaches, amusement parks and zoos,

Above Sign indicating parking space reserved for disabled drivers

and plenty of open spaces to keep kids amused. However, the main challenge is keeping kids entertained on long distance drives. Obviously, games, MP3, and DVD players are useful devices for when the drives are not at their most interesting. Use your stops wisely, choosing to stop and refuel at places that offer something entertaining for children.

Disabled Drivers

Rental companies are required by law to accommodate disabled drivers. However, you may need to make arrangements well in advance; usually at least 72 hours. All parking lots have designated priority zones for disabled drivers, indicated with a blue sign displaying a wheelchair. Contact the California Department of Motor Vehicles to check if you are eligible for a Disabled Drivers Parking Permit; at the very least a certified medical documentation of impairment will be required.

Car and Campervan Hire

International car hire companies, such as **Avis**, **Budget**, **Dollar**, and **Hertz**, have offices at airports, railway

Above Camping in the Yosemite Valley **Above right** Campervan at the entrance to Death Valley National Park

stations, upscale hotels, and popular tourist destinations. A range of vehicles is available, from subcompact sedans to large 4WDs and passenger vans. Apart from differences in price, consider what vehicle would most suit your journey. Renting a 4WD, for example, might be best if you plan on significant back country driving. Local companies may offer cheaper deals but can be less convenient in terms of picking up and dropping off vehicles at different locations, or in providing substitute vehicles in case of a breakdown. It is necessary to present a passport and a valid driving license to rent a car. Drivers must be over 25 years. Book well in advance during peak season for better rates and a greater chance of securing the type of vehicle you want.

Many visitors to the US choose to rent a campervan for touring the state. The main company that rents out campervans is **CruiseAmerica**, which has four sizes of vehicles sleeping 3 to 7 people. Fitted with toilet, shower, and kitchen, they provide all the comforts of home. However, larger vehicles may not be suited for some mountain areas, where restrictions on vehicle length exist for switchback roads.

Driving in Winter

Mountain areas receive ample snow in winter months – as much as 30 ft (10 m) or more in the High Sierras, where the roads across the mountain passes can be closed to traffic indefinitely. Take snow chains if you plan on winter driving above 4,000 ft (1,220 m) anywhere in the state, or in the far north of California. Snow chains can be bought or rented on key routes that lead to ski resorts. Check the Caltrans *(see p19)* and the CHP *(see p17)* websites for weather conditions and any mandatory snow chain requirements. Carry warm clothes, a blanket, and food and water in case of delays or a breakdown.

Winter storms can bring torrential rains to coastal areas in winter; drive with caution. In high-altitude regions, you may encounter ice. In desert areas, watch for flash-flood warnings. Reduce your speed in adverse conditions, as you will need a longer breaking distance on slippery roads, and poor visibility gives less time to react. Slow down for curves and turns, and keep your actions steady to avoid sliding out of control. If the car skids, take your foot off the accelerator – do not brake – and turn the wheel into the skid until the car corrects itself.

DIRECTORY

BUYING GAS

Biofuels
www.nearbio.com

Fuel prices
www.californiagasprices.com

CARAVANS, CAMPERVANS, AND MOBILE HOMES

KOA
www.koa.com

MOTORCYCLES

Eaglerider
www.eaglerider.com

CAR AND CAMPERVAN HIRE

Avis
www.avis.com

Budget
www.budget.com

CruiseAmerica
www.cruiseamerica.com

Dollar
www.dollar.com

Hertz
www.hertz.com

Below far left Children playing on Muir Beach **Below left** Gas station, Randsburg **Below center** Road closed due to snow, Mammoth Lakes **Below** Exploring San Diego County on motorbikes

Where to Stay

California has a wide variety of accommodations, from charming family-run country B&Bs to stylish boutique hotels and exclusive golf resorts. There are also many simple, no-frills budget motels, so that you are never very far from a place to stay if you don't have a reservation. Campsites abound, and virtually every state or national park in California has at least one campground where it is possible to park your campervan or pitch a tent. Lodging can be expensive in the center of cities. However, smaller towns located in tourist areas often have rooms to rent at reasonable rates; usually, the more popular a place, the higher the rates.

Above Wooden interior of one of the cabins at Pinewood Cove, Trinity Lake, *see p100*

Hotels

Hotels are loosely categorized according to the number of stars awarded for facilities and standard of services. However, the rating is no guide to the more subjective charms of a hotel, such as the style of the decor or the welcoming touches offered. In larger cities, it is not difficult to find accommodation in upscale hotels that are often part of an international chain, such as **Hyatt**, **Hilton**, **Intercontinental**, **Sheraton**, and **Westin**. There are many smaller hotels too, offering good affordable lodgings. These tend to be individually owned, and range from the quirky to avant-garde, such as the **Viceroy**. Several of the deluxe lodgings are resort hotels centered on golf courses; these usually have a spa and gourmet restaurant. Some resort properties in the rugged wilderness double as horse ranches.

The chain motels that populate the main stops on the driving trips include **Best Western**, **Days Inn**, and **Motel 6**. They are reliable and clean, and many have restaurants with a typical American menu.

Guest Houses and B&Bs

Guest houses are usually located in private homes. Most are in quaint, usually historic, properties, often furnished with antiques; many are heritage-listed mansions set in lovely gardens. Located in smaller towns and villages, they are typically cheaper than hotels.

B&Bs may also be the choice lodgings in areas such as Napa Valley, the Gold Country, and Mendocino, and prices reflect their popularity. They usually have only a few bedrooms and offer an intimacy unmatched by hotels.

Camping

Summer is the best time for a camping trip in California, as the weather is at its best, and since many campsites close Nov–Apr. Commercial campsites can be found across the state and often offer better access to the sights and wilderness than the nearest hotel accommodations. Well-equipped, campsites usually have electrical and water hook-ups for RVs, plus shared bathroom and shower facilities. Many also have pools, kids'

playgrounds, and grocery stores. There are often sites for pitching tents, or cabins with self-catering facilities, in addition to sites for motorhomes and caravans. Reserve a spot well in advance if visiting during the busy summer season, especially at popular destinations. In state and national parks, some camping areas are free, but may offer little in the way of facilities – so come well prepared.

Self-catering

Along the country roads, spectacular natural backdrops provide perfect settings for picnics. Supermarkets are well stocked and offer all that travelers will need for an enjoyable outing, such as a great variety of food and camping crockery. Many supermarkets have delicatessens selling pre-prepared salads, sandwiches, and other picnic foodstuffs. Outdoor markets, found in most towns and villages on certain days of the week, are also a good place to pick up fresh, locally grown produce.

Vacation rentals are an increasingly popular alternative to hotel stays. Found in or close to virtually every

Above La Costa Resort and Spa, Carlsbad, *see p232* **Above right** Spacious but cozy lobby at The Ahwahnee, Yosemite Valley, *see p168*

popular sight in California, these private homes are rented out by their owners for short- or long-term stays and offer a true "home-from-home" experience. They range from simple mountain cabins to deluxe villas on the coast, and offer exceptional value for long-term stays compared to the cost of hotels. **Vacation Rental By Owner** (VRBO) lists thousands of properties on its website.

Booking

Reservations for accommodations can be made directly with the hotel by telephone, Internet, letter, or fax. Visitors can also have their travel agent make the arrangements, or use an online booking site such as **Expedia** or **Hotels.com**. A written confirmation may be required to make a reservation, along with a credit card number, and sometimes a deposit, which will be forfeited for non-arrival. Websites such as **Cheap Tickets** offer great rates if you are flexible about travel dates. If traveling during busy periods, it is wise to book months in advance. Keep in mind that mobile phone reception

can be a problem in remote country areas, if you are trying to book while on the road.

Facilities and Pricing

With a range of accommodations on offer, the facilities available mostly reflect the price paid. Air conditioning is standard in most hotels, except in mountain areas. Coffee-making facilities and a TV are also a norm in all price categories. Luxuries such as bathrobes, spas, and tennis courts are more often available in high-end hotels. For simple accommodations, guest-houses are a good option. However, prices are also heavily influenced by other factors, such as location and time of year. In resort areas, prices are highest in summer, while in larger cities, spring and fall are more expensive. Prices may also increase if the city or region is hosting a major event. Weekend rates are usually higher than midweek rates.

Below left Mt Shasta Ranch B&B, *see p90* **Below center** Murphys Historic Hotel, *see p158* **Below** Camping at Yosemite Valley

DIRECTORY

HOTELS

Best Western
www.bestwestern.com

Days Inn
www.daysinn.com

Hilton
www.hilton.com

Hyatt
www.hyatt.com

Intercontinental
www.ichotelsgroup.com

Motel 6
www.motel6.com

Sheraton
www.sheraton.com

Viceroy
www.viceroypalmsprings.com

Westin
www.westin.com

SELF-CATERING

Vacation Rental By Owner (VRBO)
www.vrbo.com

BOOKING

Cheap Tickets
www.cheaptickets.com

Expedia
www.expedia.com

Hotels.com
www.hotels.com

PRICE CATEGORIES

The following price bands are based on one night in a standard double room in high season including tax and service:

inexpensive – under $100
moderate – $100–200
expensive – over $200

Where to Eat

Of all the states in the US, California has perhaps the widest variety of dining options. "California cuisine" typically features dishes made with fresh local ingredients prepared in a range of international styles. In addition, the plethora of Italian, Japanese, Middle Eastern, Mexican, and Thai restaurants reflect the state's cosmopolitan nature. There is also no shortage of classic diners serving all-American breakfasts plus hearty steaks, burgers, and French fries. A locally produced bottle of wine or a regional beer will further enhance the meal.

Above Sign for a coffee shop, San Clemente

Practical Information

Most restaurants are open from noon until 9 or 10pm, but may close for a break mid-afternoon. Many cafés serving breakfast open at 7am. On Sundays, brunch is served in many restaurants until 3pm, and eateries typically close early. Some are also closed on one day during the week, usually Monday. Reservations are recommended for popular city hotels.

The cost of a meal depends on factors such as location and the fame of a chef. While a three-course meal in some restaurants may cost $25, it will be more expensive in an equivalent restaurant in downtown areas of larger cities. In more upscale restaurants expect to pay $75 or more. Alcoholic drinks are priced according to the restaurant's standard. Upscale places usually offer an extensive menu of quality local and international wines.

The bill will include local sales tax, and a service charge of 15 or 20 percent for large parties. Note that a 15 percent tip is a norm. Most restaurants accept credit cards.

California law requires that all new restaurants and those undergoing renovation provide wheelchair access and bathroom facilities, and those that offer parking usually reserve spaces for the disabled.

Restaurants

Restaurants in California range from humble "mom-and-pop" roadside diners to fine-dining establishments, regarded as some of the best in the world. Many restaurants specialize in ethnic dishes, with every type of regional cuisine represented.

The major cities, plus the Napa Valley wine region, have chefs that are highly regarded on the world stage. Meals at these restaurants are often extremely expensive, but some offer great value. Many of these chefs specialize in health-conscious fusion or "California cuisine," marrying their expert use of the techniques and ingredients of European and Asian cooking to local Californian ingredients, such as fresh-picked artichokes, oysters, and dates from the desert. Most such restaurants offer vegetarian dishes. Some of the best chefs are graduates of the Napa Valley's **Culinary Institute of America**, where it is possible to dine and learn from the masters at cooking demonstrations.

Eating at a classic American diner is an experience not to be missed. These restaurants evoke nostalgia for the 1950s and are often retro-fitted with period decor. These typically serve traditional pancake, ham-and-egg, and corned beef hash and hash-brown breakfasts, plus bowls of chili, burgers, hot dogs, and other American lunch staples.

Fast-food outlets are rarely more than a few minutes away. They offer filling, inexpensive food for budget-conscious diners. Chain-owned outlets such as McDonalds, Pizza Hut, and Taco Bell prepare food in bulk and may, therefore, be a little bland. You'll usually find several fast-food restaurants grouped together, typically around service stations.

Cafés and Bars

The term café can evoke a traditional coffee shop specializing in gourmet coffees and teas, or a small homey restaurant favored by locals for breakfast and lunch. There is no shortage of cafés, from the well-known **Starbucks** chain to rivals such as **Peet's** and **Coffee Bean & Tea Leaf**, selling fresh juices, smoothies, pastries, salads, and sandwiches as

Above Store selling a variety of cheeses in Sonoma **Above right** Outdoor seating at the pier in San Clemente

well as coffees, lattes, and teas. Some have comfy sofas and lounge chairs, and even outdoor patios, and most provide free Wi-Fi.

Many bars also serve food. This can range from "beer food" served in home-brew pubs – popular in Northern California – to tapas and even fusion dishes in trendy city lounge bars and specialist wine bars. In smaller towns and rural areas, bars often are limited to down-to-earth establishments that cater to truckers and local workers. Here, meals typically include pizzas, pastas, burgers, and staples.

Picnics and Outdoor BBQs

California is tailor-made for outdoor picnics and BBQs, and on weekends and national holidays, parks are full of families and groups of friends enjoying the outdoors around a BBQ. Most campsites offer BBQ facilities such as grills or fire pits plus picnic tables and benches. Note that in areas inhabited by bears, special regulations exist that mandate how and where foodstuffs and any other scented items may be stored.

Many wineries also cater to picnickers by providing tables and benches on lawns and patios overlooking the vineyards, and some

have well-stocked delicatessens selling hams, cheeses, pâtés, and breads to accompany the estate's own wines. Many large supermarkets have special deli sections where you can purchase cured meats, marinated vegetables and olives, pre-prepared salads, sandwiches, and other picnic-perfect goodies.

Shopping

An obvious thing to shop for is Californian wine. From the world-famous Napa Valley to lesser-known wine-producing regions, such as Amador County and Southern California's Temecula, you will find superb, fruity white wines and hearty reds that reflect the state's astonishing breadth of terroirs. Many wine-growing areas also produce olives and citrus.

The inland valleys are famous for their fresh produce, often sold at roadside stalls at low prices –from artichokes, apples, and apricots to cucumbers, squash, and zucchinis, depending on region. Every town has a farmers' market on at least one day a week, where you can also buy home-made bread, honey, and other enticing products. Along the coast, fishing boats bring in the catch of the day.

Below far left Farmers' market at Lake Tahoe **Below left** Dining area at a Mendocino County vineyard **Below center** Al fresco dining in Mendocino County **Below** Dishes made with local produce **Below right** Deli, San Diego

Humboldt Han

Union Town
Humboldt City

M. Shasta

TRINITY

Pitt

Shasta Town

HA

NEVADE

Range Eel R.

Clear Cr.

Cotton Wood

Feather R.

Nelson

Pe cino

M. Linn

COLUS

Hauls
Ideo R.

Sycamore

Sacramento

B

Downieville

Py

P. Delgado

MENDOCINO

Cear
L.

Russian

Butte

O. Fremont

Colusi

Potter's R.

Neal's

Hamilton

Marysville

Yuba City

Nevada

NEVADA

mouth

Carso

Barra de Arena

Sonoma

SONOMA

NAPA

Bodega

Bodego B.

Napa

Vallejo

Vernon

Auburn

PLACER

Sacramento
City

EL

COLO

DORADO

Buriland

Colama

Carse

P. de los Reyes

S. Rafael

MARIN

Benicia

SACR

SAN

CALAVERA

San Francisco B.

Martinez

CONTRA
COSTA

Double Springs

JOAQUIN

San Francisco

Stockton

Angels

S. Joaquin

Stanislaus

TUOLUM

Sonora

SANTA
CRUZ

Arroyo

Merced R.

Santa Clara

SAN JOSE

SANTA CLARA

Merced City

Agua

Santa Cruz

Baltimore

Marip

Monterey B.

P. Pinos

S. Juan

MAR

Monterey

MONTE REY

S. Buenaventura R.

Coast Range

S. J.

San Joaquin R.

Tule Lake

S. Miguel

SAN LUIS

OBISPO

San

P. del Esteros

Luis Obispo

THE
DRIVES

- Yreka
- Redding
- CALIFORNIA
- Santa Rosa
- Sacramento
- San Francisco
- Stockton
- San Jose
- Monterey
- Fresno

Romance of the Golden Gate

Fort Funston to Angel Island State Park

Highlights

- **The magic of the Golden Gate**
  See lovely vistas of the bridge from both San Francisco and Marin County

- **The great city park**
  Explore the Golden Gate Park, from the Conservatory of Flowers to fine art at de Young Museum

- **Bayside town discoveries**
  Succumb to the allure of Sausalito's and Tiburon's waterfronts – great places for shopping and dining

- **Ferry fun**
  Enjoy a ferry ride from Tiburon to historic and scenic Angel Island

The spectacular Golden Gate Bridge seen from Baker Beach, San Francisco

Romance of the Golden Gate

The Golden Gate area continues to beckon travelers just as it drew the Gold Rush miners in 1849. The beauty of the green hillsides of Marin County, the magnificent design of the Golden Gate Bridge, and the inviting beaches and parks on the San Francisco side make this area a perennial favorite. This route begins at Fort Funston, where hang gliders soar with the current, and continues along the shore to the iconic orange bridge. Cross to the lush Marin Headlands and explore the charming bayside towns of Sausalito and Tiburon, before taking a ferry to Angel Island State Park.

Above The perimeter road circling the forested hills of Angel Island State Park, see pp34–5

ACTIVITIES

Watch hang gliders taking off as Pacific winds hit the cliffs at Fort Funston

Linger at Baker Beach and watch the sunset bathe the Golden Gate Bridge

Board a ferry in Sausalito or Tiburon for a ride to San Francisco and back

Stroll through art and design shops at Tiburon's Ark Row, once a mooring for houseboats

Hike or bike around the Angel Island State Park while enjoying panoramic views of the Bay Area

KEY

 Drive route

Left View of the Golden Gate Bridge and San Francisco from a vantage point in the Marin Headlands, see p34

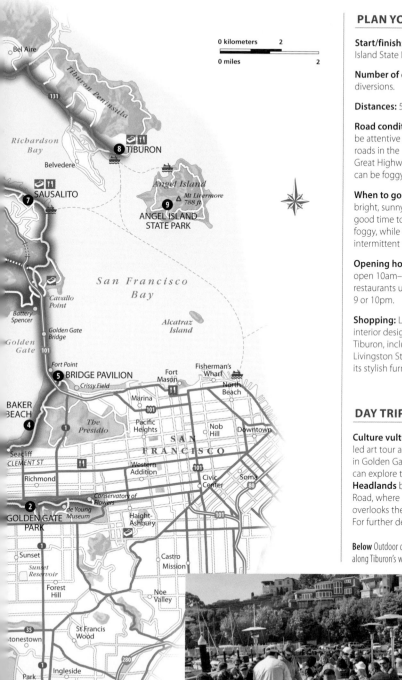

0 kilometers   2

0 miles   2

Bel Aire

Tiburon Peninsula

131

Richardson Bay

8 TIBURON

Belvedere

Angel Island

△ *Mt Livermore 788 ft*

SAUSALITO

9 ANGEL ISLAND STATE PARK

7

San Francisco Bay

Cavallo Point

Battery Spencer

Golden Gate Bridge

Alcatraz Island

Golden Gate

101

Fort Point

5 BRIDGE PAVILION

Crissy Field

Fort Mason

Fisherman's Wharf

North Beach

BAKER BEACH

4

Marina

101

The Presidio

Pacific Heights

Nob Hill

Downtown

1

SAN FRANCISCO

Seacliff

CLEMENT ST

Richmond

11

Western Addition

101

Civic Center

Soma

80

Conservatory of Flowers

2

de Young Museum

Haight-Ashbury

101

GOLDEN GATE PARK

1

Sunset

Sunset Reservoir

Castro

Mission

Forest Hill

Noe Valley

35

St Francis Wood

stonestown

280

Park Merced

Ingleside

Ocean View

PLAN YOUR DRIVE

Start/finish: Fort Funston to Angel Island State Park.

Number of days: 2 days, allowing for diversions.

Distances: 50 miles (80 km).

Road conditions: All good roads, but be attentive on the curvy, narrow roads in the Marin Headlands. The Great Highway and Marin Headlands can be foggy, especially in summer.

When to go: Spring and fall present bright, sunny weather, and are a good time to visit. Summer can be foggy, while winter may see intermittent rainfall.

Opening hours: Most businesses open 10am–6pm daily, with restaurants usually serving until 9 or 10pm.

Shopping: Lots of art, clothing, and interior design stores in Sausalito and Tiburon, including Tiburon's Ruth Livingston Studio, which is known for its stylish furniture.

DAY TRIP OPTIONS

Culture vultures will enjoy a docent-led art tour at the **de Young Museum** in Golden Gate Park. **Nature lovers** can explore the verdant **Marin Headlands** beyond Conzelman Road, where a coastal lighthouse overlooks the crashing waves. For further details, see p35.

Below Outdoor dining at one of the restaurants along Tiburon's waterfront, see p34

Above Painting of historic Sutro Baths at Cliff House Above right Hang gliders at Fort Funston

VISITING SAN FRANCISCO

Tourist Information
San Francisco Travel Association
Hallidie Plaza, 900 Market St, San Francisco, 94102; 415 391 2000; open 9am–5pm daily; www.onlyinsanfrancisco.com

VISITING FORT FUNSTON

Parking
Ample free parking in paved lots on the cliff tops at Fort Funston.

WHERE TO STAY

AROUND FORT FUNSTON

Ocean Park Motel of San Francisco *inexpensive*
One of the first motels in San Francisco, this Art Deco treasure was built in the 1930s. Comfortable, quiet accommodation near the ocean.
2690 46th Ave, San Francisco, 94116; 415 566 7020; www.oceanparkmotel.com

AROUND GOLDEN GATE PARK

Belvedere House *moderate*
This friendly, award-winning B&B has six rooms.
598 Belvedere St, San Francisco, 94117; 415 731 6654; www.belvederehouse.com

AROUND CLIFF HOUSE

Seal Rock Inn *moderate*
A modern motor inn in a quiet location near the beach. Spacious ocean-view rooms, some with kitchens.
545 Point Lobos Ave, San Francisco, 94121; 415 752 8000; www.sealrockinn.com

➊ Fort Funston
San Francisco County; 94131
A clifftop park with a sandy beach below, Fort Funston is a favorite spot for hang gliding. Visitors can stand at the viewing platform and watch enthusiasts launch their crafts. The gliders ride the bouncy sea breezes and the thermals rising from the cliffs below, as they slide past like hovering raptors just a few paces away. Fort Funston, like many of the Golden Gate area parks, was once a military property, before being handed over to the National Park Service.

🚗 **Exit Fort Funston southbound on Hwy 35; after 400 yards (365 m) double back. Turn left onto the Great Hwy. Turn right on John F Kennedy Dr into Golden Gate Park; turn left at the first stop sign and drive to the Conservatory of Flowers. There is free roadside parking.**

➋ Golden Gate Park
San Francisco County; 94117
Often celebrated as one of the great urban parks in the world, Golden Gate Park has many appealing features. The white Victorian **Conservatory of Flowers** (*www.conservatoryofflowers.org*) is an exquisite public conservatory from 1879, and the horticultural displays inside are mirrored by extensive outdoor flower gardens. Nearby, the **de Young Museum** (*www.deyoung museum.org*) is San Francisco's main repository of fine art, with collections ranging from African sculptures to American paintings.

🚗 **Drive back west to the Great Hwy and turn north a quarter mile (0.5 km). On the left is the Cliff House, with parking in front.**

➌ Cliff House
San Francisco County; 94121
A fine-dining establishment today, Cliff House (*1090 Point Lobos; www.cliffhouse.com*) has its roots in 19th-century San Francisco, when this was the location of the Sutro Baths – several large, enclosed pools of seawater, which were hubs for swimming and socializing. Look at the artwork in the restaurant to see what the Sutro Baths once looked like, and then head behind the building to gaze out at Seal Rocks, which is a haven for seals, sea lions, and birds. A short walk north of Cliff House is **Lands End**, a promontory

Below View of Golden Gate Bridge from Lands End, near Cliff House

Above left Conservatory of Flowers surrounded by well-tended gardens, Golden Gate Park
Above Colorful totem pole at Cliff House

offering a first glimpse of the awe-inspiring Golden Gate Bridge.

🚗 *Proceed uphill to 45th Ave. Turn left, then right onto Clement St, and left onto Legion of Honor Dr. Head north through Lincoln Park and continue east on El Camino del Mar, which becomes Lincoln Blvd. Look out for the turnout to Baker Beach on the left; there is ample parking in paved lots.*

④ Baker Beach
San Francisco County; 94121
Some of the best views of the Golden Gate Bridge from the San Francisco side are to be had from Baker Beach, especially in the hours before sunset, as the final glow of the day bathes the imposing structure in golden light. Baker Beach is a swath of wide sandy beach and crashing foamy surf. It is a great place for a picnic, so consider stocking up with a bottle of wine if there is a designated driver, some local blue cheese, and a loaf of San Francisco's famous sourdough bread.

🚗 *Continue on Lincoln Blvd until a signed turnoff left indicates Golden Gate Bridge. Park in the lot at the Bridge Pavilion, the south-side viewing platform for the bridge.*

⑤ Bridge Pavilion
San Francisco County; 94121
This vantage point offers a sweeping view of the bridge and San Francisco's skyline. Stop to look at the statue of Joseph Strauss, the German-American engineer who completed the Golden Gate Bridge in 1937,

before admiring the features of the classic bridge's architecture. Walk out onto the bridge and look back at the sprawling city of San Francisco. Below is **Fort Point** *(www.nps.gov/fopo)*, a brick military structure that protected the Bay Area from Confederate attack during the Civil War. To the east stretches **Crissy Field**, a landscaped park laid out on a former airstrip. Head here for a walk along the bay or to enjoy a leisurely picnic lunch.

🚗 *Exit Bridge Pavilion, following the 101 North signs, and cross the bridge to enter the Marin Headlands. Take the Alexander Ave turnoff; at the T-junction follow the sign to 101 San Francisco southbound, turn right to Conzelman Rd, signed for Marin Headlands. There is roadside parking along main stops.*

Above Hiking/biking path curving down towards the foot of the Golden Gate Bridge

EAT AND DRINK

AROUND GOLDEN GATE PARK
The Beach Chalet Brewery & Restaurant *moderate*
This restaurant serving American cuisine is set in a historic building with views of the Pacific. See the treasured 1930s-era murals on the ground floor.
1000 Great Hwy, San Francisco, 94121; 415 386 8439; open for breakfast, lunch & dinner daily; www.beachchalet.com

Mai's *moderate*
A Vietnamese establishment, Mai's epitomizes the fine ethnic restaurants on Clement Street. Try the coconut chicken or lemongrass beef entrées.
316 Clement St, San Francisco, 94118; 415 221 3046; open 11am–8:30pm daily

CLIFF HOUSE
Cliff House *expensive*
Enjoy fine dining at a historic location with ocean views. Cliff House offers a full range of seafood and meat dishes; good choices include the seared scallops and rack of lamb.
1090 Point Lobos, San Francisco, 94121; 415 386 3330; open daily, check website for timings; www.cliffhouse.com

AROUND BRIDGE PAVILION
Greens *expensive*
A leader in vegetarian cuisine, Greens is a Zen-inspired restaurant serving organic produce from its Green Gulch Farm in Marin County.
Fort Mason, Building A, San Francisco, 94123; 415 771 6222; check website for timings; www.greensrestaurant.com

Eat and Drink: inexpensive under $25; moderate $25–50; expensive over $50

Above Shops lining a street, Tiburon **Below** Yachts moored along Sausalito's waterfront

VISITING THE GOLDEN GATE NATIONAL RECREATION AREA

Tourist Information
Fort Barry, Marin Headlands, 94965; 415 331 1540; open 9:30am–4:30pm daily; www.nps.gov/goga

VISITING SAUSALITO AND TIBURON

Parking
There is ample parking on the streets and in designated lots in both towns.

WHERE TO STAY

SAUSALITO

The Gables Inn *expensive*
This elegant B&B is within easy walking distance of the waterfront.
62 Princess St, 94965; 415 289 1100; www.gablesinnsausalito.com

AROUND SAUSALITO

Cavallo Point Lodge *expensive*
An upscale lodge in the Golden Gate National Recreation Area.
601 Murray Circle, 94965; 415 339 4700; www.cavallopoint.com

TIBURON

Water's Edge Hotel *moderate*
Rooms offer views of the harbor, San Francisco Bay, and Angel Island. Shopping and dining is close by.
25 Main St, 94920; 415 789 5999; www.watersedgehotel.com

⑥ Marin Headlands
Marin County; 94965
The drive along Conzelman Road through the headlands *(www.nps.gov/ goga; see also p48)* presents three great views of the Golden Gate. The first of these is from Battery Spencer, a gun emplacement last used in World War II. The next ridge affords a classic view of the bridge with San Francisco in the background. Continue on the road and turn left at a roundabout and follow Conzelman Road to Hawk Hill and Point Bonita Lighthouse to enjoy a panoramic view of the entire bridge.
🚗 *Leave Point Bonita along Fort Barry Rd to Bunker Rd; follow signs for 101 Tunnel Route. Exiting the tunnel, go under I-101 and turn left for Sausalito.*

⑦ Sausalito
Marin County; 94965
With many restaurants built on wooden piers, Sausalito is a great place to stop for a bite by the waterside *(see also p48)*. Bridgeway is lined with street artists showcasing their talents – look out for Bill Dan, a rock-balancing maestro who sets rocks on top of each other.
🚗 *Continue north on Bridgeway till it merges with Hwy 101. Turn east on Hwy 131 into Tiburon.*

Rock-balancing act by Bill Dan, Sausalito

Naming the Golden Gate
The strait connecting the Pacific Ocean and the San Francisco Bay was named the Golden Gate by John Fremont, of the US Topographical Engineers, before gold was even discovered in California. He surveyed the rolling hillsides and the spectacular ocean views, and wrote in 1848, "To this gate I gave the name Chrysopylae, or Golden Gate."

⑧ Tiburon
Marin County; 94920
This casual town attracts visitors with its bayside walking path, restaurants atop piers, and art shops set in quaint buildings. Its harbor is also a boarding point for ferries departing for San Francisco and Angel Island. Stroll through downtown and look out for **Ark Row**, where many buildings were actually recreational houseboats in the 1890s, inhabited by sea captains, Bohemian artists, and summer residents from San Francisco. The houses on 104, 106, 108, and 116 are authentic boats.
🚗 *Leave the car in Tiburon and take the ferry from the harbor to Angel Island. The ferry shuttles back and forth from 10am to 3:30pm daily in summer and on weekends in winter.*

⑨ Angel Island State Park
Marin County; 94920
The largest island in the San Francisco Bay, Angel Island served variously as a military facility and an important immigration station before being converted into a state park *(www.angelisland.com)*. Today, the island is popular with daytrippers for its historic buildings, hiking trails, and sandy beaches. The 5-mile (8-km) perimeter road, walk affords great views of the Golden Gate, San Francisco, and the bay. Alternatively, visitors can opt for a tram ride that stops at the main sights.

A two-hour walking tour
Passengers disembark at **Ayala Cove** ①, named after the Spanish sea captain who first mapped the area. There is a small visitor center and an outfit that rents bikes and provides a Segway tour. Several hiking trails to the hilly interiors of the island depart from the visitor center. A trek to the summit of Mt Livermore, at 788 ft (240 m) above sea level, rewards with panoramic views of the Bay Area. Walk anti-clockwise on the perimeter road to **Camp Reynolds** ② to see intact troop houses and a parade ground that recall 19th-century military life. Camp Reynolds is one of many forts around the Bay Area that no longer serve a military function, and have become part of parks. After Camp Reynolds, look out for a path down

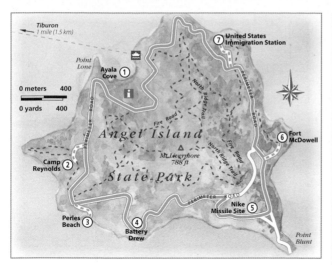

from the road to the secluded **Perles Beach** ③, which offers stunning views of the Golden Gate. A short stroll ahead on the perimeter road leads to **Battery Drew** ④, one of the many gun emplacements put up to protect San Francisco Bay. Stationary gun emplacements such as this became obsolete after the Pearl Harbor attack showed what air power could accomplish. Continue on the road to the abandoned **Nike Missile Site** ⑤, a legacy of the Cold

War days. Nike missiles were placed here and on the Marin Headlands in the 1950s to be fired at potential Soviet bombers. Farther ahead, **Fort McDowell** ⑥, or East Garrison, is a large post from where more than 300,000 soldiers were shipped out to the Pacific theater in World War II. Continue farther to the **United States Immigration Station** ⑦ (*www.aiisf. org*), a critical site for new arrivals to the US between 1910 and 1940. More than a million immigrants from 80 countries were processed here, including 175,000 Chinese. The site is a major museum, and visitors should see the barracks, which re-create the dormitories where Asian immigrants waited for interrogations that would determine if they could stay or not. Look out for the poems carved into the walls by the despairing Chinese immigrants. Return to Ayala Cove to board the ferry.

Above Golden Gate Bridge as seen from Conzelman Road **Below left** Ferry landing at Ayala Cove, Angel Island State Park

EAT AND DRINK

SAUSALITO
The Trident *moderate*
Set on wooden piers with bay views. Try the California oysters or calamari.
558 Bridgeway, 94965; 415 331 3232; open 11am–10pm daily; www.horizonssausalito.com

TIBURON
Don Antonio Trattoria *moderate*
A locals' favorite bistro with specialties such as gnocchi bolognese and risotto.
114 Main St, 94920; 415 435 0400; open 5–9:30pm Tue–Sun; www.donantoniotrattoria.com

Guaymas *moderate*
Mexican cuisine, including grilled giant shrimp marinated in lime, served on a sunny deck.
5 Main St, 94920; 415 435 6300; open 11am–9pm daily; www.guaymasrestaurant.com

DAY TRIP OPTIONS
The cultural wealth of the Golden Gate Park and the outdoor adventures in the Marin Headlands are day trips worth considering.

Arts and plants in the park
The de Young Museum at Golden Gate Park ❷ has excellent art collections, including an exhibit of ethnic arts from Oceania. Across the street, exhibits at the California Academy of Sciences

(*www.calacademy.org*) include the re-creation of a rain forest and a white alligator. Carnivorous plants can be found at the nearby Conservatory of Flowers.

Park in the public garage at the de Young Museum and walk to this cluster of sites.

Headland highlights
A lingering drive through the Marin Headlands ❻ and some great walks

amount to an enticing day trip. From Hawk Hill, descend a steep hill going west. Stop at the visitor center to pick up a map of the area. Head for an invigorating 0.5 mile (0.8 km) walk to the Point Bonita Lighthouse. The 1.5-mile (2.5-km) loop hike around Rodeo Lagoon introduces visitors to the rich birdlife in the estuary environment.

There is ample parking at the visitor center and at the walk trailheads.

Eat and Drink: inexpensive under $25; moderate $25–50; expensive over $50

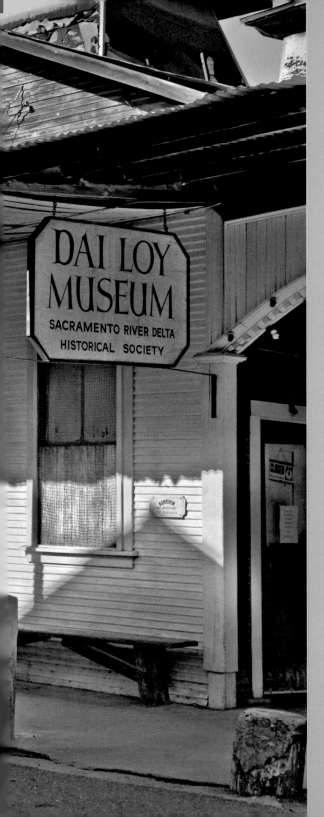

Sacramento Delta

Martinez to Wine and Pear Country

Highlights

- **Birdlife galore**
  Spot egrets, herons, and other waterfowl in Peytonia Slough Ecological Reserve at Suisun Marsh

- **Country crafts**
  Visit Rush Ranch to see a blacksmith at work and then watch out for rare birds along the wetland trails

- **Yesteryear trams**
  Ride the rails on a vintage tram at the Western Railway Museum

- **Quaint hamlet**
  Wander the dusty streets and store-museums of Locke that recall its pioneering days

One of Locke's typical wooden structures with Chinese markings

Sacramento Delta

Comprising more than 1,000 miles (1,600 km) of waterways, the Sacramento Delta, northeast of San Francisco, is where four rivers meet and flow into San Francisco Bay. Scenic byways run atop the levees, connecting historic hamlets and offering fine vistas over farmland and marshy sloughs that are a haven for migratory birds. This route meanders lazily through the delta, from the historic town of Martinez at the delta's mouth, up to a lush countryside planted with vines and fruit trees. En route, take time to stop to sample wines and fresh fruit sold roadside, and explore Locke and other tumbledown towns that are ghostly memorials to long-ago days when Chinese laborers built the levees.

Above Billboard welcoming visitors to Walnut Grove, near Locke, *see p43*

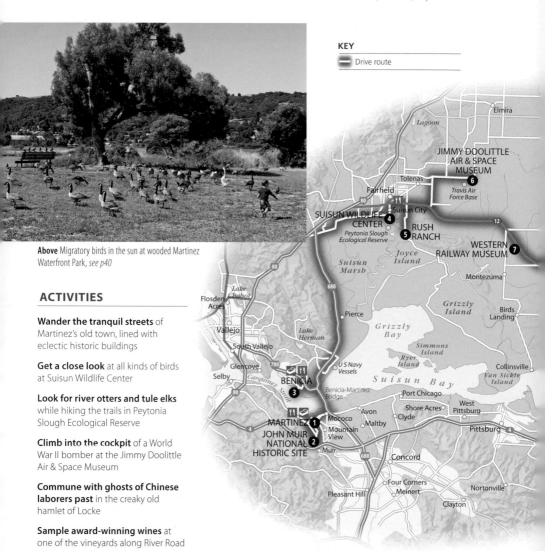

Above Migratory birds in the sun at wooded Martinez Waterfront Park, *see p40*

KEY

— Drive route

ACTIVITIES

Wander the tranquil streets of Martinez's old town, lined with eclectic historic buildings

Get a close look at all kinds of birds at Suisun Wildlife Center

Look for river otters and tule elks while hiking the trails in Peytonia Slough Ecological Reserve

Climb into the cockpit of a World War II bomber at the Jimmy Doolittle Air & Space Museum

Commune with ghosts of Chinese laborers past in the creaky old hamlet of Locke

Sample award-winning wines at one of the vineyards along River Road

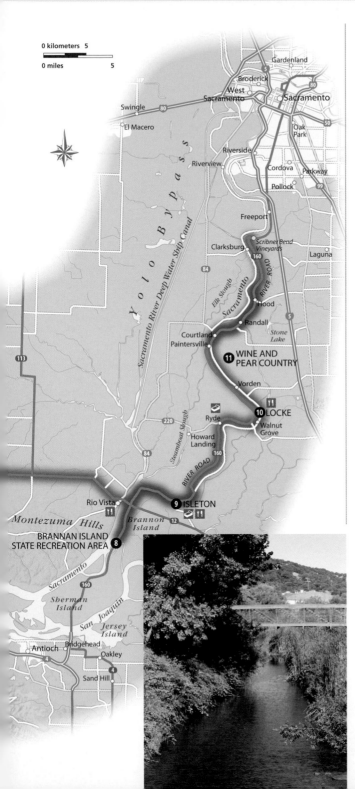

Left Alhambra Creek winding through Martinez, *see p40*

PLAN YOUR DRIVE

Start/finish: Martinez to Wine and Pear Country.

Number of days: 1–2 days, allowing half a day to explore Martinez.

Distance: 112 miles (180 km).

Road conditions: Generally excellent, with relatively little traffic. Some of the early sections of the route include freeway driving. The SR 12 and SR 160 (River Road) are unlit outside urban areas.

When to go: Spring is the perfect time, as the weather is generally sunny and temperate, the air crystal clear, and citrus and pear orchards are in bloom. Summer can get hot, but late summer is a good time to witness the fruit and grape harvest.

Opening times: Most of the sights are open daily, but timings in summer and winter vary. Call ahead to ensure that state parks are open.

Shopping: Look for fresh produce sold along SR 160 (River Road). Isleton, Locke, and Walnut Grove have antique shops.

Major festivals: Travis Air Force Base: Travis Air Show, Aug. **Isleton:** Crawdad Festival, Jun. **Courtland:** Pear Fair, Jul.

DAY TRIP OPTIONS

History buffs can wander the streets of **Benicia** and **Locke**, marvel at working trams in the **Western Railroad Museum** and at World War II aircraft at the **Jimmy Doolittle Air & Space Museum**. **Wildlife lovers** can go birding and hiking in **Peytonia Slough Ecological Reserve** and **Rush Ranch**. For full details, *see p43*.

Above Victorian building of the Martinez Museum Below Open vistas at the Waterfront Park, Martinez

VISITING MARTINEZ

Parking
There is paid street parking, or free parking at the Amtrak railway station on Estudillo St.

WHERE TO STAY

MARTINEZ

Muir Lodge *inexpensive*
This charming, well-furnished motel has an outdoor pool.
3930 Alhambra Ave, 94553; 925 228 3308; www.muirlodgemotel.com

BENICIA

Inn & Spa at Benicia Bay *moderate*
Furnished with antiques, this centenary clapboard B&B has a cozy library.
145 E D St, 94510; 707 746 1055; www.theinnatbeniciabay.com

Union Hotel *moderate*
A well-preserved historic inn, Union Hotel features antique four-poster beds and stained-glass windows.
401 1st St, 94510; 707 746 0110; www.unionhotelbenicia.com

➊ Martinez
Contra Costa County; 94553

Surrounded by wooded hills, Martinez overlooks the Carquinez Strait at the mouth of the Sacramento Delta. Laid out in 1849, its historic downtown has well-preserved buildings. Belying the oil refineries outside town, Martinez's bucolic nature is evident from the tree-lined streets and the beavers, otters, and mink in Alhambra Creek.

A two-hour walking tour

After parking at the Amtrak station lot at the north end of Estudillo Street, begin at the **Martinez Chamber of Commerce** ➊ *(603 Marina Vista)* to pick up a map and head west along Marina Vista Avenue. Stop on the bridge at Castro Street to spot beavers in **Alhambra Creek** ➋ before continuing west to Talbart Street. Turn right here, then follow Carquinez Scenic Drive to the **Alhambra Cemetery** ➌ to see graves of the county's early settlers. Retrace the route along Marina Vista Avenue and turn right on Berrellessa Street. Walk south to Henrietta Street, and continue east to **Plaza Ygnacio Martinez Park** ➍, which has a Spanish fountain and pretty flower beds. Two blocks ahead, turn left on Ferry Street, lined with historic buildings, then right at Main Street, which slopes eastward to a freestanding clock at Court Street. Turn right, passing the Neo-Classical **Contra Costa Country Courthouse** ➎ and the 1941 Art Deco **Martinez Public Library** ➏, which boasts a collection of original books by John

Muir. Cross Ward Street to view the Depression-era **post office** ➐ that has a New Deal mural by artist Maynard Dixon (1875–1946). Return along Court Street, past the Neo-Classical **Contra Costa County Finance Building** ➑, built in 1901 as the courthouse. Beyond, the Victorian **Martinez Museum** ➒ *(1005 Escobar St; 925 228 8160; open 11:30am–3pm Tue & Thu, 1–4pm Sun)* is dedicated to the city's history. Turn left on Marina Vista Avenue for Ferry Street; the **Old Southern Pacific Depot** ➓ train station is on the right. Cross the tracks, passing the **Southern Pacific 1228 steam locomotive** ⑪, to enter woodsy **Waterfront Park** ⑫, where paths lead past duck ponds to the marina and fishing pier. Head back to car.

🚗 *Exit the Amtrak lot onto Marina Vista Ave and turn left on Berrellessa St to Alhambra Ave. Continue south to John Muir National Historic Site, which has free parking.*

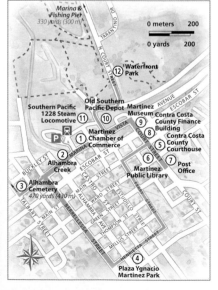

② John Muir National Historic Site

Contra Costa County; 94553

This 17-room hilltop Victorian manse *(4202 Alhambra Ave; www.nps.gov/jomu)* was the home of Scottish immigrant, environmentalist, and author John Muir for the last 24 years of his life, and houses exhibits that include his personal belongings. The visitor center shows a 20-minute film on him, and guided walks through the oak woodlands depart from here.

Stop by Martinez Adobe, a former storehouse that has an exhibit on the Juan Bautista de Anza National Historic Trail, which follows the route of a 1745 Spanish expedition from Mexico to the San Francisco Bay area.

🚗 Return north along Alhambra Ave. Turn right on Escobar St to Marina Vista Ave. Follow the signs for Benicia-Martinez Bridge (toll) via I-680. Cross the bridge. Take 780 west for Benicia. Exit at E 5th St and turn left onto 5th St, then right onto Military E St, and left at 1st St. Park along the road.

John Muir

John Muir, the father of America's National Parks, is considered the pioneer of environmentalism in the US. He became a fierce advocate of wilderness preservation after having spent years exploring California's outdoors. He gained the ear of President Theodore Roosevelt, whom he took camping in Yosemite Valley. Muir's books about nature and California's Sierra Nevada were instrumental in the creation of the National Park Service in 1899. He founded the Sierra Club – an important conservation organization – in 1892.

③ Benicia

Solano County; 94510

Founded in 1847, this riverfront city is full of historic charm. The restored **Capitol** building *(115 W G St; open 10am–5pm Sat & Sun)* served as the state's seat of government from 1853 to 1854. First Street is lined with shops and cafés, and leads to the **Benicia State Recreation Area**, a protected tidal wetland that attracts migratory waterfowl. Here, a pier offers views of

the Carquinez Strait and passing ships. A reserve mothball fleet of former US Navy vessels is anchored east of Benicia. These can be seen from the bayside.

🚗 Retrace the route east to I-780 and follow the 680 signs for Sacramento. Exit after 13 miles (21 km) onto Cordelia Rd. Take this east to Suisun City. Turn right onto Kellogg St. Park at Suisun Wildlife Center.

④ Suisun Wildlife Center

Solano County; 94585

Dedicated to the rescue of local wildlife and the preservation of the Suisun Marsh, the center *(www.suisunwildlife.org)* educates visitors about local flora and fauna and offers walks into the adjacent wetlands. It provides shelter to injured animals, that have included a coyote, golden eagle, and owls.

Walk 246 ft (75 m) east through the parking lot to enter **Peytonia Slough Ecological Reserve** *(707 944 5500)*. Part of the 116,000-acre (46,943-ha) Suisun Marsh, it is a resting and feeding ground for millions of waterfowl migrating on the Pacific Flyway, a major route for migratory birds. A trail begins at the Suisun City boat ramp and leads into the wetlands that border a meandering slough. Keep an eye out for tule elk *(Cervus elaphus nannodes)* hoof marks and badger paw prints on the trail, and for river otters among the reeds.

🚗 Take Kellogg St and Main St north through Suisun City to SR 12. Turn right, and exit onto Grizzly Island Rd. Follow this to Rush Ranch.

Below View of the Carquinez Strait from the Benicia State Recreation Area

Rescued owl at Suisun Wildlife Center

Above Tree-shaded entrance to Café Katie, Martinez

VISITING BENICIA

Tourist Information
601 1st St, 94510; 707 745 2120; www.beniciachamber.com

EAT AND DRINK

MARTINEZ

Café Katie *inexpensive*
Serves sandwiches, salads, and soups.
925 Main St, 94553; 925 229 3595; open 7am–3pm Mon–Fri

BENICIA

Lucca Bar & Grill *moderate*
Italian dishes and American comfort food in a chic, upscale setting.
439 1st St, 94510; 707 745 0943; open 11:30am–9pm Mon–Fri, 10am–noon Sat & Sun; www.luccabar.com

AROUND SUISUN WILDLIFE CENTER

Cast Iron Grill & Bar *moderate*
Modern pub-style restaurant and bar.
700 Main St, Suisun City, 94585; 707 425 1700; 11:30am–9pm Mon–Fri, 9:30am–8pm Sat, 9am–9pm Sun; www.castirongrillandbar.com

Above Rolling grasslands of Rush Ranch along the Suisun Marsh **Below** Buildings reminiscent of the Gold Rush era in Locke

5 Rush Ranch
Solano County
This historic farmstead *(open 8am–6pm daily; www.rushranch.net)* operates as a working museum and has blacksmithing demonstrations, livestock pens, a stable with a stagecoach, and an old farm equipment graveyard. Its visitor center has some natural history exhibits. A working cattle ranch, it also includes 2,070 acres (838 ha) of tidal marsh and meadow, accessed by three trails. The estuary is home to over 200 bird species, and hawks, garter snakes, and bobcats are frequently spotted.

🚗 *Return to SR 12. Continue east to Walters Rd; turn left, then right at Air Base Pkwy. Follow signs for the Jimmy Doolittle Air & Space Museum.*

6 Jimmy Doolittle Air & Space Museum
Solano County; 94535
One of the largest collections of military aircraft in the US, this museum *(Travis Air Force Base; 707 424 5605; www.jimmydoolittlemuseum.org)* exhibits B-52 Stratofortress bombers, a B-29 Superfortress, and various jet fighters. Special emphasis is given to the Korean and Vietnam wars, and to the first air raid on Japan, on April 18, 1942. Call ahead to arrange a guide. Remember to carry a valid photo ID and vehicle registration papers.

🚗 *Drive out of the Travis Air Force Base and turn left on Walters Rd. Drive south to SR 12, turn left and continue east to the Western Railway Museum.*

7 Western Railway Museum
Solano County; 94585
Step back over a 100 years in time at this living history museum *(www.wrm.org)*, where vintage electric trains, trams, and trolleybuses recall the development of urban railways. Docents in period costumes take visitors around. Stop by the Cameron Hall Visitor Center, which tells the story of electric railroading from the 1890s onward, and where restorers can be seen at work in the repair shop. Rail trips *(11am, 12:30pm, 2pm & 3:30pm)* wend their way through the Montezuma Hills.

Continue east on SR 12, which weaves through rolling hillsides carpeted in meadows and studded with hundreds of wind turbines of the Shiloh Wind Power Plant. Watch sheep and cattle graze lazily beneath the towering windmills, which stand up to 262 ft (80 m) high. The terrain is reminiscent of software company Microsoft's Windows XP screen image, shot nearby.

🚗 *Continue east on SR 12 to Rio Vista. Cross the Sacramento River via the Lift Bridge and turn right onto SR 160 (River Rd) for Brannan Island State Recreation Area.*

8 Brannan Island State Recreation Area
Sacramento County; 95476
Laced with meandering waterways, the Brannan Island State Recreation Area *(877 444 6777; www.recreation.gov)* is surrounded by the Sacramento River and sloughs on three

Trolleybus at the Western Railway Museum

sides. The park has numerous islands and is fringed by marshland that is home to beavers, muskrats, river otters, and at least 76 species of birds. The visitor center has displays on the cultural and natural history of the Sacramento Delta, as well as an interactive map. Those who enjoy the outdoors can swim, fish, or windsurf, and there are also nature trails, campsites and picnic facilities.

🚗 *Return along SR 160 (River Rd) to Rio Vista and continue north along the east side of the river to Isleton.*

9 Isleton

Sacramento County; 95641

Steamboats and paddle-wheelers once called at this formerly important river port, which was a way station for Argonauts – pioneers who headed to California during the Gold Rush of 1849. Many of the wood-and-tin structures of this 19th-century village still retain Chinese symbols and recall a bygone era when Chinese laborers formed a large part of the community. Today, this riverside hamlet is best known for the annual Crawdad Festival that draws huge crowds to gorge on different preparations of crayfish.

🚗 *Continue north for 10 miles (16 km) along SR 160 (River Rd) via Ryde, then turn right across the river signposted to Locke.*

> **Gold Rush**
>
> When gold was found in the American River in 1848, word of *Gum Shan* (Gold Mountain) led to a rush of Chinese Argonauts to California. By 1852, about 25,000 Chinese immigrants had built their own Chinese-only settlements, including Locke. Construction of the Central Pacific Railroad from Sacramento across the Sierra Nevada Mountains, and of the Sacramento Delta levees in the late 19th century, relied on Chinese workers, whose legacy can be seen to this day in delta towns.

10 Locke

Sacramento County; 95327

This quaint hamlet, built in 1915 by Chinese farm laborers, retains its early pioneer spirit more than any other town in the delta. The brothels and gambling dens are no more, but the village is still lived in and exudes an authentic, rough-around-the-edges charm. Stop at one of the rickety wooden houses that have been turned into charming one-room antique store-museums stuffed with intriguing artifacts.

🚗 *Keep following SR 160 (River Rd) through wine and pear country.*

11 Wine and Pear Country

Sacramento County; 95615

North of historic Locke, the SR 160 (River Road) passes a vast swath of farmland planted with pear orchards and vineyards, irrigated by waters from the delta's rivers and sloughs. The pear industry is centered around the tiny hamlet of **Courtland**, which celebrates the summer harvest with an annual Pear Fair, full of festivities.

Many wineries along the route are open to visits. If traveling with a designated driver, allow time for a trip to **Scribner Bend Vineyards** (*www.scribnerbend.com*), which offers complimentary tasting. Visitors can relax in its lawns and landscaped gardens while sampling its award-winning wines.

Above left Signage, Isleton Joe's **Above** Pear-laden trees in an orchard in Courtland

EAT AND DRINK

ISLETON

Rogelio's *inexpensive*
A former saloon, Rogelio's serves Chinese, Italian, and Mexican fare. *34 Main St, 95641; 916 777 5878; open 4–8pm Tue–Wed, 11am–8pm Thu & Sun, 11am–9pm Fri & Sat; www.rogelios.net*

Isleton Joe's *moderate*
The best place to enjoy crawdad (crayfish) cocktails, omelets, or platters. *212 2nd St, 95641; 916 777 6510; open 11am–9pm Mon–Fri, 8am–9pm Sat & Sun*

AROUND ISLETON

The Point Waterfront Restaurant *moderate*
A surf-n-turf restaurant, over the Sacramento River, with banquet booths. *120 Marina Dr, Rio Vista, 94571; 707 374 5400; timings vary by day and season; www.pointrestaurant.com*

LOCKE

Al's Place *inexpensive*
Try this bar-diner's steaks and pastas. *13936 Main St, 95690; 916 776 1800; open 11:30am–2pm Mon–Fri, 11:30am–9pm Sat & Sun*

DAY TRIP OPTIONS

It is possible to break up this route into several day trips.

All aboard

Train buffs can be thrilled with the toot of whistles at the Western Railway Museum 7, while aviation and military enthusiasts can admire the many World War II and later vintage military aircraft displayed at the Jimmy Doolittle Air & Space Museum 6.

From the railway museum, take SR 12 to Walters Rd for Travis Air Force Base.

Avian adventure

Get close to over 200 bird species and other rescued animals at Suisun Wildlife Center 4, then set out on a trail into waterfowl habitat at Rush Ranch 5.

Take SR 12 from Suisun City. Exit onto Grizzly Island Rd, which leads to Rush Ranch.

Memories of the Orient

Those interested in history will enjoy walking through the hamlets of Isleton 9 and Locke 10, both of which retain remnants of California's Chinese legacy.

The SR 160 (River Rd) connects the towns.

Eat and Drink: inexpensive under $25; moderate $25–50; expensive over $50

Forested Slopes and Scenic Coast

Vista Point to Point Reyes Headland

Highlights

- **Bayview boardwalk**
  Stroll Sausalito's shoreline boulevard to admire the stunning views toward San Francisco

- **Giants of nature**
  Wander the trails into Muir Woods to gaze up at the tallest trees in the world

- **Deer delights**
  Hike the Tule Elk Reserve for a close look at this endemic deer species

- **World-class whaling**
  Spot migrating California gray whales from the Point Reyes Lighthouse

Sweeping view of the coastline at Point Reyes National Seashore

Forested Slopes and Scenic Coast

The Marin County coastline is a delightful mix of contrasts, from the sublime vistas of upscale Sausalito and the soaring old-growth redwoods *(Sequoia sempervirens)* of Muir Woods to the cliff-hanger Shoreline Highway (SR 1), windswept beaches, and rugged cliffs of Point Reyes National Seashore. This route combines the best of Marin's scenic highlights, from forest to mountain and coast. Its hairpin bends and sweeping curves add thrill to the drive, and there are kaleidoscopic vistas around every turn. In addition, opportunities abound to head out on inviting hiking trails, and even the most sedentary traveler has a chance to spot tule elk, elephant seals, and whales.

Above The Tudor-style Pelican Inn set amid landscaped gardens, Muir Beach, *see p49*

ACTIVITIES

Cast a line at Stinson Beach in the hope of catching a salmon

Be a birder at Audubon Canyon Ranch and spot egrets at its Martin Griffin Preserve

Hike the Earthquake Loop Trail at Bear Valley to see how the San Andreas Fault was ripped apart in 1906

Kayak on Tomales Bay while looking out for sea lions and harbor seals

Sample oysters at Drakes Bay and then buy some for a beach barbecue

Climb the steps of Point Reyes Lighthouse to view its original Fresnel lens

Above Yachts in Sausalito's marina, *see p48*

Start/finish: Vista Point to Point Reyes National Seashore.

Number of days: 1–2 days.

Distance: 85 miles (137 km).

Road conditions: Well paved, but the Shoreline Highway (SR 1) between Muir Beach and Stinson Beach has hairpin bends and is subject to landslides. On warm weekends, traffic jams are frequent along Muir Woods Road. Fog can smother Point Reyes National Seashore at any time of year.

When to go: Spring, when wildflowers are in bloom, and late fall offer the best weather. Avoid Jul–Sep when heavy fogs are most common. Jan–Mar is a good time to spot migrating whales.

Main market days: Point Reyes Station: Jun–Nov Sat am. **Sausalito:** May–Oct Fri pm.

Opening times: Most of the sights and visitor centers along this drive are open from 10am to 5pm daily.

Shopping: Sausalito has dozens of boutique stores and art galleries.

Major festivals: Sausalito: Film Festival, Aug; Art Festival, Sep. **Point Reyes:** Birding & Nature Festival, Apr; Big Time Native American Festival, Apr.

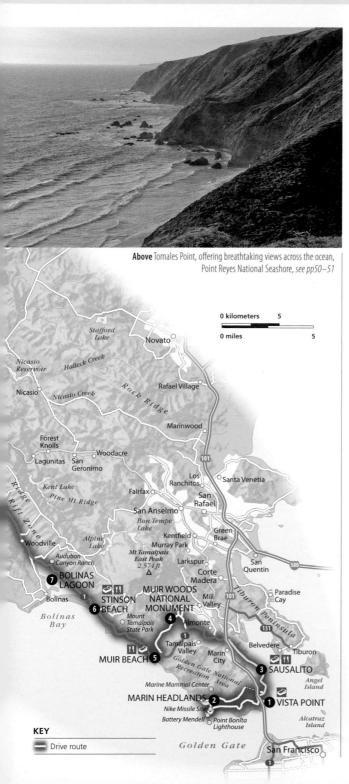

Above Tomales Point, offering breathtaking views across the ocean, Point Reyes National Seashore, *see pp50–51*

0 kilometers 5

0 miles 5

KEY

🚗 Drive route

DAY TRIP OPTIONS

Keen photographers should not miss the views from **Vista Point** and the **Marin Headlands**. Head to **Point Reyes National Seashore** and **Muir Beach** for some fun on the sand. **Animal lovers** will be in their elements at **Bolinas Lagoon** and **Tule Elk Reserve**. For full details, *see p51*.

Above View of Stinson Beach **Below** Hiking trail, Muir Woods National Monument

VISITING SAUSALITO

Tourist Information
780 Bridgeway, 94965; 415 332 0505; open 11:30am–4pm Tue–Sun

Parking
There are several parking lots with meters at Gabrielson Park.

WHERE TO STAY

VISTA POINT

Cavallo Point *expensive*
Occupying Fort Baker, a former US Army post, this hotel has great views of San Francisco and the Golden Gate. *601 Murray Circle, Fort Baker, 94965; 415 339 4700; www.cavallopoint.com*

SAUSALITO

Casa Madrona Hotel & Spa *expensive*
Spacious, well-appointed rooms with bay views, plus hillside cottages on offer. *801 Bridgeway, 94965; 415 332 0502; www.casamadrona.com*

MUIR BEACH

Pelican Inn *moderate*
On the edge of Muir Woods, this English-style inn exudes a cozy charm. *10 Pacific Way, 94965; 415 383 6000; www.pelicaninn.com*

STINSON BEACH

The Sandpiper *moderate*
Clean, pleasantly furnished rooms with quilts; and an English-style garden. *1 Marine Way, 94970; 415 868 1632; www.sandpiperstinsonbeach.com*

① Vista Point
Marin County
This lookout at the north end of the Golden Gate Bridge offers stunning views of the bridge, San Francisco, and Alcatraz. Park here for up to 4 hours.
🚗 *Drive north on I-101, exit on Alexander Ave; turn left and go under the freeway. Follow Conzelman Rd & Bunker Rd around the headlands.*

② Marin Headlands
Marin County; 94965
The wild, rugged Marin Headlands are part of the Golden Gate National Recreation Area. Conzelman Road climbs this wind-whipped headland to **Battery Mendell**, a World War II gun emplacement, and **Point Bonita**

Lighthouse, reached by a hiking trail. The views are fantastic from both. The road then descends into a valley via the **Nike Missile Site** *(415 331 1453)*, a Cold War museum, and the **Marin Headlands Visitor Center** *(415 331 1540; www.nps.gov/goga)* housed in a former World War II-era chapel. Take a tour of the nearby **Marine Mammal Center** *(www.marinemammal center.org)*, a rescue and rehabilitation hospital for marine mammals. The headlands can get cold and windy; bring proper outerwear.
🚗 *Exit Marin Headlands on Bunker Rd (one way); exiting the tunnel, go under I-101 to Alexander Ave. Turn left and continue into Sausalito. Park at the lots at Gabrielson Park, on Bridgeway.*

③ Sausalito
Marin County; 94965
This picturesque fishing village is now a trendy residential community, boasting unrivaled views across the waters of San Francisco Bay. Victorian homes dot the steep hills that rise from the bay, and below, Bridgeway forms a waterfront promenade lined with fine yacht marinas, restaurants, and fanciful houseboats.

A two-hour walking tour
Begin at **Gabrielson Park** ①, which offers a panoramic perspective of this dollhouse town and the bay. Admire the tall steel-beam sculpture, *Hermandad*, by Chilean artist Sergio Castillo, then walk south past the Sausalito ferry terminal to tree-shaded **Sausalito Town Square** ②, with its Spanish fountain. A stone's throw south on Bridgeway is **Yee Tock Chee Park** ③, a triangular boardwalk with benches. Turn west and follow Bridgeway past shops and restaurants to the **Sausalito Visitor Center & Historical Exhibit** ④ *(780 Bridgeway; 415 332 0505)*. Continue north on the waterfront side of Bridgeway, and turn right onto Marinship Way. Look out for **Bay Model Visitor Center** ⑤ *(www.spn.usace. army.mil/bmvc)*, which has a giant 3D hydraulic model of the entire San Francisco Bay area, with tides surging

in and out. If there's time for a longer walk, follow Marinship Way to Harbor Drive. Turn right, then left at Gate 5 Road, which leads to about 500 hippy-era houseboats, including the 19th-century yellow ferry – SS *City of Seattle*. Return along Bridgeway and walk west to Napa Street. Take this

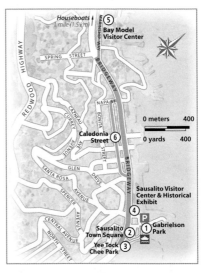

0 meters 400
0 yards 400

Above Driving through Marin County **Right** Golden Gate Bridge as seen from Vista Point

south to **Caledonia Street** ⑥, which is lined with art cafés and stores. Walk along Caledonia Street to Bridgeway to return to the lot at Gabrielson Park.

🚗 *Follow Bridgeway north to I-101; exit the freeway onto Shoreline Hwy (SR 1) and follow signs for Stinson Beach. Turn right onto Panoramic Hwy and left onto Muir Woods Rd, which descends to Muir Woods.*

④ Muir Woods National Monument
Marin County; 94941

Thousands of old-growth coast redwoods can be seen along 6 miles (10 km) of hiking trails in this forest reserve (*www.nps.gov/muwo*) created by President Theodore Roosevelt in 1908. The trees, some of which are 1,000 years old, are among the tallest in the world.

🚗 *Continue down Muir Woods Rd. Turn right onto Shoreline Hwy (SR 1) for Muir Beach. Park in the public lot.*

⑤ Muir Beach
Marin County; 94965

The hamlet of Muir Beach is nestled in a cove fronted by a swath of golden sand and cusped by craggy headlands beneath Mt Tamalpais. The marshland behind the beach is great for birding and spotting monarch butterflies. From here, SR 1 claws up the face of the cliff, snaking along the cliff-top, with occasional steep descents and ascents into river valleys. The scenery builds dramatically, with sheer drop-offs to sheltered coves protected by wave-battered crags. On clear days, the Farallon Islands seem to float on the distant horizon.

🚗 *Follow SR 1 from Muir Beach to Stinson Beach. Park in the State Beach parking lot.*

⑥ Stinson Beach
Marin County; 94970

The white sands here arc 3.5 miles (5 km) along Bolinas Bay, extending to form a spit enclosing Bolinas Lagoon. Surf washes ashore and the ocean is popular for surf fishing, but riptides, cold water, and great white shark sightings (which mandate a 5-day beach closure) make swimming unwise.

🚗 *Continue north on SR 1 via Bolinas Lagoon. Park roadside.*

⑦ Bolinas Lagoon
Marin County; 94970

This triangular tidal lagoon to the north of, and behind, Stinson Beach occupies a trough created by the San Andreas Fault. One of the most pristine coastal wetlands on the West Coast, it is an important stop on the Pacific Flyway, with millions of migratory birds stopping here twice every year. Low tide exposes over 600 acres (243 ha) of mudflats, drawing harbor seals who come here to bask and shorebirds seeking clams. In spring, herons and egrets nest in colonies in the Martin Griffin Preserve at nearby **Audubon Canyon Ranch** (*www.egret.org*). The preserve offers self-guided hiking trails, and birds can be seen from a viewing station.

🚗 *Stay on SR 1 as it snakes through eucalyptus forest, through Bear Valley to Olema, 12 miles (19 km) from Bolinas Lagoon. Park on the roadside.*

Sign for Pelican Inn

EAT AND DRINK

SAUSALITO

Venice Gourmet Market *inexpensive*
This deli serves fresh sandwiches at patio tables with bay views.
625 Bridgeway, 94965; 415 332 3544; open 9am–7pm daily; www.venicegourmet.com

Scoma's *expensive*
Overlooking the bay, this Italian restaurant specializes in fresh seafood.
588 Bridgeway, 94965; 415 332 9551; open 11:30am–9pm daily, till 10pm Fri & Sat; www.scomassausalito.com

MUIR BEACH

Pelican Inn *moderate*
Classic Tudor pub serving bangers 'n' mash, shepherd's pie, and ales.
10 Pacific Way, 94965; 415 383 6000; open 11:30am–9pm daily; www.pelicaninn.com

STINSON BEACH

Sand Dollar *moderate*
Enjoy steamed clams, fish tacos, and *cioppino* (fish stew). Live jazz on weekends.
3458 Shoreline Hwy, 94970; 415 868 0434; open 11:30am–9pm daily; www.stinsonbeachrestaurant.com

SHOPPING IN SAUSALITO

Butterflute Studios
Studio of artist Victoria Colella, who sells folk art.
2350 Marinship Way, 94966; 415 332 6608; www.butterflute.com; by appointment only

Sausalito Artists Open Studios
The Industrial Center Building houses the workspaces of about 80 artists.
480 Gate 5 Rd, 94966; 415 332 0730; www.sausalitoartistsopenstudios.com

Eat and Drink: inexpensive under $25; moderate $25–50; expensive over $50

Above Bear Valley Visitor Center, Point Reyes National Seashore's main information hub

WHERE TO STAY

OLEMA

Alta Olema Bed & Breakfast
moderate
Furnished with eclectic pieces and luxurious linens, this B&B's rooms and cottages offer plenty of charm.
9876 Sir Francis Drake Blvd, 94950; 415 663 1500; www.altaolema.com

Point Reyes Seashore Lodge
expensive
A gracious lodge with sunny rooms, down quilts, and heated floors.
10021 Coastal Hwy 1, 94950; 415 663 9000; www.pointreyesseashore.com

TOMALES BAY

Manka's Inverness Lodge *expensive*
This former hunting and fishing lodge offers rooms in a converted boathouse. Romantic cabins in the woods have vintage bathtubs.
30 Callender Way, Inverness, 94937; 415 669 1034; www.mankas.com

Below Grazing tule elk seen from Tomales Point **Below Right** Nineteenth-century Point Reyes Lighthouse

⑧ Olema
Marin County; 94950
A charming village atop the San Andreas Fault, Olema was originally a logging center in the late 19th century. Today, this sleepy settlement has a handful of antique shops, restaurants, and quaint B&Bs.

🚗 *On the north side of Olema, turn off SR 1 onto Bear Valley Rd, which leads into the Point Reyes National Seashore. Follow the signs for the Bear Valley Visitor Center.*

---

⑨ Point Reyes National Seashore
Marin County; 94956

This hook-shaped landmass jutting out into the Pacific Ocean boasts dramatic landscapes. Surf crashes ashore onto long swaths of sand that give way to headlands topped by forest and lush rolling meadows. The wind-battered Point Reyes Headland is ideal for whale-watching, while elephant seals, sea lions, and tule elk can be seen from vista points and along the many hiking trails.

① Bear Valley Visitor Center
Interactive exhibits explain the park's culture, geology, and natural history, with re-creations of various ecosystems *(open 9am–5pm daily)*. Many trails begin here; the Earthquake Loop Trail leads past a rupture that moved the Point Reyes landmass 20 ft (6 m) during the 1906 earthquake.

🚗 *Follow Bear Valley Rd north to its junction with Sir Francis Drake Blvd. Turn left and keep north along Tomales Bay, reached after 2 miles (3 km).*

② Tomales Bay
The western shore of this shallow coastal estuary is forested with pine, fir, and eucalyptus, and lined with beaches where harbor seals sunbathe. Spot ducks and bald eagles on kayak tours with **Blue Water Kayaking** *(www.bwkayak.com)*. Boats keel at low tide at the quaint community of Inverness. Heart's Desire Beach offers picnic tables and sheltered waters for swimming.

🚗 *Keep on Sir Francis Drake Blvd to the split with Pierce Point Rd. At the end of the road, park at the historic Pierce Point Ranch.*

③ Tule Elk Reserve
Stretching to the northern tip of Point Reyes, Tomales Point is roamed by tule elk. Once almost extinct, the large endemic deer species was reintroduced in 1978. They are easily spotted in the meadows and on ridges, especially in Aug–Sep, when large males fight for privileges with the females.

🚗 *Retrace the route along Pierce Point Rd to the junction with Sir Francis Drake Blvd. Turn right, and at the sign for Drakes Bay Oyster Company, turn left onto the unpaved road. Park at the lot.*

④ Drakes Estero
British explorer Francis Drake is said to have careened the *Golden Hinde* at this estuary in 1579. Waterfowl, wading birds, and white pelicans flock to the marshes, and rays, leopard sharks, and harbor seals can be seen up close on kayak trips. Learn about aquaculture at **Drakes Bay Oyster**

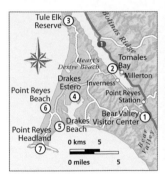

California Gray Whales

Growing upto 52 ft (16 m), these whales migrate from Alaskan waters to their breeding grounds in the warm lagoons of Mexico's Baja California each winter. They stay close to the shore as they pass California's coast on their two-month journey (each way) in mid-Dec–mid-Jan and Mar–Apr.

Company *(www.drakesbayoyster.com)*, which has an oyster farm and cannery.
🚗 *Returning to Sir Francis Drake Blvd, turn left. Continue until Drakes Beach Rd; turn left for Drakes Beach. Park at the visitor center.*

⑤ Drakes Beach

Sweeping around Drakes Bay beneath sandstone cliffs, this sheltered beach is perfect for long walks and a swim. The **Kenneth C. Patrick Visitor Center** *(open 10am–5pm Sat & Sun)* has exhibits on maritime exploration and natural history, including the skeleton of a whale. Seals use the sands as rookeries and whales are often seen close to shore.
🚗 *Back on Sir Francis Drake Blvd, turn left and then right at the sign for Point Reyes Beach South; park at the lot.*

⑥ Point Reyes Beach

This golden-sand beach, also known as the Great Beach, sees strong surf crashing ashore. Frolic in the sand dunes and tidal marsh, and spot birds such as the snowy plover during walks along the beach.
🚗 *Continue southwest to the end of Sir Francis Drake Blvd. Park in the parking lot or alongside the road, then walk to the lighthouse.*

⑦ Point Reyes Headland

Jutting 10 miles (16 km) into the Pacific Ocean, the Point Reyes Headland at the western tip of the peninsula is the windiest and second foggiest point in North America. On clear days, however, it offers sensational views over Point Reyes Beach. The visitor center has a viewing platform with binoculars for spotting passing whales. From here, take the 300-step staircase down the cliff-face to **Point Reyes Lighthouse** *(open 10am–4:30pm Thu–Mon)*, which was built in 1870 and still displays its original Fresnel lens. Chimney Rock Trail, east of the visitor center, is ablaze with wildflowers in spring. Nearby, Elephant Seal Overlook provides a vantage over the rookeries.

Above Crashing surf at Tomales Point, Point Reyes National Seashore

EAT AND DRINK

OLEMA

Farm House Restaurant *moderate*
This gourmet restaurant uses fresh local produce and has patio dining. *10021 Coastal Hwy 1, 94950; 415 663 1264; open 11:30am–9pm daily, 11:30am–10pm Sat; www.pointreyesseashore.com*

TOMALES BAY

Station House Café *moderate*
Cheerful pub ambience with live music. Try the mushroom fettuccine and pan-roasted halibut. *11180 SR 1, Point Reyes Station, 94937; 415 663 1515; check website for timings; www.stationhousecafe.com*

Vladimir's *moderate*
European nouvelle and classic dishes served indoors or in an open dining area at this cozy restaurant. *12785 Sir Francis Drake Blvd, 94937; 415 669 1021; hours vary, closed Mon*

DRAKES BEACH

Drakes Beach Café *inexpensive*
Rustic beachfront café serving burgers, sandwiches, and hot dishes. *1 Drakes Beach Rd, 94937; 415 669 1297; check website for timings; www.drakescafe.com*

DAY TRIP OPTIONS

The route can be broken down into day trips for those who want to follow a special interest.

An urban viewpoint

Photographers will find perfect angles of San Francisico from Vista Point ❶, the Marin Headlands ❷, and Sausalito ❸.

From Vista Point take Alexander Ave to cross under the freeway and link to

Conzelman Rd, which leads back via Bunker Rd to Sausalito.

Beachcomber bliss

For good surf and sand, combine Muir Beach ❺ with Stinson Beach ❻ and Heart's Desire Beach in Point Reyes National Seashore ❾.

The SR 1 highway connects the beaches. At Olema, turn left for Sir Francis Drake Blvd, and continue to Heart's Desire Beach.

Wildlife galore

Visit Bolinas Lagoon ❼, Tomales Bay, Tule Elk Reserve, and Drakes Estero to see bird and animal life in abundance.

Take the SR 1 north to Olema. Turn left for Sir Francis Drake Blvd to Tomales Bay. Continue to Point Pierce Ranch Rd, which leads to the Tule Elk Reserve. Return to Sir Francis Drake Blvd and head west for Drakes Estero.

Eat and Drink: inexpensive under $25; moderate $25–50; expensive over $50

Yreka

Redding

CALIFORNIA

Santa Rosa • Sacramento

San Francisco

San Jose

Monterey • Fresno

Wine Country
Napa to Sonoma

Highlights

- **World-class wine**
  Sample award-winning wines at eclectic wineries throughout the region

- **Contemporary art**
  Marvel at the fine works of art in the contemporary gallery at the Hess Collection winery

- **Thermal treats**
  Visit the Old Faithful geyser in Calistoga and take time to soak in therapeutic hot mud

- **Literary allusions**
  Explore the sites described by novelists Robert Louis Stevenson and Jack London in their books

Lush vineyards in front of Castello di Amorosa, Napa Valley

Wine Country

Renowned for its world-class wines, Napa Valley is just one of several scenic valleys that make up Northern California's Wine Country. The entire region is blessed with a warm, Mediterranean climate, and this route takes visitors past vine-clad vales beneath wooded mountains and to several excellent wineries. While many wineries double as art galleries and museums, others, at the edge of Healdsburg and St. Helena, are architectural wonders featuring Victorian mansions. Head to historic Sonoma to see its early mission and barracks, or visit one of Santa Rosa's many intriguing museums. Also on offer are pampering spa treatments, first-rate dining and accommodations, and activities from hiking to hot-air ballooning.

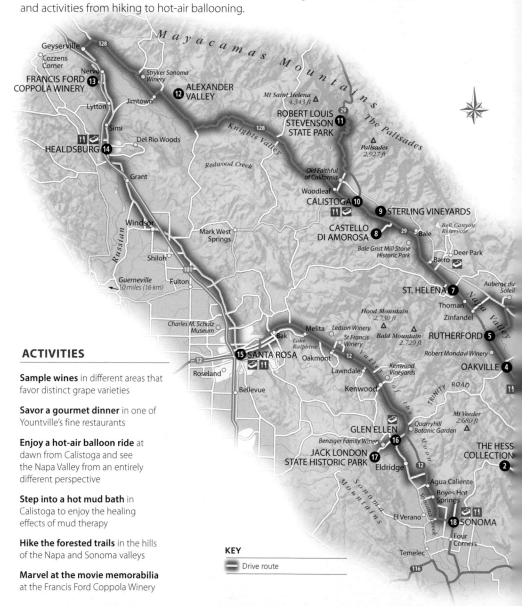

ACTIVITIES

Sample wines in different areas that favor distinct grape varieties

Savor a gourmet dinner in one of Yountville's fine restaurants

Enjoy a hot-air balloon ride at dawn from Calistoga and see the Napa Valley from an entirely different perspective

Step into a hot mud bath in Calistoga to enjoy the healing effects of mud therapy

Hike the forested trails in the hills of the Napa and Sonoma valleys

Marvel at the movie memorabilia at the Francis Ford Coppola Winery

KEY

Drive route

Above Flowers in bloom in Benziger Winery's garden near Glen Ellen, *see p60*

0 kilometers 5

0 miles 5

Above The historic Calistoga Depot, now home to wine shops and boutiques, *see p58*

PLAN YOUR DRIVE

Start/finish: Napa to Sonoma.

Number of days: 2–3 days.

Distance: 140 miles (226 km).

Road conditions: The roads are well paved. Expect heavy traffic on weekends on SR 29, and during rush hours in downtown Santa Rosa.

When to go: Wine Country is a year-round destination. In spring, lavender and mustard fields are in bloom, while summer means sunny days and fewer crowds. Fall is harvest time, when vines are crimson and gold, and wineries are at their busiest. Winter can be misty.

Main market days: Healdsburg: Sat am. **Santa Rosa:** Wed & Sat am. **Sonoma:** Fri am.

Opening times: Most wineries open daily, although hours vary. Some open by appointment only, and tours may require reservations.

Shopping: Fine wines and locally produced olive oils and cheeses can be found at the wineries. The towns have plenty of antique stores.

Major festivals: Napa: Napa Valley Wine Festival, May. **Alexander Valley:** Barrel Tasting Weekend, Mar. **Guerneville:** Russian River Jazz Festival, Aug. **Sonoma:** Sonoma County Harvest Fair, Sep.

Drinking and driving: California has strict laws against drunken driving. Visitors who plan to stop for wine-tasting along this drive should have a designated driver.

DAY TRIP OPTIONS

Art admirers can visit the **Hess Collection** and **Robert Mondavi** wineries. Those who appreciate **literature** should head to **Glen Ellen**, **Jack London State Historic Park**, and **Robert Louis Stevenson State Park**. **Wine connoisseurs** can try settle the debate about which vineyard produces the best wines. For full details, *see p61*.

VISITING NAPA

Tourist Information
*600 Main St, 94559; 707 251 5895;
www.legendarynapavalley.com*

Parking
Park at the multi-tier public lot at
5th St & Main St.

WHERE TO STAY

NAPA

Churchill Manor *expensive*
This gracious B&B recalls 19th-century
style and hospitality. The rooms are
well-appointed with antiques.
*485 Brown St, 94559; 707 253 7733;
www.churchillmanor.com*

Westin Verasa *expensive*
This deluxe hotel offers contemporary-
themed accommodations and an
excellent restaurant.
*1314 McKinstry St, 94559; 707 257
1800; www.westinnapa.com*

YOUNTVILLE

Napa Valley Railway Inn *moderate*
Cozy accommodations in antique rail
cars at this one-of-a-kind hotel.
*6523 Washington St, 94599; 707 944
2000; www.napavalleyrailwayinn.com*

AROUND RUTHERFORD

Auberge du Soleil *expensive*
A romantic hillside spa-retreat offering
world-class luxury.
*180 Rutherford Hill Rd, 94573; 707 963
1211; www.aubergedusoleil.com*

AROUND ST. HELENA

Meadowood Resort *expensive*
Set in wooded grounds, this resort-
hotel has a spa, golf course, tennis
and croquet courts, and a 3-star
Michelin restaurant.
*900 Meadowood Lane, 94574; 707 963
3646; www.meadowood.com*

Below A track cutting through sprawling
vineyards in the Napa Valley

Above The stone facade of the Culinary Institute of America at Greystone, north of St. Helena
Above right Shoppers at the Hess Collection's store

① Napa
Napa County; 94559

This former river-port town's restored
historic downtown, Main Street in
particular, is lined with Victorian
buildings that house antique stores,
art galleries, and restaurants. A hub
for shopping and dining, the
19th-century Napa Mill stands at the
heart of the Napa waterfront. Nearby,
the Italianate **Opera House**, built in
1880, is the pride of the city, while
the **First Presbyterian
Church**, erected in 1874, is a
fine example of late Victorian
Gothic architecture.

🚗 *Exit along Main St. Turn
right onto 1st St then left on
Soscol Ave to Trancas St.
Drive north and turn left after
1.5 miles (2.5 km); follow
Trancas St (later Redwood
Rd). Keep on Redwood Rd and
follow the signs for the Hess
Collection, 4 miles (6 km) uphill.*

② The Hess Collection
Napa County; 94558

Tucked high on the slopes of Mt
Veeder, this is one of the region's most
remarkable wineries *(www.hess
collection.com)*. It features a
contemporary art gallery in an avant-
garde conversion of a former
monastery. Displayed on two levels,
the collection includes works by such
renowned artists as Leopoldo Maler
and Franz Gertsch alongside other,
mostly European, artists. The ivy-clad

**Wine bottles at
Inglenook Winery**

winery also produces premium wines,
which can be sampled in the tasting
room, where a glass wall offers views
into the barrel room.

🚗 *Return via Redwood Rd to SR 29
(St. Helena Hwy), turning left onto
SR 29 north via the entrance. Continue
to Yountville; park on the roadside.*

③ Yountville
Napa County; 94599

A small, charming town, Yountville is
home to some of California's
top restaurants, most
notably The French Laundry.
Get a glimpse into the
valley's cultural heritage and
natural history at the **Napa
Valley Museum** *(www.napa
valleymuseum.org)* outside
town. Nearby, the **Domaine
Chandon** winery *(1 California
Dr; www.chandon.com)* is a
must-visit for its sparkling
wines. Nature lovers will enjoy a trip
to the **Napa Valley Ecological Reserve**
*(www.dfg.ca.gov/lands/er/region3/
napariver.html)*, an important setting
for birds and animals that find shelter
in the meadows, and willow and oak
habitats lining the river.

🚗 *From Yountville, drive north on
SR 29 to Oakville; park along the road.*

④ Oakville
Napa County; 94562

This charming hamlet evolved as
one of California's pioneer wine
centers in the 1870s. Look out for

the mission-style **Robert Mondavi Winery** (www.robertmondavi.com), which offers excellent tours, and has some fine sculptures. A stop at the **Oakville Grocery**, which has served the Napa Valley community for more than 120 years, is *de rigueur*: it sells everything visitors could possibly want for a picnic lunch.

🚗 Continue north on SR 29 to Rutherford; park on the roadside.

⑤ Rutherford
Napa County; 94573
Just 2 miles (3 km) north of Oakville, this tiny community has some superb wineries, set in one of the most famous AVAs (designated wine-growing regions) in Wine Country. The **Inglenook Winery** (www. rubiconestate.com) is one of Wine Country's most attractive estates. This ostentatious ivy-clad winery is owned by Hollywood filmmaker Francis Ford Coppola. A museum here displays artifacts from the winery's history as well as traces the invention of cinema.

🚗 Exit SR 29 east onto Rutherford Rd. Turn left onto Conn Creek Rd, and right onto the Silverado Trail. Turn left onto Sage Canyon Rd for Lake Hennessey, which has roadside lots.

⑥ Vaca Mountains
Napa County; 94573
A brief detour east into the Vaca Mountains leads to Lake Hennessey – the perfect place to beat the summer valley heat. This man-made reservoir behind the Conn Creek Dam irrigates Napa Valley and is a popular fishing spot. Enjoy stunning valley views from the switchback road. Stop at **Auberge du Soleil** (www.aubergedusoleil.com), a deluxe

spa-resort that evokes visions of the French Riviera with its olive groves, terraced sandstone-colored villas, and views over vineyards below.

🚗 Back on the Silverado Trail, drive north to Zinfandel Lane and turn left. After 1 mile (1.6 km), turn right onto SR 29. Drive 2 miles (3 km) into St. Helena and park on Main St.

⑦ St. Helena
Napa County; 94574
Peaceful, tree-shaded St. Helena is undoubtedly the prettiest town in the region. Its old-fashioned Main Street is lined with antique stores, upscale wine bars, and restaurants set in Victorian-era buildings. Take at least one hour to explore downtown, including the **Silverado Museum** (1490 Library Lane; www. silveradomuseum.org), dedicated to author Robert Louis Stevenson, who spent his honeymoon in St. Helena in 1880.

On the north side of town, **Beringer Winery** (www.beringer.com) is an ornate stone-and-timber, 17-room Victorian mansion that doubles as a wine-tasting room. Visit the historic, castle-like Greystone Cellars, the former winery of the **Culinary Institute of America** (www.ciachef.edu/california). Greystone's attractions include a huge corkscrew collection, a Vintners Hall of Fame, and cooking and wine-appreciation demonstrations. Stop at the **Bale Grist Mill Stone Historic Park** (www.parks.ca.gov/), a short distance north of town, to see a restored 19th-century mill and its 36-ft (118-m) high waterwheel.

🚗 Continue north on SR 29 to the Castello di Amorosa winery, signed on the left of the highway; it has parking.

Above One of the sculptures in the grounds of the Robert Mondavi Winery, Oakville

EAT AND DRINK

NAPA

ZuZu *moderate*
This cozy tapas restaurant serves bite-sized treats and has an attentive staff.
829 Main St, 94559; 707 224 8555; open 11:30am–10pm Mon–Thu, 11:30am–11pm Fri, 4:30–11pm Sat, 4:30–9:30pm Sun; www.zuzunapa.com

YOUNTVILLE

Hurley's *moderate*
This casual Mediterranean restaurant uses fresh local ingredients and has a communal dining table. It offers a *prix fixe* lunch.
6518 Washington St, 94599; 707 944 2345; open 11:30am–9pm Mon–Thu & Sun, 11am–10pm Fri & Sat; www.hurleysrestaurant.com

The French Laundry *expensive*
Chef Thomas Keller's restaurant is widely acclaimed for its French-inspired dishes. Reserve two months in advance.
6640 Washington St, 94599; 707 944 2380; open 5:30–9:15pm Mon–Thu, 11am–1pm Fri–Sun; www. frenchlaundry.com; by reservation only

AROUND YOUNTVILLE

Mustards Grill *moderate*
A diner-style restaurant with a wood-burning grill. Try the chipotle-rubbed quail, or crispy calamari with a slaw.
7399 St. Helena Hwy, 94558; 707 944 2424; open 11:30am–9pm Mon–Thu, 11:30am–10pm Fri, 11am–10pm Sat, 11am–9pm Sun; www.mustardsgrill.com

Left The Rhine House at Beringer Winery, set amid lush gardens

Above Medieval-style turrets of Castello di Amorosa

VISITING CALISTOGA

Tourist Information
1133 Washington St, 94515; 707 942 6333; www.calistogavisitors.com

WHERE TO STAY

CALISTOGA

Brannan Cottage Inn *moderate*
This 1860 B&B with gingerbread trim and a wraparound porch has rooms with fireplaces and four-poster beds.
109 Wapoo Ave, 94515; 707 942 4200; www.brannancottageinn.com

Calistoga Ranch *expensive*
Tucked in a private canyon, this resort hotel offers 48 cabins in the woods.
580 Lommel Rd, 94515; 707 254 2800; www.calistogaranch.com

HEALDSBURG

Healdsburg Inn *moderate*
Located next to the plaza, Healdsburg Inn boasts large and luxurious rooms.
112 Matheson St, 95448; 707 433 6991; www.healdsburginn.com

The Raford Inn *moderate*
This Victorian inn, overlooking vineyards, offers antique-furnished rooms, gourmet breakfasts, and a spa.
10630 Wohler Rd, 95448; 707 887 9573; www.rafordinn.com

Right The tree-lined road leading up to Sterling Vineyards

8 Castello di Amorosa
Napa County; 94515
The dream of vintner Dario Sattui, the castle *(www.castellodiamorosa. com)* has a working drawbridge, turrets, and a 500-year-old fireplace, as well as a torture chamber with antique torture devices. A state-of-the-art facility behind the castle makes award-winning wines. Step into the underground tasting rooms and a barrel cellar, which hosts a midsummer Medieval Festival, or take a horse-drawn carriage tour through the vineyards.

Return to SR 29 and continue north to Dunaweal Lane; turn right for Sterling Vineyards, which has parking.

9 Sterling Vineyards
Napa County; 94515
Perched on a 300-ft (91-m) high knoll, Sterling Vineyards is a local landmark and offers spectacular views of Napa Valley. An aerial tram ride whisks visitors up to this Mediterranean-style winery. View the "Winemaker's Video Tour", and enjoy a leisurely self-guided tour.

Return to SR 29 and continue north to Calistoga. Turn right on Lincoln Ave and park anywhere along the street.

10 Calistoga
Napa County; 94515
Located on the site of thermal springs, this charming resort-town was laid out as a spa destination in the 1860s by millionaire businessman Sam Brannan. Lincoln Avenue retains the town's original character and is lined with eclectic stores, inns, and eateries. Do not miss the historic **Calistoga Depot** train station, where six restored antique railroad carriages house boutique stores. Relax in a therapeutic thermal mud bath at **Dr Wilkinson's Hot Springs Resort**

(www.drwilkinson.com), and on the way out of town, visit **Old Faithful of California** *(Tubbs Lane; www.oldfaithful geyser.com)*, one of only three geysers in the world that erupt at regular intervals; to get there, turn left off Stevenson Street onto Grant Street, and continue for 1 mile (1.6 km).

From the geyser, follow Tubbs Lane east to Lake County Hwy (SR 29). Turn left and follow the road uphill. Park at the turnout signed for the Robert Louis Stevenson State Park.

Judgment of Paris
In 1976, British wine merchant Steven Spurrier organized a blind tasting in Paris, where the best Bordeaux and Burgundy wines were pitted against wines from California. Chateau Montelena's chardonnay and Stag's Leap Wine Cellars' cabernet were named the best wines, bringing instant recognition to California wines.

11 Robert Louis Stevenson State Park
Napa County; 94515
This forested park enshrining Mt Saint Helena has a signed Stevenson Memorial Trail that snakes up a slope to a granite open book, marking the spot where the Scottish author and his bride honeymooned in a cabin in 1880. Walk 5 miles (8 km) uphill along a well-graded fire road to the summit, which offers panoramic views spanning Napa Valley and San Francisco Bay. On clear days, the snow-capped peaks of the High Sierra can be seen glistening in the sun.

Return to Tubbs Lane and after 1.5 miles (2.5 km) turn right on SR 128 for Alexander Valley. After 15 miles (24 km), turn right at the junction of Alexander Valley Rd, W Sausal Lane, and SR 128.

⑫ Alexander Valley

Sonoma County

North of Calistoga, the highway snakes through twin forested ridges to traverse this long, narrow valley drained by the Upper Russian River. Sheltered from the moist coastal air, the Alexander Valley produces opulent wines. Stray from SR 128 to explore this bucolic vale full of vineyards, apple orchards, and green meadows. Wine lovers will appreciate the **Stryker Sonoma Winery** (www.strykersonoma.com), where a glass-walled tasting room overlooks the vineyards and valley. Continue north 6.5 miles (10 km) to the attractive hamlet of **Geyserville**, where wineries offer some of the region's best wines for tasting.

🚗 *In Geyserville, turn left onto Geyserville Ave. Stay on it as it passes under I-101 freeway twice. Turn right onto Independence Underpass. Pass under the freeway to enter Francis Ford Coppola Winery.*

Above Stairs leading up to the Francis Ford Coppola Winery

⑬ Francis Ford Coppola Winery

Sonoma County; 95441

Famous Hollywood film director Francis Ford Coppola owns this namesake winery (www.francis coppolawinery.com). View the movie memorabilia displayed on two levels, including a rare 1948 Tucker automobile, from *Tucker: A Man and his Dream* (1988), which dominates the entrance lobby. Other iconic mementos from

Coppola's movies, screened throughout the winery, include the giant martini glass from *One from the Heart* (1982), costumes from Bram Stoker's *Dracula* (1992), plus Vito Corleone's desk from *The Godfather* (1972). The winery also has swimming pools, bocce ball courts, and a poolside amphitheater that hosts live concerts.

🚗 *Continue south on Geyserville Ave. Turn left at Lytton Spring Rd then immediately right onto Healdsburg Ave, which leads into Healdsburg. Park at the plaza or on side streets.*

⑭ Healdsburg

Sonoma County; 95448

One of Wine Country's most serene towns, Healdsburg resembles a living museum of handsome Victorian homes. The 19th-century plaza has a gazebo shaded by towering coast redwoods and palms, and the tree-shaded streets are lined with upscale restaurants and wine-tasting rooms. Many artists and musicians have settled here, invigorating this town with a vibrant culture. **Healdsburg Museum** (www.healdsburgmuseum. org), in the Neo-Classical Healdsburg Library on Matheson Street, profiles Sonoma County's history.

🚗 *Leave town heading south on Healdsburg Ave, which veers east to become the Old Redwood Hwy. Stay on this through Windsor (8 miles/ 13 km S of Healdsburg). Pass under I-101 and continue on Old Redwood Hwy, which becomes Mendocino Ave, leading into downtown Santa Rosa (10 miles/ 16 km S of Windsor).*

Above left The interior of Cyrus in Healdsburg
Above Vineyards seen from the Francis Ford Coppola Winery

VISITING HEALDSBURG

Tourist Information
217 Healdsburg Ave, 95448; 707 433 6935; www.healdsburg.com

EAT AND DRINK

CALISTOGA

Calistoga Inn *inexpensive*
This small brewpub delights beer lovers. Dishes include meats from a wood-fired grill.
1250 Lincoln Ave, 94515; 707 942 4101; open 11am–midnight daily; www.calistogainn.com

HEALDSBURG

Barndiva *moderate*
Wholesome nouvelle California dishes using sustainably sourced food served in a casual yet sophisticated ambience.
231 Center St, 95448; 707 431 0100; open noon–11pm Wed & Thu, noon– midnight Fri & Sat, 11am–10pm Sun; www.barndiva.com

Zin Restaurant & Wine Bar *moderate*
Minimalist decor features bare cement floors and walls, and exposed roof beams. It serves seasonal American dishes using farm fresh local produce. In winter, try the signature Coq au Zin.
344 Center St, 95448; 707 473 0946; open 11:30am–2pm & 5:30–9pm Mon–Fri, 5:30–9pm Sat & Sun; www.zinrestaurant.com

Cyrus *expensive*
Celebrated for its creative fusion fare, this elegant restaurant requires reservation well in advance.
29 North St, 95448; 707 433 3311; open 5:30–9:30pm Thu–Mon, 11:30am– 1:30pm Sat; www.cyrusrestaurant.com

Eat and Drink: inexpensive under $25; moderate $25–50; expensive over $50

Above Detail at one of Sonoma's wineries
Above right Tractor ride through a vineyard near Glen Ellen **Below** Lotus flowers in bloom at the Quarryhill Botanical Garden, Glen Ellen

VISITING SANTA ROSA

Tourist Information
*9 4th St, 95401; 707 577 8674;
www.visitsantarosa.com*

VISITING SONOMA

Tourist Information
*453 1st St E; 707 996 1090;
www.sonomavalley.com*

WHERE TO STAY

SANTA ROSA

Hotel La Rose *moderate*
A century-old hotel in the Railroad Square Historic District offering comfort in gracious environs.
*308 Wilson St, 95401; 707 579 3200;
www.hotellarose.com*

GLEN ELLEN

The Gaige House Inn *expensive*
This deluxe hotel has stylish Asian-inspired furnishings and a spa.
*13540 Arnold Dr, 95442; 707 935 0237;
www.gaige.com*

SONOMA

The Sonoma Hotel *moderate*
Antiques furnish the rooms at this 19th-century hotel on the plaza.
*110 W Spain St, 95476; 800 468 6016;
www.sonomahotel.com*

⑮ Santa Rosa
Sonoma County; 94501
The largest city in Wine Country, Santa Rosa is a hub for arts, fine dining, and entertainment. The **Charles M. Schulz Museum** *(www.schulzmuseum.org)* celebrates the *Peanuts* cartoon characters and the life of the cartoonist with hundreds of his original works. The **Sonoma County Museum** *(www.sonomacountymuseum. org)* has exhibits on the art, culture, and history of Wine Country. Head south to the revitalized **Railroad Square Historic District** *(Davis St between 3rd St & 6th St; railroadsquare. net)*, built by Italian stonemasons in 1904. Today, the buildings here have been turned into restaurants, boutiques, and trendy bars. Close by, explore the former home of famous horticulturist Luther Burbank and the gardens where he conducted plant-breeding experiments at the **Luther Burbank Home & Garden** *(www.lutherburbank.org)*.

🚗 *Follow Sonoma Ave east to Summerfield Rd. Turn left, then right*

on Montgomery Dr, left on Mission Blvd, and right onto SR 12 for Glen Ellen. Park at the lot at Arnold Dr and London Ranch Rd.

⑯ Glen Ellen
Sonoma County; 94501
Nestled at the base of forested hills, Glen Ellen is a peaceful and scenic town. Oak trees shade its winding streets lined with 19th-century brick-and-timber buildings. The **Quarryhill Botanical Garden** *(12841 Sonoma Hwy; www.quarryhillbg.org)*, on the north side of town, delights with its collection of Asian plants.

🚗 *Head west out of town along London Ranch Rd, which ends at a lot.*

⑰ Jack London State Historic Park
Sonoma County; 95442
This forested park *(2400 London Ranch Rd; www.parks.ca.gov/)* preserves the former ranch of writer Jack London, who built his home here in 1905. Trails wind through the 1,400-acre (567-ha) park, connecting his cottage residence with a lake and bathhouse, the remains of "Wolf House", and "The House of Happy Walls", which hosts a museum on his life. En route, stop at the **Benziger Family Winery** *(www.benziger.com)*, which offers tractor-drawn tram tours through the vineyard.

🚗 *Return to Glen Ellen, then exit on Arnold Dr and turn left on Madrone Rd. At SR 12, turn right for Sonoma. In town, turn left on W Spain St and follow signs to Sonoma State Historic Park. Park at the visitor center.*

⑱ Sonoma
Sonoma County; 95476
The picturesque town of Sonoma is graced with carefully preserved historic buildings dating back to 1823, when Franciscan *padres* built the last of the 21 Spanish missions in California. A historic ensemble of Mexican adobe buildings recalls the city's formative years when it was the political center of Northern California. With plenty of cafés, restaurants, and galleries, central Sonoma is tailor-made for a stroll.

A two-hour walking tour
Begin at the Sonoma State Historic Park's visitor center at **Lachryma Montis** ① *(363 3rd St W; 707 996 1090; www.parks.ca.gov/)*, the former Gothic Revival home of Sonoma's founder,

General Mariano Vallejo (1808–1890). Admire the ornamental trim, pointed arches, and large windows of this restored Victorian-era house. The grounds are planted with vines and shady fruit trees, and feature a stone-

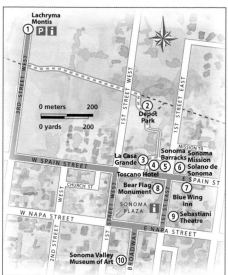

Lachryma Montis

0 meters 200
0 yards 200

W SPAIN STREET
La Casa Grande ③
Toscano Hotel
Bear Flag Monument ⑧
SONOMA PLAZA
W NAPA STREET
Sonoma Valley Museum of Art ⑩

3RD STREET WEST
1ST STREET WEST
1ST STREET EAST
Depot Park ②
MISSION TR
Sonoma Barracks ④⑤
Sonoma Mission ⑥
Solano de Sonoma ⑥
E SPAIN ST
Blue Wing Inn ⑦
Sebastiani Theatre ⑨
E NAPA STREET
CHURCH ST
2ND STREET WEST
1ST STREET WEST
1ST STREET EAST
BROADWAY

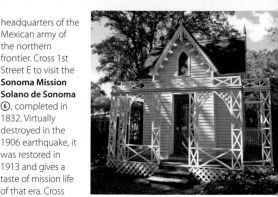

Above El Delirio, garden pavilion in the grounds of Lachryma Montis, Sonoma

and-brick reservoir, where turtles and ducks swim. After exploring the estate, walk south along the tree-lined driveway and turn left onto the bridal path that leads east through a meadow to **Depot Park** ②, where the town's history is regaled in the old train station. Turn south and pass through a car park to reach **La Casa Grande** ③. This adobe structure, once the servants' quarters, is all that remains of General Vallejo's first home, destroyed by fire in 1867. To its east, peek into the historic **Toscano Hotel** ④. Today a museum evoking the early-20th century, it is furnished as if guests are expected. Just ahead, **Sonoma Barracks** ⑤ was the

California State Parks signage

headquarters of the Mexican army of the northern frontier. Cross 1st Street E to visit the **Sonoma Mission Solano de Sonoma** ⑥, completed in 1832. Virtually destroyed in the 1906 earthquake, it was restored in 1913 and gives a taste of mission life of that era. Cross the street to view the venerable adobe **Blue Wing Inn** ⑦, which housed soldiers assigned to the mission. Walk 165 ft (50 m) west to view the **Bear Flag Monument** ⑧ at the northeast corner of the Sonoma Plaza. It recalls the rebellion of 1846 that sparked California's independence from Mexico, and its subsequent adoption as a US state. Follow 1st Street E south past the Art Deco **Sebastiani Theatre** ⑨, built in 1933. Turn right onto E Napa Street, then left onto Broadway for the **Sonoma Valley Museum of Art** ⑩, which exhibits multi-media works by local and interna-tional artists. Return to Sonoma Plaza and follow it clockwise to W Spain Street. Turn left and walk the 440 yards (400 m) to 3rd Street W. Turn right and follow it along the driveway that leads back to Lachryma Montis.

WHERE TO EAT

SANTA ROSA

Petite Syrah *expensive*
Stylish decor and an inventive menu emphasizing Wine Country dishes, such as beet salad and duck breast.
205 5th St, 95401; 707 568 4002; open 5–9pm Mon–Fri, 5–10pm Sat & Sun; www.petitesyrah.com

SONOMA

Della Santinas *moderate*
Romantic Tuscan ambience at this restaurant seving excellent Italian fare.
133 E Napa St, 95476; 707 935 0576; open 11:30am–3pm & 5–9:30pm daily; www.dellasantinas.com

The Girl & the Fig *expensive*
A casual French-style bistro, this restaurant gets packed with patrons seeking wholesome, delicious Wine Country fare.
110 W Spain St, 95476; 707 938 3634; open 11:30am–10pm Mon–Thu, 11:30am–11pm Fri & Sat, 10am–10pm Sun; www.thegirlandthefig.com

---

DAY TRIP OPTIONS
This area can be divided into three day trips, each catering to a specific interest.

For art lovers
For a perfect one-day artsy trip, start at The Hess Collection ②, then stop at Robert Mondavi Winery in Oakville ④, and at Clos Pegase Winery *(www.clospegase.com)* in Calistoga ⑩.

To get to Hess, take Redwood Road west off SR 29 north and follow the signs. Return to SR 29 which leads

north past Mondavi. Continue north and turn right on Dunaweal Lane for Clos Pegase.

For book buffs
Combine visits to Glen Ellen ⑯, Jack London State Historic Park ⑰, and Robert Louis Stevenson State Park ⑪ for a novel journey.

To get to Glen Ellen, take SR 12 north from Sonoma; London Ranch Rd leads to Jack London State Historic Park. From Glen Ellen, take snaking Trinity Rd

(which becomes Oakville Rd) east to SR 29, then north to Calistoga; turn right on Lincoln Ave and follow signs for Robert Louis Stevenson State Park.

For oenophiles
Sample some of the region's best wineries in Sonoma Valley. Look out for Kenwood, Ledson, and St. Francis Wineries.

SR 12 connects Santa Rosa and Sonoma via Sonoma Valley; the three wineries are signed along the highway.

Wine Valleys and Coastal Vistas

Healdsburg to Boonville

Highlights

- **Small town California**
  Stroll through downtown Healdsburg to admire this charming Victorian farming and railroad town

- **A Russian affair**
  Visit Fort Ross, the former Russian headquarters for hunting sea otters

- **Bucolic Russian River Valley**
  Explore wineries and redwood forests on one of California's most scenic riverside routes

- **Farms and vineyards**
  Buy a bottle of the region's fine pinot noir and sample the locally grown apples at Philo

Relaxing by the Russian River near Guerneville, on a sunny day

Wine Valleys and Coastal Vistas

This drive begins in Healdsburg, home to the tasting rooms of some of California's top wineries. From here, the route takes visitors through redwood parks and small resort towns scattered across the winding Russian River Valley. Next, drive along the Sonoma Coast, where beaches merit relaxing seaside walks. Stop at Jenner to watch seals basking in the sun and take in stunning ocean views from the historic lighthouse at Point Arena. The route finally snakes inland through the rustic Anderson Valley, another paradise for oenophiles.

Above Colorful shops lining the street, Guerneville, *see p66* **Below** Historic Point Arena Lighthouse and former lighthouse keepers' quarters, *see p70*

ACTIVITIES

Canoe or kayak a lazy stretch of the Russian River, aided by an outfitter in Guerneville

Spot a sea otter in the kelp beds at Fort Ross State Historic Park

Spend a night at a historic lighthouse property at Point Arena

Hike in the hush of a redwood forest in one of the many parks along this route

Sip the region's famed red wine varietals including pinot noir and zinfandel

0 kilometers 10

0 miles 10

Above Highway weaving through the dramatic coastal landscape north of Jenner, *see p67*

KEY

⬤ Drive route

PLAN YOUR DRIVE

Start/finish: Healdsburg to Boonville.

Number of days: 2–3 days.

Distance: 175 miles (280 km). Allow plenty of time as roads can be narrow and winding, and the attractions are many.

Road conditions: All paved and in good condition, but with lots of bends, so drive carefully, especially along the cliff roads of the Sonoma Coast. The coast road can be foggy in summer.

When to go: This drive is good anytime during the year but spring and fall are especially delightful.

Opening times: Most shops open from 10am to 6pm daily; restaurants usually serve until 9pm.

Shopping: Healdsburg is home to shops selling antiques, tasting rooms offering the area's best wines, and art galleries displaying scenic photos and paintings of the vineyards and coast.

Major festivals: Healdsburg: Antique fairs; Memorial Day & Labor Day. Guerneville: Russian River Jazz & Blues Festival, Sep. Fort Ross: Culture Heritage Day, Jul.

DAY TRIP OPTIONS

Healdsburg will engage day trippers with its Victorian charm and flourishing food scene. The Anderson Valley around **Boonville** attracts **wine** and **outdoor lovers** with its personalized wine tasting, boutique farming, and redwood parks. For full details, *see p71*.

Below Navarro Vineyards nestled in the Anderson Valley, near Philo, *see p71*

VISITING HEALDSBURG

Tourist Information
Healdsburg Chamber & Visitor Bureau
*217 Healdsburg Ave, 95448; 707 433
6935; open 9am–5pm daily;
www.healdsburg.com*

VISITING GUERNEVILLE

Tourist Information
Russian River Chamber & Visitor Center
*16201 1st St, 95446; 707 869 9000;
open 10am–5pm Mon–Sat, 10am–
4pm Sun; www.russianriver.com*

WHERE TO STAY

HEALDSBURG

Camellia Inn *expensive*
An Italianate Victorian B&B located
within walking distance of restaurants.
*211 North St, 95448; 707 433 8182;
www.camelliainn.com*

AROUND HEALDSBURG

The Raford Inn *moderate*
This Victorian manor house, encircled
by vineyards, has rooms named after
medicinal and culinary herbs.
*10630 Wohler Rd, 95448; 707 887 9573;
www.rafordinn.com*

MONTE RIO

Village Inn and Lodge *moderate*
This relaxed historic lodge is set in a
redwood grove near the Russian River.
*20822 River Rd, 95462; 707 865 2304;
www.villageinn-ca.com*

JENNER

Jenner Inn and Cottages *expensive*
Lodgings range from rooms to
furnished vacation homes.
Unparalleled river views.
*10400 Coast Hwy 1, 95450; 707 865
2377; www.jennerinn.com*

Above Stores along one of the streets in Guerneville

1 Healdsburg
Sonoma County; 95448
A progressive yet quiet riverfront
town, Healdsburg is centered
around a classic 19th-century
Spanish-style plaza, which is
surrounded by several antique shops
and hosts two antique fairs each
year. The town *(see also p59)* is
home to the tasting
rooms of many fine
wineries in the region
and boasts a fine-
dining scene. Park
roadside in town.

🚗 *Take Westside Rd
18 miles (29 km) west
from Healdsburg until
it becomes River Rd
and then merges with Hwy 116. Stop
at Guerneville; ample roadside parking.*

Below left Charming exterior and garden of
Camellia Inn, Healdsburg **Below** Canoeing on
the Russian River near Guerneville

Picnic food selection at a
deli in Healdsburg

2 Guerneville
Sonoma County; 95446
A thriving town of vacation rentals
and tourist lodgings along the
Russian River, Guerneville is a popular
getaway for the residents of San
Francisco. The town is an intimate
place brimming with small shops
and boutiques. Walk out on the
pedestrian bridge to enjoy
breathtaking views
of the Russian
River. The more
adventurous can
rent kayaks and canoes
from outfitters such
as **King's Sport &
Tackle** *(16258 Main
St; 707 869 2156;
www.kingsrussianriver.com)* and
tackle a section of the river.

🚗 *Exit Guerneville and continue
north on Armstrong Woods Rd to
Armstrong Redwoods State Natural
Reserve; park near the entrance.*

Where to Stay: inexpensive under $100; moderate $100–200; expensive over $200

Above left Picnicking at Armstrong
Redwoods State Natural Reserve
Above Mustard fields, Guerneville

③ Armstrong Redwoods State Natural Reserve

Sonoma County; 95446

The 700-acre (283-ha) Armstrong Redwoods State Natural Reserve (*www.parks.ca.gov/*) preserves a small portion of the ancient old-growth redwoods that lined the Russian River before logging operations began here in the 19th century. The reserve's tallest tree is the 1,300 year-old Parson Jones Tree, which towers to a staggering 310 ft (95 m).

Take the self-guided Pioneer Trail, which starts at the park entrance and weaves through the dense redwood forest habitat. Gazing up at the massive trees in the hushed quiet of a redwood grove is an unforgettable experience.

🚗 *Return to Guerneville on Armstrong Woods Rd and turn west on Hwy 116. Drive to Monte Rio; there is free roadside parking.*

④ Monte Rio

Sonoma County; 95462

Another little river town, Monte Rio is lined with charming Victorian buildings and offers plenty of quiet places to stay. Head to its riverside beach to sunbathe or to enjoy a swim. Look out for the town's funky theater set in a mural-covered Quonset hut (a semi-circular corrugated structure).

The town is perhaps best known for its proximity to the campground of the exclusive private men's club, the Bohemian Club, whose members include some well-known figures of the business and government elite.

🚗 *Leave the Russian River with a 10 mile (16 km) drive west on Hwy*

116. When the highway meets Coast Hwy 1, turn north and drive to Jenner; park roadside.

⑤ Jenner

Sonoma County; 95450

The Russian River broadens out at Duncans Mills and empties into the sea at Jenner. A sandy spit formed at the mouth of the river serves as a massive breeding ground for seals. Their numbers spiral in April, with the birth of new pups. Watch these gentle creatures from a perch above the water or get a closer look while strolling across the driftwood-strewn sand at Goat Rock Beach. Enjoy the refreshing sea breeze and keep an eye out for the offshore rock pedestals here, known as "sea stacks."

🚗 *Proceed north from Jenner on Coast Hwy 1 for 12 miles (19 km) to Fort Ross State Historic Park.*

Above Wooden cabin on the forested shores of the Russian River, Monte Rio

EAT AND DRINK

HEALDSBURG

Baci Café & Wine Bar *moderate*
Try the shrimp chilled with lime, oven-roasted duck, and home-made gnocchi.
336 Healdsburg Ave, 95448; 707 433 8111; open 5–9pm Thu–Mon; www.bacicafeandwinebar.com

Zin *moderate*
Using fresh ingredients from its own farm, Zin serves seasonal American food in a coastal ambience.
344 Center St, 95448; 707 473 0946; closed for lunch Sat & Sun; www.zinrestaurant.com

GUERNEVILLE

Taqueria La Tapatia *inexpensive*
A favorite for Mexican food; try the *camarones rancheros* (shrimp in butter-garlic sauce with jalapeños), *carne asada* (roasted meat), or vegetarian options.
16632 Main St, 95446; 707 869 1821; open 11am–9pm daily

AROUND MONTE RIO

Blue Heron Restaurant & Tavern *inexpensive*
Grab a burger, a skewer of salmon, or fish taco at this local favorite.
25300 Steelhead Blvd, Duncans Mills, 95430; 707 865 2261; open 3–9pm Mon–Fri, 11am–10pm Sat & Sun; www.blueheronrestaurant.com

JENNER

River's End *expensive*
With a dining legacy dating to 1927, River's End serves regional Valley Ford lamb and Petaluma poultry.
11048 Hwy 1, 95450; 707 865 2484; open noon–3:30pm & 5–9pm daily; www.ilovesunsets.com

Eat and Drink: inexpensive under $25; moderate $25–50; expensive over $50

Above The winding, well-paved Coast Highway 1 near Gualala

❻ Fort Ross State Historic Park
Sonoma County; 95450

One of the most compelling symbols of California's historic culture, Fort Ross (www.parks.ca.gov/) flourished as the southernmost Russian settlement in North America from 1812 to 1841. Named for *Rossia* or Russia, it was established as a hunting base as well as an agricultural colony to sustain the Russian stations in Alaska. The extensive fortified stockades are impressive and the restored buildings and museum exhibits offer an insight into what life was like for the Russians who lived here in the early 19th century. Enjoy a walk through the rustic countryside and the breezy oceanfront.

A one-hour walking tour

Turn off Coast Highway 1 at Fort Ross and park in the lot north of the fort. Start at the excellent **Visitor Center and Museum** ①, where displays orient visitors to the contested world of 19th-century California, when many nations, including Russia, Spain, and England had designs on the territory. Look out for the Aleut sealskin kayak that was used in the hunt for sea otters, the prized fur of that era. A 10-minute scenic walk brings visitors to the imposing wooden **fort** ② constructed from local trees. Stop at the Kuskov House, which displays weaponry and agricultural tools, including the muskets, cannons, and wooden rakes that were used by the Russians. Continue to the northeast corner of the fort, where a wooden chapel is adorned with icons. Once an outpost of Russian Orthodox Christianity, its structure sharply contrasts with the adobe Spanish mission churches of that time. The Officials' Quarters is the most

Bell at the Russian Orthodox Chapel

elaborate building, with rooms devoted to the crafts that the Russians needed to survive here, including blacksmithery, tanning, weaving, and carpentry. The fort commandant's restored residence, Rotchev House, is also worth a stop to see what life was like for the leaders of the Russian-American Company, as the business was then called. The two blockhouses served as high observation points from where the Russians could watch for any potential adversaries, including pirates, the Spanish, or any disgruntled Native Americans.

Walk out of the main gate of the fort and stroll down a quarter mile (0.5 km) to **Sandy Cove** ③, where skilled Russian shipwrights built ships, using wood from the Douglas fir, oak, and redwood trees growing in the vicinity. Enjoy a leisurely stroll on the bluff, while taking in the panoramic seaside views. Douglas iris wildflowers bloom here in spring, while migrating gray whales might be

WHERE TO STAY

FORT ROSS STATE HISTORIC PARK

Fort Ross Lodge *moderate*
This modern condo-type lodging overlooks the sea. Units have private patios, fireplaces, and grills, plus a communal hot tub and sauna.
20706 Coast Hwy 1, 95450; 707 847 3333; www.fortrosslodge.com

GUALALA

St. Orres *expensive*
A coastal lodging, St. Orres offers cottages and a central building that echoes the onion-domed Russian architectural traditions of Fort Ross.
36601 Coast Hwy 1, 95445; 707 884 3303; www.saintorres.com

Below View of restored 19th-century Fort Ross as seen from the oceanfront

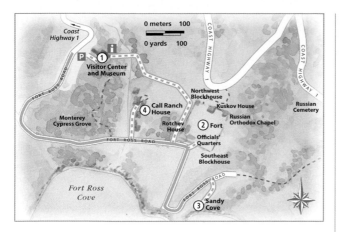

Above Carpentry tools displayed at Officials' Quarters, Fort Ross

The Sea Otter

The 18th century saw the beginnings of a flourishing fur trade. Stirred by the rising demands of the European fashion industry for sea otter furs, Russian hunting expeditions moved south from their base in Alaska and established a colony in Fort Ross in 1812. They brought skilled Aleut hunters from Alaska who hunted the otters to near extinction. Fortunately, the numbers have increased over the years and, today, these endangered animals live freely in the kelp beds along California's coast.

visible offshore in fall and winter, and possibly even the inquisitive heads of some California sea otters.

Walk back to the parking lot, pausing at the **Call Ranch House** ④, now a museum that shows how the Calls, a pioneering ranching family, took over the Fort Ross area in the 19th century and survived with lumber and dairying operations.

Half a mile's (0.8 km) drive south on Coast Highway 1 lies the Russian Cemetery. Park alongside the road and take a walk through this poignant graveyard peppered with wooden crosses.

🚗 *Continue another 26 miles (41 km) north along Coast Hwy 1 to Gualala, and park roadside.*

⑦ Gualala

Mendocino County; 95445
This relaxed coastal town is noted for its restaurants and B&Bs, as well as the Gualala Point Park, which has a good beach and offers excellent

hiking. Pronounced "wa-la-la" by the locals, the town's name is derived from a Pomo Indian word that means "water flows down," referring to the Gualala River that meets the sea here. The town started as a lumbering outpost in the 1860s and witnessed a boom after the 1906 San Francisco earthquake, which created a huge demand for lumber to rebuild the city. In recent decades, tourism has become the economic mainstay here, as it has all along the coast. The town is home to several inns, hotels, and B&Bs, as well as an array of eateries and fine-dining restaurants, making it a good place to stay for a night.

🚗 *Continue 19 miles (30 km) north on Coast Hwy 1 through Point Arena, and after 2 miles (3 km) turn left for Point Arena Lighthouse.*

Below Russian-inspired architecture at St. Orres, near Gualala **Below right** Waves crashing against the rocky shore, south of Gualala

EAT AND DRINK

AROUND FORT ROSS STATE HISTORIC PARK

Alexander's *moderate*
This restaurant serves regional specialties, such as Monterey calamari or red abalone starters, followed by Sonoma lamb or local albacore. Excellent views of the Sonoma Coast.
Timber Cove Inn, 21780 Coast Hwy 1, Timber Cove, 95450; 707 847 3231; open 8am–9pm Sun–Thu, 8am–10pm Fri & Sat; www.timbercoveinn.com

GUALALA

St. Orres *expensive*
A pioneer in North Coast cuisine, St. Orres offers nightly fine-dining specials that could include stuffed pheasant breast, grilled quail, baked wild boar, or medallions of venison. Excellent service and an elegant setting.
36601 Coast Hwy 1, 95445; 707 884 3335; open summer: 5–9pm daily, 10am–2:30pm Sat & Sun; www.saintorres.com

Eat and Drink: inexpensive under $25; moderate $25–50; expensive over $50

Above Point Arena Lighthouse overlooking the rugged Pacific coastline

whale migration season. In fall, the whales swim south to Mexico, while in spring, they travel north to Alaska. Visitors can stay in the former lighthouse keepers' houses and pick up souvenirs from the gift shop.

🚗 *Continue north from the lighthouse for 19 miles (30 km) on Coast Hwy 1 to the Elk/Albion area.*

⑨ Elk
Mendocino County; 95432
The coastline around Elk is famous for its jagged land features and islands that jut out from the shore. At Elk itself, walk out along the cliffs above **Greenwood State Beach** to enjoy stunning coastal views. On a sunny day, buy fixings for a picnic from the Elk Grocery & Deli and enjoy it by the beach. North of Elk, **Albion** is a small commercial fishing hub for sea urchins and abalone.

🚗 *Six miles (10 km) north of Elk, turn inland on Hwy 128 to Navarro River Redwoods State Park.*

WHERE TO STAY

POINT ARENA LIGHTHOUSE

Point Arena Lighthouse *moderate*
Experience the thrill of staying in the historic lighthouse keepers' houses. The three-bedroom, two-bath houses have fireplaces and full kitchens.
45500 Lighthouse Rd, 95468; 707 882 2809; www.pointarenalighthouse.com

ELK

Harbor House Inn *expensive*
This luxurious former home of a lumber baron has been converted to rooms with ocean views and fireplaces. The dining room is in a romantic setting overlooking crashing surf.
5600 South Hwy 1, 95432; 800 720 7474; www.theharborhouseinn.com

AROUND ELK

Albion River Inn *expensive*
An ideal sunset-watch lodging, this modern all-amenities facility includes a fine-dining restaurant. View rooms are set on a bluff overlooking the Albion River and a rocky coastline.
3790 North Hwy 1, Albion, 95410, 707 937 1919; www.albionriverinn.com

BOONVILLE

Boonville Hotel *moderate*
A modern hotel with small-town charm. Fifteen rooms and an excellent family-style restaurant. All attractions are within walking distance.
14050 Hwy 128, 95415; 707 895 2210; www.boonvillehotel.com

⑧ Point Arena Lighthouse
Mendocino County; 95459
An architectural gem on California's coast, the 115-ft (35-m) high Point Arena Lighthouse *(45500 Lighthouse Rd, Manchester; www.pointarenalighthouse.com)* is one of the tallest lighthouses on the Pacific Coast. Climb the 146 steps to the top of the lighthouse to enjoy spectacular panoramic views. The original Fresnel lens of the lighthouse could amplify a kerosene lamp such that it could be seen from 20 miles (32 km) at sea. Point Arena Lighthouse is also one of the most popular whale-watching points on California's coast, especially during the Pacific gray

Colorful fish net floats displayed in Point Arena

⑩ Navarro River Redwoods State Park
Mendocino County
This state park *(www.parks.ca.gov/)*, preserving 660 acres (268 ha) of towering redwoods, stretches for 11 miles (17 km) along the Navarro River. The campground at **Paul M. Dimmick Park** is a great place to enjoy a picnic lunch or a refreshing swim in

Above Oak tree canopy over the road entering Philo

Where to Stay: inexpensive under $100; moderate $100–200; expensive over $200

Top left Everyday items on display in one of Boonville's stores **Above left** Picnic tables with sea views at Elk **Above right** Oak trees along a stream in Boonville

the river. Highway 128 continues under a canopy of oaks to the small town of Navarro.

🚗 Continue for 8.5 miles (14 km) on Hwy 128 to Philo; free street parking.

11 Philo
Mendocino County; 95415
Farther along the road, a picturesque drive along thick oak trees leads to the apple-growing town of Philo. Here, the **Hendy Woods State Park** (www.parks.ca.gov/) offers excellent hiking and walking trails through virgin redwood groves along the Navarro River. Look out for the family-run Navarro Vineyards, known for its

excellent pinot noir, chardonnay, and gewürztraminer.

🚗 Drive for 8 miles (13 km) on Hwy 128 for Boonville; free street parking.

12 Boonville
Mendocino County; 95415
Part of Boonville's charm is that it has its own language, called boontling, which developed in the late 19th century. With over 1,000 eccentric words, boontling was probably formed to keep conversations private from outsiders. Today, this farming town boasts tasting rooms – open to the public – of 16 Anderson Valley boutique wineries (www.avwines.com).

EAT AND DRINK

AROUND POINT ARENA LIGHTHOUSE
The Pier Chowder House and Tap Room *moderate*
Try fried calamari or Dungeness crab cakes, and sole or rock cod entrées.
790 Port Rd, Point Arena, 95468; 707 882 3400; open 11am–9pm daily; www.thepierchowderhouse.com

ELK
Harbor House Restaurant *expensive*
Nightly changing menu, which might include squash soup, pencil asparagus, petrale sole, and chocolate souffle.
5600 South Hwy 1, 95432; 800 720 7474; open dinner daily; www.theharborhouseinn.com; reserve 24 hrs ahead

AROUND ELK
Albion River Inn Restaurant *expensive*
Start with steamed shellfish or wild mushroom soup, then proceed to the lime and ginger grilled prawns.
3790 North Hwy 1, 95410; 707 937 1919; open 5:30–8:30pm daily; www.albionriverinn.com

BOONVILLE
Mosswood Market *moderate*
Try the home-made carrot cake and blueberry muffins, the goat's cheese panini, or the mango chicken wrap.
14111 Hwy 128, 95415; 707 895 3635; open 7am–3pm daily

Table 128 *moderate*
Prix fixe family-style meals emphasizing seasonal, local ingredients. A typical dinner includes curried cauliflower soup, polenta, and pan-seared steak.
Boonville Hotel, 14050 Hwy 128, 95415; 707 895 2210; open 6:30–8:30pm Wed–Mon; www.boonvillehotel.com

---

DAY TRIP OPTIONS
The small town of Healdsburg and the food-and-wine rich Anderson Valley are pleasing day trips.

Healdsburg highlights
Drive to Healdsburg 1 and park at its central plaza, before heading to the Healdsburg Chamber & Visitor Bureau (see p66) to pick up a map. History buffs will enjoy a stroll through downtown Healdsburg to admire its restored Victorian buildings. The Healdsburg Museum (see p59) offers an insight into the town's history. Get supplies for a riverfront picnic from outlets such as the Oakville Grocery

(124 Matheson St) or head to one of the town's dozen fine-dining establishments (see p67). Rent a canoe or kayak from River's Edge (www.riversedgekayakandcanoe.com) and head down the Russian River for a watery adventure. On the way out, stop to explore the Dry Creek Road region, known for its red varietals and hospitable tasting rooms. Dry Creek Vineyard is a good place to start.

Healdsburg is on 101 Freeway, 70 miles (112 km) north of San Francisco.

Epicurean feast
The less-explored Anderson Valley,

stretching between Navarro and Boonville 12 is a gourmand's idea of bliss. Artisan food delights palates, and pinot noir-producing vineyards await oenophiles. Navarro Vineyards, located in Philo 11, is among the region's best wineries. The area is also famous for its apples. Try a Sierra Beauty variety at a roadside stand or join a cooking class or cottage stay at The Apple Farm (www.philoapplefarm.com), where chutneys, jams, jellies, and other organic food is celebrated.

Drive on Hwy 128 between Navarro, Philo, and Boonville.

Eat and Drink: inexpensive under $25; moderate $25–50; expensive over $50

Redwood Empire Route

Mendocino to Crescent City

Highlights

- **Craggy headlands**
  Admire the jagged coastline, crashing surf, and sea life at Mendocino headlands

- **Majestic redwoods**
  Wander in the dense, ancient groves in Redwoods National and State Parks

- **The Lost Coast**
  Take a leisurely meander around this tract of undeveloped California coast

- **Animal planet**
  Spot herds of wild Roosevelt elk grazing in the meadows of Prairie Creek or watch a pod of migrating whales from Mendocino's coast

The scenic Avenue of the Giants winding through Humboldt Redwoods State Park

Redwood Empire Route

From arty, picturesque Mendocino and the craggy, windswept headlands of Fort Bragg, this drive snakes northward – running parallel to the Pacific Ocean and featuring appealing seaside settlements, pastoral towns, and lumbering communities. Sea otters can be spotted in the kelp forests along the Mendocino coast. When the drive meanders inland, it takes visitors through majestic Redwood country. Humboldt Redwoods State Park and the combined Redwood National and State Parks protect thousands of acres of virgin timber, and are perfect for hiking and camping. Some of the most sophisticated B&B lodging in the state can be found along this rewarding drive, which strikes a fine balance between coastal and inland delights.

Above Foamy surf in one of the coves at the Mendocino Headlands, *see p77*
Below The Eel River making its way through dense redwood forest, near Leggett, *see p77*

ACTIVITIES

Admire the blue Douglas iris wildflowers that grow on the Mendocino Headlands

Take a ride on the Skunk Train from Fort Bragg to Willits

Marvel at the magnificent Founder's Tree in Humboldt Redwoods State Park

Shoot the giant Roosevelt elk with a camera at Prairie Creek Redwoods State Park

Stroll amid stands of huge redwoods in Jedediah Smith Redwoods State Park

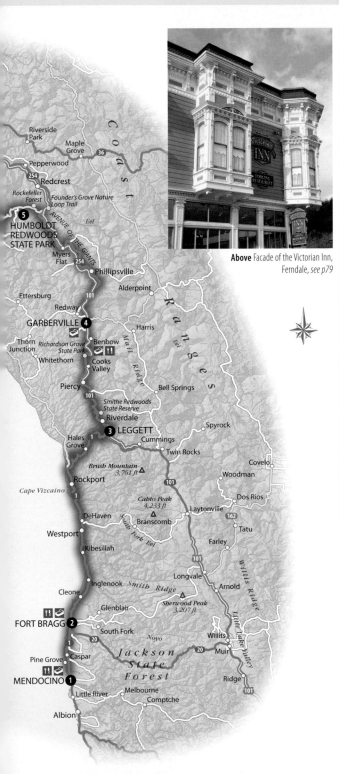

Above Facade of the Victorian Inn,
Ferndale, *see p79*

PLAN YOUR DRIVE

Start/finish: Mendocino to
Crescent City, *see p80 for Ferndale
to Crescent City map.*

Number of days: 4–5 days.

Distance: Approx 300 miles (483 km).

Road conditions: Highway 101 is part
freeway and part two-lane road. Roads
that lead to Honeydew and the Lost
Coast are precarious and deteriorated;
drive slowly and cautiously. Fogs are
frequent in summer.

When to go: Late spring, summer,
and early fall are the best times to
visit, although they are also the
busiest. Much of the region closes
down from late fall through winter
because of rain and snow.

Opening hours: During the summer
season, most businesses open
10am–6pm daily, with restaurants
usually serving until 9 or 10pm daily.

Shopping: "Burls" – bud growths on a
redwood tree that can sprout a new
tree – can be bought at gift shops.
Look out for wood crafts, from
redwood bowls to table slabs.

Major festivals: Mendocino: Wine &
Mushroom Festival, Nov. **Ferndale:**
Kinetic Sculpture Race, May. **Arcata:**
The Godwit Days Shorebird Migration
Festival, Apr.

DAY TRIP OPTIONS

With its many galleries showcasing
works by up-and-coming artists,
Mendocino is a haven for **fans of art**,
while **nature enthusiasts** can explore
the myriad secrets of the **Redwood
National and State Parks**. For full
details, *see p83*.

Above The charming MacCallum House in Mendocino

VISITING MENDOCINO COUNTY

Tourist Information
120 South Franklin St, Fort Bragg, 95437; 707 462 7417; www.visitmendocino.com

WHERE TO STAY

MENDOCINO

The Mendocino Hotel & Garden Suites *moderate*
This historic hotel, established in 1878, has 51 units spread over a 2-acre (1-ha) property amid splendid gardens.
45080 Main St, 95460; 707 937 0511; www.mendocinohotel.com

MacCallum House *expensive*
This charming B&B is housed in a historic structure, with extensive gardens. Gourmet breakfast, spa services, and free Wi-Fi.
45020 Albion St, 95460; 707 937 0289; www.maccallumhouse.com

FORT BRAGG

The Beachcomber Motel *moderate*
A modern motel right on the waterfront, the Beachcomber delights with its park-like setting and location. All rooms have decks and ocean views.
1111 N. Main St, 95437; 707 964 2402; www.thebeachcombermotel.com

❶ Mendocino
Mendocino County; 95460

Poised on a broad-shouldered promontory surrounded by the Pacific, provincial Mendocino is undeniably beautiful. The headlands present a most stunning aspect of the ocean and crashing surf, while the town abounds in New England-style architecture – a legacy of the early settlers of this community. Although tourism is Mendocino's main industry, it also has a thriving contemporary art scene.

A two-hour walking tour

Park on Albion Street at the **Kelley House Museum** ① *(www.kelleyhousemuseum.org)*, which recounts the town's history as a logging and shipping center. Once the abode of a pioneering lumberman, Kelley House now displays photographs, historical maps, and Native American artifacts. The museum also conducts walking tours of the town *(11am Sat)*. Leave the musuem via its oceanside exit onto Main Street and turn right to find **The Mendocino Hotel** ② *(www.mendocinohotel.com)*. Constructed in 1878, this period hotel overlooks the Pacific Ocean and brims with Victorian charm. The inviting Lobby Lounge is good for a drink and the dining room offers excellent coastal cuisine. From here, walk along Main Street and turn right on Kasten Street, then right on Albion Street to arrive at the **MacCallum House** ③, one of the loveliest and most ornate B&Bs in the area. The building is surrounded by flower gardens and boasts a gray whale sculpture at the entrance, a reminder that migrating whale celebrations

are central to Mendocino, with a Whale Festival every March. Next, continue to Lansing Street and turn left toward **Moody's Organic Coffee Bar** ④ *(www.moodyscoffeebar.com)*, which offers beverages and pastries, plus Internet access. Walk down Lansing Street to Ukiah Street and turn left. To the left of the street, a red building – formerly a Baptist church – houses **Corners of the Mouth** ⑤ *(www.cornersofthemouth.com)*, a natural foods store. A worker-owned collective since 1975, the store has deep roots in the organic food movement in Northern California. Farther along the street, at the junction with Kasten Street, the large yellow **Odd Fellows Hall** ⑥ is a major arts display space; temporary exhibits include paintings, sculptures, and woodwork. From here, continue on Kasten Street to Little Lake Street. Stop at the sprawling **Mendocino Art Center** ⑦ *(www.mendocinoartcenter.org)*, an institute that is at the heart of the arts movement in this little town. The center conducts workshops and showcases exhibitions by local and national artists. Receptions are held

Sculpture on display at Mendocino Art Center

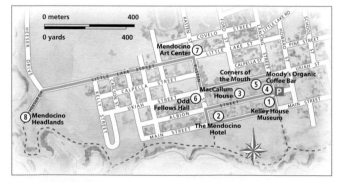

Above left The Chandelier Drive-Thru Tree, Leggett **Above** Quaint Mendocino perched on the headlands **Below left** The Eel River winding between Leggett and Garberville

on the second Saturday of each month from 5 to 8pm.

From the center, walk half a mile (0.8 km) left to the intersection with Heeser Drive to reach the **Mendocino Headlands** ⑧. Nothing compares to the haunting beauty of the landscape here. The ceaseless surf pounds against the promontory, saturating the air with ocean spray. Spring is peak migrating season for gray whales, which can be spotted from headlands aglow with a scattering of blue Douglas iris wildflowers. Black brandt ducks skim across the water and sea otters play in the kelp beds, as painters working *en plein air* attempt to capture the seascapes. The path on Heeser Drive continues all along the western and northern sides of the headlands. If short of time, retrace the route through town to the car.

🚗 *Return to Coast Hwy 1 and continue 9 miles (15 km) northward to Fort Bragg; there is ample parking.*

② Fort Bragg
Mendocino County; 95437

In many ways, Fort Bragg is the flip side to serene Mendocino. Founded as a military fort, it became a working city with the incorporation of several lumbering companies in the vicinity. Today, Fort Bragg is a popular destination owing to its rugged coastline, which affords great views of the Pacific Ocean, and an abundance of budget accommodations. The **Guest House Museum** *(Main St; www.fortbragghistory.org)* is housed in a former lumber baron's residence and has displays on the town's history. Adjacent is the **Skunk Train Depot** *(www.skunktrain.com)* where the Skunk Train, so named because of

its stinky wood smoke fumes, takes visitors through scenic redwood country out to Willits and back. On the southern outskirts of town, **Noyo Harbor** is crammed with fishing and whale-watching boats.

🚗 *Continue on Coast Hwy 1 for 43 miles (69 km) as it skirts the ocean and then turns inland and meets Hwy 101 at Leggett. Follow signs for the Drive-Thru Tree.*

③ Leggett
Mendocino County; 95585

This little hamlet is where redwood country begins in earnest, but it is the drive itself – from Fort Bragg to Leggett – that is the appeal. The vistas along California Coast Highway 1 are amazing and the final 9 miles (15 km) inland along the **Eel River** are the most winding section of road along the entire route. Drive through the **Chandelier Drive-Thru Tree**, which is part of a scenic park and picnic area.

🚗 *Drive north from Leggett along Hwy 101 for about 20 miles (32 km) before taking Exit 639A toward Garberville; free roadside parking.*

EAT AND DRINK

MENDOCINO

MacCallum House Restaurant
expensive
MacCallum House boasts exquisite regional dining. Start with the yam bisque or a platter of oysters, and move on to the mackerel wasabi or a rack of lamb.
45020 Albion St, 95460; 707 937 0289; open 8:30–10:30am & 5:30–9pm daily; www.maccallumhouse.com; call ahead for reservations

Victorian Dining Room *expensive*
Inventive cuisine served in a cozy setting; try the signature crab and oysters Mendocino, or the Maple Creek Farms crispy skin duck.
Mendocino Hotel, 45080 Main St, 95460; 707 937 0511; open 6–9pm Sun–Thu, 6–9:30pm Fri & Sat; www.mendocinohotel.com

FORT BRAGG

Cliff House Restaurant *moderate*
Noted for outstanding ocean and Noyo Harbor views, Cliff House specializes in local seafood and produce, such as oysters grilled in a scampi sauce or wild chanterelle mushrooms in risotto.
1011 South Main St, 95437; 707 961 0255; open 4–9:30pm Sun–Fri, 4–10pm Sat; www.fortbragg cliffhouse.com

Eat and Drink: inexpensive under $25; moderate $25–50; expensive over $50

Right Hikers in the Founder's Grove, Humboldt Redwoods State Park

VISITING THE REDWOODS PARKS AND LOST COAST

Tourist Information
Garberville-Redway Area Chamber of Commerce *782 Redwood Dr, Garberville, 95542; 707 923 2613; www.garberville.org*

WHERE TO STAY

GARBERVILLE

Best Western Humboldt House Inn
moderate
The inn has rooms with all basic amenities. Additional draws are a pool, hearty breakfasts, and proximity to the Avenue of the Giants. Reservations are essential.
701 Redwood Dr, 95542; 707 923 2771; www.humboldthouseinn.com

AROUND GARBERVILLE

Benbow Hotel and Resort *expensive*
This classic Tudor-style country inn offers comfortable rooms adorned with antiques. Tea and scones are served in the stately lobby.
445 Lake Benbow Dr, Benbow, 95542; 707 923 2124; www.benbowinn.com

FERNDALE

Victorian Inn *expensive*
A restored historic building in downtown Ferndale, the Victorian Inn is close to shops, galleries, and museums. The high-ceilinged rooms are decorated with period wallpaper.
400 Ocean Ave, 95536; 707 786 4949; www.victorianvillageinn.com

④ Garberville
Humboldt County; 95542

As Highway 101 approaches this town, it leads past **Richardson Grove State Park** *(6 miles/10 km S of Garberville)*, while the Eel River surges along adjacent to the road. Notorious as the "marijuana heartland of the US," Garberville is a small town with few attractions but makes a good base for hiking trips into the enchanting Redwood Empire. Small commercial enterprises abound, selling, among other things, table slabs cut from redwood trunks.

🚗 *Drive north on Redwood Dr and turn right to merge onto Hwy 101. Then take Exit 645 and drive along the SR 254 (Ave of the Giants) for 20 miles (32 km) to reach Humboldt Redwoods State Park visitor center.*

⑤ Humboldt Redwoods State Park
Humboldt County; 95542

Established in 1921 by the Save the Redwoods League, this 53,000-acre (21,448-ha) expanse of majestic coast redwoods is the third largest park in the California State Park System. The **Avenue of the Giants** is a scenic, serpentine parkway that runs along a choice stretch of this ancient forest, meandering through primeval redwoods that overshadow the road. Allow time to walk around the groves to appreciate the sheer height and majesty of these trees. The visitor center has excellent displays on the flora and fauna and logging history of the region. The **Founder's Grove Nature Loop Trail** begins about 4 miles (6 km) north of the visitor center and goes past the **Founder's Tree**, honoring the founders of the Save the Redwoods League. A swath of dense forest lies on the western side of the Avenue of the Giants along Bull Creek Flats Road: the drive west passes the **Rockefeller Forest** – an impressive old growth stand of trees with a fern-rich groundcover – that thrives along **Bull Creek**. The entire park offers over 100 miles (161 km) of hiking trails.

🚗 *Drive along Bull Flat Creek Rd, which becomes Mattole Rd, to exit the park westward. The deteriorated road switchbacks over several mountains to descend to the Lost Coast.*

Top right A Victorian building in Ferndale **Below right** Roadside shops selling redwood souvenirs, Garberville **Far right** Eel River along the Avenue of the Giants

Left Lost Coast landscape near Honeydew
Below left Dairy equipment on display at the Ferndale Museum

The Redwood Tree

California's coast redwood trees *(Sequoia sempervirens)* are the tallest tree species on earth. The tallest among these giants is a redwood – about 370 ft (113 m) in height – in the Redwood Creek watershed in Redwood National Park *(see pp82–3)*. These trees flourish in a moist environment, deriving about 30 percent of their water from fog drip. They have surface roots that lock together, and the bark is extremely resistant to fire damage, allowing the trees to survive forest fires.

⑥ Lost Coast

Humboldt County; 95545
This section of the Northern California coast remains the last stretch of undeveloped shoreline in the state, hence the name. The **Kings Range**, running parallel to the coast, ensures the inaccessibility of the coastal wilderness with its impassable sea cliffs that drop steeply to the Pacific Ocean. **Honeydew** and **Petrolia** are forgotten, bucolic towns en route to Ferndale, offering a calm repose for the weary traveler. The magnificent archways of redwoods, Douglas fir, and oak along the winding Mattole Road are matched by the splendor of the Kings Range and riverbed grazing lands around Honeydew and Petrolia. **Cape Mendocino**, farther north from Petrolia, has miles of pristine, sandy coastline.

🚗 *Head northeast from Cape Mendocino on Mattole Rd and drive for approximately 17 miles (27 km) to reach Ferndale; turn right on Ocean Ave.*

⑦ Ferndale

Humboldt County; 95536
An attractive town of gingerbread Victorian houses, Ferndale's appealing 19th-century architecture has resulted in the town being designated a State Historical Landmark. Learn more about the town's history at the **Ferndale Museum** *(www.ferndale-museum.org)*, which displays artifacts, documents, and old newspaper reports from the Gold Rush through the logging era. The museum also houses an exceptional collection of equipment used in the dairy industry – an activity that bolstered the town's economy and sustained settlers along the grasslands of this Eel River delta from the 1880s onwards.

🚗 *From Main St drive north toward Fernbridge Dr and turn right to join Hwy 101 southbound. Drive for about 11 miles (18 km) before Exit 679 toward Scotia; there is ample parking.*

EAT AND DRINK

AROUND GARBERVILLE

Flavors *inexpensive*
A favorite with locals for home-made soups, Flavors also has inventive salads such as feta and apple, plus turkey sandwiches and wraps.
767 Redwood Dr, Benbow, 95542; 707 923 7717; open 7am–7pm daily

Benbow Hotel and Resort Dining Room *expensive*
Considered one of the finer dining options in redwood country since 1926, the Benbow Dining Room tempts with its beet salad or leek soup starters, and rib-eye steak or lamb shank entreés.
445 Lake Benbow Dr, Benbow, 95542; 707 923 2124; open 8am–1:30pm & 6–9pm daily; www.benbowinn.com

FERNDALE

VI *moderate*
This is the gourmet restaurant at the Victorian Inn. Try the artisan mac and cheese crock, with local Loleta cheeses, or pair a cup of clam chowder with the grilled salmon.
400 Ocean Ave, 95536; 707 786 4949; open 8am–9pm daily; www.victorianvillageinn.com

Eat and Drink: inexpensive under $25; moderate $25–50; expensive over $50

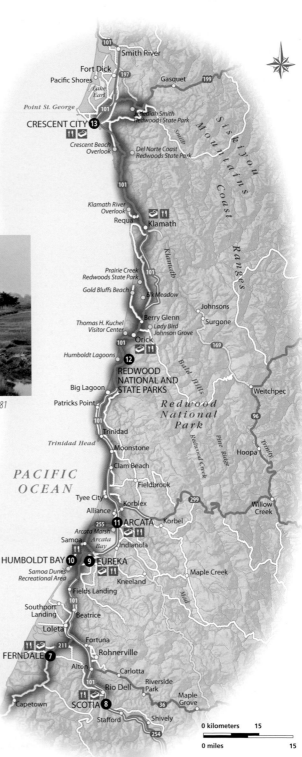

Yreka

Redding

See p75

CALIFORNIA

Santa Rosa

Sacramento

San Francisco

Stockton

San Jose

Monterey

Fresno

Smith River

101

Fort Dick

197

Pacific Shores

Gasquet

199

Lake Earl

101

Point St. George

CRESCENT CITY ⑬

Jedediah Smith Redwoods State Park

Smith

Siskiyou Mountains

Crescent Beach Overlook

Del Norte Coast Redwoods State Park

101

Coast

Klamath River Overlook

Requa

Klamath

Klamath

Ranges

Prairie Creek Redwoods State Park

101

Gold Bluffs Beach

Elk Meadow

Johnsons

Surgone

Thomas H. Kuchel Visitor Center

Berry Glenn

Lady Bird Johnson Grove

Orick

101

Humboldt Lagoons

⑫

169

REDWOOD NATIONAL AND STATE PARKS

Bald Hills

Big Lagoon

Redwood National Park

Weitchpec

Patricks Point

101

Trinidad

96

Trinidad Head

Moonstone

Redwood Creek

Pine Ridge

Hoopa

Trinity

Clam Beach

PACIFIC OCEAN

Fieldbrook

Tyee City

Korblex

299

Willow Creek

Alliance

Korbel

255

⑪ ARCATA

Arcata Marsh

Samoa

Arcata Bay

Indianola

HUMBOLDT BAY ⑩ ⑨ EUREKA

Samoa Dunes Recreational Area

Kneeland

Maple Creek

Fields Landing

Maul

101

Southport Landing

Beatrice

Loleta

211

Fortuna

Rohnerville

FERNDALE ⑦

Alton

Carlotta

Riverside Park

Maple Grove

101

Rio Dell

Capetown

⑧ SCOTIA

36

Stafford

Shively

254

0 kilometers   15

0 miles   15

Above Sprawling grasslands around Humboldt Bay, *see p81*

KEY

Drive route

Above Fanciful Victorian architecture, Carson Mansion, Eureka, *see p81*

⑧ Scotia

Humboldt County; 95565

Founded as a company town, Scotia was owned and built for the employees of the Pacific Coast Lumber Company (PALCO) – once the largest logging operation in Humboldt County. Most structures in town are built of redwood timber, including the stately Greek columns supporting the town theater and **Scotia Museum** building. Displayed outside the museum are a railroad engine and logging apparatus.

🚗 *Get back on Hwy 101 and drive 27 miles (44 km) north to Eureka; park on the road.*

⑨ Eureka

Humboldt County; 95501

Founded in 1850, Eureka is the northern coast's largest commercial center. The **Old Town** is situated along the waterfront, bound by C Street and M Street. Take a horse-drawn carriage ride around this area to explore the 19th-century buildings that have been converted into cafés and restaurants. The **Clarke Museum** *(www.clarkemuseum. org)*, on 3rd Street and E Street, has displays on Native American culture. Other delights include the **Carson Mansion** – former home of lumber magnate William Carson – on 2nd Street and M Street, one of the finest specimens of Victorian architecture in California, as well as the **Fisherman's Plaza** at the foot of C Street, where commercial fishermen bring in fresh catch.

🚗 *Take 5th St east and turn left at R St (Hwy 155) to take the bridge over Humboldt Bay. At the T-junction, follow the sign for Samoa for a drive along the peninsula.*

⑩ Humboldt Bay

Humboldt County; 95501

The drive along Humboldt Bay's northern peninsula is evocative of the area's lumber milling history. Stop at the **Samoa Cookhouse**, a restaurant that is also a museum about the logging era. Then drive to the tip of the peninsula to arrive at the **Samoa Dunes Recreation Area**, a 300-acre (121-ha) park that offers surfing, hiking, bird-watching, and beachcombing.

Rail engine displayed outside Scotia Museum

🚗 *Retrace the route along the peninsula and keep straight on Hwy 255 for Arcata; ample parking.*

Above Carter House Inn, Old Town Eureka
Below A horse-drawn carriage ride in Eureka

VISITING HUMBOLDT COUNTY

Tourist Information
Humboldt County Convention & Visitors Bureau *1034 2nd St, Eureka, 95501; 707 444 6634; www.redwoods.info*

WHERE TO STAY

SCOTIA

Scotia Inn *moderate*
A historic inn close to the Scotia Museum, the Scotia Inn has a lovely lobby. The rooms are basic with affordable rates.
100 Main St, 95565; 707 964 5338; www.scotia-inn.com

EUREKA

Best Western Humboldt Bay Inn *moderate*
This modern motel-style lodging offers all basic amenities. Reservations can be made online. It is only a short walk away from the Old Town.
232 West 5th St, 95501; 707 443 2234; www.humboldtbayinn.com

Carter House Inn *expensive*
Offering upscale lodging, Carter House Inn is located in several Victorian buildings in downtown Eureka, close to shops, museums, art galleries, and the Carson Mansion.
301 L St, 95501; 707 444 8062; www.carterhouse.com

EAT AND DRINK

SCOTIA

Scotia Inn Dining Room *moderate*
Local handcrafted beers and southern pecan chicken are the specialties here. Other favorites are grilled rib-eye steak or Mediterranean turkey burger.
100 Main St, 95565; 707 764 5338; open 11:30am–9:30pm Tue–Sat, 11:30am–10:30 pm Fri & Sat; www.scotia-inn.com

EUREKA

Restaurant 301 *expensive*
The premier fine dining choice in Redwood Country at the Carter House Inn. Try the rabbit or pepper steak.
301 L St, 95501; 707 444 8062; open 7:30–10am & 6–9pm daily; www.carterhouse.com

AROUND EUREKA

Samoa Cookhouse *moderate*
Enjoy buttermilk pancakes for breakfast, meatloaf for lunch, and a roast pork dinner.
908 Vance Ave, Samoa, 95501; 707 442 1659; open 7am–9pm daily; www.samoacookhouse.net

Above A herd of Roosevelt elk at Prairie Creek
Above right The lighthouse at Crescent City
Below right The unusually shaped Elephant Tree, Trees of Mystery at Redwood National and State Parks

VISITING THE NORTHERN REDWOODS

Tourist Information
Redwood National & State Parks: Kuchel Visitor Center *Hwy 101, Orick, 95555; 707 465 7765; www.nps.gov/redw*

WHERE TO STAY

ARCATA

Plaza View Stay *expensive*
These one-of-a-kind apartment-style lodgings are located on the edge of the Arcata Plaza. Some units have full kitchens.
Arcata Plaza, 95521; 877 822 0935; www.arcatastay.com

REDWOOD NATIONAL AND STATE PARKS

Elk Meadow Cabins *moderate*
Large remodeled cabins of former mill workers, in an elk meadow. Each cabin has three bedrooms, two baths, full kitchen. The proprietors organize adventure tours.
7 Valley Green Camp Rd, Orick, 95555; 707 488 2602; www.redwood adventures.com

Requa Inn *moderate*
This charming inn overlooks the mouth of the Klamath River. Owned by a Yurok Indian family, the inn offers hearty breakfasts and Yurok crafts in a gift shop.
451 Requa Rd, Klamath, 95548; 707 482 1425; www.requainn.com

CRESCENT CITY

Oceanfront Lodge *moderate*
This clean, modern facility includes a heated indoor pool, spa, and sauna. The oceanfront location presents a view of the Battery Point Lighthouse.
100 A St, 95531; 707 465 5400

⓫ Arcata
Humboldt County; 95521
The drive into Arcata passes through moist grasslands populated by innumerable milk cows and wild Canadian geese. Home to the **Humboldt State University**, Arcata is a typical college town, and consequently a hub of liberal thought. **Arcata Plaza** has stores epitomizing the youthful, bookish, artistic, and progressive community, such as Rookery Books and Arcata Artisans Fine Arts. Also worth a visit, **Arcata Marsh** (*www.arcatamarsh friends.org*) is one of the richest birding habitats in redwood country.
🚗 *Return to Hwy 101 and drive northward for about 30 miles (48 km) along the coast to arrive at the visitor center located right by the southern entrance of Redwood National Park.*

⓬ Redwood National and State Parks
Humboldt & Del Norte County
Established in 1968 by US President Lyndon B. Johnson, this long corridor of protected parks comprises old-growth coast redwoods, vast prairies, oak woodlands, and nearly 40 miles (64 km) of beautiful coastline. It promotes the preservation of biotic diversity – demonstrated by various ecosystems coexisting here harmoniously.

This region is home to gigantic coast redwood trees, protected within the **Redwood National Park** and three nearby state parks. Stop at the **Thomas H. Kuchel Visitor Center** for orientation and admire the Yurok Indian canoe – made from a hollowed out redwood log – on display. From the visitor center drive along the highway toward **Orick**, a small town with a couple of cafés and motels. Just past Orick, a large sign marks the Bald Hills Road turnoff. Turn right onto the road and drive till the parking lot appears toward the right. The trail that winds to the **Lady Bird Johnson Grove** begins here. This grove, dedicated to President Johnson's wife, "Lady Bird" Johnson, is a delightful mix of both old-growth redwood trees and showy red rhododendrons, which bloom May through June. Get back on Highway 101 and take the westward exit to Davison Road. The route leads into the **Prairie Creek Redwoods State Park**, toward the **Elk Meadow**, where herds of Roosevelt

ELEPHANT TREE

Where to Stay: inexpensive under $100; moderate $100–200; expensive over $200

elk *(Cervus canadensis roosevelti)* graze in green meadows. Farther ahead, the isolated, driftwood-littered **Gold Bluffs Beach** beckons.

Return to the highway and then exit onto the **Newton B. Drury Scenic Parkway**, a stretch noted for its exceptional stands of redwoods. The road rejoins Highway 101 after 10 miles (16 km). The **Klamath River Overlook** is the next stop, located about 7 miles (11 km) ahead at the Requa Road turnoff. This is a great location for watching migrating whales. A host of other marine mammals and seabirds can also be spotted here year round. Legendary runs of salmon in the river were managed adroitly by the Yurok Indians for a long time till dams and excessive fishing reduced the salmon population.

The highway painstakingly snakes northward to reach the **Del Norte Coast Redwoods State Park**, which boasts stunning views of the Pacific Ocean from the **Crescent Beach Overlook**. To get here, keep on the highway after Klamath River Overlook for about 15 miles (24 km) before turning left onto Enderts Beach Road (5 miles/8 km round-trip).

The last of redwood country, **Jedediah Smith Redwoods State Park**, is the northernmost point of this corridor and is named for the explorer who traversed this terrain in the 1820s. Return to Highway 101; cross onto Humboldt Road before taking a right onto unpaved Howland Road, which leads through the finest primeval stands in the region.

Above A well-maintained road through redwood groves, Jedediah Smith Redwoods State Park

🚗 *Drive for about 7 miles (12 km) along Howland Hill Rd; at South Fork Rd turn left for Hwy 199. Turn left onto Hwy 199, then take the ramp onto Hwy 101 that leads into Crescent City.*

⑬ Crescent City
Del Norte County; 95531

This city boasts proximity to both the Del Norte Coast Redwoods and Jedediah Smith Redwoods State Parks, but is otherwise a laid-back small town. Most of its buildings sustained severe damage during the tsunami after the Alaska earthquake in 1964. Park at Battery Point and walk for a quarter of a mile (0.5 km) over a sandy, rocky, and driftwood-strewn path to see the **Battery Point Lighthouse** – Crescent City's main attraction – built in 1856. The city has some good accommodation and dining options.

EAT AND DRINK

ARCATA
Plaza Grill *moderate*
Plaza Grill presents casual dining on the third floor of the historic, well-preserved Jacoby's Storehouse building on a corner of Arcata Plaza. Try the portobello mushroom or char-grilled chicken sandwiches with a local Arcata beer.
Jacoby's Storehouse, Arcata Plaza, 95521; 707 826 0860; open 5–9:30pm Sun–Thu, 5–10pm Fri & Sat; www.plazagrillarcata.com

REDWOOD NATIONAL AND STATE PARKS
The Palms Café *moderate*
A local diner serving hearty home-made comfort food such as burgers, fries, biscuits and gravy. Try their famous pies.
21130 Hwy 101, Orick, 95555; 707 488 3381; open 6am–8pm daily

Bailey's Dining Room *moderate*
An imaginative menu features seasonal ingredients procured locally. Yurok specialties include Klamath River smoked salmon.
Requa Inn: 451 Requa Rd, Klamath, 95548; 707 482 1425; open dinner Wed–Sun; www.requainn.com; reserve in advance

CRESCENT CITY
Good Harvest Cafe *moderate*
This popular highway-side establishment presents fresh red snapper fish, burgers made from beef, and vegetarian soups. Try the spinach artichoke omelet breakfast.
575 South Hwy 101, 95531; 707 465 6028; open 7:30am–9pm Mon–Sat, 8am–8pm Sun

---

DAY TRIP OPTIONS
This drive can easily be broken up into two themed itineraries.

Artistic sojourn
Drive through the scenic coast route from Mendocino ① to Fort Bragg ②, to explore numerous unspoiled beaches with outstanding ocean views. Stop at the many art galleries that thrive all along the coast, and include fine art photography as well. The Mendocino Coast Photographer Guild & Gallery *(343 N Main St; www.mcpgg.com)*,

showcases gorgeous photographs of coastal landforms and wildlife.

Drive between Mendocino and Fort Bragg on Coast Highway 1.

Nature's bounty
Spend a day exploring the many attractions of the Redwoods National and State Parks ⑫. South of Orick, the Humboldt Lagoons are a major birding habitat, with plenty of sighting opportunities. North of Orick, Fern Canyon in Prairie Creek Redwoods State Park has a lush

undergrowth of mosses, ferns, and other plants. This narrow canyon has a 2-mile (3-km) walking path with 50-ft (15-m) walls covered with oxalis clover and maidenhair ferns. Prairie Creek is also home to the Big Tree, measuring 21.6 ft (6.6 m) in diameter. Three trailheads from Big Tree Wayside invite visitors to wander amid the redwood groves.

Explore the Redwoods National and State Parks stretching south and north from the visitor center at Orick on Hwy 101.

Eat and Drink: inexpensive under $25; moderate $25–50; expensive over $50

Land of Fire and Ice

Redding to Red Bluff

Highlights

- **Sacred river**
  Admire the magnificent Sacramento River as it flows through the Turtle Bay Exploration Park in Redding

- **A day on the lake**
  Visit the Shasta Dam and rent a day boat or houseboat to explore enormous Shasta Lake

- **Alpine beauty**
  Enjoy breathtaking views of Mt Shasta, considered sacred by Native Americans

- **Fiery volcanoes**
  Drive through the Lassen Volcanic National Park, famous for its geological attractions

Snow-capped Mt Shasta rising over forested slopes and green pastures

Land of Fire and Ice

The scenic river beauty, forested alpine grandeur, and geological wonders of the Shasta-Lassen region are truly awe-inspiring. This drive meanders alongside the wild, trout-filled Sacramento River, offering ample opportunities for fishing. To take a break from driving, rent a houseboat and explore the serene Shasta Lake. Farther ahead, the rugged and unruly Castle Crags and the snow-topped Mt Shasta are laced with trails for both beginners and seasoned hikers. A hotbed of geothermal activity, the Lassen Volcanic National Park intrigues with its steaming geysers, bubbling fumaroles, and the active Lassen Peak, which last erupted in 1917.

Above Road weaving through Lassen Volcanic National Park, *see pp92–3*

ACTIVITIES

Rent a bike at the Turtle Bay Exploration Park in Redding and pedal down the Sacramento River Trail

Go wild-trout fishing after renting gear in Redding

Spend a night on a houseboat on Shasta Lake

Sleep in a railroad caboose at the Railroad Park in Dunsmuir

Take in the breathtaking views of Mt Shasta from Panther Meadows

Hike Bumpass Hell trail to see Lassen Volcanic National Park's amazing geothermal features

Above Homey interior of the popular Old Mill Eatery in Shasta Dam, *see p89*

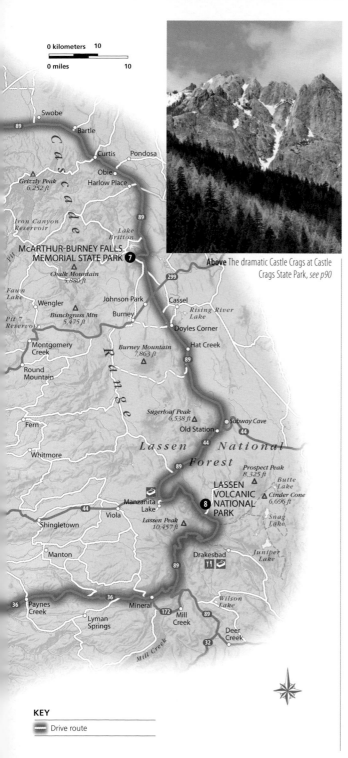

Above The dramatic Castle Crags at Castle Crags State Park, see p90

KEY

Drive route

PLAN YOUR DRIVE

Start/finish: Redding to Red Bluff.

Number of days: 4–5 days, allowing half a day each to explore Redding and Lassen Volcanic National Park.

Distance: 335 miles (540 km).

Road conditions: All roads, including those through mountainous areas, are well paved. It is essential to carry snow chains from October to June, and to be alert to temporary road closures due to snow. Depending on the amount of snowfall, the Lassen Park road may be completely closed from October to early June.

When to go: The summer and fall seasons, from June to October, are the best time to visit the area.

Opening times: Most shops open from 10am to 6pm, while the last seating at restaurants is usually by 9pm.

Shopping: Redding's shops are well known for their fly-fishing paraphernalia and other outdoor gear.

DAY TRIP OPTIONS

Cyclists can use **Redding** as a base to explore the town as well as **Shasta Lake**, while families will enjoy a picnicking on the banks of the Sacramento. **Mt Shasta** attracts **photographers** as well as **hikers**. Those interested in **geology** should not miss the chance to explore **Lassen Volcanic National Park**. For full details, see p93.

Above Unique Sundial Bridge, Redding
Below right A houseboat on Shasta Lake

VISITING REDDING & SHASTA DAM

Tourist Information
Shasta Cascade Wonderland
Association *1699 Hwy 273, Anderson,
96007; 530 365 7500;
www.shastacascade.com*

Parking in Redding
Ample space is available at the parking
lots adjacent to the Sundial Bridge.

WHERE TO STAY

REDDING

Bridgehouse Bed & Breakfast
moderate
This modern B&B has four rooms with
private baths and offers home-made
breakfasts. There is also direct access
to river walk trails.
*1455 Riverside Dr, 96001; 530 247
7177; www.reddingbridgehouse.com*

Oxford Suites *expensive*
Amenities here include a heated pool,
Jacuzzi, and fitness center. The hotel
also offers buffet breakfasts, and
appetizers and wine in the evenings.
*1967 Hilltop Dr, 96002; 800 762 0133;
www.oxfordsuitesredding.com*

AROUND SHASTA DAM

Bridge Bay Resort *moderate*
A resort with a restaurant and a
marina, the Bridge Bay Resort is located
on the banks of Shasta Lake. The resort
also rents out house-boats, fishing
boats, and fishing gear.
*10300 Bridge Bay Rd, 96003; 800 752
9669; www.sevencrown.com/lakes/
lake_shasta/bridge_bay/*

❶ Redding
Shasta County; 96003

This walk, through Redding's centerpiece – the sprawling Turtle
Bay Exploration Park *(www.turtlebay.org)* – highlights the natural
beauty and history of the Shasta-Lassen region and takes visitors
across the Sacramento River on the strikingly designed Sundial
Bridge, dating from 2004. The town itself offers opportunities for
excellent trout fishing, and the Art Deco Cascade Theatre *(1733
Market St; www.cascadetheatre.org)* in downtown Redding is a
venue for major music and entertainment events.

A two-hour walking tour

Park next to Sundial Bridge on the
south side of the river, off Sundial
Bridge Drive. Pick up a map at the
Visitor Center ① and pay the all-day
fee to see all attractions.

From the south side of the river,
look at the pedestrian **Sundial
Bridge** ②, an imaginative and
artistic representation of a sundial
by the contemporary Spanish
architect Santiago Calatrava. Walk
out to the middle of the bridge and
look down at the
Sacramento River ③,
known for its
legendary salmon
runs and as a year-
round rainbow trout
habitat. Look out for

**Rainbow trout on display,
Turtle Bay Museum**

anglers in driftboats. Proceed across
the bridge and turn left into the
**McConnell Arboretum and Botanical
Gardens** ④ *(open 7am–5pm daily)*, an
impressive cluster of a dozen major
gardens sprawled out over 200 acres
(80 ha). Follow the path to the
California Garden ⑤, which
celebrates plants native to California,
such as the orange poppy, blue

lupine wildflower, and red-barked
madrone tree. Walk down the path
and then turn right to reach the
Sounds of Water Fountain ⑥, which
serves as a gentle reminder that
water preservation plays an
important role in this arid area's
history, politics, and prosperity. Spot
the colorful flutter at the **Butterfly
Garden** ⑦, which delights children
and adults alike.

Continue down the path back to
the Sundial Bridge. Both ends of
the bridge provide
access to the paved,
forested Sacramento
River Trail, which can
be explored on foot or
on bicycle if time
permits. Bicycles can be
rented from the Visitor Center.

Cross the bridge and proceed to
the **Turtle Bay Museum** ⑧ *(open
9am–4pm daily)*, located adjacent to
the south end of the bridge, to get
an overview of the natural history
and the lumbering and mining past
of this region. Visit the bark house,
similar to that used by local Wintu, for
a glimpse into Native American

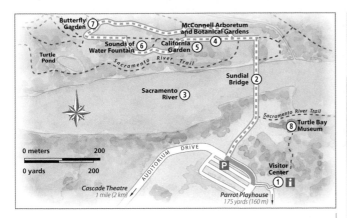

Above Anglers fishing for rainbow trout on the Sacramento River **Below left** Poppies and lupines at the McConnell Arboretum and Botanical Gardens, Redding

culture. The museum also has displays on the most celebrated local Native American, Ishi, a member of the Yana tribe, who was the last of his people and whose life story was recorded in the book *Ishi in Two Worlds* (1961). Fishing enthusiasts should not miss the stream profile with examples of the large rainbow trout that populate the streams of this region.

If there is time, walk to the Visitor Center and follow signs to the Parrot Playhouse (*open 9:30–11:45am, 1–5 pm daily*), a year-round walk-through aviary, where visitors get a chance to interact with and feed colorful lorikeets. Retrace the route to the Visitor Center and then to the parking lot.

🚗 *Proceed north from Redding to the I-5 for 10 miles (16 kms) to the Shasta Dam Rd (Hwy 151 west) turnoff. Continue on the Shasta Dam Rd to the unsigned Vista Point, above the dam. Park at the visitor center.*

② Shasta Dam
Shasta County; 96019
The Vista Point, located above Shasta Dam, offers breathtaking views of the dam, a major feat of engineering in its day. Next, drive down to the visitor center. The dam was completed in 1945 and is the second largest dam in the US, surpassed only by the Grand Coulee Dam across the Columbia River. The dam's waters are used to irrigate the naturally arid Central Valley of California in summer for agriculture, and for generating hydroelectricity. If time permits, take a free guided tour (*www.shastalake.com*), which includes a

walk across the dam. Shasta Dam's reservoir – **Shasta Lake** – is the largest in California and is an interesting body of water to explore. Several major rivers, such as the Sacramento, McCloud, and Pit, converge at the lake. With its 360-mile (580-km) long shoreline, the lake also offers great opportunities for fishing and boating.

The many resorts on the banks of the lake arrange sightseeing tours and rent boats and fishing gear. A popular option is the Jones Valley Resort (*www.houseboats.com*), located around 20 miles (32 km) northeast from the dam, where visitors can rent a pontoon day boat and go sightseeing or fishing on the lake. Fully furnished self-guided houseboats are available for overnight stays on the lake.

🚗 *Return to the I-5 and drive 51 miles (82 km) north. Watch out for the signed turnoff, which leads west, off the highway, to the Castle Crags State Park.*

EAT AND DRINK

REDDING
Tortuga Bay Grill *inexpensive*
Try the fish tacos or barbecued pulled pork sandwich.
1815 Park Marina Drive, 96001; 530 229 0755; open 11am–9pm daily

C. R. Gibbs American Grill *moderate*
Redding's iconic restaurant features an open-viewing kitchen; the bar here offers specialty drinks.
2300 Hilltop Dr, 96002; 530 221 2335; open 11am–9pm Mon–Fri, 11am–10pm Sat & Sun; www.crgibbs.com

Moonstone Bistro *moderate*
This restaurant uses fresh, locally sourced ingredients. Sample the fish tacos, garden tomato salad, and blue crab cakes.
3425 Placer St, 96001; 530 241 3663; open 11am–9pm Tue–Thu, 11am–10pm Fri & Sat, 10am–2pm Sun; www.moonstonebistro.com

SHASTA DAM
Old Mill Eatery *moderate*
This restaurant, a favorite with the locals, has a friendly atmosphere. Serves large portions of delicious home-made food, including breakfast omelets and lunch sandwiches.
4132 Shasta Dam Blvd, 96019; 530 275 0515; open 7am–3pm Wed–Sun

Above Granite peaks of Castle Crags, Castle Crags State Park **Below right** View of the crags from the Railroad Park Resort, Dunsmuir **Below far right** Church of St. Joseph, McCloud

WHERE TO STAY

DUNSMUIR

Railroad Park Resort *moderate*
Fun for anyone with a touch of rail nostalgia, this "caboose" motel of restored, antique Southern Pacific railroad cars stretches in a circle around a pool.
100 Railroad Park Rd, 96025; 530 235 4440; www.rrpark.com

AROUND MT SHASTA

Mt Shasta Ranch B&B *moderate*
This elegant B&B has spacious rooms, a carriage house, a cottage, and offers great views of Mt Shasta.
1008 W. A. Barr Rd, Mount Shasta, 96067; 530 926 3870; www.stayinshasta.com

Mt Shasta Resort *expensive*
The resort's luxurious chalets and woodland rooms are surrounded by pine trees. There is also an 18-hole golf course and a clubhouse with views of Mt Shasta.
1000 Siskiyou Lake Blvd, Mount Shasta, 96067; 530 926 3030; www.mtshastaresort.com

MCCLOUD

McCloud River Mercantile *moderate*
This historic property has rooms with high ceilings on the upper floor, and a restaurant and a general store selling new and antique goods.
241 Main St, 96057; 530 964 2330; www.mccloudmercantile.com

③ Castle Crags State Park
Shasta County; 96017

Soaring spires of ancient granite, along with breathtaking views of Mt Shasta and the forested region, greet visitors in the Castle Crags State Park *(www.parks.ca.gov)*. There are 28 miles (45 km) of mainly easy hikes such as the River Trail; the fit and energetic can make the steep ascent to the top of the crags for a bird's-eye view of Mt Shasta. It is also possible to swim or fish in the Sacramento River, which twists through the park.

🚗 *Return to I-5 and drive north to Exit 729 for Dunsmuir.*

④ Dunsmuir
Siskiyou County; 96025

A major railroad town in the north–south corridor, Dunsmuir *(www.dunsmuir.com)* has a roundhouse that was built to repair workhorse steam engines. The town has a lively dining and art scene, with galleries located in historic buildings. Stop at Brown Trout Cafe & Gallery *(5841 Sacramento Ave)* for coffee and to browse some excellent art.

From Dunsmuir, drive north on Dunsmuir Avenue, and turn left on Mott Road before it goes under Interstate-5. Look out for signs for **Hedge Creek Falls Park**, which boasts great views of Mt Shasta, the Upper Sacramento River, and the surrounding canyon. Follow the trail that leads from the park to the Hedge Creek Falls. Legend has it that Black Bart, a stagecoach robber, once hid from a posse in the cave behind the falls.

🚗 *Return to I-5 and drive north to Mt Shasta, turning off the road at the town of Mt Shasta. In town, Lake St*

Where to Stay: inexpensive under $100; moderate $100–200; expensive over $200

*leads north to become Everett
Memorial Hwy. Follow this road
15 miles (24 km) uphill to its end at
Vista Point.*

⑤ Mt Shasta
Siskiyou County; 96067

Towering above its namesake town, regal Mt Shasta dominates this region visually. Its Vista Point affords stunning panoramas of this snowy peak and the watersheds from where the flood waters run south into the Sacramento River or west into the Klamath River.

Get closer to the mountain by stopping at the **Panther Meadows** campground, 1 mile (1.6 km) below Vista Point. From here, there are several walks ranging from gentle hikes around the base to rigorous mountaineering treks up to the peak. The mountain may be snow covered until late May, when the road is open only to Bunny Flats.

🚗 *Return to I-5 and drive south, turning east on to Hwy 89. Drive to McCloud, 10 miles (16 km) to the east.*

The Sacramento River

Gabriel Moraga (1765–1823), a Spanish explorer, first named the Sacramento *Rio del Santissimo Sacramento* (River of the Most Blessed Sacrament). The largest river in California, it covers a distance of 400 miles (643 km) from the mountains west of Mt Shasta to San Francisco Bay. The river was once legendary for the abundant runs of chinook salmon. A campaign to restore the Sacramento as an aquatic habitat, and to reinstate its fisheries is in progress.

---

⑥ McCloud
Siskiyou County; 96057

A historic logging town, McCloud offers breathtaking views of Mt Shasta. Drive around the town for stunning panoramas of the region, and to take in its attractions, such as the log church of St. Joseph.

Also worth considering is a tour of three waterfalls – Lower, Middle, and Upper Falls – located 5 miles (8 km) east of town on the McCloud River. Lower Falls is a family favorite, Middle Falls is the most photogenic, and Upper Falls is a great place to swim or picnic.

🚗 *Continue east on Hwy 89 to McArthur-Burney Falls State Park.*

Above left Lower Waterfalls on the McCloud River **Top** Golfers at the Mt Shasta Resort **Above** Deer on Mt Shasta

---

EAT AND DRINK

DUNSMUIR

Café Maddalena *expensive*
Gourmet Mediterranean fare is the focus here. Sample the roasted beet salad and beef tenderloin.
5801 Sacramento Ave, 96025; 530 235 2725; open 5–10pm Thu–Sun; www.cafemaddalena.com

AROUND MT SHASTA

Lily's *moderate*
The cuisine includes home-made soups and fresh fish. Try the Shasta turkey sandwich lunch or Lily's classic eggplant parmigiana dinner.
1013 South Mt Shasta Blvd, Mount Shasta, 96067; 530 926 3372; open 8am–9:30pm daily; www.lilysrestaurant.com

Wayside Grill *moderate*
The menu includes steaks, BBQ ribs, salads, soups, and pastas.
2217 South Mt Shasta Blvd, Mount Shasta, 96067; 530 918 9234; open 3:30–9pm Mon–Thu, 11am–10pm Fri–Sun; www.waysidegrill.com

Vivify *moderate*
Sample the spicy tuna poke, the quinoa timbale, tempura, and teriyaki chicken at this Japanese restaurant.
531 Chestnut St, Mount Shasta, 96067; 530 926 1345; open 5–8pm Wed–Sun; www.vivifyshasta.com

Above Hikers on snow-covered Mt Shasta in May

Eat and Drink: inexpensive under $25; moderate $25–50; expensive over $50

VISITING LASSEN VOLCANIC
NATIONAL PARK

Tourist Information
*Mineral, 96063; 530 595 4444;
www.nps.gov/lavo*

WHERE TO STAY

LASSEN VOLCANIC
NATIONAL PARK

Manzanita Lake Cabins *inexpensive*
These rustic but functional cabins are
located along the Main Park Road.
*Manzanita Lake Campground,
96063; 877 444 6777;
www.lassenrecreation.com*

Drakesbad Guest Ranch *expensive*
Featuring bungalows and a pool, this
lodge is Lassen Park's only overnight
accommodation option that has a
restaurant attached to it.
*End of Warner Valley Rd, Drakesbad
96020; 866 999 0914; open early Jun–
early Oct; www.drakesbad.com*

RED BLUFF

Best Western Antelope Inn *moderate*
This motel is within walking distance of
restaurants. Rooms have all basic
amenities and there is also a pool.
*203 Antelope Blvd, 96080; 530 527
8882; www.bestwestern.com*

Below The scenic Manzanita Lake, Lassen
Volcanic National Park **Right** A cabin at the
Manzanita Lake Campground

⑦ McArthur-Burney Falls
Memorial State Park
Shasta County; 96013
Burney Falls, the main attraction of
the McArthur-Burney Falls Memorial
State Park *(www.parks.ca.gov/)* is a 129-ft
(40-m) high gush of water arising from
the underground rivers that converge
here. The falls are not rain-fed, so a
visit is rewarding even at the height
of summer. Beyond Burney Falls is
Subway Cave, another intriguing
stop on the road south to Lassen
Park. Here visitors can take a walk in
a lava tube that once had a molten
river of lava coursing through it.
🚗 *Continue south on Hwy 89
for another 48 miles (77 km) to the
northwestern entrance of Lassen
Volcanic National Park.*

⑧ Lassen Volcanic National Park
Shasta County and Lassen County; 96063
A destination both severe and enchanting, Lassen Volcanic National
Park is renowned for its range of geological features. The Main Park
Road *(open mid-Jun–Oct)*, curves its way through the park, past the
most impressive features – Lassen Peak, the largest plug dome volcano
in the world; the numerous mountain lakes that reflect the peaks,
which are snow covered even in the early summer; and bubbling
mud pots and steam vents at Sulphur Works and Bumpass Hell.

① Manzanita Lake Trail
The walk along the shoreline path
around Lake Manzanita, a high
alpine lake, starts at the ranger
station check-in at the northwest
entrance of the park. Walk a quarter
mile (0.5 km) out along the pine-
forest path by the lake to be
rewarded with classic views of
Lassen Peak reflected in the clear
waters of Lake Manzanita and framed
by a wide sky and pine trees along
the bank. Many believe that this is
the most beautiful view in the park.
🚗 *Continue down the Main Park Rd,
the only road going through
the park, to the Manzanita Lake
Campground.*

② Manzanita Lake Campground
The main hub of activity in the park is
the Manzanita Lake Campground and
Loomis Museum. The museum offers
detailed explanations of the volcanic
eruptions that occurred between
1914 and 1917, and displays many
historic photographs of the eruptions.
The campground has cabins and a
store that is the only supply of food
in this part of the park.
🚗 *Continue on the Main Park Rd to
Chaos Jumbles. Roadside parking
near the viewpoint.*

③ Chaos Jumbles
As its name suggests, Chaos Jumbles
is a heap of volcanic rock debris and
a testament to the explosive force
with which a volcano can hurl out

boulders during an eruption. Another debris field, the aptly named Devastated Area, is located nearby.

🚗 *Continue on the Main Park Rd to Summit Lake.*

④ **Summit Lake**
Located near the center of the park, the clear Summit Lake is ideal for a refreshing swim. There is also a campground for backpackers and hikers, which offers access to a number of hiking trails, some of which are part of the Pacific Crest Trail that extends all the way from Canada to Mexico.

🚗 *Continue on the Main Park Rd to the parking lot near Bumpass Hell.*

⑤ **Bumpass Hell**
Hike in to Bumpass Hell, which presents a range of geothermal features from bubbling mudholes and gaseous fumaroles to geysers. Those who want to trek to the 10,457-ft (3,187-m) high Lassen Peak can take the turnout for the steep trail near Bumpas Hell; park in the designated lot. Once back on the Main Park Road, drive on to the Sulphur Works, where boiling mud pots and steam vents can be viewed from a sidewalk.

🚗 *Continue on the Main Park Rd to the Kohm Yah-Mah-Nee Visitor Center.*

⑥ **Kohm Yah-Mah-Nee Visitor Center**
Lassen Volcanic National Park's modern visitor center has displays on the park's geology, flora, and fauna, as well as the only restaurant on the Main Park Road. The center is named

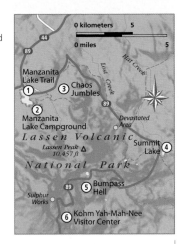

after the Mountain Maidu Native American name for Lassen Peak, Kohm Yah-Mah-Nee, which means "snow mountain."

🚗 *Exit the park southward on Hwy 89, then turn west on Hwy 36 to Red Bluff.*

⑨ **Red Bluff**
Tehama County; 96080
An agricultural town to the south of Redding, Red Bluff has some Victorian-era buildings in the Cone & Kimball Plaza, in the central part of the town. Located on the banks of the Sacramento on the outskirts of the town is the **William B. Ide Adobe State Historic Park** *(www.parks.ca.gov/)*. Explore the historic adobe buildings and visitor center to get an idea of what life was like for the settlers and pioneers who converged in the area at the time of the Gold Rush, when it was a busy river crossing.

Above Alpine trees and wildflowers in Lassen Volcanic National Park

---

DAY TRIP OPTIONS
This region gives a choice of several day trips.

Riverside tour
Use Redding ① as a base for a day of cycling. Rent a bike at the Turtle Bay Exploration Park and enjoy a ride either on the Sacramento River Trail or on the 16-mile (26-km) long road to Shasta Dam ②. It is also possible to settle down for a picnic on the forested banks of the river.

Redding is on I-5, 162 miles (260 km) north of Sacramento.

Admiring Mt Shasta
The town of Mount Shasta is a good place for a day trip to Mt Shasta ⑤. Drive down the Everett Memorial Highway to the base of the mountain, stopping at the vista turnoffs on the way that show the regional mountain water divides. Pack a picnic lunch and drive west from Mt Shasta to Castle Lake to see some spectacular views of the peaks.

From the town of Mount Shasta, follow the Everett Memorial Hwy to the mountain. Take the the W. A. Barr

Rd southwest, and then the Castle Lake Rd to the picturesque Castle Lake.

Geological wonders
Drive through the Lassen Volcanic National Park ⑧ and visit its many attractions including Chaos Jumbles, Bumpass Hell, and the Cinder Cone in the northeast corner of the park.

Drive down the Main Park Rd to see most of the sights. For the Cinder Cone, drive east on Hwy 44 along the north side of Lassen Park and turn south on the road to Butte Lake.

Mountains, Lakes, and Ranchlands

Shasta City to Yreka

Highlights

- **The great outdoors**
  Hike around Whiskeytown Lake
  or take an organized tour into the
  forested Trinity Alps

- **Rivers of gold**
  Discover how scores of Chinese
  miners dredged for gold in the
  Trinity River

- **Waterside recreation**
  Kayak the Trinity River for an
  adrenaline rush, then relax on
  a houseboat on the reservoir

- **A cowboy's life**
  Watch the Etna rodeo for a taste of
  the wild, wild West, and then bite
  into a local, medium rare steak

East Boulder Creek rushing through a
mountain meadow, Trinity Alps

Mountains, Lakes, and Ranchlands

This scenic, forested route winds past glittering reservoir lakes, along the picturesque Trinity River, and through the northern Gold Rush towns that still retain their historic legacy, including charming Weaverville. Take in the panoramic views of the Trinity Alps and the Marble Mountains and admire the sprawling grasslands of the Scott Valley around Etna and Fort Jones. History lovers will get a glimpse of Northern California's halcyon Gold Rush days, and outdoor enthusiasts can make good use of the ample hiking, camping, fishing, and rafting opportunities this region offers.

Above Religious items at Joss House, Weaverville, see pp98–9 **Below** Serene landscape around Highway 3, near Etna, see p100

ACTIVITIES

Discover the historic Gold Rush legacy in the museums and brick buildings of Shasta City and Weaverville

Raft a section of the wild Trinity River

Fish for the wily rainbow trout in the Trinity River

Watch some real deal cowboys rope a calf at the Etna rodeo in July

Explore the Marble Mountain Wilderness on horseback from Etna

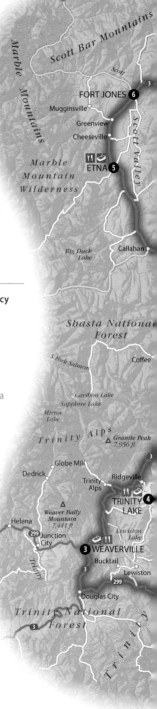

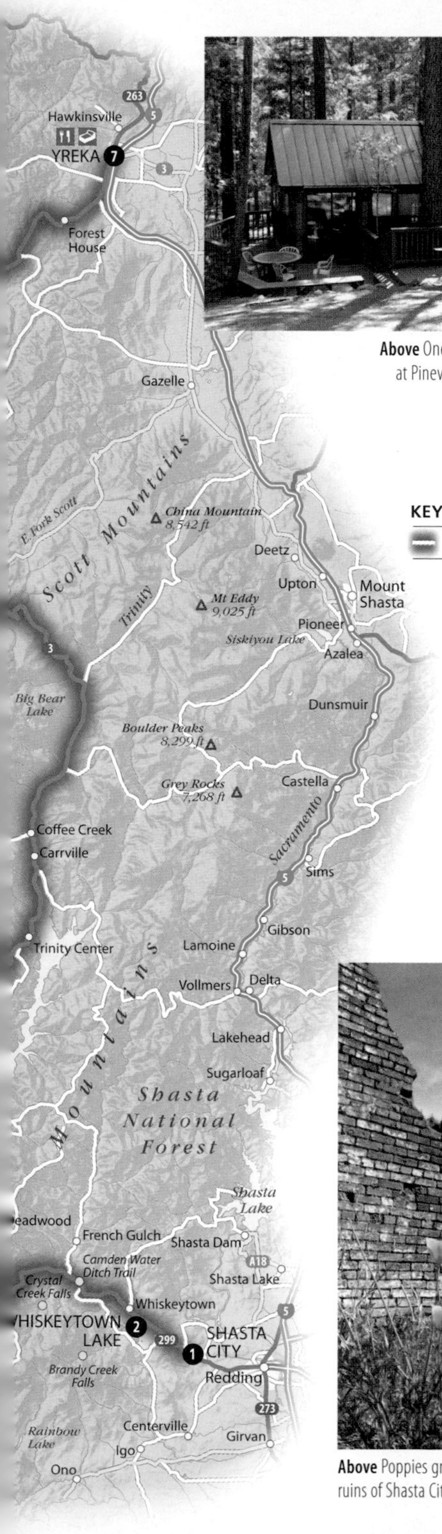

Above One of the pretty wooden cabins for rent at Pinewood Cove, near Trinity Lake, *see p100*

KEY

Drive route

0 kilometers   10

0 miles   10

Above Poppies growing wild among the brick ruins of Shasta City, *see p98*

PLAN YOUR DRIVE

Start/finish: Shasta City to Yreka.

Number of days: 2–3 days, allowing half a day to explore Weaverville.

Distance: 156 miles (251 km).

Road conditions: Roads are well paved, but safe only in the summer and fall travel season. The mountain roads can sometimes be temporarily impassable until plowed in winter and spring. Inquire locally and carry tire chains in winter and spring. Check road conditions with the California Department of Transportation (800 427 7623; www.dot.ca.gov/cgi-bin/roads.cgi).

When to go: Jun–Oct is the best time to visit this area.

Opening times: Most shops and services in this back country area are open from 9am to 5pm daily, with restaurants winding down about 9pm. Regional museums are usually open 10am–4pm daily.

Accommodation: Plan lodging along this route carefully. Redding, near the start of this drive, and Yreka, at the end, have plenty of places to stay, but there is not much in between. When traveling in summer, it is best to have a confirmed reservation for Weaverville and Etna.

DAY TRIP OPTIONS

History enthusiasts should visit **Shasta City** and **Weaverville** to find out about the northern Gold Rush period. For **outdoor activities**, head to **Whiskeytown Lake** and enjoy scenic views, hikes, fishing, and kayak trips. For full details, *see p101*.

Right Panoramic view of serene Whiskeytown Lake **Below** Brick ruins of historic Shasta City, Shasta State Historic Park

VISITING WEAVERVILLE

Download the Walking Tour of Historic Weaverville map from the town website *(www.weavervilleinfo.com)* in advance of a visit.

WHERE TO STAY

WEAVERVILLE

Weaverville Hotel & Emporium *moderate*
Located close to several restaurants, this historic hotel has seven rooms named after local gold mines.
481 Main St, 96093; 530 623 2222; www.weavervillehotel.com

The Whitmore Inn *moderate*
This B&B offers rooms with shared or private baths, an outdoor veranda, a Jacuzzi, and gourmet breakfast.
761 Main St, 96093; 530 623 2509; www.whitmoreinn.com

Weaverville Victorian Inn *moderate*
A modern full-service motel with breakfast, Internet access, and a pool.
2051 Main St, 96093; 530 623 4432; www.trinitycounty.com/weaverville victorianinn/VictorianInn.htm

① Shasta City
Shasta County; 96087
Called the Queen City of the Northern Mines during the Gold Rush days, Shasta City is now a skeleton of scattered brick buildings that make up the Shasta State Historic Park *(www.parks.ca.gov/)*. Some of these ruins have been restored – the 1861 **County Courthouse**, which is now a museum with a range of historic artifacts on display. Do not miss the Boggs Collection, displaying Californian art dating from 1850 to1950.

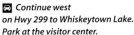

Historic stagecoach on display at the Shasta Sate Historic Park

🚗 *Continue west on Hwy 299 to Whiskeytown Lake. Park at the visitor center.*

② Whiskeytown Lake
Shasta County; 96095
The jewel of the Whiskeytown-Shasta-Trinity National Recreation Area *(www.nps.gov/whis)*, Whiskeytown Lake is a great destination for watersports, with 36 miles (58 km) of shoreline offering lots of opportunities for boating, fishing, and sailing. Enjoy ranger-led free kayak tours on the lake, picnic under the shaded old-growth trees, or hike to the four major waterfalls in the vicinity, of which the **Crystal Creek Falls** are the most accessible. A Waterfalls Weekend, held each April, encourages participants to explore all four waterfalls. Another excellent trek, the 1.1 mile (1.7 km) **Camden Water Ditch Trail** loop takes hikers past abandoned mining machinery and historic fruit orchards.

🚗 *Continue west on Hwy 299 to the junction with Hwy 3. Turn north on Hwy 3 to Weaverville and park on Main St near Jake Jackson Museum.*

③ Weaverville
Trinity County; 96093
This former mining and ranching town still retains its historic charm, with its original brick and wood buildings now occupied by lively restaurants, art and antique shops, and small inns. Weaverville has a thriving arts, theater, and music scene, and is also the regional hub for hiking, biking, rafting, and fishing. Learn about the Taoist beliefs of the Chinese workers who lived here, have a look at the delightful bandstand, or browse through the many excellent art galleries.

A two-hour walking tour
Start at the **Jake Jackson Museum** ① *(www.trinitymuseum.org)*, one of the more elaborate regional museums in Northern California. Walk the grounds and see displays of clothing, firearms, musical instruments, and daily items from the world of ranching, farming, and mining. Look out for the stamp mill, a device used to crush gold-bearing rock, then head to the carriage barn to see a

restored 1885 stagecoach that passed through Weaverville as it made the run from Sacramento to Portland. There are also on-site demonstrations of black-smithing and tinsmithing. Walk north of the museum to **Joss House** ② *(www.parks.ca. gov/)*, which served as a place of worship for the 2,000 Chinese gold miners who worked the Trinity River. Docents explain the symbolism in the architecture of the building and the concept of "spirit screens" to keep out evil spirits. Just north of Joss House was the actual Chinatown site where Chinese miners lived in cramped quarters. Continue to the Historic District, stopping at **Pacific Brewery** ③, an 1854 brick structure where locals gathered until Prohibition laws closed brewing operations in 1917. A short stroll ahead is the **Old Firehouse** ④, which has a red-painted wood exterior, but side walls that show the rammed earth construction of the early period. Three buildings on Main Street have **ornate exterior spiral staircases** ⑤ which were a good way to evade taxes that were levied on the interior staircases in a structure in the 19th century.

Downtown Weaverville is also a lively place for art galleries and musical performances. If time permits, drop into the Mamma Lamma Coffeehouse *(490 Main St)* to catch visiting performers. Continue to the **Weaverville Hotel &**

Emporium ⑥ which was first built in 1861. A quaint lodging, it features high ceilings and wooden floors. Farther ahead, the **bandstand** ⑦ is a classic small town element built in 1901. The **courthouse** ⑧ across the street dates from 1856, making it one of the oldest courthouses in California. Walk down two blocks of **Court Street** ⑨ to see some of the town's more lavish Victorian homes, then retrace the route to the car.

🚗 *Leave Weaverville and proceed north on Hwy 3 to Trinity Lake.*

The Northern Gold Rush

While the main Gold Rush of 1849 took place in the foothills east of Sacramento, there were also sizable gold discoveries in far Northern California. In the 1850s, a discovery could lead to a horde of prospectors arriving in no time. A gold discovery in Yreka *(see p101)* in 1851, for example, brought in 5,000 miners within months. The first prospectors sought gold with pans, but later large hoses with trapped stream water were used to wash down hillsides in search of gold.

(see p101)

EAT AND DRINK

WEAVERVILLE

Garden Café *moderate*
Located in the Historic District, Garden Café offers pancakes for breakfast, and salads, sandwiches, and wraps for lunch.
570 Main St, 96093; 530 623 2400; open 8am–3pm Tue–Sun

Johnson's Steakhouse *moderate*
Sample the home-made soup, cuts of steaks, and prime ribs at this steakhouse located on a golf course.
160 Golf Course Rd, 96093; 530 623 6209; open 11:30am–2:30pm & 5–9pm daily; www.trinityalpsgolf.com/dining.html

La Grange Café *expensive*
Fine-dining restaurant with a charming decor, La Grange Café offers a varied menu and a lively bar. Try the braised lamb shank, beef ravioli, or hazelnut pork chop.
520 Main St, 96093; 530 623 5325; open 11:30am–9:30pm daily

Below left Taoist items of worship displayed at Joss House **Below** Weaverville's historic bandstand

WHERE TO STAY

TRINITY LAKE

Trinity Lake Resort and Marina
moderate
This full-service resort has furnished cabins, houseboats, and a restaurant.
45810 State Hwy 3, 96091; 530 286 2225; open all year; www. trinitylakeresort.com

ETNA

Alderbrook Manor *moderate*
A large house from 1877, Alderbrook is nestled amid tranquil grounds with extensive lawns and a pond. There are regular guest rooms and a hostel-style hiker's hut with bunks.
836 Sawyers Bar Rd, 96027; 530 467 3917; www.alderbrookmanor.com

YREKA

Baymont Inn & Suites Yreka
moderate
Hometown hospitality, as well as an indoor pool, spa, and fitness center. Breakfast with waffles and French toast. Restaurants, shopping, and recreation are close by.
148 Moonlit Oaks Ave, 96097; 530 841 1300; www.baymontinn.com

Yreka Third Street Inn *moderate*
This 1897 Victorian inn has four rooms decorated with vintage lace curtains, and with private baths. The inn also serves a hearty breakfast in the elegant dining room.
326 3rd St, 96097; 530 598 0615; www.yrekabedandbreakfast.com

Above right Trinity Lake, edged by thick alpine forest **Below** Horses grazing in the sprawling pastures around Etna

④ Trinity Lake
Trinity County; 96091
Formed by the Trinity Dam, this lake is a major recreational destination for outdoor activities including swimming, boating, waterskiing, and camping. Resorts such as the Trinity Lake Resort (*www.trinitylakeresort. com*) and Pinewood Cove (*www.pinewoodcove.com*), 17 miles (27 km) north of Weaverville, offer boats, houseboats, and cabins for rent. The more adventurous can head to Big Flat, 20 miles (32 km) west of Weaverville, where local outfitters such as Trinity River Rafting (*www.trinityriverrafting.com*) offer rafting and kayaking tours. Trinity Lake is also a popular spot for fishing trout in spring and bass in summer.

🚗 *Continue another 70 miles (114 km) north on Hwy 3 to Etna; exit at Main St to enter town.*

⑤ Etna
Siskiyou County; 96027
The drive from Trinity Lake to the town of Callahan passes through magnificent forests, laced with cascading rivulets that feed into the Trinity River. The road climbs over Scott Mountains, offering panoramic vistas of the Trinity Alps. It then winds through scenic Scott Valley, which is lined with hay and alfalfa fields, to the charming town of Etna. Nestled at the foot of the Marble Mountain Wilderness (a designated 378-sq mile/978-sq km wilderness area), Etna is a popular base for hikers, backpackers, and rafters, though it is perhaps better known for the annual professional rodeo that takes place here each May. Held on the first weekend of the month, the event attracts professionals on the rodeo circuit and includes a parade and dinner. In July, the town hosts the more casual Old Time Rodeo, which is followed by an Old Timer Dinner.

Deer antlers on a ranch barn in Scott Valley

🚗 *Continue on Hwy 3 to Fort Jones; park roadside.*

⑥ Fort Jones
Siskiyou County; 96032
Established as a frontier outpost to protect the stagecoach route, Fort Jones got an early boost with gold mining, but its lasting economy was from ranching and farming. Stop at the **Fort Jones Museum** (*11913 Main St; www.fortjonesmuseum.com*) to learn about the history of the Scott Valley. The museum has a fine collection of

Far left Exhibit in Fort Jones Museum
Left Victorian exterior of Alderbrook
Manor, Etna **Below left** Cozy interior of
Grandma's House Restaurant in Yreka

EAT AND DRINK

TRINITY LAKE

Timbers Restaurant & Lounge at Trinity Lake Resort *moderate*
Hearty portions of steaks, prime ribs, and seafood served in a casual atmosphere. Barbecue on Saturday nights during summer months.
45810 State Hwy 3, Trinity Center, 96091; 530 286 2225; open May–Labor Day: 5–9pm Wed–Sun; www.trinitylakeresort.com

ETNA

Etna Brewing Company *moderate*
This small-town craft brewery sells nine private labels. The menu features sandwiches, wraps, burgers, salads, soups, and chili con carne.
131 Callahan St, 96027; 530 467 5277; open 11:30am–4pm Tue, 11:30am–8pm Wed, Thu & Sun, 11:30am–9pm Fri & Sat; www.etnabrew.net

YREKA

The Dutchman *inexpensive*
Set in a historic building with Dutch decor. Try the biscuits and gravy for breakfast and the burgers or daily special for lunch.
155 North 11th St, 96064; 530 459 5397; open 8am–2pm Wed–Sat, 8am–1pm Sun

Grandma's House Restaurant *moderate*
A friendly, family atmosphere, generous portions, and good value make this a local favorite.
123 East Center St, 96097; 530 842 5300; open 7am–8pm daily

Native American artifacts, including basketry from Northern Californian tribes, as well as photographs, clothing items, and other objects that belonged to the trappers, placer miners, and immigrant pioneers who lived in the area in the Gold Rush days. Visitors can also head out to explore the Marble Mountain Wilderness on a horse-packing trip, organized by local providers, such as S&E Outfitters *(www.sandeoutfitters.com).*

🚗 *Continue on Hwy 3 to Yreka. Park outside Siskiyou County Museum.*

⑦ Yreka
Siskiyou County; 96097
Pronounced Y-reeka, this small town was an important settlement during the Gold Rush era. Every June, the town hosts the "Yreka Gold Rush Days," which celebrates that period with street fairs, feasting, and music. The Chamber of Commerce *(www.yrekachamber.com)* is a good place to start a self-guided walking tour of the brick buildings that line Miner

Street. Look out for the "the largest gold display south of Alaska" in the lobby of the **Siskiyou County Courthouse** *(311 4th St)*. The gold nuggets are from around the area, and recall the fabulous gold strike in and around Yreka. Take a tour of the **Siskiyou County Museum** *(910 South Main St; 530 842 3836)*, where exhibits range from the mountain man and trapping era to the frontier and pioneer period.

DAY TRIP OPTIONS
Spend a day exploring the Gold Rush at Shasta City and Weaverville, or the outdoors at Whiskeytown Lake.

Museum mania
In Shasta City ❶ start at County Courthouse, which has a special collection of early Californian art, including Percy Gray's *Landscape with Oaks*. The Pioneer Barn's highlights include 19th-century farming equipment, while the Litsch General Store re-creates a shop from the 1880s. Weaverville, ❸ farther west

on Highway 299, will also interest history buffs. Allow time to visit the Jake Jackson Museum, the Joss House, as well as the Historic District.

Shasta City is 6 miles (10 km) and Weaverville is 45 miles (72 km) west of Redding on Hwy 299.

Lakeside recreation
The visitor center at Whiskeytown Lake ❷, where J. F. Kennedy Memorial Drive intersects with Highway 299, is worth an orientation stop. Gaze across the lake to see

mountainous back country beyond a tree-lined shore. From Brandy Creek, on the southern shore, take a walk to Brandy Creek Falls or join one of the ranger-led kayak trips that leave from the Brandy Creek Marina. At the north end of the lake, rent a boat for fishing at Oak Bottom Marina. Farther north, hike the Camden Water Ditch Trail through orchards, or walk to the easily accessible Crystal Creek Falls, on Crystal Creek Road.

Whiskeytown Lake is 10 miles (16 km) west of Redding on Hwy 299.

California's Undiscovered North

Yreka to Graeagle

Highlights

- **Time travel**
  Walk the streets of the Gold Rush town of Yreka and admire its 19th-century buildings

- **Bird-watchers' paradise**
  Take a tour of the Lower Klamath and Tule Lake Refuges to see the thousands of migratory birds

- **War and volcanoes**
  Walk around the Lava Beds National Monument, known for its volcanoes

- **Mountain meanders**
  Get an adrenaline high while hiking through the stupendous South Warner Wilderness

Flight of snow geese in March, Lower Klamath Lake National Wildlife Refuge

California's Undiscovered North

Northern California presents its visitors with a varied, diverse, and virtually unexplored landscape. This driving tour begins at the historic town of Yreka, and then takes drivers through thick conifer forest to the California/Oregon border, where birdlife flourishes in the Lower Klamath and Tule Lake Wildlife National Refuges. From the plush greenery of the refuges, the tour leads southward to the stark and barren landscape of the Lava Beds National Monument. Farther down, take in the sheer grandeur of the South Warner Mountains before continuing to the grasslands of the western edge of the Great Basin, where wildlife, from antelope to grouse, abounds.

KEY

▬ Drive route

Above The ponderosa pine forest at Mill Creek Camp in South Warner Mountains, *see p108*

ACTIVITIES

Pick up binoculars and go bird-watching at the Tule Lake National Wildlife Refuge

Explore a lava labyrinth at the Lava Beds National Monument

Bike or walk down the Bizz Johnson Trail in Susanville

Cast a line in the trout-filled Eagle Lake, near Susanville

Above Fishing in the Feather River at Graeagle, *see p109*

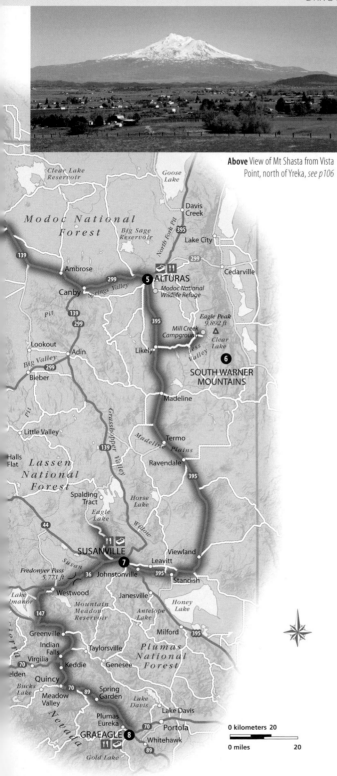

Above View of Mt Shasta from Vista Point, north of Yreka, *see p106*

see p106

PLAN YOUR DRIVE

Start/finish: Yreka to Graeagle.

Number of days: 3–4 days, allowing half a day to explore the Lava Beds National Monument.

Distance: 460 miles (740 km).

Road conditions: Though the area is remote, the roads are paved and well maintained. June–November is the best time for driving. Carry snow chains in winter and spring (Dec–May). Some roads can close temporarily between December and February due to heavy snowfall. There is no fuel station for 90 miles (145 km) south of Alturas on Hwy 395.

When to go: The best times to visit are late spring (May), summer (Jun–Aug), and fall (Sep–Nov). December–February can be snowy and March rainy.

Opening times: Most shops in these remote areas are open from 9am to 5pm. The museums tend to be open from 10am to 4pm. Restaurants generally close around 9pm.

Accommodation: Plan lodging for this drive in advance – the route is long and lodgings are limited. There are many places to stay in the bigger towns such as Yreka, Alturas, and Graeagle, but the stretches in between have few places to stay and reservations have to be made in advance. It is best to start early in the morning and complete a major part of the exploring by mid-afternoon.

DAY TRIP OPTIONS

History buffs can explore **Yreka, Lava Beds Monument**, and **Alturas**. **Wildlife enthusiasts** can visit the **Lower Klamath National Wildlife Refuge** and **Tule Lake National Wildlife Refuge** to get a closer look at waterfowl and other wildlife. For full details, *see p109*.

see p109

Above View of Mt Shasta from Vista Point, north of Yreka **Below** Captain Jack's Stronghold, Lava Beds National Monument

VISITING LAVA BEDS NATIONAL MONUMENT

Tourist Information
1 Indian Well Headquarters, Tulelake, 96134; 530 667 8113

WHERE TO STAY

YREKA

Mountain View Inn *moderate*
With views of Mt Shasta, this small inn has rooms with basic amenities.
801 N Main St, 96097; 530 842 1940; www.mountainviewinnyreka.com

AROUND LOWER KLAMATH LAKE NATIONAL WILDLIFE REFUGE

Hospitality Inn & Dinner House *moderate*
The decor at this inn is pleasant and homey, and the staff accommodating.
200 S California St, Dorris, 96023; 530 397 2097

Fe's Bed & Breakfast *moderate*
This bed and breakfast offers four comfy rooms. The owners are helpful.
660 Main St, Tulelake, 96134; 530 667 5145; www.fesbandb.com

① Yreka
Siskiyou County; 96097
A small settlement nestled in the Shasta Valley, Yreka *(see also p101)* offers stunning views of Mt Shasta. It was established as a "boomtown" during the Northern California Gold Rush in the 1850s, and has retained much of its 19th-century architecture.

🚗 *Drive south on I-5 to Weed (Exit 748), then turn northeast on Hwy 97. After 55 miles (88 km), turn east on Hwy 161 for Lower Klamath Refuge.*

② Lower Klamath Lake National Wildlife Refuge
Siskiyou County; 96134
A part of the Klamath Basin National Wildlife Refuge Complex *(www.fws. gov)*, this refuge was established as America's first waterfowl refuge in 1908. Its 46,900 acres (19,000 ha) of marshes, vast lakes, and grassy uplands provide the ideal habitat for waterbirds. A 10-mile (16-km) self-guided auto tour lets visitors see a variety of birds in their habitat.

Continue east on Highway 161, then turn southeast on Highway 139, and drive 16 miles (26 km) to Tulelake. Stop here for a meal and overnight stay before heading to the Tule Lake National Wildlife Refuge.

🚗 *Drive west from Tulelake on the East West Rd, turning south on Hill Rd to reach the Visitor Center near the entrance to the Tule Lake National Wildlife Refuge.*

③ Tule Lake National Wildlife Refuge
Modoc & Siskiyou County; 96134
Spread over 39,100 acres (15,800 ha), this refuge is an important stop for nearly 250 species of birds that migrate along the Pacific Flyway from Canada to the tropics annually. Spot waterfowl and other birds on a driving tour or a leisurely walk.

🚗 *Continue south on Hill Rd to enter Lava Beds National Monument. Turn left at the Y-junction, and follow signs for Captain Jack's Stronghold, which has ample parking.*

④ Lava Beds National Monument
Modoc & Siskiyou County; 96134
The scene of the Modoc War (1872–3) – a conflict between the US Army and Native American Modoc tribe led by Captain Jack (also known as Kientpoos) – Lava Beds National Monument *(www.nps. gov/labe)* encompasses a rugged terrain fraught with volcanic eruptions, which have led to the formation of over 700 caves. This walk highlights Captain Jack's defensive positions, known as Captain Jack's Stronghold, on the northern edge of the monument. Other activities include exploring the monument's lava tube caves, hiking its trails, and viewing the Native American cave drawings.

A two-hour walking tour
From the parking lot, follow signs along the Short Trail and to the **Modoc Outpost** ①, a typical hidden lookout that enabled the Modocs to defend themselves. Continue down the trail to **main defense line** ②, the inner perimeter of the defensive positions, and to the **firing position** ③, one of the many places that Modoc sharpshooters used as a vantage point. During the war, over 100 Modoc families lived in the numerous caves around the Stronghold, surviving the harsh winter with limited fuel, food, and water. Stop by the **shelter** ④, one such typical small cave, to visualize how the hardy Modocs lived, then continue to **Sally Way** ⑤, a

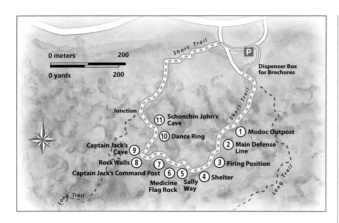

Junction

⑪ Schonchin John's Cave

⑩ Dance Ring

Captain Jack's Cave ⑨

Rock Walls ⑧

Captain Jack's Command Post ⑥ ⑤

Medicine Flag Rock Sally Way

⑦

① Modoc Outpost

② Main Defense Line

③ Firing Position

④ Shelter

Dispenser Box for Brochures

Short Trail

0 meters 200

0 yards 200

Long Trail

strategically located defensive postion. **Medicine flag rock** ⑥, a short walk away, is where the Modoc shaman, Curly-Headed Doctor, hung a flag made of mink skin and hawk feathers, which he claimed would protect the tribe.

Ahead lie **Captain Jack's command post** ⑦, where Captain Jack deployed his small force to hold off the army, and the **rock walls** ⑧ built by the Modocs to enhance their defense. Walk on to **Captain Jack's cave** ⑨, where Captain Jack, his two wives, and a daughter survived the winter during the war. Walk around the **dance ring** ⑩ to get a feel of the Modoc ritualistic dance, then head north to **Schonchin John's cave** ⑪, the lodgings of the Modoc second-in-command. Walk back along the short trail to the parking lot.

🚗 *Return to the Y-junction and keep straight on Hill Rd to the*

Lava Beds National Monument park entrance and visitor center. Drive through the park and exit onto Hwy 139. Turn right for Canby, then turn left onto Hwy 299 for Alturas; park roadside.

Modoc War

The Modoc War was a result of the conflict arising from white settlers encroaching on Native American lands. The Modocs were unwilling to live on a reservation. A group under Captain Jack (Kientpoos) left the reservation and returned to their homeland, which led to a bitter fight. The Modocs withdrew to Lava Beds for a final stand. Despite fierce fighting, US Army troops eventually overpowered them and three, including Captain Jack, were hanged. The war, however, is remembered for the small group of Modocs who held off large US troops for months.

EAT AND DRINK

YREKA

Pat's BBQ *moderate*
Feast on slow-smoked meats cooked over juniper wood. Try the pork ribs, chicken, beef ribs, sandwiches, such as pulled pork and BBQ beef, or home-made potato salad.
1421 S Main St, 96097; 530 841 0300; open 11am–7pm Tue–Sat

AROUND LOWER KLAMATH LAKE NATIONAL WILDLIFE REFUGE

Captain Jack's Stronghold *moderate*
This quality restaurant serves prime ribs, pasta, fresh seafood, home-made soups, and desserts.
45650 State Hwy 139 A, Tulelake, 96134; 530 664 5566; open 8am–8pm Tue–Fri, 8am–9pm Sat, 9am–8pm Sun; www.captainjackslaststand.com

Below left A Victorian house on Miner Street, Yreka **Below** The stunning Tule Lake National Wildlife Refuge

Eat and Drink: inexpensive under $25; moderate $25–50; expensive over $50

Top right A Victorian house from the 1860s in Susanville **Below right** A historic railroad locomotive at the Western Pacific Railroad Museum near Graeagle **Far right** The Feather River, Graeagle

WHERE TO STAY

ALTURAS

Best Western Trailside Inn *moderate*
Located close to the Modoc Historical County Museum, this modern inn in downtown Alturas provides breakfast and has an outdoor swimming pool.
343 N Main St, 96101; 530 233 4111; www.bestwesterncalifornia.com

Rim Rock Motel *moderate*
This clean motel offers all the modern amenities. Ask the owners for tips on hiking, fishing, and wildlife viewing.
22760 Hwy 395N, 96101; 530 233 5455; www.rimrockmotelalturas.com

SUSANVILLE

High Country Inn *moderate*
This modern and independent motel has an outdoor heated pool, an indoor exercise room, breakfast, and free Wi-Fi.
3015 Riverside Dr, 96130; 530 257 3450; www.high-country-inn.com

Roseberry House B&B *moderate*
Housed in a lovely, antique-rich Victorian building, Roseberry House serves home-cooked breakfasts in a quaint dining hall.
609 North St, 96130; 530 257 5675; www.roseberryhouse.com

GRAEAGLE

River Pines Resort *moderate*
A family-owned resort, River Pines has a variety of lodgings. The on-site Coyote Bar & Grill restaurant is popular with the locals.
8296 Hwy 89, 96103; 530 836 2552; www.riverpines.com

Chalet View Lodge *expensive*
Set in a forest, this luxurious lodge offers spa treatments and fine dining.
72056 Hwy 70, 96103; 530 832 5528; www.chaletviewlodge.com

⑤ Alturas
Modoc County; 96101
Set in a landscape of grasslands and plateaus, the town of Alturas has a high desert climate. The Lassen-Applegate Trail Marker indicates the converging point of two historic trails that brought pioneers into Northern California. The **Modoc County Historical Museum** *(600 Main St)* has exhibits on the rich heritage of the Modoc tribe, including an exceptional display of Native American artwork; do not miss the arrowheads fashioned from volcanic obsidian.

Located on the southern edge of Alturas, the **Modoc National Wildlife Refuge** *(www.fws.gov)* was established in 1961. It has a large freshwater lake that provides habitat for migrating waterbirds. Over 246 species of birds have been sighted here.

🚗 *Drive 18 miles (29 km) south from Alturas on Hwy 395 to Likely, then continue east on the Jess Valley Rd toward the South Warner Mountains.*

⑥ South Warner Mountains
Modoc & Lassen County; 96116
East from Likely, the South Warner Wilderness offer miles of untouched natural beauty and pristine wilderness. Pass through cattle ranching country on the Jess Valley Road along the South Fork of the Pit River, known for trout fishing. Turn north onto West

Above Lake at the Modoc National Wildlife Refuge, Alturas, popular with migrating waterbirds

Warner Road for stunning views of the South Warner Mountains. Continue on this road and follow the signs for Mill Creek Campground, a good picnic spot in a ponderosa pine forest. A half-mile (1-km) long walk from Mill Creek Campground leads to Clear Lake, the starting point for walking and hiking trails into the South Warner Wilderness.

🚗 *Return to Likely, then drive southward for 85 miles (137 km) on Hwy 395 to Susanville; roadside parking.*

7 Susanville
Lassen County; 96127

The town of Susanville is a center for outdoor adventures. The town is the main access point for the 25-mile (40-km) long **Bizz Johnson Trail**, which runs along the Susan River. The trail was once a railroad line which has been converted into a recreation path. Rent a bike at Bicycle Bananas *(702 Main St)* and pedal down the trail. The best time to visit is in fall, when the aspens take on hues of yellow, orange, and gold.

Exit Susanville on Hillcrest Road, and turn right on Eagle Lake Road after 5 miles (3 km). Drive 14 miles (23 km) to California's second largest natural lake. **Eagle Lake** is favored by bird-watchers and fishing enthusiasts who visit it for its golden and bald eagles, and trophy trout. In winter, snowmobiling and skiing are popular activities here.

Return to Highway 136 and continue 30 miles (51 km) west, then turn south on Highway 147 for

Above A pasture en route to Graeagle

Lake Almanor. This man-made alpine resort lake is a great place to hike and picnic.

🚗 *Continue south on Hwy 147 and turn east on Hwy 89 to reach Graeagle.*

8 Graeagle
Plumas County; 96103

Nestled in the Plumas and Tahoe National Forests, this central resort town is a great getaway. The area is blessed with mountain scenery, conifer trees, numerous lakes and streams, and many hiking- and mountain-biking trails.

Visit Gold Lake, one of the most scenic lakes in California, and the town of Portola, known for its **Western Pacific Railroad Museum** (*www. wplives.org*), which has a collection of rail locomotives and passenger cars.

DAY TRIP OPTIONS
This route can be divided into day trips geared for specific interests.

A taste of history
Those who appreciate history can wander the streets of Yreka ❶, which evoke its Gold Rush heyday. Then head to the Lava Beds National Monument ❹ where Captain Jack led the Modoc in a fierce battle against US troops in 1872–73. After exploring Captain Jack's Stronghold, continue to Alturas ❺ to learn more about the brave Modoc tribe at the Modoc County Historical Museum.

From Yreka, take the I-5 to Weed, then head toward Lava Beds via Hwy 97 and Hwy 161. From here, drive southeast on Hwy 139, and then east on Hwy 299 to Alturas

Wildlife paradise
With Tulelake as the base, take the self-guided auto tours around the Lower Klamath Lake National Wildlife Refuge ❷ and the Tule Lake National Wildlife Refuge ❸ known for their migrating waterbird populaton. The two refuges come to life at dawn and dusk, when the waterbirds are at their most active.

Photo blinds can be reserved in advance by photography enthusiasts. The two refuges also have a variety of flora and fauna, including endangered species, such as bald eagles, sandhill cranes, and peregrine falcons that can be viewed during the tour.

From Tulelake drive northwestward on Hwy 139 and then turn westward on to Hwy 161 to reach the Lower Klamath National Wildlife Refuge. For the Tule Lake National Wildlife Refuge, retrace the route to Tulelake and then drive westward on the East West Rd, turning south on Hill Rd.

Santa Cruz Sojourn

San Francisco shoreline to Salinas

Highlights

- **Capital surf**
  Watch surfers "hang ten" at Santa Cruz, Northern California's surfing hub

- **Ride the rails**
  Journey through redwood forests on a 19th-century steam train at Roaring Camp Railroad

- **Humble mission**
  Soak up history at San Juan Bautista Historic Park, once home to California's largest Spanish mission

- **A novel place**
  Visit the National Steinbeck Center in Salinas for an insight into the life and works of Nobel-prize winner John Steinbeck

Windsurfers riding the waves at Santa Cruz

Santa Cruz Sojourn

Twining south from San Francisco, the Pacific Coast Highway clings to a rugged shore. This drive takes in seal rookeries, coast wetlands, sand dunes, daunting cliffs, and lonesome beaches ideal for leisurely walks. While the water is generally too cold for swimming, surfers don wet suits to brave the chilly waves, notably in Santa Cruz, which enchants with its Spanish Mediterranean architecture, popular Boardwalk Amusement Park, and scenic Cliff Drive. A detour into the mountains leads into soaring redwoods, while the Salinas Valley is the source of fresh strawberries and artichokes sold in stores across the US. Novelist John Steinbeck grew up here, wrote about the region in his many novels, and is honored in his birthplace, Salinas.

Above Elephant seals on the beach at the Año Nuevo State Reserve, *see p116*
Below Tidal pools at Fitzgerald Marine Reserve at Moss Beach, *see p115*

ACTIVITIES

Ride on horseback along the shore of Half Moon Bay

Hike to see elephant seals up close at Año Nuevo State Reserve

Stroll the boardwalks at Natural Bridges State Beach to see the monarch butterflies that migrate here every winter

Learn to surf or rent a board and show off in Santa Cruz

Hop aboard a 1890s-era steam train for a ride in the redwoods at the Roaring Camp Railroad

Spot birds in the wetlands at Watsonville

Be immersed in culture at Salinas' National Steinbeck Center, which has lectures, films, and special events that bring the legacy of John Steinbeck to life

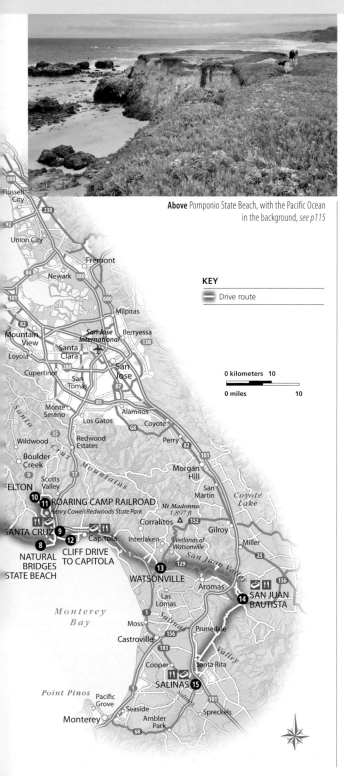

Above Pomponio State Beach, with the Pacific Ocean in the background, *see p115*

KEY

--- Drive route

0 kilometers 10

0 miles 10

PLAN YOUR DRIVE

Start/finish: San Francisco Shoreline to Salinas.

Number of days: 2–3 days, allowing half a day to explore Santa Cruz.

Distance: 144 miles (232 km).

Road conditions: The roads are well-maintained, but the coast road is subject to fog and strong winds, and SR 9 is mountainous and winding.

When to go: The best time is between March and September with a preference for late spring to catch the wildflower blooms. Summer weekends can be busy in Santa Cruz.

Opening times: Museums along this route are usually open 10am–5pm daily. Shops tend to open 9am–5pm Mon–Sat, restaurants around 9pm. State parks typically open 8am–sunset daily.

Main market days: Half Moon Bay: Sat. Santa Cruz: Wed pm. Salinas: 9am–2pm Sat.

Shopping: Look for strawberries, artichokes, and other seasonal, freshly picked produce.

Major festivals: Half Moon Bay: Art & Pumpkin Festival, Oct. **Santa Cruz:** Shakespeare Santa Cruz, Jul–Aug; Cold Water Classic, Oct. **Capitola:** Art & Wine Festival, Sep.

DAY TRIP OPTIONS

It is possible to make this drive in a number of day trips. **Literary fans** will enjoy exploring sites associated with John Steinbeck in **Salinas**, while **nature lovers** should head to **Año Nuevo State Park**, **Pescadero State Beach**, and **Natural Bridges State Beach**. **History buffs** and the **ecclesiastically minded** can visit the **Santa Cruz** and **San Juan Bautista** missions. For full details, *see p121*.

Above Wildflowers along San Gregorio Creek San Gregorio State Beach **Top right** Dangerous cliffs sign at Devil's Slide, near Point Montara Lighthouse **Above right** Whale jawbone outside the Half Moon State Beach visitor center

---

WHERE TO STAY

MOSS BEACH

Seal Cove Inn *moderate*
This English cottage-style inn weds modern luxuries with a touch of old England.
221 Cypress Ave, 94038; 800 995 9987; www.sealcoveinn.com

HALF MOON BAY

Pacific Victorian B&B *moderate*
A charming Victorian-style inn with antique furnishings.
325 Alameda Ave, 94019; 650 712 3900; www.pacificvictorian.com

Ritz-Carlton Half Moon Bay
expensive
The epitome of luxury, this large resort perches atop cliffs at the edge of the sea. The vistas are priceless.
1 Miramontes Point Rd, 94019; 650 712 7000; www.ritzcarlton.com

Right San Francisco's Ocean Beach, a favorite with surfers

---

❶ San Francisco Shoreline
San Francisco County
Perched on cliffs at the very northwest tip of the San Francisco peninsula, **Cliff House** *(see pp32–3)* makes a good starting point. Run by the National Park Service as a restaurant, it has fine views over Seal Rocks and windswept Ocean Beach, a broad swath of gray popular with surfers. The Great Highway (SR 1) runs along the shore as part of the 49-Mile Scenic Drive. At the south end of the beach the road curls around Lake Merced, merges with Skyline Boulevard, and climbs to **Fort Funston** *(see p32)*. Keep right at the split with John Muir Drive for the fort, which was initiated as a coastal battery in World War I, enlarged

during World War II, and later served as a Nike missile site. Built on top of hard-packed sand dunes, it is laced with trails. Hang gliders launch from the cliffs around the fort.
🚗 *From Fort Funston, continue south on Skyline Blvd, then exit onto SR 1 south for Pacifica.*

❷ Pacifica
San Mateo County; 94044
The coast highway is hemmed by houses until Pacifica, where a headland affords great views of crescent-shaped Pacifica State Beach and the town nestled in a bay cusped by forests. The **Portolá Expedition Historical Marker**, on the east side of SR 1 by the beach, marks a campsite of the expedition led by Spaniard Gaspar de Portolá that on Oct 31, 1769, sighted San Francisco Bay – the first Europeans to do so – from nearby Sweeney Ridge. The Mexican-era **Sánchez Adobe** *(1000 Linda Mar Blvd)* was built atop the foundations of an early mission outpost in 1846 and is the oldest building in San Mateo County.
🚗 *Keep south on SR 1 to Moss Beach.*

Elephant Seals
The world's largest fin-footed mammal, the male elephant seal – whose long, pendulous proboscis gives the species its name – can grow to 16 ft (5 m) and weigh 6,000 lb (2,700 kg). Males reach maturity at five years and fight bloody battles for control of harems during mating season. The species was hunted to the brink of extinction in the 19th century, but the population has now rebounded.

Where to Stay: inexpensive under $100; moderate $100–200; expensive over $200

❸ Moss Beach
San Mateo County; 94038

South of Pacifica, SR 1 claws along a steep, rocky coastal promontory famous for landslides – the source of its name, "Devil's Slide"– that often make the road impassable. Drive with caution, as the road has sharp corners and sheer drop-offs, and the views can be a distraction. Stopping is forbidden along much of the route.

Gray Whale Cove State Beach (www.parks.ca.gov/) is named for the whales that can often be seen close to shore (Nov–Apr). The 1875 **Point Montara Lighthouse**, overlooking the golden sands of Montara Beach, is a good spot for whale-watching.

Continue 1 mile (1.6 km) south to the small coastal village of Moss Beach. In town, turn off SR 1 at California Avenue to reach the **Fitzgerald Marine Reserve** (www. fitzgeraldreserve.org), a coastal habitat where a bluff-top trail leads through ancient cypress groves. Below, unique shale formations form intertidal pools where visitors can look for anemones, sea urchins, and crabs. Harbor seals are present in spring, and sea otters can sometimes be spotted foraging offshore.

🚗 **Continue south on SR 1 to Half Moon Bay.**

❹ Half Moon Bay
San Mateo County; 94019

Tucked at the sheltered north end of long scimitar-shaped Half Moon Bay is the lively fishing port and resort of **El Granada**, with a large harbor that was once a whaling station. Take Capistrano Road to reach Pillar Point by a trail that leads past **Pillar Point Marsh**, where one-fifth of all North American bird species have been spotted. The point offers an unmatched view of the harbor and of surfers tackling the world-famous Mavericks wave, which breaks over an offshore ocean reef. Sea lions can be seen basking on the jagged rocks below. To the south, four interconnected white-sand beaches curl around the bay for 4 miles (7 km) and make up **Half Moon Bay State Beach** (www.parks. ca.gov/), centered on the community of Half Moon Bay. A paved track and

a parallel horse trail run alongside the beaches. Inland, the Santa Cruz Mountains form a fantastic backdrop.

🚗 **Follow SR 1 (Cabrillo Hwy) south to San Gregorio State Beach.**

❺ The State Beaches
San Mateo County; 94074

South from Half Moon Bay, the road runs along a cliff top and dips down to a series of coves and beaches. At **San Gregorio State Beach** (www.parks. ca.gov/), the San Gregorio Creek feeds a freshwater lagoon and driftwood-strewn estuary. A plaque records that Spanish explorer Gaspar de Portolá's expedition camped here in 1769. Framed by high sandstone bluffs, **Pomponio State Beach** (www.parks. ca.gov/) also has a lagoon, a habitat for creatures such as blue heron, raccoon, fox, and skunk. Kite-surfers favor wind-whipped **Pescadero State Beach** (www.parks.ca.gov/).

🚗 **From Pescadero, continue for 6 miles (10 km) on SR 1 (Cabrillo Hwy) to Pigeon Point Lighthouse, park roadside.**

Left Horseback riders at Half Moon State Beach, Half Moon Bay **Below** Point Montara Lighthouse near Moss Beach

EAT AND DRINK

MOSS BEACH

Moss Beach Distillery *moderate*
A rum-runner's hangout during Prohibition, it has an oceanfront patio for enjoying great food and cocktails. *140 Beach Way, 94038; 650 728 5595; open noon–8:30pm Mon–Thu, noon–9pm Fri & Sat, 11am–8:30pm Sun; www.mossbeachdistillery.com*

HALF MOON BAY

Pasta Moon *moderate*
In the heart of the Half Moon Bay community, this elegant restaurant serves delicious Italian fare, such as tagliatelle with fresh sea scallops. *315 Main St, 94019; 650 726 5125; open 11:30am–2:30pm & 5:30–9pm Mon–Thu, 11:30am–2:30pm & 5:30–9:30pm Fri, noon–3pm & 5:30–9:30pm Sat, noon–3pm & 5:30–9pm Sun; www.pastamoon.com*

Miramar Beach Restaurant *moderate*
Three-course fresh seafood dinners, live music, and superb ocean vistas from a glass-enclosed outdoor patio. *131 Mirada Rd, 94019; 650 726 9053; open noon–3:30pm & 5–9pm Mon–Fri, 11:30am–3pm & 4:30–9pm Sat & Sun; www.miramarbeachrestaurant.com*

Eat and Drink: inexpensive under $25; moderate $25–50; expensive over $50

Above Pigeon Point Lighthouse **Below** Watching elephant seals on the beach at Año Nuevo State Reserve

VISITING SANTA CRUZ

Tourist Information
Santa Cruz County Conference & Visitors Council *303 Water St, Suite 100, 95060; 831 425 1234; www.visitsantacruzca.org*

WHERE TO STAY

PIGEON POINT

Pigeon Point Lighthouse Hostel *inexpensive*
Private rooms and shared dorms in the restored lighthouse keepers' quarters, with kitchens and hot tub. Free Wi-Fi. *210 Pigeon Point Rd, Pescadero, 94060; 650 879-0633; www.norcalhostels.org/pigeon*

SANTA CRUZ

West Cliff Inn *moderate*
This enchanting B&B features spacious and comfy rooms with gracious furnishings. Fantastic location overlooking the boardwalk. *174 W Cliff Dr, 95060; 831 457 2200; www.westcliffinn.com*

Babbling Brook Inn *expensive*
Set in a lush garden, this lovely B&B has a fireplace and down quilts in rooms themed for famous painters. A 15-minute walk from the shore. *1025 Laurel St, 95060; 831 427 2437; www.babblingbrookinn.com*

⑥ Pigeon Point Lighthouse
San Mateo County; 94060
The tallest operating lighthouse on the West Coast stands at Pigeon Point, named for the *Carrier Pigeon*, a clipper ship that ran aground here in fog in 1853. Built in 1872, the 115-ft (35-m) tall structure is outfitted with its original (and still functioning) Fresnel lens. Its signature beam still flashes every 10 seconds. Sea lions bask on the rocks below the point, and a boardwalk overlook lets visitors look out for passing whales in winter.

🚗 *Continue south on the SR 1 (Cabrillo Hwy) to Año Nuevo State Reserve. Park in the lot.*

⑦ Año Nuevo State Reserve
San Mateo County; 94060
This reserve (*www.parks.ca.gov/*) protects a breeding rookery of elephant seals. In winter, hundreds of these giant mammals gather to mate and give birth on a large offshore island and on two small sandy beaches reached by a 3 miles (5 km) round-trip trail from the visitor center. Seals are also seen in spring and summer, when they waddle ashore to shed their outer skin and fur. Guided walks are compulsory in the mid-Dec–Mar breeding season, the best time to visit. Absent for nearly a century after being hunted to virtual extinction, elephant seals first returned to Año Nuevo in 1975.

🚗 *Follow SR 1 (Cabrillo Hwy) along the shore to the outskirts of Santa Cruz. After 20 miles (32 km), turn right on Western Dr and follow the signs for Natural Bridges State Beach.*

⑧ Natural Bridges State Beach
Santa Cruz County; 95060
At the western limit of Santa Cruz, this beach (*www.parks.ca.gov/*) is named for the offshore stack with an arch forming a natural bridge. Moore Creek flows to the ocean through a freshwater marsh, and crabs and sea anemones can be seen in the tide pools. A eucalyptus grove behind the beach is home to the **Monarch Butterfly Natural Preserve**, one of the largest monarch butterfly habitats in fall and winter, when thousands of butterflies migrate and cluster on the trees. A wheelchair-accessible boardwalk loops through the preserve.

🚗 *Exit onto Delaware Ave, then right onto Swanton Blvd. At the shore, turn left onto W Cliff Dr for Santa Cruz boardwalk.*

Above The impressive mudstone arch at the Natural Bridges State Beach

⑨ Santa Cruz
Santa Cruz County; 95060-95067
Regarded by some as California's quintessential beach town, Santa Cruz combines a Mediterranean climate with superb coastal vistas, fabulous surf, broad beaches, plus a pier and boardwalk famous for its thrill-ride amusement park. The University of California Santa Cruz campus ensures that this small resort town retains a youthful character, despite its 18th-century mission and historic downtown.

A three-hour walking tour
Park in the public lots on Cliff Drive and head to the tiny **Surfing Museum** ① (*701 W Cliff Dr; 831 420 6289; www.santacruzsurfingmuseum. org*) set in a lighthouse overlooking the beach. The museum traces the history of surfing back to 1885 when three Hawaiian princes rode the waves off Santa Cruz and introduced board surfing to the US mainland. After watching surfers catching waves immediately below at **Lighthouse Point** ②, walk north along W Cliff Drive to the *To Honor Surfing* **statue** ③ (*Pelton Ave*), depicting a surfer with a longboard. The viewpoint here offers a fantastic view over Cowell Beach, the pier, and Santa Cruz Beach Boardwalk.

Where to Stay: inexpensive under $100; moderate $100–200; expensive over $200

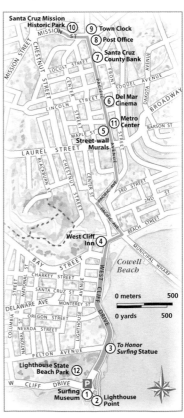

EAT AND DRINK

SANTA CRUZ

Café Campesino *inexpensive*
Outside patio dining and delicious, authentic Mexican fare at this walk-up kiosk café.
1130 Pacific Ave, 95060; 831 425 5979; open 11:30am–6:30pm Thu–Tue

Kianti's Pizza & Pasta Bar *moderate*
A popular and contemporary themed Italian restaurant with an open kitchen. Pizzas and pastas rarely disappoint. Live entertainment.
1100 Pacific Ave, 95060; 831 469 4400; open 11am–10pm Mon–Fri, 10am–10pm Sat & Sun; www.kiantis.com

Above left *To Honor Surfing* statue on the Santa Cruz waterfront **Top right** Surfers at Lighthouse Point **Above right** Street-wall mural on the exterior of Andy's Auto Supply

Catching a Wave

Surfing was invented by ancient Polynesian cultures, who revered the sacred sport they called *he'enalu* in the Hawaiian language. Chiefs were expected to demonstrate special prowess and bravado. Surfing was first recorded by Lt. James King during the third and fatal voyage of British explorer Captain James Cook in 1769. The sport is said to have been introduced to California in 1885.

Continue north past the **West Cliff Inn** ④ to Pacific Avenue and follow this to downtown. Look for the **street-wall murals** ⑤ at Jazz Alley and Andy's Auto Supply *(corner of Maple St)*. Pacific Avenue is lined with historic buildings – survivors of the 1989 earthquake that leveled many others. Do not miss the Art Deco **Del Mar cinema** ⑥ *(1124 Pacific Ave)* and

Above The Del Mar cinema, an Art Deco gem in Santa Cruz

the **Santa Cruz County Bank** ⑦ *(1502 Pacific Ave)*, built in 1895, whose handsome Neo-Classical facade today hides a modern interior. Standing at the corner of Front Street, the **Post Office** ⑧ is a fine example of Renaissance Revival architecture. The **Town Clock** ⑨, to the north at Harvey West Park across Mission Street, was built in 1900 and relocated here in 1976 from farther down Pacific Avenue. Turn left and walk the 110 yards (100 m) to **Santa Cruz Mission Historic Park** ⑩ *(144 School St; 831 425 5849)*, where a half-scale replica of the original church stands; an adobe building beside the visitor center has a museum. Return down Pacific Avenue to the **Metro Center** ⑪ *(831 425 8600; www.scmtd.com)*, from where hourly shuttles run to **Lighthouse State Beach Park** ⑫ *(Pelton Ave & National St)*. Get off here and walk through the park to return to the car.

🚗 *Exit downtown Santa Cruz on Chestnut St and merge south onto SR 1 (Cabrillo Hwy). Turn left at SR 9 (River St) for Henry Cowell Redwoods State Park Felton; this road has switchback bends. Turn right on Graham Hill Rd and continue north to Felton; park roadside.*

Eat and Drink: inexpensive under $25; moderate $25–50; expensive over $50

Above Santa Cruz & Felton Railroad's trestle bridge at Felton **Below** Historic steam train at Roaring Camp Railroad

WHERE TO STAY

CAPITOLA

Inn at Depot Hill *expensive*
Now a romantic inn, this former railroad depot has luxurious rooms with decor representing European destinations, such as St. Tropez, Paris, and Portofino.
250 Monterey Ave, 95010; 831 462 3376; www.innatdepothill.com

⑩ Felton
Santa Cruz County; 95018
Deep in the Santa Cruz Mountains, this down-to-earth former logging town is surrounded by redwood forests, which can be explored along trails in **Henry Cowell Redwoods State Park** (*101 N Big Trees Park Rd, 95018; 831 335 7077; www.parks.ca.gov/*). The entrance is well-signed 1 mile (1.6 km) before entering Felton. Take time to visit the nature center and to hike some of the 15 miles (24 km) of trails beneath old-growth redwoods towering up to 285 ft (87 m) overhead. The "Big Trees" here were the first stand of coastal redwoods to be protected from logging. Redwoods supplied the lumber for the tallest covered bridge in the US, which still stands at **Felton**

Sign, Henry Cowell Redwoods State Park

Covered Bridge Park (*Graham Hill Rd & Mt Hernon Rd*), and for the former Santa Cruz & Felton Railroad's trestle bridge southeast of town alongside SR 9. Many locals believe an ape-like bipedal creature called Sasquatch or Bigfoot roams the mountains. To learn more, visit the **Bigfoot Discovery Museum** (*5497 SR 9; 831 335 4478; www.bigfootdiscoveryproject.com*).
🚗 *Follow Graham Hill Rd to Roaring Camp Railroad, signed on the right; it has a parking lot.*

⑪ Roaring Camp Railroad
Santa Cruz County; 95018
Narrow-gauge steam trains that once hauled lumber today take passengers on hour-long round-trip tours through the redwood forests here. Bring warm clothing for the journey in open carriages to the top of Bear Mountain. It is a fun ride as the train puffs uphill and over trestles while a narrator presents a history of the train and lumbering. The seven working steam locomotives date back to 1870, although only three are in service. Trains depart Roaring Camp (*831 335 4484; www.roaringcamp.com*), a re-creation of a 1880s logging camp and train depot of the former South Pacific Coast Railroad, complete with a saloon, general store, and blacksmith workshop, all staffed by interpretative docents in period costume. Call ahead to reserve rail trips.

Above The jagged coast along Cliff Drive

CAPITOLA

Zelda's *moderate*
Enjoy fresh seafood and roasted prime ribs on a beachfront patio; Thu is "Lobster Night". Live music Thu–Sun.
203 Esplanade, 95010; 831 475 4900; open 7am–3pm & 5–10pm daily; www.zeldasonthebeach.com

Shadowbrook Restaurant *expensive*
A little cable car delivers guests to this creekside restaurant serving international dishes. Try the black truffle gnocchi or Alaskan halibut.
1750 Wharf Rd, 95010; 831 475 1511; open 5–8:45pm Mon–Thu, 5–9:15pm Fri, 4–9:45pm Sat, 4–8:45pm Sun; www.shadowbrook-capitola.com

Puffing Billies

The three antique locomotives that today haul passengers at Roaring Camp Railroad are a National Mechanical Engineering Historical Landmark. Built in 1912, *Dixiana* worked a narrow-gauge mining railroad before being the first engine acquired by Roaring Camp Railroad. The *Tuolumne*, dating from 1899, has a geared drive that allowed it to negotiate steep grades with a heavy load. The 60-ton *Sonora*, built in 1911, was a museum piece when purchased and restored in 1977.

🚗 *Take Graham Hill Rd downhill to Santa Cruz. Pass beneath SR 1 (Cabrillo Hwy) and continue south on Ocean St to E Cliff Dr. Turn left here and follow it to the shore for a fine perspective over Santa Cruz boardwalk and beach.*

12 Cliff Drive to Capitola
Santa Cruz County; 95010
From the shore, follow Cliff Drive east 230 yards (200 m) to the tiny **Santa Cruz Museum of Natural History** *(1305 E Cliff Dr; 831 420 6115; www. santacruzmuseums.org)*, where the highlight is a life-sized sculpture of a gray whale. Other exhibits include native artifacts, dioramas of native fauna and habitats, and a touch pool filled with intertidal marine life. Next, turn left on Mott Avenue, then right on Murray Street and right again on Lake Avenue to return to E Cliff Drive, which passes through upscale residential neighborhoods of eastern

Santa Cruz. A detailed map from the Santa Cruz County Conference & Visitors Council *(see p116)* is a wise investment. The road runs inland along headlands, occasionally dipping to the shore as it passes Schwan Lagoon then Sunny Cove Beach County Park and Corcoran Lagoon and, finally, Moran Lake before reaching the coast at Pleasure Point Park. Stop here to admire the view along the Opal Cliffs toward **Capitola**, tucked in a cove at the base of sandstone cliffs. Resembling a Mediterranean coastal village, this charming and popular little resort town is known for its many B&B inns and restaurants overlooking a broad beach. It is a great place to take a break for kayaking, fishing, or surfing.

🚗 *Exit Capitola on Monterey Ave. Turn right on Park Ave to SR 1 (Cabrillo Hwy). Follow the freeway to SR 152 and exit for Watsonville. After 1.5 miles (3 km), turn right onto Main St for Watsonville Plaza and park here.*

Below left View over Capitola from Cliff Drive in Santa Cruz **Below** Re-created general store at the Roaring Camp Railroad

Eat and Drink: inexpensive under $25; moderate $25–50; expensive over $50

Right Rooster crossing Main Street, San Juan Bautista **Far right** Field of mustard, San Juan Valley **Below** Colorful mural in oldtown Salinas **Below right** Shrine at Mission San Juan Bautista, San Juan Bautista

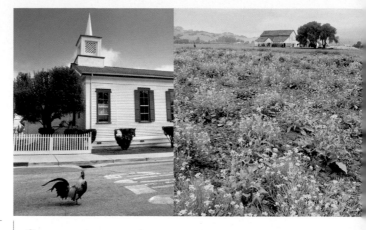

VISITING SALINAS

Tourist Information
222 Main St, 93901; 831 435 4636;
www.destinationsalinas.com

WHERE TO STAY

SAN JUAN BAUTISTA

San Juan Inn *inexpensive*
No frills at this otherwise cozy motel-style property with a swimming pool and free Wi-Fi.
410 The Alameda, 95045; 831 623 4380; www.sanjuaninnca.com

Posada de San Juan *moderate*
A modern inn in Spanish colonial style, graciously furnished in the fashion of yesteryear.
310 4th St, 95045; 831 623 4030; www.paseodesanjuan.webs.com

SALINAS

Vision Quest Ranch *expensive*
African-style bungalows, set inside an animal sanctuary, offer the comfort of a luxury hotel. A truly unique experience.
400 River Rd, 93908; 800 228 7382; www.visionquestranch.com

⑬ Watsonville
Santa Cruz County; 95076
Founded in 1852, this agricultural town is laid out in a grid around a spacious town square, Watsonville Plaza, which features a bronze bust of George Washington, plus a Civil War-era field cannon. Main Street is lined with gracious centenary buildings, including the Art Deco Wells Fargo Bank.

A series of freshwater sloughs on the west side of town comprise the **Wetlands of Watsonville** *(www.wetlandsofwatsonville.org)*, which are accessed by trails. East of Watsonville, the Riverside Drive snakes through agricultural flatlands that widen into the sprawling San Juan Valley. Together with the neighboring Salinas Valley, this region is known as the "Salad Bowl of the Nation" for its vast production of lettuce, artichokes, strawberries, grapes, and other produce. The vale is a patchwork quilt of fields irrigated by tapping subterranean waters. Stop to buy fresh produce at stalls along the route.

🚗 *Leave town eastbound on Main St, and continue left on SR 129 (Riverside Dr) through San Juan Valley. Cross over the I-101 freeway and turn right onto San Juan Hwy, which leads into San Juan Bautista, where there is ample free parking.*

⑭ San Juan Bautista
San Benito County; 95045
This tiny town is remarkable for its historic buildings, many of which date back to the early Spanish period. At its heart, **San Juan Bautista State Historic Park** *(www.parks.ca.gov/)* preserves many buildings that formed a once-important crossroads on the Camino Real, the road connecting the 21 Spanish missions in California. Laid out around the grassy town square, these include the Plaza Hotel; the Zanetta House, furnished as it was when hotel owner Angelo Zanetta and his family lived here; José Castro adobe, built in 1840 for the Comandante General of Alta California; soldiers' barracks; stables with old carts and coaches; and the old city jail.

Located on the plaza's west side, the **Mission San Juan Bautista** was built in 1797 as the largest Spanish mission in California. Well-preserved today, it retains an exquisite church and an impressive museum.

The town's Main Street is lined with buildings of architectural note. Look out for the sturdy sandstone Galacoma Building, erected in 1830

Where to Stay: inexpensive under $100; moderate $100–200; expensive over $200

John Steinbeck

One of America's outstanding 20th-century writers, John Steinbeck (1902–68) was born in Salinas and became nationally famous after publishing *Tortilla Flat* (1935). His writings focused on the people and places around Salinas and Monterey, particularly the struggles of working farm life. He won the Pulitzer Prize for *The Grapes of Wrath* (1939), and was awarded the Nobel Prize for Literature in 1962, becoming the only US writer to win both prizes.

as a hotel, and the Masonic Hall, topped by a cupola. Roosters and and chickens strut along the streets.
🚗 **Exit east along 3rd St (The Alameda). Cross Hwy 156 and turn right onto Salinas Rd (County Rd 3) that becomes San Juan Grade Rd. Keep straight at the junction with Crazy Horse Canyon Rd and continue to Salinas. Turn left onto Main St. Park outside National Steinbeck Center.**

⓯ Salinas
Monterey County; 93901
Named after the Spanish word for a salt marsh, this charming town at the north end of the Salinas Valley grew wealthy as a vegetable- and fruit-packing center. The recently revived **Oldtown Salinas** is worth exploring for its many restored historic buildings, which today function as offices, restaurants, and cafés, including the stylishly Art Deco Fox Theater *(241 Main St)*. Salinas is most intimately associated with novelist John Steinbeck, whose life, literature, and legacy are the theme of the modern, and not-to-be-missed, **National Steinbeck Center** *(1 Main St; 831 775 4721; www.steinbeck.org)*. The state-of-the-art main Exhibition Hall brings Steinbeck's works to life with movie clips and dioramas that re-create scenes from such novels as *Cannery Row* (1945), *East of Eden* (1952), and *Travels with Charley* (1962). The center also hosts the Rabobank Agricultural Museum, with interactive exhibitions that explore the history of farming in Salinas Valley from "field to fork." A new Asian Cultural Center honors the important contribution made by Salinas' large Japanese population to the town's economy and culture. Don't leave town without visiting **Steinbeck House** *(132 Central Ave; www.steinbeck house.com)*, the beautifully preserved Victorian mansion where Steinbeck was born in 1902. Today, it serves as a tearoom and restaurant. To round out a Steinbeck tour, visit his grave at the **Garden of Memories Cemetery** *(768 Abbott St)*, south of town.

EAT AND DRINK

SAN JUAN BAUTISTA

Jardines de San Juan *inexpensive*
This Mexican restaurant delivers great food and service at budget prices.
115 3rd St, 95045; 831 623 4466; open 11:30am–9pm Sun–Thu & till 10pm Fri & Sat; www.jardinesrestaurant.com

Joan & Peter's German Restaurant *inexpensive*
Classic Teutonic dishes such as breaded pork chops and apple strudel.
322 3rd St, 95045; 831 623 4521; open 11:30am–2:30pm & 5–8pm Thu–Sat, 11:30am–5pm Sun; www.joanandpeter.com

SALINAS

Steinbeck House Restaurant *inexpensive*
The menu is limited to soups, salads, and sandwiches, but the historic venue is priceless.
132 Central Ave, 93901; 831 424 2735; open 11:30am–2pm Tue–Sat; www.steinbeckhouse.com

Above left Corridor at Mission San Juan Bautista, San Juan Bautista **Below** Steinbeck House in Salinas

DAY TRIP OPTIONS
This route can be divided into day trips to satisfy special interests.

In the footsteps of fame
Spend time in **Salinas** ⓯ to visit the National Steinbeck Center and Steinbeck House, and view the author's grave at the Garden of Memories Cemetery. Then explore the San Juan Valley between San Juan Bautista ⓮ and Watsonville ⓭, which featured in Steinbeck's works.

From Salinas, head north on Main St, then east on San Juan Grade Rd to reach San Juan Bautista and the San Juan Valley.

Wildlife wonders
The lagoons behind The State Beaches ❺ are good for birding, and in winter, whales can be spotted from Pigeon Point Lighthouse ❻. To view elephant seals, head to Año Nuevo State Reserve ❼, while Natural Bridges State Beach ❽ offers a chance to see monarch butterflies en masse.

The SR 1 (Cabrillo Hwy) lead past all the sites on this route. Turn off SR 1 onto Western Dr and follow the signs to reach Natural Bridges State Beach.

Religious order
Begin in Santa Cruz ❾ and its Santa Cruz Mission Historic Park, then head to San Juan Bautista for its well-preserved mission buildings.

From Santa Cruz, follow Cliff Dr to SR 1. Exit at SR 152 via Watsonville. Turn left onto SR 129, which leads to San Juan Bautista.

Eat and Drink: inexpensive under $25; moderate $25–50; expensive over $50

Enchanting Big Sur

Monterey to Morro Bay

Highlights

- **Marine marvels**
  Be awed by the fish, marine mammals, and other magnificent creatures at Monterey Aquarium

- **Magnificent vistas**
  Enjoy amazing ocean views and ever-changing shoreline panoramas along the scenic 17-Mile Drive and Big Sur

- **Mountain highs**
  Marvel at the stunning architecture of Hearst Castle, while enjoying its mountaintop views

- **World's largest seals**
  Delight in close-up views of elephant seals at their rookeries along the coast

Bixby Bridge, one of the landmarks on the stunning Big Sur coastline

Enchanting Big Sur

California's coastal beauty is nowhere more diverse nor stunning as along the shoreline south of Monterey, a seaside city and fishing port famous for its world-class aquarium. Reached by the scenic 17-Mile Drive, the nearby village of Carmel-by-the-Sea delights with its forested hillside setting, superb art galleries, attractive beaches, and a well-preserved Spanish mission. Follow the Pacific Coast Highway (SR 1) as it snakes along beaches, leaps across coastal canyons, and weaves through headlands beneath rugged mountains. Along the route, cozy inns, redwood forests, sea otter colonies, and elephant seal rookeries provide plenty of opportunity to break the journey, while Hearst Castle, a fantasy in stone that sits perched on a mountain, is one of California's premier touristic attractions.

KEY

⬤ Drive route

*PACIFIC
OCEAN*

Above Tide pool at the Monterey Bay Aquarium, *see p127*

ACTIVITIES

Walk downtown Monterey and discover historic attractions before visiting its spectacular aquarium

Savor fresh seafood along Monterey's Fisherman's Wharf

Browse for art in the galleries of Carmel-by-the-Sea

Learn to surf in the relatively sheltered bay at Carmel-by-the-Sea

Hike the coastal trails to spot seals and shorebirds at Point Lobos State Reserve

Ramble among the redwoods at Julia Pfeiffer Burns State Park

Go sea-kayaking at Morro Bay for eye-to-eye encounters with sea otters and seals

Above Sea-kayaking past Morro Rock, Morro Bay, *see p131*

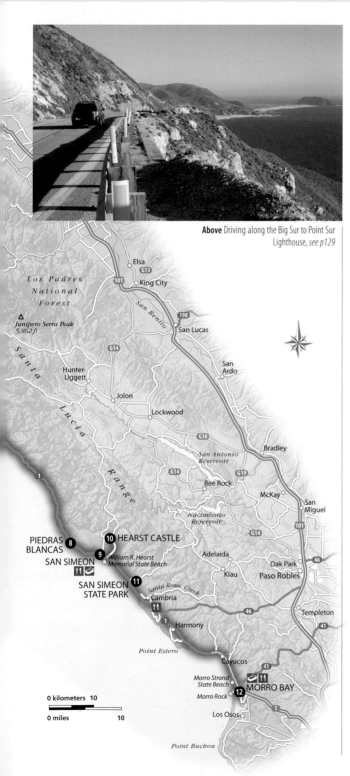

Above Driving along the Big Sur to Point Sur Lighthouse, *see p129*

Map labels:

Los Padres National Forest

Elsa G13

King City 101

San Benito

San Lucas 198

△ Junipero Serra Peak 5,862 ft

G14

Santa Lucia Range

Hunter-Liggett

Jolon

Lockwood

San Ardo

G18

Bradley

San Antonio Reservoir

G14 G19

Bee Rock

McKay

San Miguel

101

PIEDRAS BLANCAS **8**

HEARST CASTLE **10**

SAN SIMEON **9**
William R. Hearst Memorial State Beach

SAN SIMEON STATE PARK **11**

Cambria

Santa Rosa Creek

Harmony

1

Point Estero

Cavucos

Morro Strand State Beach

Morro Rock

MORRO BAY **12**

Los Osos

Point Buchon

Nacimiento Reservoir

G14

Adelaida

Klau

Oak Park

Paso Robles 46

Templeton

41

46

1

0 kilometers 10

0 miles 10

PLAN YOUR DRIVE

Start/finish: Monterey to Morro Bay.

Number of days: 2–3 days, including half a day to explore Monterey.

Distance: 139 miles (224 km).

Road conditions: The Coast Highway is well maintained, but the Big Sur stretch is subject to frequent landslides which can close the road for weeks at a time. Check road conditions with the California Department of Transportation (Caltrans) *(800 427 7623; www.dot.ca. gov/cgi-bin/roads.cgi).*

When to go: Jan–Apr is the best time for viewing whales and elephant seals, while wildflowers are at their prime Mar–May. Spring and late fall months offer the best weather. Be prepared for cold, biting winds, and the possibility of fog year round.

Main market days: Monterey: Fri am. Carmel-by-the-Sea: May–Sep: Tue am. Morro Bay: Sat pm.

Opening times: Art galleries typically open 10am–6pm daily. Small shops tend to open 9am–5pm Mon–Sat. Museum hours vary widely.

Shopping: Carmel-by-the-Sea is a world-class venue for quality art, sold at galleries around town. Look for more rustic art at studios along SR 1.

Major festivals: Monterey: Jazz Festival, Sep. **Carmel-by-the-Sea:** Bach Festival, mid-Jul. **Morro Bay:** Harbor Festival, Oct.

DAY TRIP OPTIONS

It is possible to visit the area in a number of day trips. Those fond of **animals** will enjoy visiting the **Monterey Bay Aquarium** and **Point Lobos State Reserve**. Those who admire **art** can explore the galleries in **Carmel-by-the-Sea**, and along the coast. **Photography buffs** will thrill to the opportunities along the **17-Mile Drive**, **Big Sur**, and at **Hearst Castle**. For full details, *see p131*.

VISITING MONTEREY

Tourist Information
401 Camino El Estero, 93940; 877 666 8373; www.seemonterey.com

Parking
Monterey has plenty of public, fee-based parking lots. Metered parking is available on most streets.

WHERE TO STAY

MONTEREY

Casa Munras *moderate*
A cozy hotel inspired by a Spanish hacienda. Many rooms have fireplaces.
700 Munras Ave, 93940; 831 375 2411; www.larkspurhotels.com

Portola Hotel & Spa *expensive*
A stylish hotel with comfortable rooms, a microbrewery, plus spa.
Two Portola Plaza, 93940; 866 711 1534; www.portolahotel.com

17-MILE DRIVE

Lodge at Pebble Beach *expensive*
This deluxe hotels overlooks a cove and the hotel's signature golf course. Fine restaurants.
1500 Cypress Dr, Pebble Beach, 93593; 831 624 3811; www.pebblebeach.com

➊ Monterey

Monterey County; 93940

This large seaside town combines a beautiful setting in Monterey Bay with plenty of attractions: from an old whaling station and Cannery Row to the world-class Monterey Bay Aquarium. Established by the Spanish in 1770, the town served as California's capital under Spanish and Mexican rule. It later lost political importance, instead developing into a thriving fishing port, a role made famous by novelist John Steinbeck's *Cannery Row* (1945). Downtown, well-preserved 19th-century buildings recall its heyday while Fisherman's Wharf caters for visitors' needs, from seafood dining to boat trips.

A three-hour walking tour

Park in the lot on the waterfront east of Fisherman's Wharf and head to **Custom House Plaza** ➀, where the US flag was first officially raised in California on July 7, 1846. Next door, Custom House is the oldest government building in California. Dating from 1822, when it served as a Mexican inspection post, it stands at the gateway to Monterey State Historic Park, a collection of notable buildings dotted around town. Walk south to the **Museum of Monterey** ➁ which traces the past of the city and the bay. On the west side of the plaza, explore the **Pacific House Museum** ➂, dedicated to local history and home to the Museum of the American Indian. Next, follow Alvarado Street south, passing the **Old Monterey Hotel** ➃ *(Franklin St)*, built in 1904, and the Art Deco **State Theatre** ➄ *(417 Alvarado St)*. Turn left on Pearl Street, then right onto Houston Street to pass **Stevenson House** ➅

Anchor outside the Custom House, Monterey

(530 Houston St), the former French Hotel, where novelist Robert Louis Stevenson convalesced in 1879; a museum recalls his stay. At Webster Street turn left, then right at Abrego Street and left on Church Street for the **Royal Presidio Chapel** ➆. Founded by Father Junipero Serra in 1770, this well-preserved church is the oldest in California. Take Church Street and turn right on Abrego Street, then left on Webster Street and right on Hartnell Street to visit the **Monterey Museum of Art** ➇ *(www.montereyart. org)*, a trove of contemporary art displayed in eight galleries. Across the street, manicured lawns lead up to **Colton Hall** ➈, the handsome limestone building where California's constitution was signed in 1849. Note the brass seal of California embedded at the base of the steps. Continue north along Pacific Street to the tiny weathered wooden **First Theatre** ➉ *(corner Scott St)* which has hosted Victorian vaudeville theater since 1847. Turn right, then left onto Oliver St. At the end the **Old Whaling Station** ⑪, on the left, displays

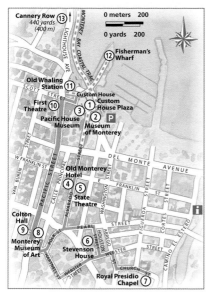

Map labels:
- Cannery Row ⑬
- 440 yards (400 m)
- 0 meters 200
- 0 yards 200
- Fisherman's Wharf ⑫
- MONTEREY BAY COASTAL TRAIL
- LIGHTHOUSE AVE
- Old Whaling Station ⑪
- Custom House ①
- Custom House Plaza
- Museum of Monterey ②
- ③
- P
- First Theatre ⑩
- Pacific House Museum
- SCOTT STREET
- PACIFIC STREET
- OLIVIER STREET
- W FRANKLIN ST
- DEL MONTE AVENUE
- Old Monterey Hotel ④
- ⑤
- FRANKLIN STREET
- State Theatre
- VAN BUREN
- CALLE PRINCIPAL
- ALVARADO STREET
- WASHINGTON STREET
- FIGUEROA STREET
- CORTES STREET
- Colton Hall
- PEARL STREET
- Monterey Museum of Art ⑨ ⑧
- ⑥
- ABREGO STREET
- HOUSTON STREET
- CAMINO EL ESTERO
- Stevenson House
- WEBSTER STREET
- CHURCH ST
- Royal Presidio Chapel ⑦
- i

hang overhead, and real-life jellyfish, octopus, barracudas, sharks, and schools of sardines amaze.

🚗 *Head west along Ocean View Blvd, which becomes Sunset Dr. Turn right onto 17-Mile Drive toll road; pay the entrance fee and pick up a map at the Pacific Grove Gate. Allow 2 hours for the 17-Mile Drive, with stops along the way.*

❸ 17-Mile Drive

Monterey County

One of the most scenic drives in North America, the 17-Mile Drive weaves around exquisite white-sand coves, with sea otters feeding in the kelp forests just offshore, and over craggy headlands topped by wind-bowed Monterey cypress and pines. The area is favored by millionaires who have built extravagant homes and is the setting for four championship golf courses. **Bird Rock** is populated by countless seabirds, and lots of seals and sea lions bask on the rocks. Be sure to stop at **Cypress Point**, a headland offering sensational views along the coast. Nearby, the iconic **Lone Cypress** is instantly recognizable for its much-photographed wind-swept cypress tree, which stands atop a lonesome rocky perch. Built in 1919, the deluxe **Lodge at Pebble Beach** is home to the world-famous Pebble Beach Golf Links, and hosts the annual Concours d'Elegance classic car event each August.

🚗 *Exit at the Carmel Gate. Follow Carmel Way, then San Antonio Ave. Turn left onto Ocean Ave for the beach at Carmel-by-the-Sea. Park curbside.*

> ### Monterey Cypress
> This short cypress tree species – *Cupressus macrocarpa* – is endemic to California's central coast, where it is confined to the Monterey Peninsula and Carmel. It thrives in the cool, damp climate and is often found in exposed granitic headlands subject to salt spray and winds. Its typically flat-topped crown is shaped by high winds.

mementos of the 19th-century whaling industry. Cross Oliver Street to **Fisherman's Wharf** ⑫. The boardwalk is a lively venue for shops and seafood restaurants, and seals and sea lions can be seen below. The Monterey Bay Coastal Trail leads from the wharf to **Cannery Row** ⑬. Made famous by American author John Steinbeck's eponymous novel, the old fish canneries have metamorphosed into souvenir stores, boutiques, hotels, and restaurants.

🚗 *Drive west along Lighthouse Ave then go right on Hoffman Ave and left on Foam St. Park roadside or in one of the lots along Foam St.*

❷ Monterey Bay Aquarium

Monterey County; 93940

This awe-inspiring aquarium *(www.montereybayaquarium.org)*, occupying a former cannery, is the largest aquarium in the US. More than 600 species of Monterey Bay marine creatures swim in huge tanks that replicate their natural environments. The daily feeding time for the penguins and sea otters is a highlight. Other exhibits include an enclosed kelp forest, a Splash Zone that reproduces a wave-bashed habitat, and touch pools where kids can handle sea stars, bat rays, and other sea creatures. Life-size replicas of various whale and shark species

EAT AND DRINK

MONTEREY

Crabby Jim's *moderate*
Dine with a view over the harbor at this seafood restaurant famous for its clam chowder. The menu includes Mexican and Italian dishes as well.
25 Fisherman's Wharf, 93940; 831 372 2064; open 11am–9:30pm Mon–Fri, 11am–10:30pm Sat & Sun; www.crabbyjimsmonterey.com

Monterey Fish House *moderate*
Away from the tourist hordes of Fisherman's Wharf, this seafood restaurant serves delicious fresh-caught seafood, including fish blackened on an oak-fired grill. Begin with plump oysters in the half-shell or grilled artichokes.
2114 Del Monte Ave, 93940; 831 373 4647; open noon–10pm Mon–Sat, 4–11pm Sun

Sardine Factory *expensive*
A sumptuous European-style surf-and-turf restaurant serving Chef Rachael Ray's award-winning steaks and seafood.
701 Wave St, 93940; 831 373 3775; open 5–9:30pm Sun–Thu & 5–10pm Fri–Sat; www.sardinefactory.com

Below The Lone Cypress perched high above the sea along the 17-Mile Drive

Eat and Drink: inexpensive under $25; moderate $25–50; expensive over $50

Top Bird Island at Point Lobos State Reserve
Above Charming building in Carmel-by-the-Sea **Above right** Tilework in courtyard garden of Mission San Carlos Borroméo del Río Carmelo, Carmel-by-the-Sea

VISITING CARMEL-BY-THE-SEA

Tourist Information
San Carlos St between 5th & 6th, 93923; 831 624 2522; open 10am–5pm daily

WHERE TO STAY

CARMEL-BY-THE-SEA

Lamp Lighter Inn *moderate*
Set in lush gardens, it has exquisite furnishings in cozy wooden cottage rooms. Friendly and helpful owner.
Ocean Ave & Camino Real, 93921; 831 624 7372; www.carmellamplighter.com

Pine Inn *moderate*
Opened in 1899 as the first hotel in town, Pine Inn offers a lavish lounge, and spacious, comfortable rooms. Gourmet restaurant plus coffee shop.
Ocean Ave & Lincoln Ave, 93921; 831 624 3851; www.pineinn.com

BIG SUR

Big Sur Lodge *moderate*
This modern yet back-to-nature hotel has comfy cabins tucked beneath the redwoods. No telephones, TVs, or alarm clocks.
47225 SR 1, 93920; 831 667 3100; www.bigsurlodge.com

Where to Stay: inexpensive under $100; moderate $100–200; expensive over $200

④ Carmel-by-the-Sea
Monterey County; 93921
A fairytale village of clapboard homes and picket fences, Carmel-by-the-Sea abounds with intriguing shops, art galleries, quaint B&Bs, and fine-dining restaurants. Ocean Avenue slopes down to **Carmel Beach**, known for great surfing and fabulous sunsets. From the bottom of Ocean Avenue, Scenic Road wriggles around the Carmel Peninsula to **Carmel River Beach**, which straddles the Carmel River and is backed by a wetland reserve; swimming is discouraged due to strong currents. Continue on Scenic Road as it becomes Carmelo Street, and turn right onto 15th Avenue (which becomes Lausen Drive) to **Mission San Carlos Borroméo del Río Carmelo** *(3080 Rio Rd; 831 624 3600)*. Built in 1770 and restored and furnished as it was two centuries ago, "Carmel Mission" recalls the days when it served as the administrative center for all the California missions.
🚗 *Follow Rio Rd southeast to SR 1, and turn right for Point Lobos State Reserve; ample parking.*

⑤ Point Lobos State Reserve
Monterey County; 93923
This magnificent coastal reserve *(831 624 4909; www.parks.ca.gov/)* was created to protect a large grove of

Monterey cypress, which can be explored on the **Cypress Grove Trail**. Other short, easy trails lead past fascinating geological formations to **Sea Lion Point**, named for the sea lions that gather on the rocks offshore, and to a viewpoint over **Bird Island** where thousands of Brandt's cormorants nest close together. Sea otters are frequently seen resting and feeding in the kelp offshore, harbor seals like to haul out onto the beaches, and whales are often spotted in coastal waters. Serving as home to whalers a century ago, **Whaler's Cabin** houses a small cultural history museum today.
🚗 *Continue south along SR 1 towards Bixby Bridge.*

⑥ Big Sur
Monterey County
The spectacular coastal settings of central California's Big Sur offer one of the world's most sensational drives, with more than 110 km (65 miles) of stunning headlands, rocky coves, and surf-pounded beaches. It is no surprise that novelist Robert Louis Stevenson (1850–94) called it the "greatest meeting of land and water in the world." The entire shore forms part of the California Sea Otter State Game Refuge. Drive with caution, as the road includes many cliff-top switchbacks and sharp turns. It is advisable to plan ahead, as settlements, hotels, and restaurants are few and far between. The hamlet of Big Sur is a great stop to browse through art galleries and handicrafts made by local artisans.

Below Sea Lion Point, a popular spot to observe sea lions, Point Lobos State Reserve

Probably the most photographed object along the scenic Big Sur coastline, the single-arch **Bixby Bridge** is an engineering masterpiece and a classic landmark. Erected in 1932, the 714-ft (218-m) long concrete structure stands 280 ft (85 m) above a canyon. Its beauty is matched by its setting, with ocean waves crashing on the rocky coastline below. Countless people come to photograph the bridge, whose mood changes with weather conditions and time of day. Sunset is a particularly good time, when the slanting sun reflects off the white structural supports.

The **Point Sur Lighthouse** (www. parks.ca.gov/), built in 1889, stands above the remnant of a volcanic cone and still functions to warn ships of the treacherous Big Sur coast. It's open to the public through docent-led tours; call ahead. Take a break to hike hillside meadows or beachcomb in **Andrew Molera State Park** (www.parks.ca. gov/), a 10-minute drive north of the community of Big Sur.

🚗 *Continue south on SR 1 and turn left at the sign for Pfeiffer Big Sur State Park; park in the lot.*

California Sea Otters

Once numbering in the millions, these marine mammals were hunted to near extinction for their fur. Although the population is slowly recovering, sea otters (Enhydra lutris) are now found only in Alaskan waters and along the Big Sur coast-line, south of Monterey. They inhabit sheltered coastal waters and are often seen floating on their backs amid kelp, and in groups called rafts.

🕖 Pfeiffer Big Sur State Park
Monterey County; 93920
Groves of towering redwood trees are the key draw to this park (www. parks.ca.gov/), which stretches from the shoreline to more than 3,000 ft (900 m) up the mountains. Valley View Trail leads along the Big Sur River canyon to Pfeiffer Falls; the 3-mile (5-km) round-trip hike is steep in sections. Black-tail deer, raccoons, and bobcats are occasionally sighted, as are endangered California condors soaring far overhead.

Above Cattle grazing in the sprawling pastures along Big Sur

Some 10 miles (16 km) further south, the **Julia Pfeiffer Burns State Park** (www.parks.ca.gov/) is a smaller mirror image of Pfeiffer Big Sur State Park and a very popular destination. Besides the 400-ft (120-m) tall redwoods, its main attraction is McWay Falls, which plunge 80 ft (25 m) from the cliffs into the Pacific. A 10-minute hike from the parking lot via the Overlook Trail leads to a bluff with views over the falls, which is also a good place for spotting sea otters, harbor seals, California sea lions, as well as migrating whales in winter.

🚗 *Continue for 79 km (49 miles) south on SR 1 to Piedras Blancas.*

WHERE TO EAT

CARMEL-BY-THE-SEA
Em Le's *moderate*
This village landmark is considered by locals *the* place to breakfast on French toast, pancakes, and omelets. Its dinner menu is heavy on seafood, such as linguini with mussels, clams, and salmon.
Dolores St between 5th & 6th, 93921; 831 625 6780; open 7am–3pm daily, 4:30–8pm Wed–Sun; www.emlescarmel.com

Porta Bella *expensive*
The "Cuisine du Soleil" served at this romantic restaurant focuses on Mediterranean-inspired fare, such as Dungeness crab bisque or duck and feta cheese ravioli. Owner Csaba Ajan is usually in attendance to offer a warm welcome.
Ocean Ave between Lincoln St & Monte Verde St, 93921; 831 624 4395; open 11:30am–11pm daily; www.portabellacarmel.com

BIG SUR
Big Sur Deli & General Store *inexpensive*
This full-service deli makes burritos, specialty sandwiches, and salads, and is a good place to enjoy early morning coffee and croissants.
47520 SR 1, 93910; 831 667 2225; open 7am–8pm daily; www.bigsurdeli.com

Nepenthe *moderate*
Dramatic coastal vistas are a bonus at this acclaimed restaurant. Its eclectic menu ranges from burgers to roast chicken. The owners also run Café Kevah, serving granola breakfasts and other coffee-shop treats.
48510 SR 1, 93920; 831 667 2345; open 11:30am–10pm daily; www.nepenthebigsur.com

Above Elegant Bixby Bridge spanning a canyon along Big Sur

Eat and Drink: inexpensive under $25; moderate $25–50; expensive over $50

Right Elephant seals basking on Piedras Blancas Beach **Far right** The Classical-themed Neptune Pool, Hearst Castle

VISITING HEARST CASTLE

Tourist Information
750 Hearst Castle Rd, 93452; 1 800 444 4445; www.hearstcastle.org

WHERE TO STAY

SAN SIMEON

Best Western Cavalier Oceanfront Resort *moderate*
This family-run motel enjoys a fantastic oceanfront locale. Spacious rooms have stylish modern furnishings, and some have kitchens and Wi-Fi.
9415 Hearst Dr, 93452; 805 927 4688; www.cavalierresort.com

The Morgan *moderate*
Graciously appointed with modern furnishings, this boutique hotel has a heated indoor pool plus spa.
9135 Hearst Dr, 93452; 800 451 9900; www.hotel-morgan.com

MORRO BAY

Back Bay Inn *moderate*
Thirteen refined rooms with king beds overlook wild gardens and a beach on the southern shores of Morro Bay. Some rooms have fireplaces.
1391 2nd St, Los Osos, 93402; 805 528 1233; www.backbayinn.com

Inn at Morro Bay *moderate*
A Cape Cod-style hotel with rooms and an elegant restaurant overlooking the bay, and also a spa.
60 State Park Rd, 93442; 805 772 5651; www.innatmorrobay.com

⑧ Piedras Blancas
San Luis Obispo County
Rising up from meadows, the **Piedras Blancas Lighthouse** dates back to 1875 and is named for the three white, guano-splattered rocks just off the point. The Bureau of Land Management offers public tours; call ahead for schedules *(805 927 7361)*. The beaches immediately south of the lighthouse are populated by hundreds of elephant seals. Park in the signed lot at North Vista Point, at **Piedras Blancas Beach**, where boardwalks lead to viewing decks with interpretive signs. Blue-uniformed docent guides are sometimes present to assist visitors. December to April is the best time to visit, when males arrive and battle for dominance over harems, and females give birth on the beach.
🚗 *Continue south on SR 1 to San Simeon. Turn right on San Simeon Rd to park on the street in the hamlet.*

⑨ San Simeon
San Luis Obispo County; 93452
Located in a protected cove, this tiny hamlet was established in 1852 as a whaling station. In the late 19th century, Senator George Hearst, who owned most of the land, built a pier here. His son, William R. Hearst, added Spanish-style homes for employees who worked at Hearst Castle. Today, a handful of the original 45 buildings remain, including the one-room schoolhouse and Sebastian's General Store *(805 927 3307)*, which operates as a coffee shop and gift store. The crescent-shaped **William R. Hearst Memorial State Beach** *(www.parks.ca.gov/)* has a grassy picnic area behind the cove, where kayaks can be rented. The **Coastal Discovery Center** *(open 10am–4pm Fri–Sun)* has environmental and nature exhibits.
🚗 *Return to SR 1 and cross onto Hearst Castle Rd. Park in the lot at Hearst Castle Visitor Center.*

⑩ Hearst Castle
San Luis Obispo County; 93452
Perched above the hamlet of San Simeon, the fantasy castle-home of media tycoon and art collector William R. Hearst is one of California's top man-made attractions *(www.hearstcastle.org)*. Designed by renowned architect Julia Morgan and completed in 1947, his Mediterranean Revival-style home is a one-of-a-kind museum. The twin-towered **Casa Grande** and three guest houses totalling 115 rooms, set amid lavish gardens, can be visited on group tours *(depart every 15 mins;*

Above The restored single-room schoolhouse at San Simeon

Where to Stay: inexpensive under $100; moderate $100–200; expensive over $200

book ahead). Stocked with European antiques and art, Casa Grande was designed to resemble a medieval cathedral. It has a Gothic-style Great Hall, where several famous guests have dined. The billiards room features an early 16th-century French tapestry, and a movie theater is lined with caryatids. The grounds include orchards, palm groves, and classical statuary. Do not miss the white marble **Neptune Pool** which features a Greek temple facade. The visitor center's **Hearst Castle Theater** shows "Building the Dream," which profiles the castle's construction.

🚗 *Return to San Simeon, then continue south on the SR 1. Park in the day-use lot on SR 1 to enter San Simeon State Park.*

Julia Morgan

Born in San Francisco in 1872, Julia Morgan graduated as a civil engineer from the University of California, Berkeley, and was the first woman to graduate as an architect from the École des Beaux-Arts in Paris. She designed more than 700 homes and buildings across California, including for William Randolph Hearst, who became her patron. Morgan designed every aspect of Hearst Castle during a span of 28 years.

---

⑪ San Simeon State Park

San Luis Obispo County; 93428
Perfect for easy hikes, this nature reserve *(www.parks.ca.gov/)* protects seasonal coastal wetlands and wooded bluffs shaded by Monterey cypress against a backdrop of the Santa Lucia mountain range. From the lot, a coastal trail offers breathtaking views and gives access to tide pools and seal rookeries. Trails

and boardwalks that begin across the highway from the lot lead into the marshland and riverside woodlands of the **Santa Rosa Creek Preserve** – a wintering site for monarch butterflies, which gather in their thousands. Interpretive panels provide information on wildlife and habitat.

🚗 *Continue south through Cambria to Morro Bay. Exit onto Main St and turn right onto Pacific St. At the waterfront, turn right onto Embarcadero and park in the public lot or on the street.*

⑫ Morro Bay

San Luis Obispo County; 93442
Although marred by an ungainly coastal power station, this otherwise charming seaside fishing town is a great place for close-up encounters with marine-life. Pelicans perch on the piers where fishing boats anchor, and sea lions haul out onto the docks to snooze and sunbathe. An extinct volcanic plug, **Morro Rock** juts up from the ocean, protecting Morro Bay harbor. This great monolith, which was named by the Juan Rodríguez Cabrillo expedition in 1542, is a nesting site for endangered peregrine falcons.

The Harborwalk pedestrian and bicycle path enfolds Morro Bay Harbor, connecting Embarcadero to Morro Rock and **Morro Strand State Beach**, a popular surfing spot. Whale-watching trips and bay cruises depart from Embarcadero, and visitors can rent kayaks to explore the bay. Inquisitive sea otters and seals often pop up alongside. To learn about the local ecosystem, visit the **Morro Bay Estuary Nature Center** *(www.mbnep.org)*.

Above The winding access road leading to Hearst Castle

WHERE TO EAT

SAN SIMEON

Manta Rey Restaurant *moderate*
The De Alba family serves fresh seafood, such as coconut shrimp, locally caught sand dabs, and chardonnay poached salmon.
9240 Castillo Dr, 93452; 805 924 1032; open 5–9pm daily; www.mantareyrestaurant.com

AROUND SAN SIMEON

Sow's Ear Café *inexpensive*
Set in an old wooden cottage, this restaurant offers favorites such as baby pork ribs and steak with gravy, all served with marbled bread.
2248 Main St, Cambria, 93428; 805 927 4865; open 5–9pm daily; www.thesowsear.com

MORRO BAY

Giovanni's Fish Market & Galley *moderate*
The menu at this casual Italian seafood restaurant also includes sushi, and Mexican-inspired dishes such as grilled prawn quesadillas and halibut burritos.
1001 Front St, 93442; 805 772 1276; open 9am–6pm daily; www.giovannisfishmarket.com

---

DAY TRIP OPTIONS

The sights along this single, long road could be divided into themed day trips.

Creatures great and small

Allow at least two hours to fully appreciate Monterey Bay Aquarium ❷ before setting out to view seals, sea otters and seabirds at Point Lobos State Reserve ❺.

From Monterey, follow 17-Mile Drive

along the shore to reach SR 1 and turn right for Point Lobos State Reserve.

Masterful art

Lovers of art and collectibles will enjoy the many fine-art galleries in Carmel-by-the-Sea ❹, while the village of Big Sur ❻ is a haven for talented artists producing jewelry, sculpture, ceramics, and handblown glass.

In Carmel, take Ocean Ave east to link

with SR 1, which leads south to Big Sur.

Picture perfect

Capture some of North America's most stunning coastal scenery along the 17-Mile Drive ❸, Big Sur ❻, and Hearst Castle ❿.

After the 17-Mile Dr, Ocean Ave leads east to SR 1, which passes all the sites (for Hearst Castle, turn off near San Simeon).

On the Royal Road

San Luis Obispo to Ojai

Highlights

- **Cultured town**
  Admire the late 18th-century mission of San Luis Obispo and absorb the town's lively cultural scene

- **Beach fun**
  Ride a horse along the sands at magnificent Pismo Beach

- **A little bit of Spain**
  Discover the Spanish-influenced art and architecture of the seaside city of Santa Barbara

- **Rejuvenating Ojai**
  Stroll around this pretty town with its relaxing ivy-clad B&Bs, deluxe spas, and sunny climate

Waters of the Pacific Ocean lapping the shore of Pismo State Beach

On the Royal Road

Extending from the wind-battered shores of Pismo Beach to the sheltered bays of Santa Barbara, this section of California's coastline has long been a vacation playground, with lovely seaside towns known for fishing and clamming, and some of the state's best surfing. Inland, tawny hills rise to rugged mountains that cusp lakes and bucolic vales farmed with orchards and vineyards. The region's Spanish heritage is displayed in San Luis Obispo and Santa Barbara, named for their missions that were once linked by El Camino Real, or the historic Royal Road. Danish-themed Solvang offers a fascinating, somewhat kitschy contrast, and is also the gateway to the Santa Ynez and Los Olivos wine country.

ACTIVITIES

Kite-surf the waves at Pismo Beach

Stroll the streets of Lompoc to admire its wall mural art

Take a journey back in time at Mission La Purísima Concepción

Follow the wine route around Santa Ynez and Los Olivos to sample the wines

Surf the breakers that roll ashore at Santa Barbara

Fish off Stearns Wharf in Santa Barbara

Picnic by sparkling Lake Casitas

Steep in a wrap at Ojai Valley Inn & Spa

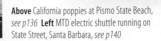

Above California poppies at Pismo State Beach, see p136 **Left** MTD electric shuttle running on State Street, Santa Barbara, see p140

Above Driving to Ojai, *see p141* **Below** The Art Deco Fremont Theater in San Luis Obispo, *see p136*

KEY

 Drive route

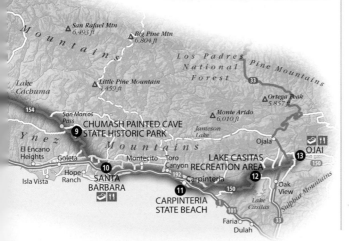

PLAN YOUR DRIVE

Start/finish: San Luis Obispo to Ojai.

Number of days: 2–3 days, allowing half a day for San Luis Obispo, plus a full day for Santa Barbara.

Distance: 161 miles (260 km).

Road conditions: The roads here are well-maintained but can be tricky to negotiate. East of Santa Ynez, the route climbs over the San Marcos Pass and has steep grades and sharp bends, as does the Casitas Pass Road, west of Ojai; the road to Chumash Painted Cave State Historic Park requires extra caution.

When to go: Mar–May is a good time for wildflowers, Sep–Oct is the wine harvesting season, while winter is good for spotting whales offshore.

Main market days: San Luis Obispo: 6–9pm Thu & 8–10:30am Sat. Solvang: 2:30–6pm Wed. **Santa Barbara:** 4–7:30pm Tue & 8:30am–1pm Sat. **Ojai:** 9am–1pm Sun.

Opening times: Wineries typically open 10am–5pm daily. The missions open 9am–5pm daily, as do most shops and museums.

Shopping: Santa Barbara is a good place to seek out fine art. The farmers' markets sell artisanal candles and soaps, plus organic breads, honey, and fresh produce.

Major festivals: San Luis Obispo: Greek Festival, Jun; Festival Mosaic (music festival), Jul. **Solvang:** Danish Days, Sep. **Santa Barbara:** Old Spanish Days Fiesta, Aug; Sandcastle Festival, Sep. **Ojai:** Music Festival, Jun; Wine Festival, Jun.

DAY TRIP OPTIONS

Ecclesiastical enthusiasts can take the mission route, stopping by the missions of **San Luis Obispo**, **La Purísima Concepción**, and **Santa Barbara**. **Outdoorsy visitors** can opt to surf, kite-surf, hike, or ride horses at **Pismo Beach**, while the **Guadalupe-Nipomo Dunes** will delight **birdwatchers**. For full details, *see p141*.

Above Horseback riders on Pismo Beach
Above right Detail on the facade of the History Center, San Luis Obispo

VISITING SAN LUIS OBISPO

Tourist Information
1039 Chorro St, 93401; 805 781 2777; open 10am–5pm Sun–Wed, 10am–7pm Thu–Sat; www.visitslo.com

Parking
There is metered street parking downtown, and a secure paid parking lot at 873 Marsh St.

VISITING PISMO BEACH

Tourist Information
California Welcome Center *333 Five Cities Dr, Suite 100, 93449; 805 773 7924; open 10am–9pm Mon–Sat, 10am–7pm Sun; www.visitcwc.com*

Parking
Follow Pomeroy Ave to the paid lot by the pier. W Grand Ave and Pier Ave have parking as well.

WHERE TO STAY

SAN LUIS OBISPO

San Luis Creek Lodge *moderate*
This smoke-free, family-run B&B has 25 well-furnished and spacious rooms. Walking distance from downtown. *1941 Monterey St, 93401; 1 800 593 0330; www.sanluiscreeklodge.com*

Madonna Inn *expensive*
Famous for its whimsical decor, with all-rock grotto rooms and waterfall showers, this inn has a top-class spa, and a pool with walk-in beach access. *100 Madonna Rd, 93405; 805 543 3000; www.madonnainn.com*

PISMO BEACH

Cottage Inn by the Sea *moderate*
Set in a superb cliff-top location, with comfy guest rooms. *2351 Price St, 93449; 805 773 4617; www.cottage-inn.com*

① San Luis Obispo
San Luis Obispo County; 93401
Charming San Luis Obispo is laid out in a grid around the **Mission San Luis Obispo de Tolosa** (*www.missionsan luisobispo.org*). Founded in 1776, this mission includes a functioning church and a museum dedicated to the Chumash Native American culture. It overlooks **Mission Plaza**, the cultural heart of the city and a setting for the **Museum of Art** (*www.sloma.org*). The landscaped plaza hosts many festivals and has benches overlooking tree-lined San Luis Creek. To its southwest, the Gothic sandstone-and-granite Carnegie Free Library is now a **History Center** (*www. historycenterslo.org*), with fascinating exhibits about the city's past; pick up a podcast tour. Downtown is replete with adobes and other notable historic buildings, such as the Art Deco **Fremont Theater** (*1025 Monterey St*). Across from the theater, the **County Courthouse** is fronted by an antique four-face clock.

🚗 *Leave west on Marsh St to I-101 south. After 11 miles (18 km), exit the freeway on Pismo Beach SR 1. Continue 3 miles (5 km) south to turn right on Pier Ave; park by the beach.*

② Pismo Beach
San Luis Obispo County; 93448
This small resort town is best known for its remarkable 17-mile (23-km) white-sand beach, most of which is within **Pismo State Beach** (*www.parks. ca.gov/*). Kite-surfing, horseback riding, surf fishing, and digging for once-abundant Pismo clams are popular activities along the windswept beach. Monarch butterflies return annually to their wintering site (Oct–Feb) in the

tiny **Pismo Beach Monarch Butterfly Grove**, and huge sand dunes rise over the southern end of the beach, where the **Oceano Dunes State Vehicular Recreation Area** (*340 James Way; 805 773 7170; open 6am–11pm daily*) draws fun-seekers for the thrill of driving ATV quad bikes, which can be rented here, up and down giant dunes.

🚗 *Return to SR 1 and turn right. Stay on SR 1 for 13 miles (21 km) south to Guadalupe. Park on SR 1.*

③ Guadalupe
Santa Barbara County; 93434
Set in the Santa Maria River Valley, this town resembles a 1950s Hollywood movie set. Stop at **City Hall** (*918 Obispo St*) to take in the four wall murals of local life by Judy Baca. The town is surrounded on three sides by a quilt of fields farmed with lettuce, strawberries, and artichokes. To the west, the **Guadalupe-Nipomo Dunes** (*end of W Main St; open 7am–7:30pm daily*) form one of the world's largest coastal sand dune ecosystems. They are separated into north and south sections by the Santa Maria River. The southern dunes, in Rancho Guadalupe Dunes Preserve, reach 550 ft (168 m) and were the setting for scenes in the *Ten Commandments* (1956) and *Pirates of the Caribbean: At World's End* (2007). The **Guadalupe-Nipomo Dunes Center** (*www.dunescenter.org*), in town, features educational exhibits. Oso

Above Historic church at Mission San Luis Obispo de Tolosa, San Luis Obispo

Above Colorful buildings lining Guadalupe's Main Street

Flaco Lake Road, north of town, leads to the Oso Flaco wetlands, with a boardwalk for spotting birds, such as the endangered Western snowy plovers and California least terns.
🚗 *Continue south on SR 1; turn right, follow the signs for Vandenburg AFB to stay on SR 1 (Cabrillo Hwy). Turn onto N H St for downtown Lompoc (29 miles/46 km from Guadalupe). Park at the lot at Ocean St and S I St.*

④ Lompoc
Santa Barbara County; 93436
Called "The City of Arts and Flowers", Lompoc nests amid the sprawling flower fields of the Lompoc Valley and thrives on the production of cut flowers and flower seeds. Walk the downtown streets painted with more than 30 impressive wall murals relating to Lompoc's history and culture *(www.lompocmurals.com)*. The Chamber of Commerce *(11 S I St; www.lompoc.com)* has maps of the murals and offers a flower tour of the nearby fields. The town also has many wine-tasting rooms at **Lompoc Wine Ghetto** *(N 7th St & Chestnut Court; www.lompocghetto.com)*.
🚗 *Exit on E Ocean Ave which becomes Buelton-Lompoc Rd (SR 246). Turn left on Purisima Rd, and right into the mission's parking lot.*

⑤ Mission La Purísima Concepcíon
Santa Barbara County; 93436
The most completely restored of California's 21 missions, Mission La Purísima Concepcíon *(www.parks.ca. gov/)* offers authentic insight into mission life two centuries ago.

Founded in 1787, the original mission was destroyed by an earthquake in 1812. Its replacement also fell into ruin and was rebuilt as a Depression-era work project. The mission has 37 rooms with period-style furnishings, and volunteers here hold candle-making and loom-weaving demonstrations. Wander through the restored gardens, and stop by the corral, which houses livestock as it did in the old days. Guided tours are offered daily at 1pm.
🚗 *Turn left onto Purisima Rd. Keep straight for 18 miles (29 km) through wine country to Solvang.*

Lompoc Murals
Conceived in 1988 as a means of encouraging tourism and boosting a stagnating "Old Town" economy, the Lompoc Murals project has encouraged the creation of colorful murals. Today there are more than 30 commissioned murals, from the *Flower Industry* by Santa Monica artist Art Mortimer, to *Temperance*, artist Dan Sawatsky's portrayal of women busting up an illegal saloon, reflecting the days when Lompoc was founded as a Temperance Community.

EAT AND DRINK

SAN LUIS OBISPO
Novo *moderate*
With open-air decks overlooking San Luis Creek, this stylish restaurant is *the* place to dine al fresco in town. Enjoy Mediterranean, Brazilian, and Asian-inspired tapas. It serves dozens of international beers, wines, and sakes.
726 Higuera St, 93401; 805 543 3986; open 11am–10pm Mon–Sat, 10am–10pm Sun; www.novorestaurant.com

PISMO BEACH
Steamers *moderate*
Panoramic coastal vistas from banquet booths are a bonus at this cliff-top restaurant serving excellent seafood and steaks. Try the local steamed clams, fish 'n' chips, or calamari steaks. Leave room for warm strawberry lemon cake.
1601 Price St, 93449; 805 773 4711; open 11:30am–3pm & 4:30–9pm daily, 11:30am–3pm & 4:30–10pm Fri & Sat; www.steamerspismobeach.com

LOMPOC
Sissy's Uptown Café *moderate*
This bright and cheery family-run restaurant delivers wholesome fusion dishes, such as coconut-encrusted salmon with Asian tamarind sauce, coconut jasmine rice, and sautéed fresh veggies, made from farm-fresh local ingredients. A huge wine cellar holds more than 300 labels.
112 S I St, 93436; 805 735 4877; open 11am–2:30pm Mon–Wed, 11am–2:30pm & 5–8:30pm Thu–Sat; www.sissysuptowncafe.com

Below left Red-tile roof at Mission La Purísima Concepcíon **Below** *Temperance* wall mural, Lompoc

VISITING SOLVANG

Tourist Information
1639 Copenhagen Dr, 93463; 805 688 6144; www.solvangusa.com

Parking
There is metered street parking.

WHERE TO STAY

SOLVANG

Hadsten House *moderate*
This motel has gracious furnishings, stylish marble-topped bathrooms, and excellent amenities.
1450 Mission Dr, 93463; 1 800 457 5373; www.hadstenhouse.com

Solvang Gardens *moderate*
Many of the 24 individually furnished rooms at this Danish-style, Wi-Fi-enabled country inn have fireplaces.
293 Alisal Rd, 93463; 1 888 688 4404; www.solvanggardens.com

LOS OLIVOS

Fess Parker Inn & Spa *expensive*
This deluxe hotel in the heart of town offers differently themed rooms with down comforters, antiques, and fireplaces. Its gourmet restaurant is a highlight.
2860 Grand Ave, 93441; 805 688 7788; www.fessparker.com

AROUND LOS OLIVOS

The Ballard Inn *expensive*
A cozy country-style hotel with a renowned restaurant, The Ballard Inn is a popular getaway. Book well ahead.
2436 Baseline Rd, Ballard, 93463; 1 805 688 7770; www.ballardinn.com

6 Solvang
Santa Barbara County; 93463
It may look like a kitschy Walt Disney false-front village, but Solvang was founded as a colony by Danish immigrants with windmills and half-timbered buildings that recalled their homeland. Virtually the entire town is made up of Danish Provincial-style structures, drawing a steady stream of tourists. Locals dressed in traditional costume attend visitors in restaurants and shops selling Danish specialties, and at the **Elverhøj Museum** *(www.elverhoj.org)*, where exhibits celebrate the Danish heritage. On the east side of town, **Mission Santa Inés** *(1760 Mission Dr; 805 688 4815; open 9am–5:15pm daily)* is a reconstruction of the original 1804 mission, destroyed by an earthquake in 1812. It still functions as a church under the care of Franciscan friars, and has an ecclesiastically themed museum.

Township of
Santa Ynez sign

🚗 **Exit east on Mission Dr (SR 246). Turn left onto Alamo Pintado Rd. Drive through Ballard to Grand Ave; turn left for Los Olivos. Roadside parking.**

7 Los Olivos
Santa Barbara County; 93441
This delightful village occupies the heart of the Santa Ynez wine and horse-breeding district. Sprinkled with prairie-style Victorian buildings,

Los Olivos is famous for its eclectic mix of art galleries, epicurean restaurants, wine-tasting rooms, and quaint B&Bs. Many of the best wineries can be visited along the "Foxen Canyon Wine Trail"*(www.foxencanyonwinetrail.com)*, which leads north from Los Olivos; the Neverland ranch, former home of Michael Jackson, is about 5 miles (8 km) north of town. **Blackjack Ranch** *(www.blackjackranch.com)*, immediately south of town, has a tasting room where some of the best wines of the region are served.

🚗 **At the north end of Grand Ave turn right onto SR 154; exit at Edison Rd for Santa Ynez. Park roadside.**

8 Santa Ynez
Santa Barbara County; 93460
Los Olivos' charming, sleepy neighbor, Santa Ynez features typical 1880s Western wooden architecture, including saloons, a jail, library, and Wells Fargo stagecoach office. **Santa Ynez Valley Historical Society Museum & Parks-Janeway Carriage House** *(www.santaynez museum.org)* showcases a barn full of old wagons and buggies, plus eight rooms of historic memorabilia that includes guns, saddles, and Chumash Native American artifacts. The Chumash tribal property, on the south side of town, houses the

Above left The landmark Antique Center in the Danish-themed town of Solvang
Below A typical Danish Provincial-style building in Solvang

Sideways

In 2004, the Hollywood hit movie *Sideways* made viewers aware that California has wine regions beyond Napa Valley. The comedy-drama, which follows two middle-aged men on a roadtrip through the Santa Ynez Valley, was filmed at real sights. It won critical acclaim and also served, inadvertently, as a travelogue and national advertisement that delivered the region a tourist bonanza. Many locations in the area have the unmistakable *Sideways* logo posted on their signs.

Chumash Casino Resort *(www.chumashcasino.com)*. It is possible to easily spend a day touring the region's wine country; pick up a map at the Santa Barbara County Vintners' Association *(3669 Sagunto St; 805 688 0881; www.santaynezwinecountry.com)*.

🚗 *At the south end of Edison Rd, turn left onto SR 246. Turn right onto SR 154 (San Marcos Pass Rd), and follow it south past Lake Cachuma to Santa Barbara. After 20 miles (32 km), turn left onto Painted Cave Rd. Be extra cautious, as this narrow*

mountanious road has many blind curves. The caves are 2 miles (3 km) uphill; park on the left side of the road.

❾ Chumash Painted Cave State Historic Park

Santa Barbara County

High in the Santa Ynez Mountains, this park *(www.parks.ca.gov/)* preserves a remote cave embellished with Native American Chumash pictographs painted in ochre, white, black, and rust. Visitors can view these 1,000-year-old pictographs through a grill that protects the cave. Educational signs help identify lizards, snakes, scorpions, and sacred symbols, although their meaning is unclear. The cave, in a sandstone cliff-face, is accessed by a short, stepped path that leads up through a boulder field at the side of the road.

🚗 *Return to Hwy 154 and continue downhill to Santa Barbara. Exit Hwy 154 at the Cathedral Oaks Rd exit and turn left onto Foothill Rd. Turn right onto Mission Canyon Rd, opposite Ocho Robles, and continue to Mission Santa Barbara. Park in the free parking lot.*

Above left Wine-tasting room in Los Olivos
Above Old Los Olivos Market in Los Olivos
Below left Chumash pictographs, Chumash Painted Cave State Historic Park **Below right** Back at the Ranch antique store, Solvang

WHERE TO EAT

SOLVANG

Greenhouse Café *moderate*
Danish folk run this Nordic bistro with an outdoor terrace and Danish and American dishes, plus Danish pastries and handmade chocolates.
487 Atterdag Rd, 93463; 805 688 8408; open 8am–5pm daily; www.greenhousesolvang.com

LOS OLIVOS

Wine Merchant Café *expensive*
This local institution famously featured in the movie *Sideways*. Lightweight wine country dishes are served tapas-style, and entrées include braised lamb shank with *panzanella* (Italian bread salad), feta, olives, and lemon aioli.
2879 Grand Ave, 93441; 805 688 7265; open 11:30am–8:30pm daily; www.losolivoscafe.com

AROUND LOS OLIVOS

The Ballard Inn & Restaurant *moderate*
Start with hamachi sashimi with avocado and soy-yuzu vinaigrette, followed by Australian rack of lamb with polenta, roasted beets, and goat's cheese. Superb service and an excellent wine list.
2436 Baseline Rd, Ballard, 93463; 1 805 688 7770; open 5:30–9pm Wed–Sun; www.ballardinn.com

SANTA YNEZ

Vineyard House *moderate*
In a Victorian-era home, this restaurant has outdoor decks and cozy indoor dining. Choose from salads and sandwiches to baked Brie, crab cakes, or fusion-style venison and pork entrées.
3631 Sagunto St, 93460; 805 688 2886; open 11:30am–9pm Mon & Wed–Sat, 10am–9pm Sun; www.thevineyardhouse.com

Eat and Drink: inexpensive under $25; moderate $25–50; expensive over $50

Above Santa Barbara's impressive County Courthouse **Below right** The sprawling city of Santa Barbara as seen from Stearns Wharf

VISITING SANTA BARBARA

Tourist Information
1 Garden St, 93101; 805 965 3021; open 9am–5pm Mon–Sat, 10am–5pm Sun; www.sbchamber.org/visitor-center.php

WHERE TO STAY

SANTA BARBARA

Bath Street Inn *moderate*
An English-style B&B, Bath Street Inn has 12 individually themed rooms, a cozy parlor, and a dining room.
1720 Bath St, 93101; 1 800 549 2284; www.bathstreetinn.com

Santa Barbara Inn *moderate*
With a fabulous shorefront setting, this motel has spacious rooms and suites with deluxe linens and flat-screen TVs.
901 E Cabrillo Blvd, 93103; 1 800 231 0431; www.santabarbarainn.com

OJAI

Ojai Valley Inn & Spa *expensive*
A full-service resort with an esteemed history, this deluxe hotel has its own golf course. Its 308 rooms and suites boast sumptuous furnishings.
905 Country Club Rd, 93023; 805 646 1111; www.ojairesort.com

Su Nido Inn *expensive*
Set in the heart of town, this warm and inviting hotel has one- and two-bedroom suites, lavishly furnished in contemporary style.
301 N Montgomery St, 93023; 1 866 646 7080; www.sunidoinn.com

⑩ Santa Barbara
Santa Barbara County; 93101

A beautiful, palm-studded seaside town, Santa Barbara is called the American Riviera for its Mediterranean climate and setting in a beach-fringed bay overlooked by forested mountains. Many early 19th-century adobes survive alongside Spanish Colonial Revival buildings. This cultured city is also home to the world-class Museum of Art and lively festivals such as the Old Spanish Days Fiesta.

A three-hour walking tour

Begin at **Mission Santa Barbara** ① *(www.santabarbaramission.org)*, the only one of California's 21 missions to be continuously in use since its founding in 1786. Admire the only remaining Native American-made altar in the California missions, a fine Colonial art collection, and restored living quarters. Follow Laguna Street downhill to Mission Street. Turn left at Anacapa Street. (Drive to avoid the uphill return walk; park in the lot at the junction with Figueroa Street.) Stop at the Colonial-style **County Courthouse** ② *(www.santabarbara courthouse.org)*, graced by Tunisian tiles, wrought-iron grillwork, and bas-reliefs. Take the antique elevator to the top of El Mirador clock tower for a fine perspective over downtown, then walk through the **Sunken Garden** ③, planted with specimens from around the world, to Santa Barbara Street. Turn right and walk two blocks to **El Presidio State Park** ④ *(www.sbthp.org/presidio.htm)*, founded in 1782 as the last of four military fortresses built by the Spanish along the coast of the Alta California frontier. Explore the adobe structures that enclose a central parade ground, then walk one block south to **Santa Barbara Historical Museum** ⑤ *(www.santabarbaramuseum.com)*, which

Sign of the Granada Theatre, Santa Barbara

has exhibits relating to the city's history. Turn right on E De La Guerra Street and continue to State Street. Turn left for **Stearns Wharf** ⑥ *(www.stearnswharf.org)*, 1 mile (1.4 km) away; alternatively, catch the MTD electric shuttle that runs along State Street. The wooden pier lined with seafood restaurants is a popular spot for fishing; do not miss the Ty Warner Sea Center *(805 962 2526)*, with touch tanks filled with marine creatures. Return along State Street to the **Santa Barbara Museum of Art** ⑦ *(www.sbmuseart.org)*, with works spanning 4,000 years. One block north, **Granada Theatre** ⑧ *(1214 State St)* is the city's tallest building and home to the Santa Barbara Symphony and State Street Ballet. A block farther, pass the 1931 Mission Revival-style **Arlington Theatre** ⑨ *(www.thearlingtontheatre.com)*. Turn right onto E Sola St to return to Anacapa Street; **Our Lady of Sorrows Church** ⑩ stands on the northwest corner. Turn either left or right on Anacapa Street to return, depending on which parking spot was used.

🚗 *Take State St south to E Cabrillo St. Turn left, and left again at Garden St. Enter I-101 east and exit at Carpenteria Ave. Turn right onto Palm Ave and continue to the Carpinteria State Beach car park.*

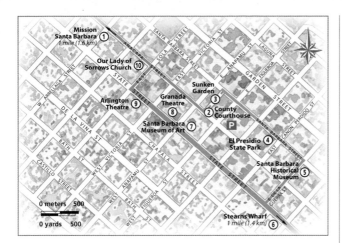

Map labels:
Mission
Santa Barbara ①
1 mile (1.6 km)

Our Lady of
Sorrows Church ⑩

Sunken
Garden ③

Arlington
Theatre ⑨

Granada
Theatre ⑧

County
Courthouse ②

Santa Barbara
Museum of Art ⑦

El Presidio ④
State Park

Santa Barbara
Historical ⑤
Museum

0 meters 500
0 yards 500

Stearns Wharf ⑥
1 mile (1.4 km)

⑪ Carpinteria State Beach

Santa Barbara County; 93013
This beach *(805 968 1033; open 7am–sunset)* was named by the Spanish for the Chumash Native American carpenters who made canoes, sealed with the tar that bubbles to the surface at the southern end of the beach. Nearby, rocky tidepools reveal starfish and sea anemones during low tide, while harbor seals and sea lions bask on the rocks. At the northern end, the Carpinteria Creek estuary forms a wetland habitat for coots, mallards, and herons.
🚗 *Return to Carpinteria Ave and turn right. Cross I-101 freeway. Keep along SR 150 (Rincon Rd) that merges into Casitas Pass Rd. Drive for 15 miles (24 km) to Lake Casitas Recreation Area. The ranger station has parking.*

⑫ Lake Casitas Recreation Area

Ventura County; 93001
Formed by Casitas Dam, Lake Casitas reservoir is where anglers cast for bass, catfish, crappie, and rainbow trout. This area is a lovely spot for hiking, picnicking, or camping, and also has RV hook-ups *(805 649 1122)*. **Casitas Water Adventure** *(www.casitaswater.org)* has waterslides, a lazy river ride, and other attractions.
🚗 *Continue east on SR 150 (Baldwin Rd) to N Ventura Ave; turn left and follow into Ojai. At the junction with Maricopa Hwy, veer right onto W Ojai Ave. Park curbside.*

⑬ Ojai

Ventura County; 93023
Enfolded by mountains on three sides, Ojai enjoys a reputation as a New Age resort for the wealthy; **Ojai Valley Inn & Spa** draws celebrities to partake of healing treatments. Its main street is lined with a Mission Revival-style arcade. **Ojai Valley Museum** *(www.ojaivalleymuseum.org)* honors Chumash Native Americans, in whose language Ojai means moon. **Cluff Vista Park** *(W Ojai St & Rincon St)* showcases a variety of plants, while in spring the town is fragrant with the blossoms of orange groves that surround it.

VISITING OJAI

Tourist Information
201 S Signal St, 93024; 888 652 4669; open 10am–4pm Mon–Fri; www.ojaivisitors.com

WHERE TO EAT

SANTA BARBARA

Our Daily Bread *inexpensive*
A charming café-restaurant serving breads and pastries, chicken breast paninis, and vegetable pot pie.
831 Santa Barbara St, 93101; 805 966 3894; open 6am–5:30pm Mon–Fri, 7am–4:30 Sat; www.ourdailybread.net

OJAI

Feast Bistro *moderate*
Try the frittata specials, white bean soup, and the citrus olive oil cake at this London-style bistro.
254 E Ojai Ave, 93023; 805 640 9260; open 11:30am–2:30pm & 5:30–9pm Tue–Sat, 10:30am–3pm Sun; www.feastofojai.com

Suzanne's Cuisine *expensive*
The fusion fare here includes crab and corn cake with lemon cream sauce, and stuffed Cornish game hen with apricot Madeira sauce.
502 W Ojai Ave, 93023; 805 640 1961; open 11:30am–2:30pm & 5:30–10pm Wed–Mon; www.suzannescuisine.com

Below Lake Casitas surrounded by forested shores

DAY TRIP OPTIONS

This region can be explored on different day trips geared to specific interests.

El Camino Real
The old Camino Real, or the Royal Road, linking California's 21 missions passed through this region. Visitors with a fascination for history or religious sites can explore four of the Spanish missions along the route, beginning in San Luis Obispo ❶, then La Purísima Concepción ❺ in Lompoc, Santa Ínes in Solvang ❻, and ending at Mission Santa Barbara ❿.

From San Luis Obispo, take SR 1 to Lompoc, then SR 246 to Mission La Purísima Concepción and Solvang, then SR 154 to Santa Barbara.

Outdoor adventures
Hop in the saddle for horseback rides or strap into a harness to kite-surf at Pismo Beach ❷. Then continue to the Guadalupe-Nipomo Dunes near Guadalupe ❸ for great birding opportunities.

SR 1 connects Pismo Beach to Guadalupe, then take W Main St to the Guadalupe-Nipomo Dunes.

Eat and Drink: inexpensive under $25; moderate $25–50; expensive over $50

The Tahoe Loop

Sacramento to Placerville

Highlights

- **Old Town Sacramento**
  Walk through historic downtown Sacramento and relive the Gold Rush days

- **Wealth of an empire**
  Visit the Empire Mine State Historic Park, once the richest gold mine in California

- **Natural jewel**
  Enjoy awe-inspiring lake views and splash about in the crystal-clear waters of Lake Tahoe

- **Sweet hike**
  Breathe in the crisp mountain air while walking the trails of Sugar Pine Point State Park above Lake Tahoe

Stunningly beautiful Lake Tahoe, North America's largest alpine lake

The Tahoe Loop

A year-round destination for hiking, and a popular spot for fishing in summer and skiing in winter, Lake Tahoe is the jewel in the crown of the High Sierra. This drive forms a perfect loop combining several fascinating Gold Rush-era towns, the major sights around Lake Tahoe, plus Sacramento – the sophisticated, history-packed state capital. In winter, tire chains are sometimes mandatory due to snow and sudden blizzards, and access roads are frequently temporarily closed. The beauty of the mountains, however, is unparalleled during this time.

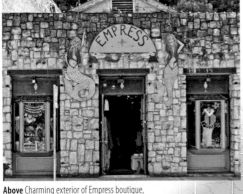

Above Charming exterior of Empress boutique, Placerville, *see p151* **Below** Street in 19th-century town of Grass Valley, *see p148*

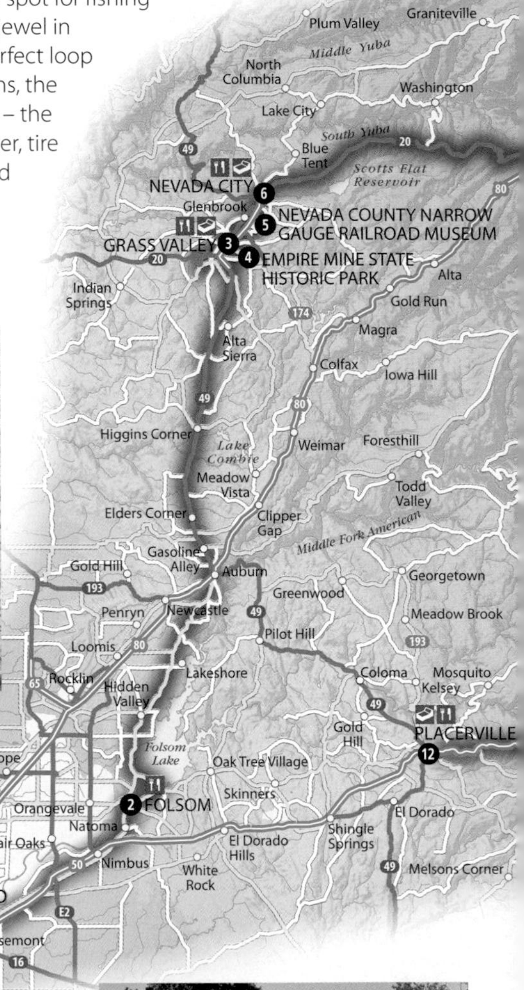

0 kilometers 10

0 miles   10

ACTIVITIES

Walk the streets of Old Sacramento on which the Pony Express riders sped

Stroll the gardens and trails of Empire Mine State Historic Park to learn about the largest and richest gold mine in California

Swap the car for a bike and pedal past the beaches, marinas, and exquisite coves of Lake Tahoe

Hike the forested trail to Vikingsholm, near Lake Tahoe, and admire its Scandinavian architectural features

Kayak or sail at Lake Tahoe, then warm up by sunbathing on a beach

Get a rush skiing at one of Lake Tahoe's superb ski resorts

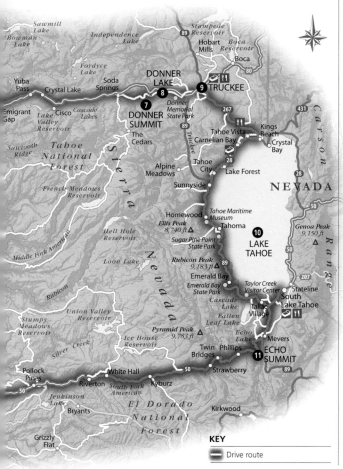

KEY

⊟ Drive route

PLAN YOUR DRIVE

Start/finish: Sacramento to Placerville.

Number of days: 3–4 days, including a full day in Sacramento and at least one day around Lake Tahoe.

Distance: 234 miles (377 km).

Road conditions: Mostly well-paved roads, with some freeway. Sections of mountain roads with steep grades and switchback bends require caution, especially during wintry conditions. Elevations above 4,000 ft (1,200 m) are often snowbound in winter, and snow chains are often compulsory. Roads at higher elevations may be closed for long periods following heavy snowfall.

When to go: Although winters here are breathtaking, spring and fall are the best times, especially late fall, when the foliage turns every shade from red to gold, and the weather is generally perfect.

Main market days: Sacramento: Sun. Folsom: 8am–noon Fri. **South Lake Tahoe:** 8am–1pm Tue. **Placerville:** mid-May–early Oct: Wed pm.

Opening times: Most museums open 9am–5pm Tue–Sun. Shops usually operate from 10am–7pm daily; restaurants close around 9pm.

Major festivals: Sacramento: Music Festival, May; California State Fair, Aug; Arts Festival, Oct. **Auburn:** Wine & Food Festival, Oct. **Lake Tahoe:** Shakespeare Festival, Jul–Aug; Music Festival, Jul. **Placerville:** Crafts Faire, Aug.

DAY TRIP OPTIONS

This tour can be easily treated as a series of day trips. A large section of the route weaves through foothill Gold Rush-era towns that will delight **history buffs**. **Outdoor lovers** can swap the car for hiking, biking, and water-based recreation around Lake Tahoe. For full details, *see p151.*

Above Pier at Sugar Pine Point State Park, Lake Tahoe, *see p150*

Above The landmark yellow Tower Bridge, across the Sacramento River

VISITING SACRAMENTO

Tourist Information
Sacramento Convention & Visitors Bureau *1608 I St, 95814; 1800 292 2334; www.discovergold.org*

Parking
Metered street parking is limited to 90 minutes. Downtown Sacramento has plenty of paid parking, including lots at either end of Old Sacramento.

Old Sacramento Visitor Center *J St & 2nd St, 95814; 916 442 7644; www.oldsacramento.com*

Discounts
Several hotels offer free VIP Gold Cards, which grant discounts at restaurants and shops plus two-for-one entry to select museums. Check at front desks.

WHERE TO STAY

SACRAMENTO

Amber House B&B *moderate*
A classy inn with 10 rooms named for famous composers and poets. Serves gourmet breakfasts.
1315 22nd St, 95816; 916 444 8085; www.amberhouse.com

Citizen Hotel *expensive*
This boutique hotel offers luxury furnishings, state-of-the-art technology, and a gourmet restaurant.
926 J St, 95814; 916 447 2700; www.citizenhotel.com

Delta King *expensive*
Tied to the wharfside, this historic paddleboat steamer is elegantly furnished, and has a fine restaurant.
1000 Front St, 95814; 916 444 5464; www.deltaking.com

❶ Sacramento
Sacramento County; 95814

The capital of California, Sacramento is also one of its most fascinating and cosmopolitan cities. Founded in 1839 as Sutter's Fort, it boomed as a commercial center and major railroad terminus during the Gold Rush era, and the wealth that ensued graced the city with magnificent buildings. This walk through Old Sacramento takes visitors past buildings that date back to the wild and formative Gold Rush days. The city also offers several excellent museums, fine-dining restaurants, and boutique hotels.

A three-hour walking tour
Park at the fee lot on L Street and 10th Street, and head to the **State Capitol** ① *www.capitolmuseum.ca.gov)*, the city's most notable landmark. This Neo-Classical building was completed in 1874 and the lavish interior, with its impressive rotunda, State Senate Chamber, and Governor's Office, plus historic offices furnished as museums, is best explored on a hour-long guided tour, offered hourly. Exit the Capitol and walk down the Capitol Mall, passing the **California Peace Officers' Memorial** ②, on the left. **Pony Express Monument** Do not miss the **Wells Fargo Museum** ③ *(916 440 4161; open 9am–5pm Mon–Fri)*, in the lobby of the Wells Fargo Center, displaying an original stagecoach among other historic exhibits. Turn left onto 3rd Street and right at O Street. Allow at least an hour to explore the **Crocker Art Museum** ④ *(www.crockerart museum.org)*, with superb collections spanning art from around the world

and through the centuries. Continue west, crossing to the riverfront. Turn right and walk past the iconic yellow **Tower Bridge** ⑤. Cross Capitol Mall to enter Old Sacramento Historic State Park *(www.parks.ca.gov/)* and the **Waterfront Boardwalk** ⑥ to admire the **Delta King** Steamboat ⑦ *(www.deltaking.com)*, a former paddle-wheel steamboat that is now a floating hotel and restaurant. Walk up K Street and turn left onto Front Street. At the end awaits the **Sacramento History Museum** ⑧ *(www. historicoldsac.org)*, which gives an insight into the town's history. The museum also offers underground tours *(Thu–Sun)* of the sidewalks and ground floors built before the city was raised in the 1860s to protect it from flooding. Next door, the **California State Railroad Museum** ⑨ *(www.csrmf.org)* has magnificent historic dioramas and 21 restored locomotives dating back to 1862.

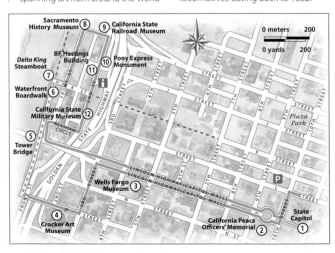

Left Horse-drawn carriage outside the BF Hastings Building, Sacramento **Below** Statue of Queen Isabella and Christopher Columbus in the State Capitol, Sacramento

Walk one block and turn right onto 2nd Street, lined with buildings that re-create the atmosphere of the 19th century. At J Street, note the **Pony Express Monument** ⑩ showing a life-size bronze rider in gallop. Walk diagonally to the **BF Hastings Building** ⑪, containing the Old Sacramento Visitor Center *(916 442 7644)*, the Wells Fargo History Museum *(916 440 4263)*, and a re-creation of the California Supreme Court, which sat here 1954–69. Continue along 2nd Street to the **California State Military Museum** ⑫ *(www.militarymuseum.org)*, where exhibits span from the early Spanish period to today. Walk around Neasham Circle and return to the parking lot via Capitol Mall.

🚗 *Exit south along 15 St. Pass under the I-50 freeway and turn left on X St. After one block, enter I-80 eastbound, then I-50 eastbound. After 19 miles (30 km), exit onto Folsom Blvd; turn left and continue into Folsom. Take Sutter St to Reading St to Leidesdorff St and park in the covered lot.*

❷ Folsom
Sacramento County; 95630

This town was a gold miners' way-stop with Transcontinental Railroad and Pony Express depots. Its historical core, around Sutter Street, is lined with red-brick buildings and boardwalks, and makes for delightful strolling, recalling the days when Pony Express riders galloped down the street and gold prospectors boarded stagecoaches in search of better fortunes. The **Folsom History Museum** *(www.folsomhistorymuseum.org)* displays railroad memorabilia and exhibits on Native America Maidu culture.

The town was made famous by Johnny Cash's 1955 song "Folsom Prison Blues". Folsom State Prison, immediately northeast of downtown, is equally famous for having held many celebrity prisoners, such as mass murderer Charles Manson, and a visit to its **Folsom Prison Museum** *(www.folsomprisonmuseum. org)* is quite fascinating. To reach it from Leidesdorff Street, drive south on Wool Street and turn left on Natoma Street for Prison Road.

Head northeast of town to **Folsom Lake** *(www.parks.ca.gov/)*. Created by the Folsom Dam, built in 1956, it is one of Northern California's premier recreational spots for hiking, biking, and aquatic sports.

🚗 *Natoma St leads to Folsom Lake Crossing; after 2.5 miles (4 km) turn left and pass the dam. After 2 miles (3 km) turn right on Folsom-Auburn Rd, which leads 16 miles (26 km) to Auburn (see p156). Pass through town, exiting right on Lincoln Way. After two blocks, turn left on SR 49 (I-80 signs). After 23 miles (37 km), exit onto S Auburn St for Grass Valley. Turn left into town; park along the street.*

Pony Express
Initiated on April 3, 1860, the Pony Express was a fast mail service using horse riders who delivered mail between the eastern states and California. Riders operated in relays that covered 250 miles (402 km) in a 24-hour day and took 10 days for the journey. More than 100 stations had been opened by October 24, 1861 when completion of a telegraph line ended the need for its existence.

EAT AND DRINK

SACRAMENTO

Fat City Bar & Café *moderate*
In the heart of Old Sacramento, this 150-year-old venue retains its Gold Rush ambience. Dishes range from light appetizers to hearty fusion entrées.
1001 Front St, 95814; 916 446 6768; open 11:30am–2:30pm & 4–9pm Mon–Fri, 10:30am–3:30pm & 5–10pm Sat & Sun; www.fatsrestaurants.com

Ella *expensive*
This lofty downtown restaurant offers fine dining in chic surrounds. Sample the yellowfin tuna carpaccio, followed by braised spiced lamb shank with couscous, ginger mint confit and spring onions.
1131 K St, 95814; 916 443 3772; open 11:30am–2pm & 5:30–9pm Mon–Thu, 11:30am–2pm & 5:30–10pm Fri, 5:30–10pm Sat; www.elladiningroomandbar.com

FOLSOM

Karen's Bakery & Cafe *moderate*
This casual café serves gourmet baked goods plus light fare such as cauliflower soup, beef bourguignonne, and egg salad and prosciutto sandwich.
705 Gold Lake Dr, 95630; 916 985 2665; open 6am–4pm Mon–Fri, 7am–4pm Sat; www.karensbakery.com

Above Firehouse Number 1 Museum, Nevada City **Above right** Blacksmithing demonstrations, Empire Mine State Historic Park **Below** Sign at the Empire Mines

VISITING GRASS VALLEY

Tourist Information
248 Mill St, 95945; 530 273 4667;
www.grassvalleynevadacitycvb.com

WHERE TO STAY

GRASS VALLEY

Holbrooke Hotel *moderate*
Antique-furnished rooms, a traditional
salon, and fine dining at this historic inn.
212 W Main St, 95945; 530 273 1353;
www.holbrooke.com

NEVADA CITY

Broad Street Inn *moderate*
Lovely B&B with exquisite furnishings.
517 W Broad St, 95959; 530 265 2239;
www.broadstreetinn.com

TRUCKEE

Larkspur Hotel *moderate*
This modern hotel has well-appointed
rooms and a cozy restaurant-bar.
11331 Broadway Rd, 96161; 530 587
4525; www.larkspurhotels.com

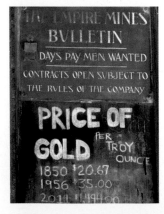

❸ Grass Valley
Nevada County; 94945
At its peak, in the 1890s, this Gold
Rush town was surrounded by mines
and stamp mills, and almost two-
thirds of its population comprised
miners from Cornwall, England.
Gracious 19th-century buildings still
line its streets. Look out for the glass-
domed **Nevada County Bank Building**
(131 Mill St), the town's most impressive
building, and the Art Deco **Del Oro
Theatre** *(165 Mill St)* with its iconic
illuminated spire. The **Grass Valley
Museum** *(410 S Church St; 530 273 5509;
Apr–Dec: open 12:30–3:30pm Wed–Sat)*
provides an introduction to the Gold
Rush era with re-creations of a
classroom, doctor's office, and parlor
of the period. For a fuller immersion,
drive south along Mill Street to the
North Star Mining Museum *(10933
Allison Ranch Rd; 530 273 4255; open
May–Oct: 10am–4pm Tue–Sun)*, demon-
strating mining artifacts, including a
working stamp mill and the largest
Pelton Wheel (a water turbine used
for generating electricity) ever built.

🚗 *Exit the museum onto McCourtney
Rd, then right onto Empire St; follow
the signs to Empire Mine State Historic
Park; continue uphill to the main Penn
Gate entrance.*

❹ Empire Mine State Historic Park
Nevada County; 95945
Buildings and mining equipment
associated with one of the richest
and longest-surviving gold mines in
California are preserved in this
784-acre (317-ha) park *(www.parks.
ca.gov/)*. Admire the original mine
buildings, Bourn Cottage – the
owner's English manor-style granite

house with its extravagant redwood
interior, and the landscaped gardens.
Explore some of the 367 miles
(590 km) of underground tunnels, and
hike or bike the 14 miles (219 km) of
trails through the site and surrounding
forests. One of the best options is the
Hardrock Trail, which begins at the
Penn Gate parking lot and leads past
several mining sites displaying
equipment from the Gold Rush era.

🚗 *Return down Empire St and after 1
mile (1.5 km) turn right onto the SR 49
freeway for Nevada City. Exit on Gold
Flat Road, and turn right. Immediately
turn left on Hollow Way and right on
Bost Ave for the Nevada County
Narrow Gauge Railroad Museum.*

❺ Nevada County Narrow Gauge Railroad Museum
Nevada City; 95959
An impressive collection of railroad
memorabilia, including four Baldwin
steam trains dating from 1875 are on
display here *(www.ncngrrmuseum.org)*.
Visit the maintenance shop, where
the volunteer staff is usually busy
restoring vintage rolling stock.

🚗 *Return to SR 49 and continue to
Nevada City.*

❻ Nevada City
Nevada City; 95959
Once known as the "Queen of the
Northern Mines", Nevada City
evolved into one of the largest
northern Gold Rush towns, before
finally declining in the late 19th
century. Its renovated core is a
National Historic District with maple-
lined streets lit by gas lamps and
bordered by Victorian buildings,
many graced by delicate gingerbread
trim. Look out for the **National Hotel**

Where to Stay: inexpensive under $100; moderate $100–200; expensive over $200

(211 Broad St), one of the oldest hotels in California, the **Nevada Theatre** *(401 Broad St; www.nevadatheatre.com)*; and, one block north, the **Firehouse Number 1 Museum** *(214 Main St; 530 265 5468)*, with gingerbread trim and a cupola bell tower. The interior displays eclectic historic pieces that include Maidu Native American artifacts and a Chinese temple altar.

🚗 *Exit on SR 49 which becomes SR 20. After 29 miles (46 km) through the Sierras, merge onto the I-80 freeway. Exit at Historic US Hwy 40 for Donner Summit.*

⑦ Donner Summit
Nevada County; 96161

This peak looms over the Euer Saddle, or the Donner Pass, which crosses the Sierra crest at 7,056 ft (2,151 m). Approached by a gradual incline from the west, it plunges on the east side, where Donner Pass Road begins a switchback descent of the Truckee River Valley. Stop at the Hwy 40 Scenic Bypass to admire the views. Panels point out and describe the railroad, completed in 1868 and visible below and to the right. Look out for the tunnel and snowsheds built so that avalanches would pass over the track.

🚗 *Continue to Donner Lake, 6 miles (10 km) from the Scenic Bypass.*

⑧ Donner Lake
Nevada County; 96161

A popular resort and fishing spot, this freshwater lake is cusped on three sides by mountains and is dammed by a natural moraine deposited by ancient glaciers. The

---

Donner Party

In the winter of 1846–7, 87 pioneers – the "Donner-Reed Party" – attempted to cross the Sierra Nevada by an untested route called the Hastings Cutoff. Delayed by a series of mishaps, their wagon train got caught up in heavy snowfall in the mountains near Truckee. Trapped for months, they ran out of food. To survive, some of them resorted to cannibalism, eating those who had succumbed to starvation and sickness. Only 48 members survived.

---

forested **Donner Memorial State Park** *(www.parks.ca.gov/)* around the east end of the lake offers great hiking trails. Do not miss the park's Pioneer Monument and Emigrant Trail Museum that commemorate the Donner Party of pioneers that were famously trapped in snow while trying to haul their wagons over the Sierra in 1847.

🚗 *Stay on Donner Pass Rd as it passes over I-80. Continue into Truckee.*

⑨ Truckee
Nevada County; 96160

This small mountain town is the northern gateway to Lake Tahoe and an important stop on the I-80 trans-Sierra highway. It evolved in the mid-19th century as a railroad and lumbering town and later served as the setting for Charlie Chaplin's *The Gold Rush* (1925). The **Old Jail Museum** *(www.truckeehistory.org)* is worth a stop.

🚗 *Turn right on Bridge St (later becomes Brockway Rd), then right on SR 267. Continue 12 miles (19 km) to Lake Tahoe.*

Above Bourn Cottage, Empire Mine State Historic Park **Below left** Truckee, set amid alpine forest

VISITING NEVADA CITY

Tourist Information
132 Main St, 95959; 530 265 2692; open 9am–5pm Mon–Fri, 11am–4pm Sat, 11am–3pm Sun; www.nevada citychamber.com

VISITING TRUCKEE

Tourist Information
10065 Donner Pass Rd, 96161; 530 587 2757; www.truckee.com, www.visitcwc.com/Truckee

EAT AND DRINK

GRASS VALLEY

Marshall's Cornish Pasties *inexpensive*
Pick up home-baked savory Cornish pasties to go or eat upstairs.
203 Mill St, 95945; 530 272 2844; open 9:30am–6pm Mon–Fri, 10am–6pm Sat

NEVADA CITY

Nevada City Classic Café *inexpensive*
A 1950s American diner serving classic breakfast such as eggs Benedict and French crêpes, burgers for lunch, plus tapas for dinner.
216 Broad St, 95959; 530 265 9440; open 8:30am–2:30pm daily; www.ncclassiccafe.com

TRUCKEE

Moody's Bistro & Lounge *expensive*
Hearty California fare including roasted organic beets with crumbled cheese and olive oil and the house special "Big Ass Pork Platter". Live jazz Wed–Sat.
10007 Bridge St, 96161; 530 587 8688; open 11:30am–9:30pm Mon–Thu, 11:30am–10pm Fri, 11am–10pm Sat, 11am–9:30pm Sun (closed 2:30pm–5:30 daily); www.moodysbistro.com

Eat and Drink: inexpensive under $25; moderate $25–50; expensive over $50

Above Panning for gold at Placerville
Below Boats moored at Lake Tahoe

VISITING LAKE TAHOE

Tourist Information
Tahoe City Visitors Information Center
380 N Lake Blvd, Tahoe City, 96145; 530
581 6900, 530 544 5050;
www.visitinglaketahoe.com

WHERE TO STAY

LAKE TAHOE

Inn by the Lake *moderate*
This lakeside motel offers spacious
rooms with king-size beds.
3300 Lake Tahoe Blvd, South Lake
Tahoe, 96150; 530 542 0330;
www.innbythelake.com

Shooting Star *moderate*
A log-cabin inn with a friendly owner,
pleasant furnishings, and an upstairs
lounge with lake views.
315 Olive St, Carnelian Bay, 96140;
530 546 8903; www.shooting
starbandb.com

PLACERVILLE

Cary House *moderate*
All the rooms at this historic, ivy-clad
hotel have stylish period furnishings.
300 Main St, 95667; 530 622 4271;
www.caryhouse.com

⑩ Lake Tahoe
Placer & El Dorado County

An unparalleled natural attraction, Lake Tahoe is California's most
beautiful body of water, the largest alpine lake in North America, as
well as the second-deepest lake in the US (1,645 ft/501 m). The
western two-thirds of the lake are in California, and the eastern third
is in Nevada. The crystal clear waters of the lake, ranging from hues of
emerald to sapphire, are popular for watersports, while its white
sands draw families for beach activities. Hiking and biking trails lace
the surrounding hills, including the 165-mile (270-km) Tahoe Rim
Trail. In winter, the snow-bound peaks are famous for their ski resorts.

First stop on the lake is **Kings Beach**,
known as the lake's "banana belt" for
receiving the sun's rays from early
morning through the afternoon.
Here, the stretch of shore comprises
several public golden-sand beaches
that are lined with resort hotels.
From here, drive west counter-
clockwise on SR 28 for 3 miles
(5 km) to **Carnelian Bay**, a popular
boating center. Six miles (10 km)
ahead lies the resort area of
Tahoe City, at the
headwaters of the Truckee
River. Walk its lakeside
boardwalk, stroll across the
historic 18-ft (5-m) tall
Lake Tahoe Dam, and visit
the waterfront William B.
Layton Park. Here, the
Gatekeeper's Museum
showcases the history of
the area, while the
Steinbach Indian Basket Museum
displays more than 800 baskets from
85 tribes across North America. Veer
left in town onto SR 89 to continue
around the lake, stopping after
around 5 miles (8 km) at the **Tahoe
Maritime Museum** *(530 525 9253;
www.tahoemaritimemuseum.org)*,

**Vintage car at Tallac
Historic Site**

which traces Lake Tahoe's maritime
history and includes more than 30
historic vessels. The route grows
increasingly scenic as it snakes past a
series of bays for the next 4 miles
(6 km) before arriving at **Sugar Pine
Point State Park** *(530 525 7982;
www.parks.ca.gov/)*. Extending from
the shore into the Desolation
Wilderness, the park has trails, a
lighthouse, and the baronial
Hellman-Ehrmann Mansion
(530 525 7232), built in 1903 for
banker Isaiah Hellman.
Another 10 miles (16 km)
ahead, the road rises to
offer a stunning view
down over **Emerald Bay
State Park** *(530 541 3030;
www.parks.ca.gov/)*. The
beautiful flask-shaped inlet
is the most photogenic
part of the lake. Roadside
pullouts here have interpretive
panels; be cautious of heavy traffic.
Trails lead uphill to the Eagle and
Cascade Falls, and sharply downhill
to **Vikingsholm** *(530 525 3345)*, built in
1928 as a summer-house in the form
of a Nordic castle. Continue along
the ridge between Emerald Bay and
Cascade Lake, and drive cautiously as
the road switchbacks downhill to the
Taylor Creek Visitor Center *(530 543
2674)*. Immediately beyond, turn left
into the parking lot of **Tallac Historic
Site** *(530 541 5227)*, which preserves
three late 19th-century summer
estates. Most prominent is **Valhalla**,
featuring a renovated boathouse.
Continue 3 miles (5 km) to the
junction of US 50 and **South Lake
Tahoe**, a sprawling town with many
motels and restaurants.
🚗 *Depart South Lake Tahoe south
along US 50 (SR 89), also known as
Emerald Bay Rd, for Echo Summit.*

⑪ Echo Summit
El Dorado County

Also known as Johnson Pass, this mountain pass peaks at 7,382 ft (2,250 m) and was a favored route for the 1849 prospectors heading for the gold fields, Pony Express riders, and early pioneer immigrants. The road is carved into a granite cliff-face and features pullouts from which to enjoy the awe-inspring views down over Tahoe Basin and the sapphire waters of Echo and Upper Echo Lake. Beyond the summit, the road begins to wind down through the upper canyon of the South Fork American River. Several hairpin bends precede **Twin Bridges**, where the Pyramid Peak Trailhead leads up into a glacial U-shaped valley, made more dramatic by a fabulous waterfall.

🚗 *Continue downhill on US 50, descending past Strawberry (9 miles/ 14 km below Echo Summit). Continue through El Dorado National Forest to Placerville after 48 miles (77 km). Exit onto Bedford Ave and turn left into the historic downtown.*

⑫ Placerville
El Dorado County; 95667

This Gold Rush town named after the placer, or alluvial, gold deposits found in the hills around town was founded in 1848. The early rough-and-tumble community was known as Dry Diggings, but soon earned the name Hangtown due to the many hangings that took place. Its central location in Gold Country made it a major supply center for the nearby mining camps and is still an important crossroads on both US 50 and SR 49. Look out for the **El Dorado County Courthouse** *(495 Main St; 530 626 0773)*, built in 1912 in sober Civic style, and consider stopping at the **Placerville Historical Museum** *(524 Main St; 530 626 0773; open 11am–4pm Wed–Sun)*, housed in the old Fountain-Tallman Soda Works. Exhibits include soda-factory relics. For a more comprehensive historical profile, drive out to the **El Dorado County Historical Museum** *(104 Placerville Dr; 530 621 5865; open 1am–4pm Wed–Sat & noon–4pm Sun)* to see a stagecoach and re-created blacksmith shop; to get there, return to US 50 west-bound, drive two exits to Placerville Drive/Forni Road, and turn right.

Above left Row of shops at Placerville
Above The Historic Gold Bug Mine, Placerville
Below left Lower Eagle Falls at Emerald Bay, Lake Tahoe

EAT AND DRINK

LAKE TAHOE

Ernie's Coffee Shop *inexpensive*
An American diner serving fish 'n' chips steak sandwich, and scrambled eggs. *1207 Emerald Bay Rd, South Lake Tahoe, 96150; 530 541 2161; open 6am–2pm daily; www.erniescoffeeshop.com*

Spindleshanks *moderate*
This popular alpine-style, stone-and-timber American bistro serves nouvelle California dishes. Try the baked oysters with spinach or the roasted butternut squash ravioli. Live music on weekends. *673 N Lake Blvd, Tahoe Vista, 96148; 530 546 2191; open 5:30pm–midnight daily; www.spindleshankstahoe.com*

PLACERVILLE

Sequoia *moderate*
Artichoke dip, hot crab sandwich, and whisky peppercorn steak are popular items on the varied menu at this elegant restaurant. *643 Bee St, 95667; 530 622 5222; open 4:30–9pm Tue–Thu, 11am–10pm Fri–Sat, 9:30am–9pm Sun; www.sequoiaplacerville.com*

DAY TRIP OPTIONS
This drive can be easily broken up into two distinct day trips.

Following the Gold Rush trail
Anyone interested in the Gold-Rush era will find plenty to amuse and amaze across the region. Old Sacramento ❶, Folsom ❷, Empire Mine Historic State Park ❹, and Nevada City ❻ together provide a profile of mid- and late-19th-century evolution with their fascinating museums, buildings, and railroad memorabilia.

Exit Sacramento on I-50 to Folsom Blvd and turn left to reach Folsom, from where Auburn-Folsom Rd leads to Auburn. From here, take SR 49 to the Empire Mines and Nevada City, then SR 20 to I-80 and Truckee.

In the lap of nature
Sugar Pine Point State Park and Emerald Bay State Park at Lake Tahoe ❿ offer excellent hiking trails. Do not forget to carry a picnic lunch.

From Truckee, Brockway Rd connects to SR 267, which leads south to Lake Tahoe. Follow SR 28 and SR 89 around the lake to the two state parks.

Eat and Drink: inexpensive under $25; moderate $25–50; expensive over $50

Gold Country

Auburn to Jamestown

Highlights

- **Fields of gold**
  Explore Marshall Gold Discovery
  State Historic Park, where gold
  was found in 1848

- **Wine valley**
  Taste world-class zinfandel wines in
  the beautiful Shenandoah Valley,
  renowned for boutique wineries

- **Titans of the forest**
  Marvel at the giant sequoia trees in
  Calaveras Big Trees State Park

- **Time travel**
  Explore a well preserved Gold
  Rush-era town at Columbia State
  Historic Park, where docents dress
  in period costume

Wells Fargo Express Office and stagecoach,
Columbia State Historic Park

Gold Country

The rolling western foothills of the Sierra Nevada are dotted with small historic towns founded during the California Gold Rush of 1849. The majority of these settlements lie along scenic Highway 49, making them easy to explore. Most towns are thriving communities that retain their charming yesteryear wooden boardwalks and redbrick buildings, and boast antique stores, Western saloons, "mom-and-pop" diners, and quaint B&Bs. Side trips lead to wineries and to sights that tout such natural attractions as California's largest single-chamber cavern and some of the world's largest trees. An agreeably Mediterranean climate and gentle, pleasant countryside add to the region's irresistible and diverse appeal.

Above Antique steam engine at the Railtown 1897 State Historic Park, Jamestown, *see p161*

Above Information panel at the Indian Grinding Rock State Historic Park, *see p158*

ACTIVITIES

Hunt for antiques along the main street of Auburn

Taste the wines in the Shenandoah Valley Wineries

Thrill to white-water rafting at Angels Camp

Picnic in the shade of the leafy giants in Calaveras Big Trees State Park

Step back in time by strolling the well-preserved streets of Columbia State Historic Park

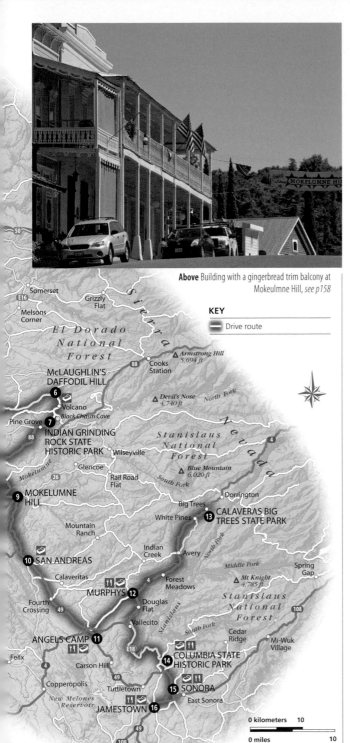

Above Building with a gingerbread trim balcony at Mokeulmne Hill, *see p158*

KEY

🚗 Drive route

Map labels:
Somerset
Grizzly Flat
Melsons Corner
El Dorado National Forest
McLAUGHLIN'S DAFFODIL HILL **6**
Volcano
Black Chasm Cave
Pine Grove **7**
INDIAN GRINDING ROCK STATE HISTORIC PARK
Glencoe
Rail Road Flat
MOKELUMNE HILL **9**
Mountain Ranch
SAN ANDREAS **10**
Calaveritas
MURPHYS **11** **12**
Fourth Crossing
Douglas Flat
Vallecito
ANGELS CAMP **11**
Felix
Carson Hill
Copperopolis
New Melones Reservoir
Tuttletown
JAMESTOWN **16**
Cooks Station
Armstrong Hill 5,694 ft
Devil's Nose 4,740 ft
North Fork
Wilseyville
Stanislaus National Forest
Blue Mountain 6,020 ft
South Fork
Big Trees
White Pines
CALAVERAS BIG TREES STATE PARK **13**
Dorrington
Indian Creek
Avery
North Fork
Middle Fork
Mt Knight 4,785 ft
Spring Gap
Forest Meadows
Stanislaus National Forest
Cedar Ridge
Mi-Wuk Village
COLUMBIA STATE HISTORIC PARK **14**
SONORA **15**
East Sonora
Sierra Nevada

0 kilometers 10
0 miles 10

PLAN YOUR DRIVE

Start/finish: Auburn to Jamestown.

Number of days: 2–3 days, allowing half a day for exploring the Shenandoah Valley Wineries.

Distance: 165 miles (266 km).

Road conditions: Roads are mostly narrow, winding, and often steep – some are single lane with infrequent passing places. The routes are well marked, and signs point the way to major sights.

When to go: A year-round destination, Gold Country is lovely in early spring when the wildflowers are in bloom. To avoid excessive heat, skip Jul–Aug, which are also the busiest months.

Main market days: Auburn: Wed & Sat am. **Sutter Creek:** Sat am. **Angels Camp:** Jun–mid-Sep: Fri pm.

Opening times: Shops generally open 9am–5pm Mon–Sat, but many stay open longer, including Sun, in summer. Wineries vary widely, but most open daily 11am–4pm or longer.

Shopping: Fresh farm produce, including grapes and local wines, are available at Shenandoah Valley, while antiques can be bought at many towns along the route.

Major festivals: Auburn: Gold Country Fair, Sep. **Angels Camp:** Calaveras County Fair & Jumping Frog Jubilee, May. **Murphys:** Calaveras Grape Stomp, first Sat in Oct.

DAY TRIP OPTIONS

Fans of history will find no end of attractions in the main **Gold Rush towns** along Highway 49. For **gourmet wines** and **fresh produce**, head into the **Shenandoah Valley** for a half-day's touring. **Calaveras Big Trees State Park** and the white-water rafting at **Angels Camp** will thrill **adventure lovers**. For full details, *see p161*.

Above Placer County Courthouse at Auburn
Above right Re-creation of Sutter's Mill, Marshall Gold Discovery State Historic Park
Below right Paved corridor at the charming historic St. George Hotel, Volcano

VISITING SHENANDOAH VALLEY WINERIES

Amador Vintners Visitor Center
9310 Pacific St, Plymouth, 95669; 888 655 8614; www.amadorwine.com

WHERE TO STAY

AMADOR CITY

Imperial Hotel *moderate*
This redbrick hotel built in 1872 boasts a fine-dining restaurant, a charming bar, and a serene garden.
The six attractive guest rooms are filled with antiques.
14202 Hwy 49, 95640; 209 267 9172; www.imperialamador.com

SUTTER CREEK

Hanford House Inn *expensive*
A downtown historic inn with renovated rooms and cottage suites boasting luxury linens, state-of-the-art amenities, and individual themes from classic 19th-century furnishings to hip 21st-century styling.
61 Hanford St, 95685; 209 267 0747; www.hanfordhouse.com

AROUND MC LAUGHLIN'S DAFFODIL HILL

Union Inn and Pub *moderate*
A charming B&B offering a choice of four well-appointed rooms with robes, Wi-Fi, luxury linens, and complimentary breakfast.
21375 Consolation St, Volcano, 95689; 209 296 7711; www.volcanounion.com

① Auburn
Placer County; 95602

A former gold mining town, Auburn was founded in 1849. The town's oldest surviving building, dating from 1851, **Bernhard House Museum** *(291 Auburn Folsom Rd; 530 889 6500; open 11am–4pm Tue–Sun)* recalls the days when the Bernhard family were pioneers in viticulture and the property served as a winery. Take the Auburn Folsom Road north and turn left on Lincoln Way. Park at the granite- and- redbrick trimmed **Placer County Courthouse** that dominates Auburn from its hilltop perch, which was once a place for public hangings. Climb the long staircase to visit the **Placer County Courthouse Museum** *(101 Maple St; 530 889 6500; open 10am–4pm daily)*, containing exhibits on Native American culture, the Gold Rush, a restored Sheriff's Office and women's jail, and a glittering gold collection. Afterwards, walk south one block to downtown, noting the plaques that tell the history of each of the firebrick buildings.

🚗 *Exit south on Auburn Folsom, then south on High St. Turn right on El Dorado St and follow the signs for Hwy 49; continue for 16 miles (25 km) to the Marshall Gold Discovery State Historic Park, with parking.*

② Marshall Gold Discovery State Historic Park
El Dorado County; 95613

This park *(www.parks.ca.gov/)* protects the site where James Marshall first spotted gold flakes in the water flume of his sawmill in January 1848, sparking the Gold Rush. Spanning 250 acres (101 ha) on both sides of

Highway 49, the site includes a full-scale re-creation of Sutter's Mill. The **Gold Country Museum** in the visitor center interprets the site's history. Marshall is buried beneath a hilltop statue of his likeness.

🚗 *Continue south on Hwy 49. Pass through Placerville (see p151) and exit along Hwy 49 via Diamond Springs. In downtown El Dorado, continue along Hwy 49 to Plymouth. Turn left on Shenandoah Rd; after 0.6 miles (1 km), turn left for the wineries.*

③ Shenandoah Valley Wineries
El Dorado & Amador County

The rolling Shenandoah Valley is the center of local viticulture due to its ideal climate and growing conditions that favor production of red wines. About three dozen small, family-owned wineries line the road, which snakes uphill past a gently undulating

sea of vines – many of them old-vine zinfandels that thrive in high summer temperatures. Stop to sample the wines, perhaps at **Sobon Estates Winery** *(www.sobonwine.com; open 10am–5pm daily)*, which is host to the Shenandoah Valley Museum, if there is a designated driver.

🚗 *Return to Plymouth and continue south on Hwy 49 for Amador City.*

❹ Amador City
Amador County; 95601

This tiny community once thrived on the wealth generated by the Keystone and Sutter gold mines. Stop to explore the **Amador Whitney Museum** *(14167 Main St; 209 267 5250; open noon–4pm Sat & Sun)*, where fascinating exhibits include a covered wagon; and the old cemetery behind the redbrick Imperial Hotel, worth a stop to enjoy lunch at one of Gold Country's finest restaurants.

🚗 *Exit town south on Old Hwy 49 and continue to Sutter Creek. Park along Main St.*

❺ Sutter Creek
Amador County; 95685

One of Gold Country's prettiest towns, Sutter Creek is known as the "Jewel of Amador County." With rich deep-rock mines, it remained a full-fledged mining town until 1942, when the mines were shut down by executive order. Today, the town's main street is lined with beautiful two-story wooden buildings fronted by boardwalk arcades. Many buildings are now antique shops and boutique B&Bs. Visit **Knights Foundry** *(Eureka St; www.knightfoundry.org)*, the only functioning 19th-century water-powered foundry and machine shop in the US, now preserved as a museum.

🚗 *Drive east on Gopher Flat Rd, which becomes Snake Ridge Rd and meets Rams Horn Grade after 13 miles (21 km). McLaughlin's Daffodil Hill Ranch is at the T-junction.*

❻ McLaughlin's Daffodil Hill
Amador County; 95689

Each spring, the McLaughlin family's 4-acre (1.6-ha) farm explodes into vibrant color when more than 300,000 daffodils bloom here. The first daffodils were planted here in 1887, and additional bulbs are

planted every year. The working farm also features an old barn with historic wagons, and mining and farming equipment. Daffodil Hill opens to the public usually from mid-March through mid-April; call ahead to verify *(209 296 7048)*.

At the farm, turn right (south) onto Rams Horn Grade. Drive with caution, as the narrow road twists downhill 3 miles (5 km) to **Volcano**. Measuring just four square blocks, this picturesque old gold-mining town is a true treasure. Its preserved buildings include the old jail, a brewery, the former Wells Fargo stagecoach office, and the redbrick **St. George Hotel**, dating from 1862. Adventure seekers should take time to explore the **Black Chasm Cave** *(www.caverntours.com/BlackRt.htm)*, 1 mile (1.6 km) south of Volcano, displaying stunning helictite crystals.

🚗 *Continue south from Volcano on Pine-Volcano Rd for Indian Grinding Rock State Historic Park.*

Black Bart
One of 19th-century America's notorious highway robbers, Charles Earl Bowles was a "gentleman bandit" who robbed 28 Wells Fargo stagecoaches between 1875 and 1883, many of them in Gold Country. He always wore a fine linen coat, plus a bowler hat on top of a sack with two eyeholes. Detectives finally tracked him down after tracing a handkerchief he had dropped at a San Francisco laundry. He was nicknamed "Black Bart" for the signature he used on the poems he left at two of his robberies.

Above left Knights Foundry, Sutter Creek **Top** Statue depicting a pioneer panning for gold, Auburn **Above** Road sign, Marshall Gold Discovery State Historic Park **Below** Wooden buildings in Sutter Creek

VISITING SUTTER CREEK

Tourist Information
71A Main St, 95685; 209 267 1344; www.suttercreek.org

EAT AND DRINK

AMADOR CITY

Imperial Restaurant *moderate*
This acclaimed restaurant serves Californian fare using organic produce. *Prix fixe* three-course offered midweek. *14202 Hwy 49, 95640; 209 267 9172; open 5–9pm Tue–Fri, noon–2pm & 5–9pm Sat & Sun; www.imperialamador.com*

SUTTER CREEK

Susan's Place Wine Bar & Eatery *moderate*
California-Mediterranean dishes served in a garden patio. Large local wine list. *15 Eureka St, 95682; 209 267 0945; open noon–9pm Thu–Sun; www.susansplace.com*

Tourist Information
Calaveras County Visitors Bureau
*1192 S Main St, 95222; 209 736 0049;
www.gocalaveras.com*

White-water Rafting Companies
OARS *2863 Main St, 95222; 800 346
6277; www.oars.com*

WHERE TO STAY

SAN ANDREAS

Robin's Nest Inn *moderate*
A delightfully Victorian mansion set in
expansive grounds offers nine guest
rooms filled with antiques. The owners
prepare lavish breakfasts.
*247 W St Charles St, 95249; 209 754
1076; www.robinest.com*

ANGELS CAMP

The Cooper House Inn *moderate*
Owner Kathy Reese and her son
Andy pamper guests at this
charming three-bedroom B&B.
*1184 Church St, 95222; 209 736 2145;
www.cooperhouseinn.com*

MURPHYS

Murphys Historic Hotel *moderate*
A local landmark and institution
operating since 1856, this hotel has
hosted famous figures from financier
J.P. Morgan to actor John Wayne.
Original rooms share bathrooms and
lack TVs and telephones; modern
rooms have more amenities. It has an
old-fashioned saloon.
*457 Main St, 95247; 209 728 3444;
www.murphyshotel.com*

Below Bark huts in a re-created Miwok
village, Indian Grinding Rock State Historic Park

⑦ Indian Grinding Rock State Historic Park
Amador County; 95665
Tucked in a valley of oak-shaded
meadows, this park *(entrance fee
includes parking; www.parks.ca.gov/)*
preserves a marbleized limestone
plateau pitted with almost 1,200
mortar holes once used by Native
Americans to grind acorns into flour.
The **Chaw'se Regional Indian Museum**
interprets the local Native American
cultures with exhibits of basketry and
clothing, and features a re-creation of
a Miwok Indian village, complete
with a *hun'ge* (roundhouse), where
ceremonial events are hosted.
🚗 *Continue along Pine Grove-
Volcano Rd to Pine Grove; turn right
onto Hwy 88 to Jackson. Turn right
onto Broadway then left for Main St,
which has metered parking.*

⑧ Jackson
Amador County; 95642
Founded in 1848, Jackson lies at the
crossroads of two Gold Rush-era
trails and evolved as a transportation,
supply, and mining center. For a take
on local history, visit the Kennedy
Mine Models of the **Amador Historical
Society** *(209 257 1485; tours 11am & noon
Sat)* and the **Kennedy Tailing Wheels
Park** *(Jackson Gate Rd)*, which preserves
two giant wheels that lifted polluted
"tailings" from the Kennedy Mine to a
storage dam. En route to the latter
look out for the hilltop **St. Sava's
Serbian Orthodox Church** *(N Main St)*,
tipped by a white steeple.
🚗 *Exit left onto Hwy 49, and
continue south to Mokelumne Hill.
Park along Main St.*

Above A typical Gold Rush-era wooden building
in San Andreas

⑨ Mokelumne Hill
Calaveras County; 95245
A sleepy and charming small Gold
Country town, Mokelumne Hill is rich
in violent historic intrigue. In its mid-
19th-century heyday, drunken
miners packed its rowdy saloons. The
separate Catholic, Jewish, and
Protestant cemeteries are replete
with graves of the dozens of miners
killed in drunken brawls. The town's
compact core includes an old Wells
Fargo stagecoach station and the
Hotel Ledger, among the few
19th-century buildings that remain
after a devastating fire in 1898.
🚗 *Stay on Hwy 49 to San Andreas.
Turn left on Court St; park on Main St.*

⑩ San Andreas
Calaveras County; 95249
The sprawling town of San Andreas
was founded in 1848 by Mexican
miners who were later forcibly
removed. A few handsome iron-
shuttered brick and wooden buildings
from the Gold Rush era remain north
of the highway. The **Calaveras County
Historical Museum** *(www.calaveras
cohistorical.com)* occupies an old
courthouse and is worth a stop.
Highway robber "Black Bart" *(see p157)*
was tried here after being arrested.
🚗 *Keep south on Hwy 49 for Angels
Camp. There is free street parking.*

⑪ Angels Camp
Calaveras County; 95222
Among the largest towns in Gold
Country, Angels Camp is today a
center for white-water rafting on the

Stanislaus River. Most famously, it was the real-life setting for Mark Twain's classic short story, "The Celebrated Jumping Frog of Calaveras County" (1865). Visitors stumble upon the leaping amphibians at every step and frog kitsch fills the town, including embedded in bronze in the sidewalks. Twain is honored with a statue in tree-shaded **Utica Park**, on Main Street.

Before heading out, check out the two 19th-century locomotives that stand outside the **Angels Camp Museum** *(753 S Main St; 209 736 2963)*, which displays buggies, minerals, mining equipment, and Native American artifacts. Also peek in the classic 1924 **Angels Theatre** *(1228 S Main St)* to admire the hand-painted Gold Rush-era murals inside.

🚗 *Turn left onto Murphys Grade Rd to Murphys. Park on Main St.*

⑫ Murphys

Calaveras County; 95229
Nestled among thick oaks and lush vineyards, the "Queen of the Sierra" has ample old-world charm from its heyday as a mining and trading center. Its streets are lined with quaint antique emporia, trendy restaurants, and wine-tasting rooms. Gold Rush memorabilia awaits at the **Old Timers Museum** *(450 Main St; 209 728 1160)*.

Typical detail depicting a frog, Angels Camp

Opposite, the **Murphys Historic Hotel** has hosted luminaries from former US President Ulysses S. Grant to Mark Twain and even "Black Bart".

🚗 *At the east end of Main St turn left onto Hwy 4. Head east to Calaveras State Park; park at the visitor center.*

⑬ Calaveras Big Trees State Park

Calaveras County; 95223
It is a humbling experience to stand beneath the planet's largest living things at this park *(www.parks.ca.gov/)*, named for the giant sequoia *(Sequoiadendron giganteum)* trees that can reach a height of 325 ft (100 m) and a diameter of 33 ft (10 m). Trails lead from the visitor center through the well-tramped North Grove, which includes the "Discovery Tree" or the "Big Stump," the first giant sequoia to be discovered, in 1852. The Walter W. Smith Memorial Parkway leads 10 miles (16 km) to the remote South Grove, which offers greater solitude among the giants. The park is often snowbound in winter.

🚗 *Return to Murphys and continue south on Hwy 4. At Vallecito, turn left onto Parrot's Ferry Rd to Columbia State Historic Park. Park in the public lot at the corner of Jackson St.*

White-water Rafting

Experiencing Gold Country on a white-water river trip is the ultimate combination of beauty and thrill. Three rivers – the North and Middle Forks of the American, and the Stanislaus – fed by spring snowmelt provide some of the most popular thrill-filled white-water runs in the US. There are quieter moments, too, with long lazy calms ideal for swimming.

Above Old equipment at the Kennedy Tailing Wheels Park, Jackson **Below left** Delightful interior of the Murphys Historic Hotel, Murphys

---

EAT AND DRINK

ANGELS CAMP

The Pickle Barrel *inexpensive*
Good for gourmet salads, panini sandwiches, soups, wraps, and delicious carrot cake.
1225 S Main St, 95222; 209 736 4704; open 11am–3pm Wed–Sun; www.pickle-barrel.com

Camps Restaurant *expensive*
An elegant fine-dining restaurant, its menu highlights farm-fresh regional produce and local wines.
676 McCauley Ranch Rd, 95222; 209 736 8197; open 11:30am–8pm Wed & Thu, 11:30am–9pm Fri & Sun; www.campsrestaurant.com

MURPHYS

Grounds *moderate*
This casual yet elegant restaurant is a great place for granola, breakfast burritos, Greek salad, BLT sandwiches, and seared swordfish steak.
402 Main St, 95247; 209 728 8663; open 7am–3pm Mon–Tue, 7am–3pm & 5–8:30pm Wed & Thu, 7am–3pm & 5–9pm Fri, 5–9pm Sat, 5–8pm Sun; www.groundsrestaurant.com

Mineral *expensive*
Inventive fusion vegetarian dishes are served at this chic modern restaurant.
419 Main St, 95247; 209 728 9743; open noon–3pm & 5–8:30pm Thu, noon–8:30pm Fri & Sat, noon–8pm Sun; www.mineralrestaurant.com

Eat and Drink: inexpensive under $25; moderate $25–50; expensive over $50

Above Parrott's Blacksmith Shop, Columbia State Historic Park

VISITING COLUMBIA STATE HISTORIC PARK

Tourist Information
11255 Jackson St, 95310; 209 588 9128; www.parks.ca.gov/

VISITING SONORA

Tourist Information
Tuolumne County Visitor Bureau
542 W Stockton Rd, 95370; 209 533 4420; www.tcvb.com

WHERE TO STAY

COLUMBIA STATE HISTORIC PARK

Fallon Hotel *moderate*
Faithfully restored to appear as it did when built in 1859, this hotel is furnished with period antiques.
11175 Washington St, 95310; 209 532 1470; www.briggshospitalityllc.com

SONORA

The Gunn House *moderate*
A heart-of-town hotel with antique furnishings and modern bathrooms.
286 S Washington St, 95370; 209 532 3421; www.gunnhousehotel.com

JAMESTOWN

National Hotel *moderate*
This delightful hotel has a fine restaurant, plus an original "soaking room" with a claw-foot tub.
18183 Main St, 95327; 209 984 3446; www.national-hotel.com

Where to Stay: inexpensive under $100; moderate $100–200; expensive over $200

⑭ Columbia State Historic Park

Tuolumne County; 95310

Once called the "Gem of the Southern Mines" and the second largest town in California, today Columbia is a lived-in museum *(www.parks. ca.gov/)* with the largest collection of Gold Rush-era brick buildings in the state. Its authentic 1850s shops, restaurants, and hotels have been preserved and are operated by staff in period attire. Stagecoach trips around town help to complete the journey back in time.

A two-hour walking tour

Park at the lot at the corner of Parrotts Ferry Road and Jackson Street and walk east on the latter. Turn right on Columbia Street, passing the **old jail** ① on the right. Turn right on State Street, where several old wagons are displayed in **Johnson's Livery Stable** ②. Across the street, the **Columbia Museum** ③ interprets the history of the town. Turn left on Main Street, dropping in at **Parrott's Blacksmith Shop** ④ to watch farriers forge horseshoes. Two shops down, consider getting a trim and traditional open-razor shave at the **Barber Shop** ⑤. This block is lined with more than a dozen shops, restaurants, and old-time saloons. The **Wells Fargo Express Office** ⑥ is maintained just as it looked 150 years ago. It is still the center for local transportation as the Quartz Mountain Stage Line *(209 588 0808; www.qmcarriage.com)*, and operates

Signage, Columbia State Historic Park

stagecoach tours from here. Located diagonally, the **Hidden Treasure Gold Mine Tour & Panning** ⑦ is a great place to try panning for gold in a sluice. After one block, Main Street curls right as Washington Street. Follow Washington Street to the **Fallon Hotel & Theatre** ⑧, with an ice cream parlor – a perfect stop on a hot summer day.

Turn right on Broadway Street, walk two blocks to State Street, and then turn right. The block is fascinating for its **Firehouse Tuolumne Engine Company** ⑨ and, immediately beyond, **Drug Store and Dentist's Office** exhibits ⑩. Turn left on Main Street. Don't miss the **Chinese Herb Shop** ⑪ and the old fire engine displayed at the **Firehouse Columbia Engine Company** ⑫. At the end of the block, turn left onto Jackson Street to return to the parking lot. If time permits, retrace the route on Jackson Street to turn left on Columbia Street. Turn right on Pacific Street, and left onto School House Street, which leads up to the old two-story schoolhouse , in front of a cemetery studded with 19th-century headstones.

🚗 **Exit south on Broadway St to the junction with Hwy 49. Turn left for Sonora. Park on S Washington St.**

⑮ Sonora

Tuolumne County; 95370

With a population of 5,000, Sonora is among the largest of the Gold Country towns. Logging

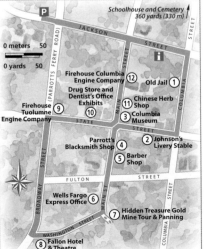

Left Exploring Columbia State Historic Park by stagecoach

remains an important industry, as it was in the gold fever days, when Sonora was founded in 1848 by Mexican miners who named it for their home state. Well-preserved Victorian buildings line its hilly, tree-shaded streets. The **Tuolumne County Museum & History Center** (www.tchistory.org), in the old city jail, is worth perusing for its collection of period firearms among its eclectic displays in former cell blocks that retain their original steel doors and bars.

🚗 *Continue on Washington St to the junction with Hwy 108; turn right for Jamestown.*

16 Jamestown
Tuolumne County; 95327
Founded only a few months after the famous discovery at Sutter's Mill, this mining camp experienced a series of booms, culminating in 1898 when a railroad was built, connecting Jamestown to nearby mining towns and the Central Valley. The **Railtown 1897 State Historic Park**

(www.railtown1897.org; hourly excursion trains Apr–Oct: 11am–3pm Sat & Sun) preserves the workshops, steam trains, roundhouse, and carriages of the still-functioning Sierra Railway. Take a stroll down Main Street with its picturesque buildings; the **National Hotel** (18183 Main St) where the bar has a stamped-tin ceiling and **The Emporium**, across the street, which is filigreed with gingerbread trim.

Wells Fargo Stagecoaches

In 1852, Vermont native Henry Wells and New Yorker William Fargo founded Wells, Fargo & Co. to provide express and banking services to California. Wells Fargo evolved as the world's largest stagecoach empire using the six-horse Concord Coach. Built to handle mountain and desert roads, the coach body rested on leather "thoroughbraces," made of strips of thick bull-hide. Valuables were kept in a green treasure box beneath the stagecoach driver's seat and guarded by an assistant with a shotgun.

WHERE TO EAT

COLUMBIA STATE HISTORIC PARK

Columbia Kate's *inexpensive*
This charming teahouse serves delectable pastries and a selection of unique tea blends in a quaint historic setting. A range of quiches, salads, and sandwiches are on the menu.
22727 Columbia St, 95310; 209 532 1885; open 11am–4pm daily; www.columbiakates.com

SONORA

Diamondback Grill *moderate*
Fine-dining restaurant specializing in California nouvelle dishes such as grilled rib-steak with blue cheese butter, and grilled salmon with cucumber *raita* (yogurt-based condiment). Separate wine bar.
93 S Washington St, 95370; 209 532 6661; open 11am–9pm Mon–Thu, 11am–9:30pm Fri & Sat, 11am–8:30pm Sun; www.thediamondbackgrill.com

JAMESTOWN

National Hotel *moderate*
Original gourmet fusion fare at this restaurant with a yesteryear ambience and attentive service. Try the crab cakes with chipotle sauce, and pork loin with green peppercorn in brandy cream sauce.
18183 Main St, 95327; 209 984 3446; open 11:30am–9pm Mon–Thu, 11:30am–10pm Fri & Sat, 10am–9pm Sun; www.national-hotel.com

---

DAY TRIP OPTIONS
Most of the main Gold Rush towns can be explored by staying on Hwy 49. Diversions into the Sierra foothills will appeal to those with special interests.

In search of gold
After re-living the Gold Rush-era history at the Amador Whitney Museum in Amador City **4** or the Kennedy Tailing Wheels Park in Jackson **8**, try panning for real gold and take a stagecoach ride in Columbia State Historic Park **14**.

From Amador City or Jackson, Hwy 49 leads south to Columbia State Historic Park, which is signed left at Springfield Rd.

Sampling zinfandels
Amador County is renowned for its hearty zinfandel wines, which can be savored on a tour of the Shenandoah Valley Wineries **3**, or at the wine-tasting rooms in Murphys **12**.

Turn east off Hwy 49 in Plymouth onto Fiddletown Rd, then turn left on

Shenandoah Rd for the Shenandoah Valley. Return to Hwy 49 and continue south to Angels Camp; turn left onto Hwy 4 for Murphys.

A taste of adventure
Thrill-seekers can spice up their tour with a half-day of white-water rafting at Angels Camp **11** or hiking in Calaveras Big Trees State Park **13**.

Turn left on Hwy 49 for Angels Camp, and then another left onto Hwy 4 to reach Calaveras Big Trees State Park.

Eat and Drink: inexpensive under $25; moderate $25–50; expensive over $50

Spectacular Yosemite

Moccasin to Bodie State Historic Park

Highlights

- **The Earth's largest trees**
  Stroll beneath giant sequoias towering to 250 ft (75 m) in Merced Grove, off Big Oak Flat Road

- **Magnificent waterfalls**
  Admire one of the world's tallest waterfall as it plunges 2,425 ft (739 m) into Yosemite Valley

- **Inspirational vistas**
  Stand in awe of the staggering view of Yosemite Valley from Glacier Point

- **Ghost town**
  Take a trip back in time to the heyday of gold mining along the deserted streets of Bodie State Historic Park

Awe-inspiring panorama from the Yosemite Valley from Tunnel View

Spectacular Yosemite

A place of incomparable beauty, Yosemite Valley is the jewel of the Sierra Nevada. Sheer granite walls, raging waterfalls, soaring redwoods, and exquisite alpine meadows set against a backdrop of magnificently sculpted peaks explain why Yosemite National Park is acclaimed as one of the most remarkable national parks in North America. The beauty and remoteness of these mountain heights are obvious in the winter months, when many of the roads are closed. The realm is a nirvana for outdoor enthusiasts, with opportunities from hiking and wildlife-spotting to rock-climbing and skiing. The sheer eastern scarp of the High Sierras plummets to Mono Lake, a haven for migratory birds, while the nearby ghost town of Bodie is preserved as it was when the gold-mining community was abandoned in 1882.

ACTIVITIES

Swim in the chilly, sparkling clear streams at Moccasin

Look out for deer, coyotes, and perhaps even bears while exploring Yosemite Valley

Hike to the top of Yosemite Falls for a fabulous view of the valley

Discover a wilderness paradise by hiking in Tuolumne Meadows

Spot the bird species at Mono Lake, where migrant avians flock in tens of thousands

Stroll the abandoned streets of Bodie State Historic Park and experience a real-life ghost town

Above The iconic Half Dome seen from Glacier Point, *see p167*

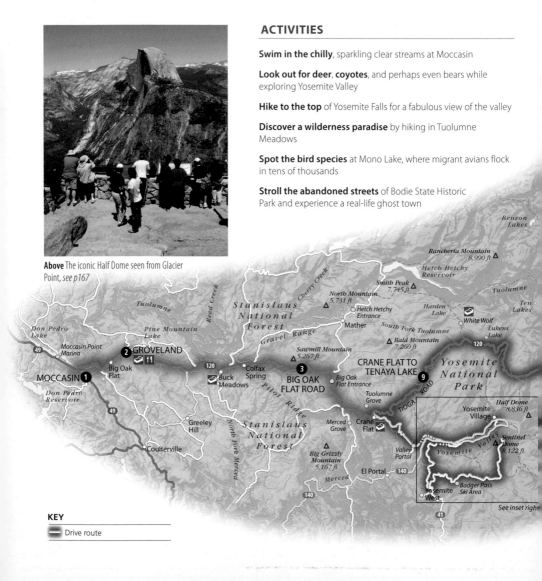

KEY

⬛ Drive route

Above Gold-mining ghost town of Bodie, preserved in Bodie State Historic Park, *see p171*

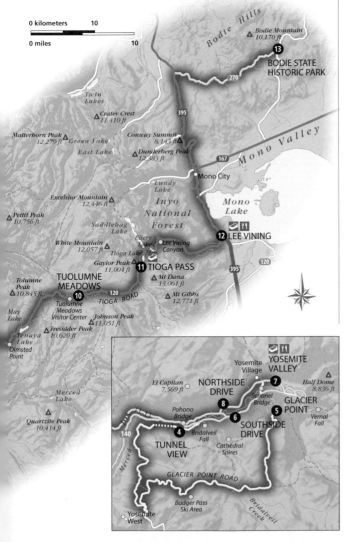

PLAN YOUR DRIVE

Start/finish: Moccasin to Bodie State Historic Park.

Number of days: 3–4 days, including 2 days to explore Yosemite National Park.

Distance: About 213 miles (343 km).

Road conditions: Well-paved except for the unpaved road to Bodie State Historic Park. The mountain access road to Yosemite is narrow and winding in places; snow chains are mandatory in winter months. Keep an eye out for falling rocks. The road to Glacier Point, and the Tioga Road (from Crane Flat to Lee Vining) are closed Nov–May or longer, due to snow.

When to go: The vast majority of visitors arrive in mid-summer, crowding Yosemite Valley. The waterfalls are at their best in late spring, when fed by snowmelt. Although the area is beautiful when crowned with snow, only part of this drive is accessible in winter.

Main market days: Groveland: 3–6pm Fri, 8am–1pm Sat.

Opening times: Yosemite National Park is open 24/7 year-round. Restaurant hours vary greatly. Most shops open 9am–5pm or longer daily.

Shopping: In Yosemite Valley, the Ansel Adams Gallery, Yosemite Museum Store, and The Ahwahnee Gift Shop sell Native American crafts and special edition prints.

Major festivals: Groveland: 49er Festival, Sep. **Yosemite National Park:** Bracebridge Dinner, Dec.

DAY TRIP OPTIONS

Wildlife lovers will be thrilled by the birds thronging **Mono Lake**, while deer, coyotes, and even black bears can be seen in **Yosemite Valley**. Those who enoy the **outdoors** can have a field day hiking to the **Yosemite Falls**. **Photographers** are spoilt for places, but key vantage vistas include **Tunnel View** and **Glacier Point**. For full details, see *p171*.

Right Don Pedro Lake, near Moccasin
Far right Hiking near Glacier Point
Below right Stunning vista of Yosemite Valley
from Tunnel View

VISITING GROVELAND

Tourist Information
Yosemite Chamber of Commerce
*11875 Ponderosa Lane, 95321; 209 962
0429; open 9am–3pm Mon–Fri;
www.groveland.org*

VISITING YOSEMITE
NATIONAL PARK

Tourist Information
209 372 0200; www.nps.gov/yose

Yosemite, Inc. handles reservations for
lodging and camping in the park, and
has information on available activities.
www.yosemitepark.com

Driving
Keep to the speed limit – the most
common human-related cause of
death for black bears is being hit by
speeding cars.

WHERE TO STAY

GROVELAND

Groveland Hotel *moderate*
This intimate B&B exuding yesteryear
charm is 23 miles (37 km) from the
park entrance.
*18767 Main St, 95321; 209 962 4000;
www.groveland.com*

AROUND GROVELAND

Blackberry Inn *moderate*
A ranch-style inn with a wraparound
porch, with individually styled rooms.
It is located 12 miles (19 km) west of
the park entrance.
*7567 Hamilton Station Loop, Buck
Meadows, 95321; 209 962 4663;
www.blackberry-inn.com*

YOSEMITE NATIONAL PARK

Crane Flat Campground *inexpensive*
Hook-ups for RVs, plus tent sites, all
with a fire ring, picnic table, and bear-
proof food locker. Showers and flush
toilets available. Reservations required.
*Crane Flat, Hwy 120, 95321; 877 444
6777; open summer only: usually Jul–
Sep; www.nps.gov/yose/planyourvisit/
campground.htm*

① Moccasin
Tuolumne County; 95347

The tiny community of Moccasin
lies at the head of **Don Pedro Lake**,
a jade-colored jewel that will
tempt visitors to sidetrack to
Moccasin Point Marina *(www.
moccasinpointmarina.com)* for an
hour or two of swimming, fishing
or watersports. Bald eagles can
sometimes be spotted perched
atop pines or scooping fish from
the water. Moccasin is owned by the
City and County of San Francisco,
which has its main power and
water project here: note the massive
pipes that drop water from the top
of Priest Grade – the switchback
mountain road above Moccasin – to
turbines below.

🚗 *From Moccasin, Hwy 120 begins a
long, sinuous ascent of the Priest
Grade to Groveland; drive cautiously
on the switchback bends.*

② Groveland
Tuolumne County; 95305

Steeped in Gold Rush-era ambience,
this erstwhile gold-mining and
lumbering town – formerly called
Garrotte for its swift and harsh
justice – abounds in old false-front
wooden and granite-block buildings.
The **Iron Door Saloon** on Main
Street, is said to be California's oldest
continuously operating saloon.
The saloon is remarkable, not least,
for its original iron doors, a 3.3-ft
(1-m) thick tin-covered natural sod
roof, and a small museum of natural
history specimens, Native American
artifacts, and historical miscellany.
Groveland is the last major
community before Yosemite
National Park and has many hotels,
restaurants, and a gas station.

🚗 *Drive 24 miles (39 km) east on Hwy
120 to Yosemite National Park's Big
Oak Flat entrance.*

Yosemite National Park

Declared America's second national park in 1906, this is undisputedly the most magnificent natural treasure in California. A visit here is *de rigueur* to admire its glacier-carved valley, granite cliffs, waterfalls, alpine meadows, and redwood forests. Accommodations within the park are limited, so book well in advance; lodgings outside the park are cheaper and easier to secure at the last minute.

Above The granite monolith, El Capitan
Below left Iron Door Saloon in Groveland
Below Sprawling oak grasslands, near Moccasin

❸ Big Oak Flat Road

Tuolumne County; 95389

Highway 120, called Big Oak Flat Road east of Groveland, is the main access road from San Francisco and the west to Yosemite National Park. From the Big Oak Flat entrance station, the road snakes through stands of Douglas fir and sugar and lodgepole pine. After 4.5 miles (7 km), turn off into the parking lot for the **Merced Grove**, where a sandy hiking trail leads downhill 1.5 miles (2 km) to a majestic stand of about 20 giant sequoias. If low on gas, stop at **Crane Flat** to fill up with fuel; there is no gas station in Yosemite Valley. From here, the highway offers sublime views as it snakes down to the valley. Just before passing through the first of three tunnels, pull into the **Valley Portal** vista point for the first view of the Yosemite Valley and Half Dome, plus a bird's-eye view of the V-shaped Merced River gorge below.

🚗 *Continue downhill to the junction with Hwy 41; turn left. Keep right and follow signs for Glacier Point (Hwy 41) park at Tunnel View vista point.*

❹ Tunnel View

Mariposa County; 95389

This vista point, with an iconic view east along the length of Yosemite Valley, is any photographer's delight. The valley is framed on the left by the sheer granite face of El Capitan, and by Cathedral Spires and Bridalveil Fall on the right, with Half Dome in the center. A bronze relief map helps identity the individual features, and signs explain the glacial and geological forces that shaped them. The vantage is named for the long tunnel that begins immediately west of the parking lot.

🚗 *Continue through the tunnel to the junction with Glacier Point Rd; turn left and continue uphill past Badger Pass Ski Area to Glacier Point. The road is closed Nov–May.*

❺ Glacier Point

Mariposa County; 95389

The paved path from the parking lot past the visitor center to Glacier Point offers great views of the Half Dome, Vernal Falls, and a sweeping panorama of the High Sierras. The views from on top of Glacier Point, however, are unmatched as Yosemite Valley unfolds in its entirety. Peer over the edge to look straight down to the valley floor 3,215 ft (980 m) below. Linger into the evening to enjoy the alpenglow, or moonrise, on the Sierra High Country.

🚗 *Return along Glacier Point Rd and Hwy 41 and turn right to follow the one-way system along Southside Rd.*

EAT AND DRINK

GROVELAND

Iron Door Saloon *moderate*
This nostalgic Western-style saloon offers filling "meat-n-potatoes" fare in winter, including bison burgers, plus Asian dishes in summer. Serves real ales. Live music.
18761 Main St, 95321; 209 962 6244; open 11am–9pm Mon–Thu, 11am–10pm Fri & Sat

VISITING YOSEMITE VALLEY

Tourist Information
*Yosemite Village, 95389; 209 372 0200;
open 9am–7:30pm daily; www.nps.
gov/yose, www.yosemitepark.com*

WHERE TO STAY

YOSEMITE VALLEY

Curry Village *inexpensive*
An official park hotel, "Camp Curry"
has been renting tented cabins with
shared bathrooms since 1899. Cabins
with private bathrooms are available
too. It can be noisy late into the night.
*Lower Pines, 95389; 801 559 4884;
www.yosemitepark.com*

Yosemite Lodge *moderate*
There are four rooms at this well-
furnished, official park lodge near
the base of Yosemite Falls.
*Northside Dr, 95389; 801 559 4884;
www.yosemitepark.com*

The Ahwahnee *expensive*
Another official hotel, the deluxe
Ahwahnee immerses guests
in history and comfort. The
renovated rooms and suites are
sumptuously appointed.
*9005 Ahwahnee Dr, Yosemite
Village, 95389; 801 559 4884;
www.yosemitepark.com*

Above right *View of the impressive Half
Dome* **Below** *The plunging Upper and
Lower Yosemite Falls*

⑥ Southside Drive
Mariposa County; 95389
Rising in the southeast corner of the
park, **Merced River** snakes along the
valley floor. This designated "wild and
scenic river" offers some calm
swimming spots; check with rangers
as it also has dangerous rapids. Rafts
can be rented at Curry Village, river
and weather conditions permitting.
Immediately east of the Tunnel View
turnoff (Highway 41), pass Bridalview
Meadow and pull in to the parking
lot for **Bridalveil Fall**. A trail leads to
the base of the fall, which plunges
617 ft (188 m) from atop a "hanging
valley." Drive on along Southside
Drive, admiring **Cathedral Spires** on
the right. Another 1.5 miles (2.5 km)
ahead, **Sentinel Beach** is a lovely

place to picnic. Continue to **Upper
Yosemite Falls Vista**, for the first
stunning views of North America's
highest waterfall. The meadow here
was the setting for the original
19th-century Yosemite Village; all that
remains of that hamlet is the Yosemite
Chapel. The road curls around to
Sentinel Bridge, famous for its views
of **Half Dome**, Yosemite's most
distinctive monument. The granite
monolith rises 8,835 ft (1,444 m)
above the valley floor to a wave-like
lip. Turn left and cross the bridge to
enter **Yosemite Village**, setting for the
visitor center, museum, and services.

🚗 *Turn right at Northside Dr. Take a
right turn into the public parking lot of
the Yosemite Valley. A shuttle takes
visitors to The Ahwahnee hotel.*

⑦ Yosemite Valley
Mariposa County
Four million visitors descend on Yosemite each year, most of them
to explore Yosemite Valley – a narrow, glacier-carved valley that
embraces one of the world's most outstanding concentrations of
waterfalls, granite formations, and breathtaking views. Visitors can
park the car to hike or bicycle the trails, or explore on valley shuttles.
Check with the visitor center or NPS website for presentations and
guided walks offered by rangers.

A three-hour walk
The Ahwahnee ① hotel is a good
place to start the walk. This historic
landmark was built of granite
boulders and huge wooden beams
in 1927. Its cavernous public hallways
and salons are furnished in Native
American style; look out for the
wood-paneled Mural Room for its
mural of Yosemite's flora and fauna.
From the hotel entrance, walk west
along Ahwahnee Drive. In spring, the
Royal Arch Cascade, to the northeast,
forms a veil over a granite cliff-face.

Turn right onto Village Drive and
follow it around the junction with
Indian Creek Road; turn left for the
Ansel Adams Gallery ② *(www.
anseladams.com)*. Owned by the
family of photographer Ansel Adams
since 1902, it displays and sells his
iconic prints. The **Wilderness Center**
③, immediately east of the gallery,
rents bear canisters *(see p171)* and
issues wilderness permits – a must
for those planning to hike the backcountry. Walk 55 yards (50 m) west to
the **Valley Visitor Center** ④ to learn

about the processes that shaped Yosemite. Exhibits here include an orientation film and a scale model of the park. Next door, the **Yosemite Museum** ⑤, an exemplary piece of "Rustic Style" architecture from 1928, focuses on interpreting the cultural history of Yosemite's Miwok and Paiute people from 1850 to the present. From the museum's west side, walk south along Oak Lane, which curls west to Northside Drive. The road's tree-lined footpath leads to **Lower Yosemite Falls Trail** ⑥, a mostly level path that leads to the base of the two-tier fall. The lower fall drops from a shelf that separates it from the Middle Cascades and, above, the Upper Yosemite Falls. Together, the cascade measures 2,425 ft (739 m) and is the sixth highest waterfall in the world. The falls are at their peak May–Jun, and by late summer they may cease flowing. Hikers in excellent physical condition can follow the Upper Yosemite Falls Trail, a 7-mile (11-km) round trip to the top of the falls; the trail begins 660 yards (600 m) west of the trailhead to Lower Yosemite Falls. Follow Northside Drive back to the car.

🚗 *From the parking lot, turn left onto Northside Dr.*

Ansel Adams

Nature photographer and environmentalist Ansel Adams is renowned for his visionary black-and-white images. He attributed his passion for photography to his first visit to Yosemite National Park in 1916. He published many books about Yosemite, the Sierras, and America's other national parks.

⑧ Northside Drive
Mariposa County; 95389
Beyond the Upper Yosemite Falls Trailhead, pass **Rocky Point**, where climbers practise their skills on a jumble of massive boulders created by a rock-fall in 1987. At Cathedral Spires Vista pullout, the views open up, providing a fine perspective of the twin Cathedral Spires and, adjacent, the hulking mass of **Cathedral Rock**, across the river. Continuing west, the road passes El Capitan Bridge. Just beyond, the emerald grasslands of El Capitan

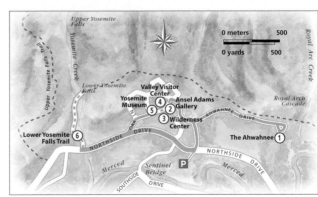

Meadow provide a neck-craning view straight up **El Capitan** ("the captain"). Be cautious here, as the roadside is usually busy with vehicles pulling in and out, and with gawkers scanning for climbers scaling the sheer granite wall that towers 3,593 ft (1,095 m) from base to summit.

Beyond the meadow, Northside Drive dips down the face of an ancient moraine, and the Merced River flows swiftly here. Breaks in the thick forest of oak and pine grant exceptional views of Bridalview Falls across the river. Stop at **Valley View**, about 1.5 miles (2.5 km) beyond El Capitan Bridge, for a perspective back along Yosemite Valley. Continue to Pohono Bridge, where visitors can turn left to return to the valley or drive on straight to continue the scenic drive (summer and fall only).

🚗 *Turn right on Big Oak Flat Rd and ascend to Crane Flat; after 9.5 miles (15 km), turn right on Tioga Rd (Hwy 120). Fill up with gas at Crane Flat.*

EAT AND DRINK

YOSEMITE VALLEY
Degnan's Deli *inexpensive*
Serves sandwiches and fresh salads. Upstairs, there is a pizza parlor and coffee shop, as well as Internet kiosks. *Village Dr & Awahnee Dr, 95389; 209 372 8454; open 7am–6pm daily; pizza parlor: closed winter*

Village Grill *moderate*
Fast food restaurant specializing in grilled dishes, from chicken to salmon burgers. *Village Dr, 95389; open 11am–6pm daily*

Ahwahnee Dining Room *expensive*
This elegant, fine-dining restaurant combines gourmet fare with a grandiose setting. *9005 Ahwahnee Dr, 95389; 209 372 1489; open for breakfast, lunch & dinner daily, 7am–3pm brunch Sun*

Below left Biking on a paved trail in Yosemite National Park **Below** White-water rafting on Merced River

Eat and Drink: inexpensive under $25; moderate $25–50; expensive over $50

Top Alpine Tenaya Lake, near Tioga Road
Above The deserted erstwhile gold-mining
town of Bodie **Above right** A marmot
spotted in Tioga Pass

VISITING MONO BASIN NATIONAL FOREST SCENIC AREA

Tourist Information
US 395, 93541; 760 647 3044; open 8am–5pm daily, closed Dec–Mar; www.monolake.org/visit/vc

WHERE TO STAY

CRANE FLAT TO TENAYA LAKE

White Wolf Lodge *inexpensive*
The official park hotel offers four cabins and 24 tented cabins nestled in an alpine meadow. No cooking facilities available.
White Wolf, Hwy 120, 95379; 801 559 4884; open Jul–mid-Sep; www.yosemitepark.com

TIOGA PASS

Tioga Pass Resort *moderate*
Rustic log cabins and a diner-style café with superb views. Owners operate a snowplow to maintain access via Lee Vining Canyon.
Saddlebag Lake Rd, 93541; www.tiogapassresort.com

LEE VINING

Lake View Lodge *Inexpensive*
Motel rooms and cozy wooden cabins set amid pine woodland.
51285 US 395, 93541; 760 647 6543; www.bwlakeviewlodge.com

9 Crane Flat to Tenaya Lake
Mariposa County; 95389
Tioga Road offers a 46-mile (77-km) scenic drive into the High Sierras in summer (usually closed Nov–May, depending on snow levels). The road rises gradually on the western slopes of the Sierras to 9,943 ft (3,031 m) at Tioga Pass before plunging steeply to Mono Lake. Park at the **Tuolumne Grove** parking lot about 0.6 miles (1 km) along Tioga Road. From here, a steep paved path leads downhill 1 mile (1.6 km) to a large stand of giant sequoias. Do not miss the **Tunnel Tree**, a dead sequoia with a road bored through it in 1878. Back on the sinuous Tioga Road, turn left to follow signs for **White Wolf**, which has accommodations and camping;

Above Trout fishing in Tenaya Lake, off Tioga Road

trails lead to Lukens Lake and Harden Lake. After another 14.5 miles (23 km), **Olmsted Point** offers a mesmerizing vista over Yosemite Valley. Descend to **Tenaya Lake**, which fills a basin gouged out by a former glacier. This scenic alpine lake is surrounded by rounded granite peaks scoured into a sheen by the ice.
🚗 *Drive east to Tuolumne Meadows.*

10 Tuolumne Meadows
Tuolumne County; 95389
Dome-studded and ablaze with wildflowers in spring, this vast alpine meadow is a starting point for some of the most rewarding hikes in the High Sierras. Stop at the **Tuolumne Meadows Visitor Center** for information; rangers can help decide which trails are right for specific abilities and interests. A short and easy trail leads to **Parsons Memorial Lodge**, a small stone building built in 1915 by the Sierra Club as its Yosemite headquarters; and to **Soda Springs**, pools of naturally carbonated water that attract deer at dawn and dusk.
🚗 *Exit the park at Tioga Pass.*

11 Tioga Pass
Mono County; 95389
The Tioga Pass Entrance to the park precedes a dramatic and memorable 12 mile (19 km) descent of Lee Vining Canyon, from High Sierra meadows at 9,741 ft (2,696 m) to the sagebrush scrub of the Mono Lake Basin, 3,000 ft (914 m) below. The entrance station occupies a saddle between Gaylor Peak and Mt Dana. The road has frequent turnouts for enjoying the views, such as man-made **Tioga Lake** and **Ellery Lake** and, beyond, the waterfall that plunges from Ellery Lake over the head of **Lee Vining Canyon**. The clear views down of the canyon are awesome. Watch for bighorn sheep on the canyon's rocky slopes.
    Drive carefully as stretches of the road have precipitous drop-offs and no guardrails, rock-falls are frequent, and the steep slopes are avalanche-prone in winter, particularly the long straight section immediately below Warren Fork, a hairpin bend at an elevation of 9,000 ft (2,743 m) .
🚗 *Descend 19 miles (30 km) to the T-junction with US 395, at Lee Vining. Turn left to enter town; park roadside.*

Store that Food

Black bears inhabit Yosemite and are drawn to easy sources of food, such as campgrounds, where they steal from tents and break into vehicles. It is illegal to leave food or *any* scented item, such as toothpaste, inside vehicles (except hard-sided RVs) at night. Use of bear-resistant food lockers is mandatory; they can be rented throughout the park. Bears often enter campsites, even when humans are present.

⑫ Lee Vining
Mono County; 93541

This small town is a major crossroads that acts as a service center for travelers arriving from or setting out to Yosemite National Park. After filling up on gas and supplies, walk over to the **Old School House Museum** *(www. historicoldhouse.com)*, next to Hess Park, to view Native American artifacts and rummage among the old farming and mining equipment. Squatting at the base of the eastern Sierra scarp, Lee Vining occupies a ledge with views down over **Mono Lake** *(see p189)*. When exiting town, stop at the **Mono Basin National Forest Scenic Area Visitor Center**, which has interactive displays on Mono Basin's

geology, ecology, and human history; trails lead from the viewing platform to the lake and its eerie tufa towers.

🚗 *Continue north 19 miles (30 km) on US 395 and turn right onto Bodie Rd for Bodie State Historic Park (signed). The last 3 miles (5 km) is unpaved; there is ample parking space.*

⑬ Bodie State Historic Park
Mono County; 93517

This park *(760 647 6445; open summer: 9am–6pm daily, winter: 9am–3pm daily)* protects a gold-mining ghost town preserved by its dry climate. Following a major strike of gold and silver ore in 1877, it exploded from a small mining community into a lawless town with a population of 10,000. It was one of the largest and wildest mining towns in the West, with more than 60 saloons and brothels. Bodie even had a small Chinatown on King Street, with its own saloons, gambling dens, and a Taoist temple. The town was abandoned almost a century ago when the gold played out. The remnants of the peak-era town were declared a National Historic Site in 1962. Many of its weathered wooden buildings are still stocked with furnishings and goods preserved in arrested decay.

Above left Unique tufa towers rising above the surface of Mono Lake **Below** Wooden chapel at Bodie State Historic Park

DAY TRIP OPTIONS

Yosemite Valley is a logical base for trips in the Yosemite National Park.

Take to the trails
It is possible to spend an entire day at Yosemite Valley ⑦ – trek to its tumbling waterfalls, look out for deer, or even a bear, and enjoy a picnic lunch with sensational views.

Make a complete loop of the valley

along Southside and Northside Drives.

Binoculars and camera...check!
Lee Vining ⑫ thrills birders with thousands of migrant birds at Mono Lake. Continue to fascinating Bodie State Historic Park ⑬ to take some excellent shots at this ghost town.

From Lee Vining, head north on Hwy 395 and follow signs for Bodie State Historic Park.

It's a snap
Tunnel View ④ and Glacier Point ⑤ are stunningly beautiful vista points that are a favorite among photographers. In winter, snap on ski boots at Badger Pass Ski Area, en route to Glacier Point.

From Tunnel View, Wawona Rd leads south to Glacier Point Rd; turn left for Badger Pass and Glacier Point.

Towering Trees and Gaping Gorges

Three Rivers to Fresno

Highlights

- **Giant sequoias**
  Stroll through groves of these massive trees in Sequoia and Kings Canyon National Parks

- **A king among canyons**
  Marvel at the sheer depth of the Kings Canyon

- **Alpine trails**
  Admire the wildflowers while walking in Crescent Meadow

- **Thundering cascades**
  Visit the dramatic waterfalls, such as Roaring River Falls, which dot this area

Gushing Clover Creek cutting across dense conifer forests, Sequoia National Park

Towering Trees and Gaping Gorges

Situated in the southern Sierra, the Sequoia and Kings Canyon National Parks are home to some of the most enormous trees in the world – the giant sequoias. The General Sherman Tree, named for US Civil War general William Tecumseh Sherman, is the most impressive, standing at a height of 275 ft (84 m). This route winds past amazingly diverse scenery, from the soaring peaks of the Sierra to exceedingly steep canyons. A fine example is the Kings Canyon, recording an 8,200-ft (2,499-m) drop between the Spanish Mountains and the Kings River. Vast areas of the parks are officially designated as wilderness, accessible only by trails, making this the perfect destination to take a break from driving and go cross-country hiking.

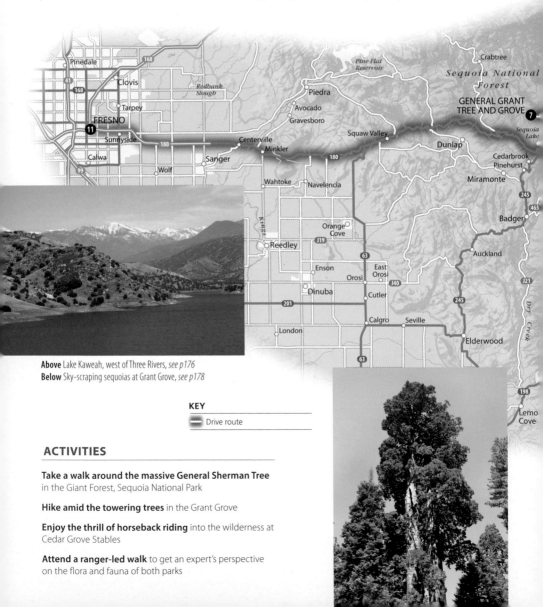

Above Lake Kaweah, west of Three Rivers, *see p176*
Below Sky-scraping sequoias at Grant Grove, *see p178*

KEY

 Drive route

ACTIVITIES

Take a walk around the massive General Sherman Tree in the Giant Forest, Sequoia National Park

Hike amid the towering trees in the Grant Grove

Enjoy the thrill of horseback riding into the wilderness at Cedar Grove Stables

Attend a ranger-led walk to get an expert's perspective on the flora and fauna of both parks

Map labels

Kennedy Mountain
11,433 ft ▲

Volcanic
Lakes

Goat Mountain
△ 12,207 ft

Mt Harrington ▲
11,009 ft

Granite
Lake

Kings

Middle Fork Kings

KINGS CANYON
SCENIC BYWAY

8

South Fork Kings

Kings Canyon
National Park

Mt Gardiner
12,907 ft
△

180

Hume Lake

Kings Canyon

Road's End

180

Hume

CEDAR
GROVE **9** **10**

Zumwalt Meadows

Bubbs Creek

6 GRANT GROVE
VILLAGE

Sentinal Ridge

ROARING
RIVER FALLS

Big Stump
Entrance

Mitchel Peak
10,365 ft ▲

Sugaloaf Creek

Deadman Canyon

Roaring

Great Western Divide

198

Big Baldy
8,211 ft
△

Kings-Kaweah Divide

Cluster Creek

Mt Silliman
△ 11,188 ft

469

GENERALS

Wuksachi

Big Bird
Lake

5 LODGEPOLE
VILLAGE

Moose
Lake

Lion
Lake

HIGHWAY

4 GIANT FOREST
CRESCENT MEADOW
3 ROAD

Sequoia
National Park

HOSPITAL
ROCK **2**

Moro Rock

Middle Fork Kaweah

Mt Eisen
12,160 ft
△

198

Kaweah

Foothills Visitor Center
Ash Mountain
Entrance

Kaweah

Hammond

1 THREE
RIVERS

East Fork Kaweah

Lake
Kaweah

South Fork Kaweah

0 kilometers   10

0 miles   10

PLAN YOUR DRIVE

Start/finish: Three Rivers to Fresno.

Number of days: 3 days, allowing at least one night in each park.

Distance: 260 miles (418 km).

Road conditions: Roads are paved and in good condition in summer through October. However, snow and rock-falls make some roads, such as Highway 180 to Cedar Grove, inaccessible in winter. Several sections in the parks are winding mountain roads with steep switchbacks. For more information call 559 565 3341 or check the park service website.

When to go: This is primarily a summer and fall drive opportunity, and rewarding drives can be undertaken until snow begins to fall around late October. However, popular winter sports, such as cross-country skiing, lure visitors to the region Nov–Mar. Note that there are sharp variations in temperature due to elevation differences, from 1,300 ft (396 m) to 14,494 ft (4,418 m).

Opening times: Visitor centers are open 9am–4:30pm in summer. Shops and restaurants usually open from 9am–9pm daily during the busy summer season.

Hiking in the wilderness: Make sure to prepare properly for any hikes in areas designated as wilderness. Check *www.fs.fed.us* or *www.nps.gov* for more information on hiking here.

DAY TRIP OPTIONS

A plethora of attractions await those who love the **outdoors** along this route. A visit to Sequoia National Park's **Crescent Meadow** offers a chance to spot bears in the wild, and the drive along the **Kings Canyon Scenic Byway** has stunning panoramas. For full details, *see p179*.

Above left Sequoia-rimmed Crescent Meadow, *see p176* **Left** Yucca plant on the roadside, Sequoia National Park, *see pp176–7*

Above Tranquil Lake Elowin Resort, Three Rivers **Above right** Tunnel Log, Crescent Meadow Road

VISITING SEQUOIA AND KINGS CANYON NATIONAL PARKS

Tourist Information
Drop-in visitor centers at Ash Mountain, Lodgepole Village, Grant Grove, and Cedar Grove provide information about the parks.

Foothills Visitor Center *47050 Generals Hwy, 93271; 559 565 3341; www.nps.gov/seki*

The Sequoia and Kings Canyon Park Services Company website provides information about authorized lodging options, plus tourist sights and activities *www.sequoia-kingscanyon.com*

WHERE TO STAY

THREE RIVERS

Buckeye Tree Lodge *moderate*
A clean motel-style lodging with a deck looking over the Kaweah River. The lodge is only a quarter mile (0.4 km) from the park entrance. The proprietors also have a sister property and house rentals.
46000 Sierra Dr, 93271; 559 561 5900

Lake Elowin Resort *moderate*
This serene resort has rustic cabins fronting a small lake in a park-like setting. Cabins are of various sizes, most with fully equipped kitchens.
43840 Dineley Dr, 93271; 559 561 3460; www.lake-elowin.com

① Three Rivers
Tulare County; 93271
This little community, located near Ash Mountain, the southern entry point into the twin parks, derives its name from the confluence of the three forks of **Kaweah River**. Hotels and restaurants are largely concentrated in and around the town. Three miles (5 km) west of the center lie the remains of the **Kaweah Colony**, a utopian socialist community that existed here in the 1880s. Highway 198 snakes along the Kaweah River, winding through chaparral landscape towards the parks' entrance. Stop for orientation at the Foothills Visitor Center, a mile (1.6 km) north of the entrance.
🚗 *Keep on Hwy 198 to Hospital Rock; there is a public parking lot.*

Sign for Sequoia National Park, near Ash Mountain Entrance

② Hospital Rock
Tulare County; 93271
A glorious alpine drive, the winding Highway 198 connects the two parks and is called the **Generals Highway**, referring to the Civil War heroes whose names have been honored by association with the largest sequoias in the parks. A roadside stop, Hospital Rock is decorated with rock drawings from an ancient Monache settlement. Archaeological evidence suggests Native American presence in this region as early as 1350. Beyond Hospital Rock, the **Four Guardsmen** – four giant sequoias – are a formidable sight.
🚗 *Drive on Hwy 198 (Generals Hwy) to the Giant Forest Museum; turn off here for Crescent Meadow.*

③ Crescent Meadow Road
Tulare County; 93271
En route to Crescent Meadow, stop at **Moro Rock**, and ascend to the top of this granite monolith to enjoy great views of the High Sierras. Back on the road, **Tunnel Log** is a tree that fell across the route in 1937. A hole has been cut through the bark for vehicles to pass under. Farther on lies the sequoia-rimmed **Crescent Meadow**. Look out for bears and the rare yellow-legged frogs at this wildflower-rich field.
🚗 *Return to the Giant Forest Museum and park here.*

④ Giant Forest
Tulare County; 93271
This grove of enormous sequoia trees was named Giant Forest by John Muir in 1875. He famously said that the trees appeared as "giants grouped in pure temple groves, or arranged in colonnades along the sides of meadows." The General Sherman Tree is in a league of its own, and gazing at this massive structure is awe-inspiring. Nearby, the Giant Forest Museum illustrates the botanical uniqueness of these big trees and recounts the story of their conservation.

A two-hour walking tour
Leave the car in the lot and head to explore the **Giant Forest Museum** ①, which provides a wealth of information about the natural history of the region. Converted from a market building, the museum makes for an interesting and informative visit. There are several exhibits on the magnificent trees, and displays trace the history of their conservation. John Muir was the first to make the case that the pioneer era of unrestrained resource exploitation, including the

rampant felling of big trees, should end. By 1885, political support became sufficient to start the process of saving some of the major groves of giant sequoias. From the museum take the park service shuttle to the General Sherman Tree parking lot, and begin the walk at the grove. It's only about 200 yards (182 m) to the **General Sherman Tree** ②, which is an essential photo-stop. This giant among sequoia trees is 275 ft (84 m) tall, with a 36.5 ft (11 m) diameter, and a circumference of 109 ft (33 m). It also contains an estimated 630,000 board feet of lumber. Walking around the base of the tree is an experience in itself. The General Sherman is also the trailhead for the **Congress Trail** ③, a 2-mile (3-km) stroll through the Giant Forest, with many marked stops at other famous sequoia trees. The altitude is 7,000 ft (2,134 m) and the terrain is undulating, so walk at a moderate pace to avoid getting tired too soon. The next famous giant is the **McKinley Tree** ④, honoring the 25th US president William McKinley. The **General Lee Tree** ⑤ is another attraction. In keeping with the tradition of honoring Civil War generals, the tree is a memorial to General Robert Edward Lee, commander of the Confederate Army of Northern Virginia. In close proximity is the handsome **President**

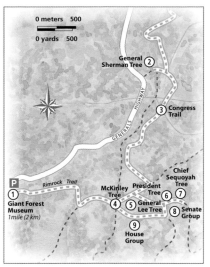

Tree ⑥, which is estimated to be at least 3,000 years old. Farther along the trail, the **Chief Sequoyah Tree** ⑦ was named for Sequoyah (around 1770–1843), a Cherokee Chief, who invented an independent Cherokee alphabet that made reading and writing possible for his people. The tree commemorates Sequoyah's contribution in facilitating the growth of literacy in the Cherokee tribe. Towards the south, six giant trees grouped together are called the **Senate Group** ⑧. Nearby, the **House Group** ⑨ is another cluster of sequoias. After exploring the Congress Trail, walk 2 miles (3 km) down Rimrock Trail to return to the Giant Forest Museum.

🚗 *Continue on Hwy 198 to Lodgepole Village. Roadside parking.*

Above Native American carvings on Hospital Rock **Below left** The enormous trunk of the General Sherman Tree, Giant Forest

EAT AND DRINK

THREE RIVERS

Anne Lang's Emporium *moderate*
This deli is a good place for lunch or to stock up for picnics in the parks. It has tables and a deck overlooking Kaweah River. Sandwiches are made to order. It is a local favorite for salads, soups, and fresh-baked goods.
41651 Sierra Dr, 93271; 559 561 4937; open 9am–4pm Mon–Sat

Right Wuksachi Lodge, near Lodgepole Village in Sequoia National Park **Below** Panoramic views of the High Sierras from an overlook, Kings Canyon National Park

WHERE TO STAY

AROUND LODGEPOLE VILLAGE

Montecito Sequoia Lodge *moderate*
A family-friendly lodge with all-inclusive packages. There are multi-day programs in summer, and snow sports in winter.
63410 Generals Hwy, 93633; 15 miles (25 km) N of the Lodgepole Village; 800 227 9900; open year-round; www.mslodge.com

Stony Creek Lodge *moderate*
This lodge on Forest Service land between the two parks can be booked through the Kings Canyon operator. The rooms have private baths.
12 miles (20 km) N of Lodgepole Village, 93633; 559 335 5500; open May–Oct; www.sequoia-kingscanyon. com/stonycreeklodge.html

Wuksachi Lodge *expensive*
An official park lodge, modern Wuksachi has a full-service restaurant, bar, and retail shops.
64740 Wuksachi Way, 93262; 888 252 5757; open year-round; www.visitsequoia.com

GRANT GROVE VILLAGE

John Muir Lodge *moderate*
The modern John Muir Lodge is an official park lodge in a woodsy setting with a stone fireplace lobby. All rooms have private baths.
93633; 559 335 5500; open year-round; www.sequoia-kingscanyon.com

CEDAR GROVE

Cedar Grove Lodge *moderate*
A timbered lodge on the Kings River, Cedar Grove has 18 rooms. A good base for exploring Kings Canyon. There is also a restaurant on site.
93633; 559 335 5500; open May–Oct; www.sequoia-kingscanyon.com

⑤ Lodgepole Village
Tulare County; 93262
Named for a pine tree species, the trunks of which were used to make lodge poles, this village is at the helm of visitor activities in Sequoia National Park. There is a visitor center and the village market is the only place within miles with a convenience store. Lodgepole is also a great base for hiking trips. Prime among the many trails that start here is the **Tokopah Valley Trail** which leads to a steep 1,200-ft (366-m) waterfall.

Farther ahead on Generals Highway, **Clover Creek**, a series of cascading streams set in conifer country, is a scenic stop with pullouts.
🚗 *Drive west on Hwy 198 (Generals Hwy) and at the intersection with Hwy 180, turn right into Grant Grove Village; park roadside.*

⑥ Grant Grove Village
Tulare County; 93633
The central stop in Kings Canyon National Park, Grant Grove Village has a visitor center and a central reservation service for lodging. Stock up on food supplies here and enjoy

a meal at the local restaurant. The General Grant Tree and Grove are the paramount attractions, but a 2.3-mile (3.7-km) drive up a ridge leads to **Panoramic Point**, a 7,520-ft (2,292-m) overlook that boasts breathtaking views of the crest of the Sierras.
🚗 *Continue north on Hyw 180 and turn left at the signed turnoff for General Grant Grove, which has a public parking lot.*

> #### The Giant Sequoia Tree
> Giant sequoias (*Sequoiadendron giganteum*) are the world's most massive trees in terms of volume. In fact, the trunk of the General Sherman Tree is equivalent in bulk to 15 adult blue whales. One giant sequoia may contain more wood than many acres of virgin timberland in the Pacific Northwest. However, the wood is brittle and not suitable for construction.

⑦ General Grant Tree and Grove
Tulare County; 93633
The Grant Grove area is home to the hefty General Grant Tree, the world's second biggest tree in total volume. It is a fairly young sequoia, aged only 1,800–2,000 years, amid a jungle of ancient 2,000–3,000 years old trees. President Coolidge designated it "the Nation's Christmas tree" in 1926, and 30 years later it was declared a living memorial to America's fallen war heroes by President Eisenhower. A couple of miles south of the grove, massive stumps cover the ground. The sight is a reminder of the extensive logging that took place in

this forest in the 19th century.

🚗 *Head back to Hwy 180, and then continue northeast towards Kings Canyon Scenic Byway.*

⑧ Kings Canyon Scenic Byway
Tulare County; 93633

This spectacular drive begins at the foothills of the western Sierras and climbs to the heart of the Kings Canyon, the South Fork of the Kings River running patiently along the road. Kings Canyon, carved by glacial and erosive forces, is the deepest in the US. Looking up at its steep, purple granite walls is an amazing experience.

🚗 *Continue east on Hwy 180 towards Cedar Grove, which has a parking lot.*

⑨ Cedar Grove
Toulare County; 93633

With its own visitor center and lodge, Cedar Grove is nestled on the valley floor, deep within the eastern interior of Kings Canyon. Amble along its trails on horseback trips arranged by the **Cedar Grove Stables**. Two granite monoliths – **Grand Sentinel** and **North Dome** – are the principal attractions, along with sensational views that extend across the canyons into the wild. John Muir compared this region to Yosemite Valley *(see pp168–9)*, observing that it is a "yet grander valley, of the same kind."

🚗 *Drive 3 miles (5 km) east on Hwy 180 to Roaring River Falls; park in the lot.*

⑩ Roaring River Falls
Tulare County; 93633

Roaring River Falls is a splendid waterfall on the south side of the road, with a turbulent stream snaking between huge granite boulders.

Next, stop at **Zumwalt Meadow**, a pasture resplendent with California black oak, incense cedar, and ponderosa pine. Farther ahead, **Road's End** is the starting point of many hiking trails into the wild.

🚗 *Backtrack by driving west through the park. Exit on Hwy 180, and continue down the west side of the foothills west to Fresno.*

⑪ Fresno
Fresno County; 93721

The road descending to Fresno passes through a conifer and broadleaf forest. A scenic 5 mile (8-km) drive south on Highway 245 to Pinehurst is recommended. Get back on Highway 180 and drive amid an oak and grassland setting.

The road to Fresno winds through Central Valley's fertile agricultural belt. Roadside stands sell local produce, including grapes, nuts and fruit, in season. If visiting during late Feb–early Mar, make sure to explore the Blossom Trail, a driving tour that meanders through fruit orchards, vineyards and citrus groves. The town has ample lodging and dining options and is a good place to stay overnight or to stop for a meal.

Above left Soaring granite walls of the Kings Canyon **Above** The drive to Pinehurst, Highway 245

EAT AND DRINK

LODGEPOLE VILLAGE

Lodgepole Market *moderate*
The Watchtower Deli and Harrison BBQ and Grill serve burgers, pizzas, sandwiches, and wraps.
63204 Lodgepole Rd, 93262; 559 565 3301; open May–Oct

AROUND LODGEPOLE VILLAGE

Montecito Sequoia Lodge Restaurant *moderate*
Buffet breakfast, lunch, and dinner for lodgers. Call ahead for drop-in dining.
63410 Generals Hwy, 93633; 15 miles (25 km) N of the Lodgepole Village; 800 227 9900; open year-round

GRANT GROVE VILLAGE

Grant Grove Restaurant *moderate*
Serves meat and fish dishes, plus pizza in summer.
93633; 559 335 5500; open year-round

CEDAR GROVE

Cedar Grove Lodge Restaurant *moderate*
Try hearty eggs and hash browns for breakfast, burgers and sandwiches for lunch, and grilled chicken, pork chops, or trout at dinner.
93633; 559 565 0100; open May–Oct

DAY TRIP OPTIONS
Both the Sequoia and Kings Canyon National Parks can be explored on day trips.

Down in the meadow
The road to Crescent Meadow ③ and a walk in the meadow itself make for a fun day's outing. Enjoy the panoramas from Moro Rock which are some of the best views in the park. Clearly marked turnoffs

along the road lead to monumental stands of giant sequoias. Enjoy a leisurely walk around this alpine meadow, where bears and rare yellow-legged frogs can sometimes be spotted. Several hiking trails into the forested back country depart from here.

The road to Crescent Meadow is a well-signed turnoff at Hyw 198 (Generals Hwy).

Canyons and cascades
Pick up the fixings for a picnic at Grant Grove Village ⑥ before setting out on the Kings Canyon Scenic Byway ⑧, which rewards with stunning canyon and river views. Stop to admire the Roaring River Falls ⑩, before picnicking at the lush Zumwalt Meadow.

Follow Hwy 180 for 34 miles (55 km) from Grant Grove to Zumwalt Meadow.

Eat and Drink: inexpensive under $25; moderate $25–50; expensive over $50

Rugged Owens Valley

Lone Pine to Mono Lake Tufa State Reserve

Highlights

- **Dizzying heights**
  Look up at the soaring peak of magnificent Mt Whitney

- **Age-old bristlecones**
  Hike amid the weather-beaten, venerable trees in the Ancient Bristlecone Pine Forest

- **Mountain wilderness**
  Get an adrenaline rush while biking, fishing, canoeing, or skiing at Mammoth Lakes

- **Jade jewel**
  Marvel at the magnificent birdlife and unique tufa towers of Mono Lake

Mt Whitney Road snaking through the jagged landscape of Whitney Portal

Rugged Owens Valley

The little-known Owens Valley, a 75-mile (120-km) long rift valley between the Sierra Nevada and White Mountains chain, offers what is probably the most dramatically scenic drive in all of California. The flat, straight valley at 4,000 ft (1,200 m) is framed by snow-capped peaks that soar to 14,000 ft (4,300 m) on either side. Short side trips into the mountains lead to majestic natural wonderlands, including towering Mt Whitney, ancient Bristlecone pines, and the sparkling lakes and volcanic marvels of Mammoth Lakes. The route along US 395 leads past several sites of historic interest and stitches together a chain of small, laid-back Old Western towns, and there are lots of great spots for hiking here too.

Above Volcanic cones and snow-capped peaks near Mono Lake, *see p189*
Below Kite-surfing on the alpine June Lake, *see p189*

0 kilometers 15

0 miles 15

KEY

Drive route

ACTIVITIES

Relive old Western movies amid the granite boulder formations of the Alabama Hills

Hike the trails to the summit of Mt Whitney along the Mt Whitney Trail

Admire the rugged resilience of the bristlecone pines while hiking above 10,000 ft (3,000 m) in the Ancient Bristlecone Pine Forest

Fish for trout in the crystal clear waters of Twin Lakes

Go kite-sailing across the jade-colored waters of June Lake

Spot birds such as pharalopes, grebes, and tundra swans at Mono Lake

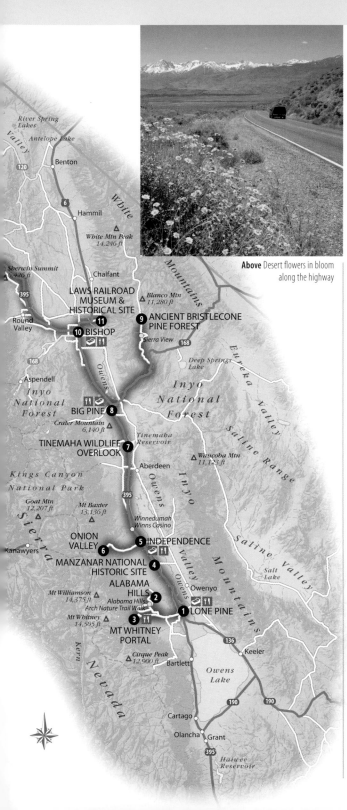

Above Desert flowers in bloom along the highway

PLAN YOUR DRIVE

Start/finish: Lone Pine to Mono Lake Tufa State Reserve.

Number of days: 2–3 days.

Distance: 258 miles (415 km).

Road conditions: The main route along US 395 is well-maintained. The mountain roads to Mt Whitney Portal and Ancient Bristlecone Pine Forest are serpentine and extremely steep in places. These two roads and the mountain pass on US 395 north of Mammoth Lakes are often snowbound and tire chains may be required. The road to Devil's Postpile National Monument is usually closed in winter and spring due to snow.

When to go: This route has something to offer year round. The climate is delightful in spring and late fall. Summer days can be hot, but the mountain roads are free of snow. In winter, fresh snow adds to the scenery and offers great opportunities for skiing, and bird-watching at Mono Lake.

Main market days: Bishop: Jul–Oct: 9am–noon Sat. Mammoth Lakes: 4–7pm Sat.

Opening times: Most museums open Tue–Sat, although some open on Sun as well. A few close in winter. Restaurants usually open until about 10pm; shops typically open from 9am–6pm Mon–Sat, but some also open Sun.

Major festivals: Lone Pine: Film Festival, Oct. Bishop: Bishop Mule Days, May. Mammoth Lakes: Jazz Jubilee, Jul; Music Festival, Jul–Aug.

DAY TRIP OPTIONS

Hikers will want to lace up their boots at **Mt Whitney** and **Alabama Hills**, while **amateur geologists** will get excited about fascinating formations of the **Devil's Postpile**, **Mono Lake**, and **Obsidian Dome**. History buffs can relive the past at **Laws Railroad Museum**, **Manzanar National Historic Site**, and various history museums across this area. For full details, *see p189*.

Above Lone Pine Film History Museum, Lone Pine **Above right** Rock formations, Alabama Hills

VISITING LONE PINE

Tourist Information
Eastern Sierra Interagency Visitor Center has superb exhibits and provides information for travelers in the Eastern Sierras and northern Mojave Desert *US 395 & SR 136, 93545; 760 876 6200; open 8am–5pm daily*

Parking
Park for free along Main St.

WHERE TO STAY

LONE PINE

Dow Villa Motel *inexpensive*
A standard motel in a great location, and near several restaurants. There is also a swimming pool.
310 S Main St, 93545; 760 876 5521; www.dowvillamotel.com

INDEPENDENCE

Ray's Den Motel *inexpensive*
A quaint motel with simply furnished rooms and landscaped grounds. Guests are well-cared for by the owner.
405 N Edwards, 93526; 760 878 2122

Winnedumah Hotel *inexpensive*
Built in the 1920s, this cozy and homey hotel has 28 rooms, a restaurant, and garden patio.
211 N Edwards St, 93526; 760 878 2040; www.winnedumah.com

BIG PINE

Glacier Lodge *inexpensive*
There are simple self-catering cabins, a RV park with hook-ups, and a general store at this alpine lodge.
Glacier Lodge Rd, 93513; 760 938 2837; www.jewelofthesierra.com

Bristlecone Manor Motel *moderate*
This tastefully furnished motel has 17 rooms with kitchenettes. A gas station and general store are attached.
101 N Main St, 93513; 760 938 2067; www.bristleconemotel.com

Where to Stay: inexpensive under $100; moderate $100–200; expensive over $200

➊ Lone Pine
Inyo County; 93545
This small town at the northern fringe of the Mojave Desert is the southern gateway to Owens Valley. Its wooden buildings dating to the 19th century lend it a frontier town feel. The tiny **Southern Inyo Museum** *(127 W Bush St; timings vary)* has a miscellany of historic memorabilia, and the **Lone Pine Film History Museum** *(www.lonepine filmhistorymuseum.org)* includes a stagecoach among its many "Westerns" mementos.
The spires of Mt Whitney and the snow-tipped southernmost peaks of the Sierra Nevada soar west of town. **Owens Lake**, 5 miles (8 km) south of town, is a dry lake that formed from glacial melt during the last ice age, but which was drained in the early 1900s to supply water to Los Angeles; it is now being rehabilitated.
🚗 **Turn west off Main St onto Whitney Portal Rd for the Alabama Hills.**

Information sign at Alabama Hills

➋ Alabama Hills
Inyo County; 93545
Movie buffs will recognize these dramatic formations from *The Lone Ranger* or the action-packed *Gladiator* (2000). More than 250 film productions have been shot in this rugged environment of unusual granite and metamorphic formations set against the sharp ridges of the Sierra Nevada. A "Movie Road" self-guided tour map can be down-loaded from the US Bureau of Land Management website *(www.blm.gov)*. The **Alabama Hills Arch Nature Trail Walk** leads to natural rock arches.
🚗 **Continue west on Whitney Portal**

Rd to Mt Whitney Portal. Note that some parking areas are for day use; others are for overnight. Remove all food and scented items from the parked car to guard against black bears breaking in.

➌ Mt Whitney Portal
Inyo County
After zigzagging uphill through conifer forest, the road ends at Whitney Portal, surrounded by granite walls at 8,360 ft (2,550 m). En route, the views down over Owens Valley and of the sheer-faced western scarp of the Sierras are magnificent, and pullouts offer a chance to photograph in safety. The **Mt Whitney Trail** is a challenging 22-mile (35-km) round-trip hike to the summit at 14,505 ft (4,421 m). Day-use and/or overnight permits are required and can be requested up to 6 months in advance *(760 873 2483; www.fs.usda.gov/inyo)*. Walk-in permits depend on the available space between May–Nov. Bear-resistant food canisters are mandatory and can be rented at Whitney Portal Store.
🚗 **Return to Lone Pine and turn left onto US 395 for the Manzanar (19 miles/ 30 km) parking lot, signed.**

➍ Manzanar National Historic Site
Inyo County; 93526
This site *(www.nps.gov/)* was created in 1992 on the site of the Manzanar War Relocation Center, where 10,000 Japanese-Americans were interred during World War II. The visitor center has superb exhibits, screens a film, and also tells the stories of Owens Valley's Paiute Native Americans, the homesteading era, and the fruit orchards that once flourished locally. Pick up a map before taking the 3.2-mile (5-km) self-guided driving tour that leads past the main sites, including a re-created guard tower. Stop at the cemetery, where a monument is draped with colorful strings of origami and strewn with mementos by survivors and visitors.
🚗 **Drive north on US 395 to Independence; park at the Interpretive Center.**

⑤ Independence

Inyo County; 93526

The town began life as US Army Fort Independence, established in 1865 to quell Native American hostilities. Today, it is the capital of Inyo County. The imposing **Inyo County Courthouse** *(N Edwards St & Center St)* dates from 1922 and is the region's only example of Neo-Classical Revival public architecture. From the courthouse, Center Street leads west to the **Eastern California Museum** *(www.inyocounty.us/ecmuseum)*, worth a visit for its collection of Paiute and Shoshone basketry, and other displays on Native American culture, natural history, and local history. The grounds are littered with old wagons and rusting farm and mining equipment.

🚗 *Turn left by the post office onto Market St (Onion Valley Rd) and follow it 13 miles (20 km) to Onion Valley Trailhead, where a fee must be paid.*

⑥ Onion Valley

Inyo County

This valley is a main gateway to the John Muir Wilderness Area and the 2,650-mile (4,265-km) long **Pacific Crest Trail**. The road switchbacks up the valley to a parking area at 9,200 ft (2,804 m), surrounded by towering peaks. Three trails weave into the eastern Sierra from Onion Valley Trailhead. The popular 11-mile (18-km) round-trip **Kearsarge Pass Trail** leads up to Little Pothole Lake – the first of many lakes in this region – then Gilbert Lake, set amid fantastic boulder formations. Continue uphill to **Kearsarge Pass** at 11,823 ft (3,604 m) for a breathtaking view over Sequoia/ Kings Canyon National Parks, *(see pp176–9)*. Campers must make reservations at least 4 days in advance *(760 937 6070; www.recreation.gov)*.

🚗 *Return to Independence and*

continue north on US 395; after 18.5 miles (29 km) turn right onto an unpaved road for Tinemaha Wildlife Overlook (not signed).

⑦ Tinemaha Wildlife Overlook

Inyo County

Created by a dam built on the Owens River in 1992, the Tinemaha Reservoir is Inyo County's best location for viewing wintering waterfowl such as Tundra swans, Canada geese, and American white pelicans. Bald eagles can also be seen in winter. The signed overlook sits above a wetland frequented by tule elk and has interpretive panels.

🚗 *Continue on US 395 to Big Pine.*

⑧ Big Pine

Inyo County; 93513

Stop at the town's **Carroll Thomas Gallery** *(www.carrollthomasgallery.net)*, where the centenarian artist still produces beautiful Plein Air paintings of the Owens Valley. The Sierra foothills east and west of town are dotted with volcanic cones, red cinder, and dark basaltic lava flows. For a close-up view of the largest cone, **Crater Mountain**, turn west on Crocker Street (it becomes Glacier Lodge Road); turn left onto McMurray Meadow Road, a dirt road to the west side of the cone. Returning to Glacier Lodge Road, turn left and follow the course of **Big Pine Creek** to the head of Big Pine Canyon, with campgrounds at about 8,000 ft (2,400 m). Two moderately strenuous hiking trails (11 mile/18 km round-trip) lead to alpine lakes with views of the Palisades Glacier.

🚗 *In Big Pine, turn east on US 168. Turn left onto White Mountain Rd and continue for 10 miles (16 km) to Ancient Bristlecone Pine Forest. The road is usually closed Dec to mid-May.*

Above Old farm machinery at the Eastern California Museum, Independence **Below left** Mt Whitney Road at Mt Whitney Portal

EAT AND DRINK

LONE PINE

Mt Whitney Restaurant *moderate*
A classic American diner serving omelets, burgers, and fries. Try the turkey with gravy and mashed potato. *227 S Main St, 93545; 760 876 5751; open 6am–10pm daily*

MT WHITNEY PORTAL

Mt Whitney Portal Store *moderate*
The only eatery in the mountains, this trailhead store serves pancakes and eggs, plus burgers and fries, hot dogs, and chicken sandwiches. *Mt Whitney Portal, 93545; open May & Oct: 9am–6pm daily, Jun & Sep: 8am–8pm daily, Jul & Aug: 7am–9pm daily; www.whitneyportalstore.com*

INDEPENDENCE

Still Life Café *moderate*
This French restaurant with a charming, bistro-like feel is famous for their onion soup and other French favorites. The menu changes daily. *135 S Edwards St, 93520; 760 878 2555; open noon–9pm Wed–Sun*

BIG PINE

Dick's Smoke Wagon *inexpensive*
This mobile wagon serves ribs with coleslaw, plus smoked chicken, pulled pork, and beef sandwiches, and bacon wrapped jalapeños stuffed with cream cheese. *310 N Main St, 93513; 760 550 2866; open 11am–7pm Wed–Sun; www.dickssmokewagon.com*

Above left The Sierra Nevada seen from Sierra View outlook, Ancient Bristlecone Pine Forest
Below Hikers setting out on the Discovery Trail through Ancient Bristlecone Pine Forest

WHERE TO STAY

BISHOP

Chalfont House B&B *inexpensive*
One block off Main Street, this B&B has seven individually styled rooms and an old-style parlor.
213 Academy Ave, 93514; 760 872 1790; www.chalfanthouse.com

Joseph House Inn *moderate*
Myriam and Hilde, the owners at this B&B, go out of their way to make guests feel at home. Set in exquisite gardens, this California Rambler-style inn has five lovely sunlit rooms.
376 W Yaney St, 93514; 760 872 3389; www.josephhouseinn.com

AROUND CROWLEY LAKE

Tom's Place Resort *inexpensive*
Rustic one- to three-bedroom log cabins with kitchens in a woodsy setting. There is a general store and restaurant as well.
8180 Crowley Lake Dr, 93546; 760 935 4239; www.tomsplaceresort.com

⑨ Ancient Bristlecone Pine Forest

Inyo County

Located high in the White Mountains, running parallel to the Sierra Nevada on the east side of Owens Valley, the Ancient Bristlecone Pine Forest offers staggering views. The wind-whipped Sierra View lookout near the parking lot offers a remarkable vista of the entire length of Owens Valley and the snow-capped Sierras. Another 2 miles (3 km) uphill, the visitor center is the starting point for trails that weave past the contorted and twisted bristlecone pines. The 4.5-mile (7.5-km) Methuselah Trail leads past "Methuselah", the oldest tree in the world – it sprouted in 2832 BC and still produces seeds.

A one-hour walking tour

Perfect for anyone not wanting to hike the longer Methuselah Trail, the 1-mile (1.6-km) Discovery Trail loops through Sherman Grove. Begin at the **visitor center** ①, which has superb exhibits on local geology, climate, and flora and fauna. The first of eight interpretive panels, **Panel One** ② provides an introduction to the trail and tells the story of Dr. Edmund Schulman's discovery of the trees in 1953. The trail then begins to switchback up the limestone slope. **Panel Two** ③, beside a fallen pine, explains about growth rings and how Schulman used them to ascertain past climatic changes. Continue to **Panel Three** ④ to read about the pines' unique adaptations. Photographers will revel in the views west across Reed Flat towards snow-capped Sierra Nevada peaks. The path climbs past some impressive pines, where Schulman discovered the first live tree known to exceed 4,000 years of age, as explained at **Panel Four** ⑤. The trail then winds through a barren **scree slope** ⑥ of shattered red rock, offering good vistas north along the crest of the range towards Blanco Mountain. Continue down the switchback on the north scarp of the scree to pass the most impressive trees of all. **Panel Five** ⑦ describes how the individual tree's genes determine their shapes. Follow the gentle grade downhill to **Panel Six** ⑧, which profiles the

Bristlecone pines

Great Basin bristlecone pines (*Pinus longaeva*) grow only at 9,800–11,000 ft (3,000–3,400 m). Scorched by high desert sun and blasted by sub-zero winds, these tenacious trees grow in limestone where rainfall averages only 10 inches (25 cm) a year. The pine grows only during a 6-week period beginning in early May. Many are kept alive by a single strip of live bark running up their trunks. Dense wood and thick resin protect bristlecones from bacteria, pests, and fungi.

work and legacy of Dr. Schulman. **Panel Seven** ⑨, a stone's throw away, points to a nearby hillside of white-colored dolomite dotted with bristlecones. **Panel Eight** ⑩ explains how the shorter, weather-beaten trees on the southern canyon slopes are older than the taller trees facing north. Continue

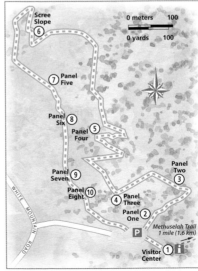

on the trail as it loops back round to the parking lot.

🚗 *Return to Big Pine and continue 14.5 miles (23 km) north on US 395 to Bishop. Park on Main St.*

⑩ Bishop
Inyo County; 93514

The largest town in Owens Valley, Bishop has plenty of restaurants, hotels, and services, and is a perfect base for recreational activities that range from biking and fishing to horsepack trips. Founded in the 1860s, it still retains many false-front 19th-century wooden buildings, and cottonwood trees line its handsome Main Street. Bishop was the home of world-renowned mountaineer and National Geographic Photographer Laureate Galen Rowell (1940–2002). Many of Rowell's amazing images of the Sierras and around the world are on display and for sale at the **Mountain Light Gallery** *(www. mountainlight.com)*, in a former bank building: note the pressed-tin ceiling and original bank vault.

Pick up a map at Bishop's Chamber of Commerce & Visitor Bureau for a self-guided tour of the town's 10 striking wall murals. The bureau is in **Bishop City Park**, where walking paths lined with quaking aspens lead past a lake.

🚗 *At the north end of Main St, take SR 6 for Laws (keep straight, as Hwy 395 swings west). Turn right on Silver Canyon Rd and park in the lot at Laws Railroad Museum.*

⑪ Laws Railroad Museum & Historical Site
Inyo County; 93515

This remarkable museum *(www.lawsmuseum.org)* preserves the legacy of the last narrow gauge railroad west of the Rockies at the original Laws Depot, complete with the turntable. It hosts a fascinating collection of railroad memorabilia, including the "Slim Princess" Baldwin 4-6-0 steam train, dating from 1909. The village's 28 buildings include a blacksmith shop, a post office, a general store, and even a dentist's

"Slim Princess", Laws Railroad Museum

Top Stark landscape around Crowley Lake
Above left Gnarled bristlecone, Ancient Bristlecone Pine Forest **Above** Laws Depot, Laws Railroad Museum & Historical Site

office, all furnished in period style. There is also a carriage horse with saddles and horse-drawn hearse.

🚗 *Return to US 395 and continue 28 miles (45 km) north over the Sherwin Summit pass to Crowley Lake. Park at the roadside lot by the lake.*

⑫ Crowley Lake
Mono County

This reservoir on the upper Owens River was created in 1941 by the Long Valley Dam and is backed by Glass Mountain and, beyond, the White Mountains – a magnificent setting. Measuring 12 miles (19 km) long by 5 miles (8 km) wide, it is the largest reservoir in the Los Angeles Department of Water & Power system. The lake is famous for its hard-fighting rainbow trout and Sacramento perch. Fishing enthusiasts can contact the **Crowley Lake Fish Camp** *(www.crowleylakefishcamp. com)*, which has the sole fishing concession at the lake, as well as a marina.

🚗 *Continue 12 miles (19 km) north to the junction with SR 203 and exit for Mammoth Lakes. Follow the signs to the California Welcome Center.*

VISITING BISHOP

Tourist Information
Chamber of Commerce & Visitor Bureau *690 N Main St, 93514; 760 873 8405; www.bishopvisitor.com*

EAT AND DRINK

BISHOP

Erick Schat's Bakery *inexpensive*
Serves fresh baked breads, pastries, split pea soup, salads, pastrami, roast beef, and corned beef sandwiches.
763 N Main St, 93514; 760 873 7156; open 6am–6pm Mon–Thu, 6am–8pm Fri, 6am–6:30pm Sat & Sun; www.erickschatsbakery.com

La Casita *moderate*
Excellent Mexican fare. The portions are huge and service is friendly. It also does takeouts.
175 S Main St, 93514; 760 873 4828; open 11:30am–9pm daily

AROUND CROWLEY LAKE

Tom's Place Resort *inexpensive*
This decades-old institution serves home-made biscuits and gravy, tuna melts, and fresh milkshakes.
8180 Crowley Lake Dr, 93546; 760 935 4239; open 7am–9pm daily; www.tomsplaceresort.com

Eat and Drink: inexpensive under $25; moderate $25–50; expensive over $50

VISITING MAMMOTH LAKES

Tourist Information
Mammoth Lakes Welcome Center
*2510 Hwy 203, 93546; 760 924 5500;
open 8am–5pm daily; www.visitcwc.
com/MammothLakes*

WHERE TO STAY

MAMMOTH LAKES

Westin Monache Resort *expensive*
Exuding class, this 230-room condo-
hotel is the most elegant in the
area. Its complete range of services
includes a spa and a ski valet.
*50 Hillside Dr, 93546; 760 934 0400;
www.westinmammoth.com*

JUNE LAKE LOOP

Gull Lake Lodge *moderate*
This motel between June and Gull
Lakes offers self-catering apartment
units with pine furnishings.
*132 Bruce Ave, June Lake, 93529; 760
648 9081; www.gulllakelodge.com*

⑬ Mammoth Lakes
Mono County; 93546

The resort town of Mammoth Lakes, surrounded by pine-clad
mountains at 7,880 ft (2,402 m), occupies the slopes of the Long
Valley Caldera – a basin formed by a massive volcanic explosion
760,000 years ago. The area is one of the most geologically active
in North America, with hot springs and lava flows that are less than
1,000 years old. One of California's premier ski destinations in winter,
it is also a popular venue for high-altitude hiking, mountain biking,
and horseback rides in summer.

After visiting the California Welcome
Center, drive west 360 yards (330 m)
on US 203, turn left at the "Hospital"
sign; continue to Meridian Boulevard
and turn left for the **Mammoth Ski
Museum** *(www.mammothlakes
foundation.org/museum.html)*, with a
huge collection of vintage artifacts
and photographs related to skiing.
The region's history as a gold-mining
center is regaled at **Mammoth
Museum** *(5489 Sherwin Creek Rd; 760
934 6918; open 10am–5:30pm daily)*,
housed in a log cabin; to get there,
take Meridian Boulevard west, turn
left on Old Mammoth Road, then left
onto Sherwin Creek Road. Now
return to US 203 and turn left. It
becomes Lake Mary Road, which
snakes uphill to **Mammoth Lakes
Basin**. The area is named for five
jade-colored lakes – popular for
fishing and boating – that fill hollows
scooped out by ancient glaciers. The
road beyond Lower Twin Lake often
remains closed until June. Snowmelt
feeds **Twin Lakes Overlook**, where
water plunges 330 ft (100 m) over a
volcanic shelf into Upper Twin Lakes.
Now return to the village and turn
left on Minaret Road, enjoying the

fabulous scenery while ascending to
the **Mammoth Mountain Ski Area &
Bike Park**, a popular downhill skiing
(winter), and hiking and mountain
biking (summer) area on the slopes
of a dormant volcanic peak. Year-
round gondola rides reward with a
sensational view. The **Top of the
Sierra Interpretive Center** has
exhibits on the area's geology,
natural history, and cultural heritage.
Beyond the ski center, Minaret Road
usually remains closed into June,
when snow abates: note that cars
must be traded for a mandatory
shuttle *(7:15am–7pm)*, which stops at
key points along the way. The road
ends in Reds Meadow Valley. Here
trails lead to **Rainbow Falls**, where
the San Joaquin River plunges 101 ft
(31 m) over a ledge, creating a
rainbow at its base, and the **Devil's
Postpile National Monument** *(www.
nps.gov/depo)*, a dramatic cliff of
hexagonal basaltic columns.
🚗 *Return along Minaret Rd; turn
left onto Mammoth Scenic Loop to
return to US 395. Exit left on unpaved
Obsidian Dome Rd for Obsidian
Dome. Drive around the dome to
its south side and park.*

Above right Mammoth Lakes, ensconced
within thick pine forest **Below** Ski run at
Mammoth Mountain Ski Area & Bike Park

⑭ Obsidian Dome
Mono County
This circular volcanic dome is one of a chain of 27 domes, three large magma flows, called *coulees*, and various other volcanic features that comprise the Mono–Inyo Craters chain, stretching 25 miles (40 km) from the Mono Lake to Mammoth Mountain. Formed within the past 5,000 years, this obsidian dome has a 1-mile (1.6- km) diameter. Hike the short trail up to the summit.
🚗 *Continue north on US 395. Turn left onto June Lake Rd.*

⑮ June Lake Loop
Mono County; 93529
Taking in a chain of four lakes beneath the steep eastern escarpment of the Sierra Nevada, this 16-mile (26-km) loop is particularly scenic in fall when the aspen trees turn to gold and maroon. Surrounded on all sides by tall snow-clad peaks, the horseshoe-shaped valley is known as the "Switzerland of California." The canyon was carved by the Rush Creek glacier, which split when it came into contact with the Reversed Peak. The alpine community of June Lake occupies a

ridge between **June Lake**, which is popular for kite-surfing, and the smaller **Gull Lake**, favored for fishing. The **June Mountain Ski Area** *(760 648 7733; www.junemountain.com)* offers downhill skiing *(Dec–Apr)* and guided nature tours *(10:30am & 1pm Fri–Sun)*.
🚗 *Complete the loop. Turn right onto US 395 and drive south 650 yards (600 m) to SR 120; turn left and continue to the public lot at South Tufa Grove.*

⑯ Mono Lake Tufa State Reserve
Mono County; 93541
This reserve was created in 1982 to protect the eerie tufa towers and other natural features of Mono Lake. This shallow, circular lake was formed at least 760,000 years ago and has no outlet to the ocean. Microscopic algae breed and photosynthesize, changing the lake's color seasonally from azure to jade and, by spring, pea-soup green. Brine shrimp thrive in the super saline waters, providing a food source for two million annual migratory birds, including American avocets, phalaropes, eared grebes, and the state's second largest nesting population of California gulls. Mono Lake's most prominent feature is the once-submerged tufa towers, exposed when the Los Angeles Department of Water & Power began diverting water from the lake in 1941. Trails lead through the **South Tufa Grove**, where these spires formed by the underwater accumulation of calcium carbonate reach heights of more than (33 ft) 10 m. **Mono Basin National Forest Scenic Area Visitor Center**, north of Lee Vining *(see p171)*, offers excellent exhibits on the local ecology and cultural heritage.

Above Tufa towers at South Tufa Grove, Mono Lake **Below** Alpine meadow near June Lake

VISITING JUNE LAKE LOOP

Tourist Information
Chamber of Commerce
www.junelakeloop.org

VISITING MONO LAKE TUFA STATE RESERVE

Tourist Information
Mono Basin National Forest Scenic Area Visitor Center *1 Visitor Center Dr, Lee Vining, 93541; 760 647 6331; www.parks.ca.gov/*

Mono Lake Committee *Hwy 395 & 3rd St, Lee Vining, 93541; 760 647 6595; www.monolake.org*

EAT AND DRINK

MAMMOTH LAKES

Slocums Bar & Grill *moderate*
Try the classic Caesar salad, Spanish paella, or beer-battered fish 'n' chips. *3221 Main St, 93546; 760 934 7647; open summer: 4–11pm daily; www.slocums.com*

JUNE LAKE LOOP

Tiger Bar & Cafe *inexpensive*
Serves pancakes, pork chops, steaks, meat loaf, and "tiger burgers". *Main St, June Lake, 93529; 760 648 7551; open 8am–10pm daily; www.thetigerbarcafe.com*

DAY TRIP OPTIONS
This drive can be broken into a series of day trips.

Head for the hills
This route abounds with hiking opportunities. For a day trip, hike among the spires and arches of the Alabama Hills ❷ then head up to Mt Whitney Portal ❸ for the ultimate high.
From Lone Pine, Whitney Portal Rd

leads through the Alabama Hills and continues uphill to Mt Whitney Portal. .

Of another time
History comes alive for visitors to the Manzanar National Historic Site ❹ and Laws Railroad Museum & Historical Site ⑪.

Manzanar is alongside US 395. Continuing north, take SR 6 from Bishop for Laws Railroad Museum.

This magnificent Earth
Travelers fascinated with physical landforms will marvel at Mammoth Lakes' ⑬ Devil's Postpile National Monument, plus the Obsidian Dome ⑭ and the tufa towers of Mono Lake ⑯.

SR 203 leads off US 395 to Mammoth Lakes. Farther north, Obsidian Dome can be accessed off US 395 via Obsidian Dome Rd, and the South Tufa Grove is signed via SR 120.

Eat and Drink: inexpensive under $25; moderate $25–50; expensive over $50

Desert Desiderata

Mojave to Badwater Basin

Highlights

- **Fiery cliffs**
  Take in the surreal flame-red cliffs at Red Rock Canyon State Park

- **Ghost town**
  View the saloons and other time-worn buildings of the erstwhile gold-mining town of Randsburg

- **Death Valley experience**
  Admire this world-renowned national park's snow-capped peaks, sculpted sand dunes, and glistening salt flats

- **Moving stones**
  Marvel at the mysterious stones and the trails that attest to their movement at The Racetrack, reachable from Ubehebe Crater

The mind-boggling sliding rocks and their tracks at The Racetrack

Desert Desiderata

Death Valley National Park is a land of geological and geographic superlatives, from sand dunes to salt pans bleached and blitzed by intense sun and other climatic extremes, including the highest ground temperature ever recorded in North America. The drive takes visitors past a variety of mesmerizing desert formations from the sculpted cliffs of Red Rock Canyon to the tufa towers of Trona. The route crosses wide, empty, desolate valleys and plains punctuated by dramatic formations and historic highlights, such as the still lively mining "ghost town" of Randsburg and Scotty's Castle. During the pleasant winter months, Death Valley's hotel rooms and campsites fill and the area bustles with outdoor activity before the searing heat of summer sets in.

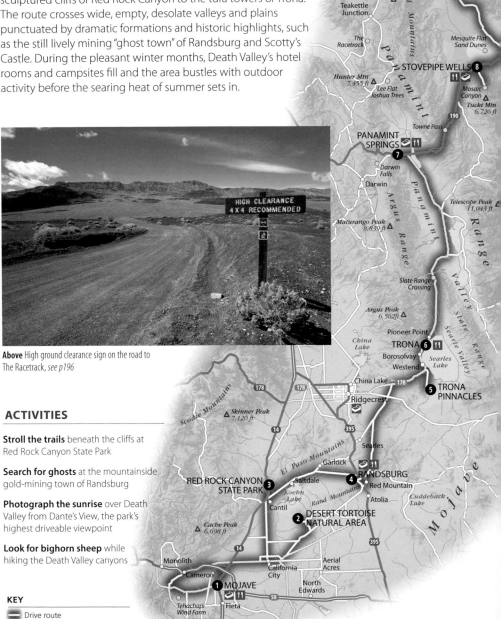

Above High ground clearance sign on the road to The Racetrack, *see p196*

ACTIVITIES

Stroll the trails beneath the cliffs at Red Rock Canyon State Park

Search for ghosts at the mountainside gold-mining town of Randsburg

Photograph the sunrise over Death Valley from Dante's View, the park's highest driveable viewpoint

Look for bighorn sheep while hiking the Death Valley canyons

KEY

━━ Drive route

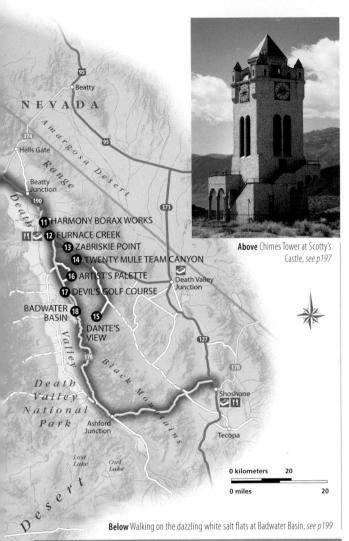

Above Chimes Tower at Scotty's Castle, *see p197*

Below Walking on the dazzling white salt flats at Badwater Basin, *see p199*

PLAN YOUR DRIVE

Start/finish: Mojave to Badwater Basin.

Number of days: 3–4 days, allowing 2 full days for exploring Death Valley.

Distance: 345 miles (555 km).

Road conditions: Generally excellent roads with relatively little traffic. The main roads through Death Valley are all two-way roads in very good condition, although park speed limits apply. The only difficult, unpaved roads are off-road tracks that require a jeep. Mountain passes into Death Valley are steep and winding, and lowland roads can be temporarily flooded and/or covered with sand after rare extreme weather. The park has gas stations at Panamint Springs, Stovepipe Wells, and Furnace Creek. Always carry plenty of water, plus a spare tire and tools to change it. Air conditioning is a must in summer.

When to go: Late fall through early spring is when weather is temperate. May–Sep is extremely hot, with temperatures reaching 100° F (38° C). Many businesses and most Death Valley campgrounds close Jun–Nov.

Opening times: The visitor centers are open daily, year-round, while most museums open in winter only, typically 8am–5pm.

Shopping: Nugget Gift Shop at Stovepipe Wells sells Native American baskets, blankets, and other crafts.

Major festivals: Death Valley: Badwater Ultramarathon, Jul; '49ers Encampment (recalling the Gold Rush of 1849), Nov.

DAY TRIP OPTIONS

History fans will enjoy visiting **Randsburg**, the **Harmony Borax Works**, and **Scotty's Castle**. For **photographers** and **nature lovers**, not-to-miss sights include **Artist's Palette**, the **Devil's Golf Course**, and **Badwater Basin**. For full details, *see p199.*

Above Santa Barbara Catholic Church, Randsburg **Below right** Magnificently colored cliffs, Red Rock Canyon State Park

WHERE TO STAY

MOJAVE

Mojave Desert Inn *inexpensive*
Offering yesteryear hospitality, this family-run no-frills motel has comfy, simply furnished rooms.
1954 Hwy 58, 93534; 888 620 3758; www.mojavedesertinn.com

Mariah Country Inn & Suites *moderate*
This business hotel's rooms are regally appointed. It has a gym and whirlpool spa.
1385 Hwy 58, 93501; 661 824 4980; www.mariahhotel.com

RANDSBURG

Cottage Hotel *inexpensive*
Surviving three town fires, this Gold Rush-era hotel has antique furnishings. The cozy restaurant (open weekends only) is warmed by a cast-iron stove. Free Wi-Fi. Also has cabins with kitchens.
130 Butte Ave, 93554; 760 374 2285; www.randsburgcottagehotel.com

AROUND RANDSBURG

Spring Hill Suites Ridgecrest *inexpensive*
Spacious, clean, and comfortable rooms. Complimentary breakfast and a fitness center.
113 E Sydnor Ave, Ridgecrest, 93555; 760 446 1630

The Carriage Inn *moderate*
Offering the most appealing lodgings in town, this motel has comfortable, well-decorated rooms.
901 N China Lake Blvd, Ridgecrest, 93555; 760 446 7910; www.carriageinn.biz

① Mojave
Kern County; 93501
Founded in the 1860s, this wind-blown desert town is today intimately associated with aerospace. **Mojave Air & Space Port** *(661 824 2433; www. mojaveairport.com; tours Mon–Fri)* hosts aviation displays and serves as a test bed for experimental aerospace craft. Continuing north, on SR 14 look back for a grand perspective of hundreds of decommissioned commercial aircraft kept in the open.

With around 5,000 wind turbines, **Tehachapi Wind Farm** is the world's second largest such collection. To pass among these towering giants sprinkled across the Tehachapi Mountains, take Oak Creek Road west from Mojave, turn right onto Tehachapi Willow Springs Road and right again onto Cameron Canyon Road, which leads to SR 58 (Blue Star Memorial Highway); take this east to reconnect with SR 14 northbound.

🚗 *Continue north on SR 14, exit on California City Blvd and continue east for 10 miles (16 km) through California City to Randsburg-Mojave Rd. Turn left and follow signs to Desert Tortoise Natural Area; park in the lot.*

② Desert Tortoise Natural Area
Kern County; 93504
This 40 sq mile (104 sq km) swath of desert has been set aside to protect the endangered desert tortoise, California's state reptile. Pick up a leaflet at the interpretive station, which has educational displays, before walking the self-guided trails. The tortoises are most active in spring, especially in early morning

and late afternoon. Keep an eye out for coyote, badgers, kangaroo rats, rabbits, and rattlesnakes as well.

🚗 *Return to California City and turn right on Neuralia Rd to the junction with Redrock-Randsburg Rd and SR 14 (16.5 miles/ 27 km). Turn left and then right to join SR 14 and follow signs to Red Rock Canyon State Park, which has a day-use lot.*

③ Red Rock Canyon State Park
Kern County; 93519
Familiar to many visitors as a setting for several Hollywood Westerns, and the opening scenes in *Jurassic Park* (1993), Red Rock Canyon State Park *(www.parks.ca.gov/)* is named for a huge gorge cut through the El Paso Mountains. Offshoot canyons to either side of SR 14 reveal beautifully colored cliffs – brown, pink, red, white, and yellow sandstones beneath layers of harder, black lava have been exquisitely folded and eroded into spires, flutes, and arches, drawing hikers along miles of trails. Take plenty of water and allow one to four hours for hiking. There is a RV camp here. The visitor center *(open spring & fall: variable hours Fri–Sun)* has educational exhibits.

🚗 *Return on SR 14 to the Redrock-Randsburg Rd junction and take this for 20 miles (32 km) east to Randsburg.*

④ Randsburg
Kern County; 93554
Although often listed as a "ghost town", this former gold-mining center in the Rand Mountains is a lived-in museum, inhabited by fewer than 100 people. Many original structures still stand

Above left The eerie Trona Pinnacles **Below left** Wall mural in Trona **Below right** The well-preserved Randsburg Inn, Randsburg

EAT AND DRINK

MOJAVE

Mike's Roadhouse Cafe *inexpensive*
This classic diner serves American comfort food. It has a great collection of antique pedal cars.
15834 Sierra Hwy, 93501; 661 824 2227; open 6am–9pm daily

Voyager Restaurant *inexpensive*
Airport views and a menu ranging from pancakes and ham and eggs, to tuna melts and Tex-Mex.
1434 Flight Line 58, 93501; 661 824 2048; open 7am–3pm Mon–Fri, 8am–2pm Sat & Sun; www.mojaveairport.com/voyager.htm

RANDSBURG

General Store *inexpensive*
It has a functioning antique soda fountain and malt machines, and serves country-style American dishes.
101 Butte Ave, 93554; 760 374 2143; open 9am–4pm Mon–Fri, 9am–5pm Sat, 10am–5pm Sun

White House Saloon *inexpensive*
A real Western saloon serving hot dogs, chili, burgers, and brews.
168 Butte Ave, 93554; 760 374 2464; open 11am–4pm Fri–Sun

TRONA

Esparza Family Restaurant *moderate*
This local favorite offers Mexican dishes and American comfort food.
13223 Main St, 93562; 760 372 5314; open 5:30am–7:30pm Mon–Sat, 5:30am–2pm Sun

Below Joshua trees in Searle Valley, near Trona

thanks to local preservation efforts, and still serve the same function as in the boom days after gold was discovered in 1895.

Park on Butte Avenue and stroll the creaky boardwalks, passing the White House Saloon, tiny **Randsburg Museum** *(open 10am–4pm Sat & Sun; www.randdesertmuseum.com)* displaying miscellany of the era, the Opera House, Santa Barbara Catholic Church, the barber shop, and the general store. Staged gunfights sometimes play out on the dusty street on weekends, when motorcyclists and off-roaders typically roar into town. The mountainside is strewn with relics of gold-mining days and tailing piles, but avoid wandering around the old mines as it is unsafe.

🚗 *Continue east through Randsburg along Butte Ave, which becomes Randsburg Cutoff Rd (then Red Mountain Rd) and drops down to SR 395. Turn left, then take Trona Rd north to SR 178 (19 miles/31 km). Turn right for Trona Pinnacles.*

⑤ Trona Pinnacles
San Bernardino County
Designated a National Natural Landmark, the Trona Pinnacles are one of the most unusual geological wonders in the Mojave Desert. Formed underwater eons ago, before Searles Lake dried out, the pinnacles comprise more than 500 tufa ridges, cones, towers, and spires sticking up from the bed of the dry Searles Lake basin. Hiking trails weave among the pinnacles, which reach up to 140 ft (43 m) and

were a setting for such movies and TV series as *Lost in Space*, *Star Trek V: The Final Frontier* (1989), and *Planet of the Apes* (2001). Access is via a 5-mile (8-km) long dirt road (RM 143) off SR 178; it is usually accessible to 2-wheel drive vehicles, but may be closed due to heavy rains or snow. Avoid the sand washes between the Pinnacles groups.

🚗 *Return to SR 178 and continue north through Searle Valley to Trona.*

⑥ Trona
San Bernardino County; 93562
Forming a deep trough between the towering Panamint Range and the Argus Range, the flat-bottomed Searle Valley was once flooded by an inland lake. The water evaporated ages ago leaving a vast snow-white, crystalline lake bed – **Searles Lake** – at an elevation of 1,000 ft (300 m). On its west shore, **Trona** was founded in 1913 to house the employees of a mining company. Its *raison d'etre* has been the extraction of borax, potash, salt, and other minerals. North of town, SR 178 climbs up **Slate Range Crossing**, atop which the **Panamint Valley** comes into view spread out below, before the road makes a long, winding descent. The tall mountain to the east is **Telescope Peak** (11,043 ft/3,366 m). The Searle and Panamint valleys are used by military aircraft for low altitude mission training.

🚗 *Continue 45 miles (72 km) north from Trona to the junction with SR 190. Turn left for Panamint Springs, just inside Death Valley National Park.*

Above Approach to Death Valley from Panamint Springs **Below** Trail weaving through the stunning Mosaic Canyon

VISITING DEATH VALLEY NATIONAL PARK

Tourist Information
The Bureau of Land Management field office has maps *300 S Richmond Rd, Ridgecrest, 93555; 760 384 5400*

The National Park Service also has a lot of information *www.nps.gov/deva/*

Driving in Death Valley
Take plenty of water, food, warm clothing, spare tires, tools, and a first-aid kit. Cellphone reception is weak or non-existent in many parts of the desert. High winds, sandstorms, sand and gravel on the road, and flash floods are potential hazards.

WHERE TO STAY

PANAMINT SPRINGS

Panamint Springs Resort *moderate*
Great views on the doorstep of Death Valley, but basic furnishings. Also has a campground and RV hook-ups.
40440 Hwy 190, 93828; 775 482 7680; www.deathvalley.com/psr

STOVEPIPE WELLS

Stovepipe Wells Village Hotel *moderate*
Spacious, modestly furnished cabins, some with views of Mesquite Flat Sand Dunes and Panamint Range.
Stovepipe Wells Village, 92328; 760 786 2387; www.escapetodeathvalley.com

Death Valley National Park

The ultimate land of extremes, this realm of desert grandeur is where summer temperatures soar to 50°C (122°F) and can plunge below freezing in winter. A kaleidoscope of physical beauty and geological wonders unfolds in this otherwise inhospitable terrain, dotted with old mines and ghost towns. In winter, when temperatures are agreeable and wildflowers bloom, the park's hotels and campgrounds are crowded. Summer visits require careful planning, and hiking is best restricted to high mountain trails. Check with the ranger stations about local conditions before setting out for explorations. There are only four hotels within the park; reserve well in advance.

⑦ Panamint Springs
Inyo County; 93828

The western gateway to Death Valley National Park *(www.nps.gov/deva)*, this tiny hamlet consists of little more than a restaurant, motel, and gas station. It is a base for exploring **Darwin Falls**, a year-round spring where willow thickets ring with birdsong, and **Lee Flat Joshua Trees**, a mountain-rimmed valley studded by iconic, wild-shaped Joshua trees as far as the eye can see.

🚗 *Continue east on SR 190 over Towne Pass to Stovepipe Wells.*

⑧ Stovepipe Wells
Inyo County; 93828

Initiated as a way-stop for miners a century ago, this small service center is home to the Western-themed Stovepipe Wells Hotel, a general store, and a gas station. Stop at the ranger station to pay the park entry fee and pick up brochures and maps. Opposite, the **Burned Wagon Point** marker recalls a group of "Forty-Niners" (gold seekers) who in 1849 were forced to eat their oxen, burn their wagons, and struggle out of the valley on foot.

The detour to **Mosaic Canyon** is richly rewarding: about 400 yards (365 m) west of Stovepipe Wells, unpaved Mosaic Canyon Road leads uphill to a car park from where a flat trail cuts through this sinuous slot canyon with marble walls polished to a slick sheen by water. The round-trip hike takes 20 minutes.

The **Mesquite Flat Sand Dunes**, 3 miles (5 km) east of Stovepipe Wells, rise to a height of 140 ft (42 m). They are best appreciated by hiking to the Star Dune summit around dawn or late afternoon. Moonlight adds a magical quality, although

sidewinder rattlesnakes are also active at night in warmer months. There is no official trail: just park the car and explore, allowing at least one hour to climb the dunes and back.

🚗 *Drive 3 miles (5 km) east on SR 190 and turn left onto Scotty's Castle Rd. After 33.5 miles (54 km) turn left onto Ubehebe Crater Rd and follow the loop to the crater.*

⑨ Ubehebe Crater
Inyo County

A testament to Death Valley's amazing grandeur, this volcanic crater measures almost half a mile (1 km) across. It is the result of a titanic explosion produced 300 years ago when fiery magma welling up from the earth's interior met underground water, which instantly flashed into steam. A trail circles the rim and leads to a cluster of smaller craters that dot the plain. Energetic hikers can also descend a trail into the 777-ft (237-m) deep crater.

🚗 *Return to Scotty's Castle Rd. Turn left for Scotty's Castle and park near the visitor center.*

The Racetrack
South of Ubehebe Crater, this flat, dry lake bed is known for the rocks that slither across its surface. No one has ever seen them move, but long, winding tracks attest to their ventures, caused perhaps by high winds and rare rain that slickens the lake bed surface. Racetrack Road begins at Ubehebe and requires a high ground clearance vehicle such as a Jeep. Midway along the road, teakettles are draped on a sign at **Teakettle Junction**. Continue to the parking lot farther south and walk to the southeast corner of the playa to marvel at the moving rocks and their tracks.

⑩ Scotty's Castle

Inyo County

The most-visited site in Death Valley, this Spanish Mediterranean "castle" is tucked into Grapevine Canyon amid an oasis of willow and palms. The fantasy in stone was built in 1922 by Chicago millionaire Albert Johnson as a winter getaway, but is named for his friend, con-man and cowboy prospector Walter Scott, who lived here after duping Johnson into investing in a non-existent gold mine. The grounds are open to the public, but the interiors, furnished with antiques, oriental rugs, and exquisite tiles, can be explored only on guided tours *(open Nov–Apr: 9am–5pm daily, May–Oct 9:30am–4pm daily)* given by rangers in 1930s costume.

Above Vehicle Boneyard at Scotty's Castle
Below left Tie Canyon Trail marker with the Chimes Tower in the background

Above The Spanish Mediterranean-style main house at Scotty's Castle

A one-hour walking tour

Set off from the car park and stroll over to the **visitor center** ① to pick up literature, including the Tie Canyon Trail guide, before turning right past the **old gas pump** ②. Continue 110 ft (100 m) to the **stables car collection** ③, which includes a 1914 Packard touring car, a 1925 Dodge pickup truck, and a 1936 Dodge sedan.

Return past the old **hacienda** ④ to the **Gas House Museum** ⑤, which recalls the castle's colorful history. Next, walk uphill and circle around the back of the **cookhouse** ⑥, stopping for the vista over the main house. Follow signs along the dirt trail up to **Scotty's grave** ⑦, where he slumbers beneath a hilltop cross. Return downhill to the **Chimes Tower** ⑧ with an Art Deco tile roof fitted with a 25-carillon-chime that plays every quarter hour. Turn right and descend the hill to join the Tie Canyon Trail, named for the more than 100,000 railroad ties that Johnson stored as firewood. Follow the trail to the **Vehicle Boneyard** ⑨, where rusty auto relics include a Ford Model A truck. Return to the trailhead and turn right to walk to the historic **main entrance** ⑩ gate. Retrace the route along the castle grounds to the unfinished **swimming pool** ⑪, with a reflecting pool and fountain, to reach the parking lot.

🚗 *Return along Scotty's Castle Rd to SR 190. Turn left and drive for 15.5 miles (25 km) to Harmony Borax Works.*

VISITING SCOTTY'S CASTLE

760 786 2392; open winter: 8:30am–5:30pm daily, summer: 9am–4:30pm

EAT AND DRINK

PANAMINT SPRINGS

Panamint Springs Resort *moderate*
The only restaurant for miles specializes in pastas and steaks and has summertime outdoor BBQs.
40440 Hwy 190, 93828; 775 482 7680; open 7am–9pm daily; www.deathvalley.com/psr

STOVEPIPE WELLS

Toll Road Restaurant *moderate*
This elegant restaurant is hewn from stone and old mine timbers. The menu includes Tex-Mex dishes, salads, and steaks. Many dishes use cactus, dates, and other local ingredients.
Stovepipe Wells Village, 92328; 760 786 2387; open mid-Oct–mid-May: 7–10am & 5–9pm daily, mid-May–mid-Oct: 7–10am & 6:30–10pm daily; www.escapetodeathvalley.com

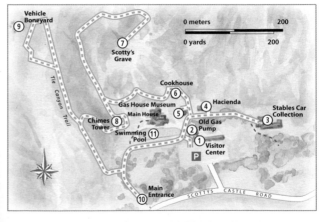

Eat and Drink: inexpensive under $25; moderate $25–50; expensive over $50

Above View of the undulating "badlands" from Zabriskie Point **Below right** The unique landscape of Artist's Palette

VISITING DEATH VALLEY NATIONAL PARK

Tourist Information
Furnace Creek Visitor Center *92328; 760 786 3200; open 8am–5pm daily*

Jeep Rental
Farabee's Jeep Rentals *Furnace Creek, 92328; 760 786 9872; www.deathvalleyjeeprentals.com*

WHERE TO STAY

FURNACE CREEK

Inn at Furnace Creek *expensive*
Gracious furnishings and fine dining amid a natural palm oasis.
Furnace Creek, 92328; 760 786 2345; www.furnacecreekresort.com

Ranch at Furnace Creek *expensive*
Built as a ranch in the 1880s, this resort boasts a pool and a golf course. Cozy rooms, spacious cabins, and RV park.
Furnace Creek, 92328; 760 786 2345; www.furnacecreekresort.com

AROUND DEATH VALLEY

Amargosa Opera House & Hotel *moderate*
Quirky historic hotel to the southeast of the park with bare furnishings.
608 Death Valley Junction, 92328; 760 852 4441; www.amargosa-opera-house.com

Shoshone Inn *moderate*
Just outside the eastern gateway to the park, this pleasant modern motel has attentive owners.
SR 127, Shoshone, 92384; 760 852 4335

---

⑪ Harmony Borax Works
Inyo County; 92328
The opening of Death Valley in the 19th century was largely due to Harmony Borax Works, which birthed the settlement of Furnace Creek and profitably extracted sodium borate from mud and salt flats. A trail with interpretive signs leads past the ruins of the processing plant and "twenty-mule team" double wagons that hauled the "White Gold of the Desert" to Mojave.

🚗 *Return to SR 190 and continue into Furnace Creek; park at Furnace Creek Ranch or at the park's headquarters.*

⑫ Furnace Creek
Inyo County; 92328
A Timbisha Native American seasonal settlement long before Europeans began to pass through the valley, Furnace Creek is a natural oasis fed by springs trickling down from the Amargosa Range. The Death Valley park headquarters and main visitor center are here. Furnace Creek also has a gas station, restaurants, the Spanish Mission-style **Inn at Furnace Creek**, and the "Western" themed **Ranch at Furnace Creek**, which houses the **Borax Museum** *(760 786 2345; open Oct–May: 9am–4pm daily)*. Its excellent displays include mule wagons, a stagecoach, and a 1920s Baldwin locomotive.

🚗 *Keep on SR 190 as it veers east for Death Valley Junction. Turn off for Zabriskie Point, which has a lot.*

---

⑬ Zabriskie Point
Inyo County
Made famous by the 1970 movie of the same name, Zabriskie Point is a popular place for watching sunrises and sunsets. The panoramic view is dramatized by the surrounding badlands – multiple layers of wildly eroded sedimentary mudstone rock, vibrantly colored in pinks, yellows, browns, and black rock bands. It is named for Christian Zabriskie, former general manager of the Pacific Coast Borax Company, whose "twenty-mule teams" were used to haul borax.

🚗 *Continue uphill 1 mile (1.6 km) on SR 190; turn off for the one-way drive through Twenty Mule Team Canyon.*

⑭ Twenty Mule Team Canyon
Inyo County
This picturesque yet desolate canyon offers a close-up look at the surreal, multicolored badlands. The unpaved 2.7 mile (4.3 km) road twists and turns through otherworldly terrain of mudstone buttes and gullies. These are a powerful testament to the erosive power of wind and rain.

🚗 *Keep on SR 190 until sign for Dante's View. Turn right and follow the narrow, steep road for 17.5 miles/ 28 km.*

⑮ Dante's View
Inyo County
From this mountain-top viewpoint at 5,475 ft (1,669 m), the entire valley is laid out in an unsurpassed panorama.

Where to Stay: inexpensive under $100; moderate $100–200; expensive over $200

Immediately below is Badwater Basin, the lowest point in North America. Telescope Peak (11,043 ft/3,366 m) can be seen across the valley. To catch sunrise here, remember the drive from Furnace Creek takes about 40 minutes.

🚌 *Return to Furnace Creek. Turn left onto SR 178 (Badwater Rd) and follow the signs for Artist's Palette.*

⑯ Artist's Palette
San Bernardino County
The technicolor hills and cliffs along this 9 mile (15 km) one-way scenic drive have a jaw dropping effect. Hike uphill from the car park for a close-up view of the blues, greens, pinks and yellows, which especially dazzle when the late-afternoon sun slants in from the west. The colors are produced by oxidation of different metals in the rocks, such as manganese, which produces purple, and mica for green.

🚌 *Continue south on SR 178, and turn off at the signs for Devil's Golf Course.*

⑰ Devil's Golf Course
Inyo County
A 1-mile (1.5-km) long gravel road leads to a vast area of large rock-salt crystals eroded by wind and rain into eerie and jagged formations. The crystals were created when Lake Manly, which once covered the valley floor, dried out ages ago, exposing the briny crust to the elements. Capillary action draws underlying water upwards to evaporate, forming salt pillars. Listen carefully to hear the musical pinging of crystals cracking as they expand and contract with varying heat. The road is often closed after rain.

🚌 *Continue south on SR 178. Park at Badwater Basin.*

Above Interpretive sign for Badwater Pool, Badwater Basin **Above right** Salt crystals on the bed of the dried Lake Manly, Devil's Golf Course

⑱ Badwater Basin
Inyo County
At 282 ft (86 m) below sea level, Badwater Basin is the lowest point in North America, and the eighth lowest in the world. Leave the car at the roadside park with interpretive signs and walk out onto the blindingly white salt pan that formed 3,000 years ago when Recent Lake dried out. A temporary lake re-forms after heavy rains but quickly evaporates and redeposits dissolved salt as sparkling new crystals. A small, marshy, highly saline spring-fed pool below the car park harbors endemic Badwater snails. The setting is made more dramatic by the sheer face of Black Mountains, soaring above the road. Follow the signs for **Shoshone** (54 miles/87 km), outside the park, which has ample hotels and restaurants.

EAT AND DRINK

FURNACE CREEK

The Wrangler *moderate*
All-you-can-eat breakfast and lunch buffet at this steakhouse specializing in grilled sirloins and seafood dishes.
Ranch at Furnace Creek; open year-round: breakfast, lunch & dinner daily; www.furnacecreekresort.com

Inn at Furnace Creek Dining Room *expensive*
Old-world elegance, exemplary service, and gourmet fusion dishes using local ingredients such as cactus.
Open year-round: breakfast, lunch & dinner daily; www.furnacecreekresort.com

AROUND DEATH VALLEY

Crowbar Café & Saloon *moderate*
Try the beef noodle soup, delicious sandwiches, or prime ribs. Slow service.
Hwy 127, Shoshone, 92384; 760 852 4123; open 8am–9:30pm daily

---

DAY TRIP OPTIONS

Death Valley National Park has ample physical attractions and historic sights to keep visitors entertained for a day or more.

Death Valley splendor
Begin at Stovepipe Wells ❽ and head east on SR 190 to marvel at the Artist's Palette ⑯, the eerie formations at Devil's Golf Course ⑰

and the lowest point in North America at Badwater Basin ⑱.

From Stovepipe Wells head east on SR 190, which leads past all the sites, in order.

A thing of the past
Roam the dusty streets of Randsburg ❹, then head to Death Valley to walk the Tie Canyon Trail at

Scotty's Castle ❿ and explore Harmony Borax Works ⓫.

Take SR 14 east to Redrock-Randsburg Rd for Randsburg. Beyond, take SR 395 west to Trona Rd. Take the SR 178 and follow signs for Death Valley. Turn left on Scotty's Castle Rd and continue north to Scotty's Castle. Return on SR 190 to Harmony Borax Works.

Eat and Drink: inexpensive under $25; moderate $25–50; expensive over $50

• Stockton
• San Jose
  • Fresno
  • Monterey
    CALIFORNIA
      • Bakersfield
Santa Barbara
  • San Bernardino
  Los Angeles
      • San Diego

Mojave Montage

Desert Hot Springs to Mojave National Preserve

Highlights

- **Stunning scenery**
  Drive past unusual rock formations and disjointed "Joshua tree" yuccas

- **Panoramic lake**
  Take to the waters of Lake Havasu for fishing, boating, or kayaking

- **Chasing memories**
  Drive down Route 66, immortalized in many Hollywood movies

- **So much sand**
  Tramp to the summit of Kelso Dunes for a great perspective over Mojave National Preserve

A rock-climber's delight in the Hidden Valley, Joshua Tree National Park

Mojave Montage

Looping through the southeast quarter of the vast Mojave Desert, this route starts in Desert Hot Springs, a humble town known for its thermal spas. Nearby, Joshua Tree National Park displays dramatic desert landscapes made surreal by the strangely shaped namesake species of yucca. Lake Havasu, formed by the Parker Dam, is a paradise for watersports centered on Lake Havasu City, in Arizona. Back in California, Route 66 retraces a path back through time en route to the Mojave National Preserve, a mosaic of sand dunes, underground caverns, and volcanic cones.

Above Hikers walking to the summit of Kelso Dunes, Mojave National Preserve, see p209

ACTIVITIES

Wander the boardwalks of Big Morongo Canyon Preserve through marsh and fan palm groves

Get a dose of the past in the former Hollywood movie set of Pioneertown

Hike the trails and climb the boulder piles of Joshua Tree National Park

Kayak on Lake Havasu after strolling across London Bridge

Dine at Roy's Motel & Café and be transported back to the 1950s

Climb the Kelso Dunes then slide down for some fun at the Mojave National Preserve

0 kilometers 20

0 miles 20

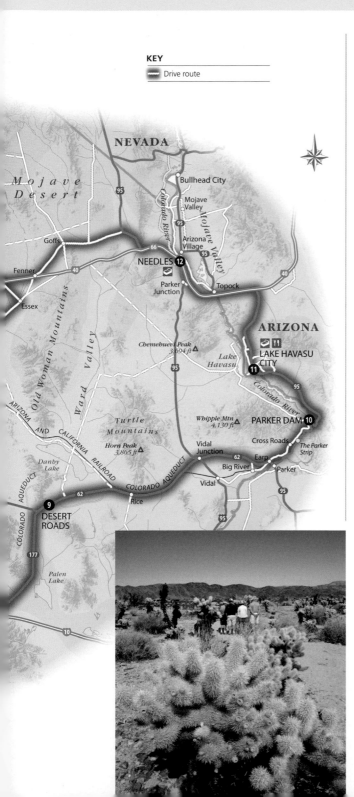

KEY

Drive route

NEVADA

Mojave Desert

Bullhead City

Mojave Valley

95

Colorado River

Goffs

Arizona Village

Mojave Valley

NEEDLES **12**

Fenner

40

Parker Junction

Topock

40

Essex

Old Woman Mountains

ARIZONA

Chemehuevi Peak
3,694 ft △

Lake Havasu

LAKE HAVASU CITY **11**

11

95

Ward Valley

95

Colorado River

ARIZONA AND CALIFORNIA RAILROAD

Turtle Mountains

Whipple Mtn
4,130 ft △

PARKER DAM **10**

Horn Peak
3,865 ft △

Vidal Junction

Cross Roads

The Parker Strip

Danby Lake

62

Earp

Big River

Parker

COLORADO AQUEDUCT

Vidal

95

AQUEDUCT

Rice

62

9
DESERT ROADS

95

177

Palen Lake

10

PLAN YOUR DRIVE

Start/finish: Desert Hot Springs to Mojave National Preserve.

Number of days: 3 days, allowing for a half-day each to explore Joshua Tree National Park and Lake Havasu.

Distance: 453 miles (729 km).

Road conditions: Generally good with some steep, winding roads in southern Joshua Tree National Park; the one to Hole-in-the-Wall is in a poor condition. Joshua Tree National Park can get infrequent snow in winter, when roads may briefly close. Gas stations are few, so fill the tank before departure and when possible during the trip.

When to go: Feb–Apr is an ideal time to visit, although many campgrounds can be fully booked at this time. Jun–Sep is extremely hot and best avoided.

Main market days: Joshua Tree: Sat am. **Lake Havasu:** Sep–May: Sun.

Opening times: Museum opening times vary widely, but most are closed on Mon. Visitor centers open 9am–5pm daily, but some close in summer.

Shopping: Joshua Tree and Pioneertown are meccas for Western-themed antiques and art. Look for Native American blankets, jewelry, and pottery around Lake Havasu.

Major festivals: Joshua Tree: Joshua Tree Music Festival, May. **Lake Havasu City:** 4x4 Desert Run, Mar; Grand Prix Pacific Offshore Powerboat Race, Apr.

DAY TRIP OPTIONS

Relive the past on the **Historic Route 66** as it passes through dusty towns that seem caught in the 1950s. Those fascinated with **geology** can explore **Joshua Tree National Park**, while **outdoor enthusiasts** can fish or kayak on **Lake Havasu**. For full details, *see p209*.

Left Exploring the Cholla Cactus Garden at Twentynine Palms, *see p206*

VISITING DESERT HOT SPRINGS

Tourist Information
11711 West Dr, 92240; 760 329 6403; open 9am–1pm Mon–Fri; www.visitdeserthotsprings.com

Parking
There is street parking outside the tourist information office and at Cabot's Pueblo Museum.

VISITING JOSHUA TREE

Tourist Information
Mojave Desert Land Trust
61732 29 Palms Hwy, 92252; 760 366 5440; www.mojavedesertlandtrust.org

WHERE TO STAY

DESERT HOT SPRINGS

Miracle Manor Retreat *expensive*
Dating from 1948, this peaceful resort combines Modernist architecture with minimalist furnishings. There is a spa.
12589 Reposa Way, 92240; 760 329 6641; www.miraclemanor.com

Two Bunch Palms Resort & Spa
expensive
This world-renowned spa resort has manicured grounds that include a waterfall grotto.
67425 Two Bunch Palms Trail, 92240; 760 329 8791; www.twobunchpalms.com

PIONEERTOWN

Pioneertown Motel *inexpensive*
Part of the old Hollywood cowboy movie set, this motel has a stable and antique wagons.
5040 Curtis Rd, 92268; 760 365 7001; www.pitowninn.com

JOSHUA TREE

The Desert Lily Bed & Breakfast
moderate
Exquisitely furnished and impeccably maintained, it has three rooms, plus five rustic cabins.
8523 Star Lane, 92252; 760 366 4676; closed Jul & Aug; www.thedesertlily. com; 2 nights minimum on weekends

Spin and Margie's Desert Hideaway
moderate
A quirky hacienda-style inn with four colorful suites and a cabin set amid a cactus garden. Flat-screen TVs, down quilts, and fluffy towels.
64491 29 Palms Hwy, 92252; 760 366 9124; www.deserthideaway.com

① Desert Hot Springs
Riverside County; 92240
This humble town on the gently sloping north side of the Coachella Valley is famous for its therapeutic thermal waters that bubble up from the San Andreas Fault, which have led to the opening of numerous deluxe spa hotels. Begin at **Cabot's Pueblo Museum** *(www.cabotsmuseum.org)*, which regales visitors with the history of pioneering homesteader Cabot Yerxa, who discovered the mineral spas in 1913. His rambling, 35-room adobe home was built of miscellaneous items scavenged from the desert. A highlight is the 22-ft (7-m) totem carved from a redwood tree. West of town, the **San Gorgonio Wind Farm** is the world's third largest wind farm, with over 4,000 turbines spun by winds channeling through the San Gorgonio Pass.

Above The Bath House, right out of the sets of an old Western movie, Pioneertown

🚗 *Exit Desert Hot Springs on Indian Canyon Rd and continue to Hwy 62. Follow the signs for Big Morongo Canyon Preserve; park in the lot.*

The Joshua Tree
The icon of the Mojave Desert, the Joshua tree *(Yucca brevifolia)* grows only here and was apparently named by Mormon emigrants for its supposed resemblance to the prophet Joshua waving his arms towards the Promised Land. It is actually not a tree, but a species of yucca plant. Adapted for desert conditions, its wild arms are tipped with waxy, dagger-like leaves.

② Big Morongo Canyon Preserve
San Bernardino County; 92256
An oasis formed by springs seeping up from the San Andreas Fault, this 31,000-acre (12,545-ha) reserve *(www.bigmorongo.org)* has trails through marshland, California fan palm groves, canyons, and desert oases, and is superb for birding and spotting bobcats, bighorn sheep, and mountain lions. The **Marsh Trail** boardwalk is wheelchair accessible and loops around a marsh shaded by cottonwoods and willows. It is a popular breeding ground for birds, including many rare birds among the 247 species seen here. The more challenging **Canyon Trail** (8.3 miles/ 13.4 km round-trip) descends through a snaking canyon to the edge of the Coachella Valley.

🚗 *Continue north on Hwy 62 to Yucca Valley. Turn left on Pioneertown Rd for Pioneertown.*

❸ Pioneertown

San Bernardino County; 92268

Created in 1946 as a permanent "Old West" Hollywood movie set, with over 200 movies and TV series having been filmed here, Pioneertown is virtually unchanged from the days when it was the Hayden Movie Ranch. Now a lived-in bohemian community, it provides visitors with a genuine Old West experience, including gunfight re-enactments on **Mane Street** *(Oct–Apr: Sat)*. Roam the dusty streets and peek into the old blacksmith's shop, jail house, post office, and Red Dog saloon, still functioning as a bar with live music. **Pioneertown Motel** still welcomes guests like it once did cowboy actors – such as Roy Rogers and Gene Autry – to a setting featuring old coaches and weathered miscellany.

🚗 *Return to Yucca Valley. Turn left on Hwy 62 for Yucca Valley.*

❹ Yucca Valley

San Bernardino County; 92284

Full of dusty antique stores, this quintessentially Western town also has a lively artistic community. Visit **Desert Christ Park** *(Sunnyslope Dr; www.desertchristpark.org)*, studded with more than 50 giant statues and tableaus of biblical scenes created by sculptor Anton Martin between 1951 and 1961. Motorcycle enthusiasts should visit the **Hutchins Harley-Davidson Museum** *(58325 29 Palms Hwy, 92284; 760 365 6311; open*

9am–7pm Tue–Fri, 9am–6pm Sat)*, displaying vintage motorcycles dating back to 1912. To learn about the Mojave Desert's flora and fauna, call in at the **Hi-Desert Nature Museum** *(www.hidesert naturemuseum.org)*, where animals such as the desert tortoise are on display.

🚗 *Drive east on Hwy 62 to Joshua Tree.*

❺ Joshua Tree

San Bernardino County; 92252

This slow-paced town is a mecca for artists and is served by the **Hi-Desert Cultural Center** *(www.hidesertplay house.com)*. Look for the avant-garde metal sculptures by local artist Simi Dabah displayed around town. Architectural buffs should stop to admire the **Joshua Tree Retreat Center** *(www.jtrcc.org)*, a famous meditation center designed by architect Frank Lloyd Wright and his son, Lloyd Wright. Rock band U2 made this small desert town world-famous with their *The Joshua Tree* album (1987). Note the giant sculpture of a desert tortoise – **Myrtle the Turtle** *(61622 29 Palms Hwy)* – beside the main drag. The town is also a gateway to the national park of the same name.

Myrtle the Turtle, Joshua Tree

🚗 *Turn off Hwy 62 onto Park Blvd. Stop at the Joshua Tree Visitor Center before continuing south to the park entrance.*

Above left Street mural of local history, Joshua Tree **Below** Turbines at San Gorgonio Wind Farm, Desert Hot Springs

EAT AND DRINK

DESERT HOT SPRINGS

South of the Border *inexpensive*
Serves some of the best Mexican food north of the border. Expect a long wait on weekends.
11719 Palm Dr, 92240; 760 251 4000; open 11am–9:30pm Sun–Thu, 11am–10pm Fri & Sat

PIONEERTOWN

Pappy & Harriets *moderate*
A real Western saloon serving veggie paninis, Caesar salads, bacon cheeseburgers, and sirloin steaks. Live country music nightly.
53688 Pioneertown Rd, 92268; 760 365 5956; open 11–2am Thu–Sun, 5–11pm Mon; www.pappyandharriets.com

YUCCA VALLEY

Diner US 62 *inexpensive*
Classic American 1950s diner with Harley-Davidson decor.
55405 29 Palms Hwy, 92284; 760 821 3618; open 6am–2pm daily

John's Place *inexpensive*
This classic American diner offers a dozen types of omelets and burgers.
56249 29 Palms Hwy, 92284; 760 365 0144; open 6am–9pm Sun–Thu, 6am–10pm Fri–Sat; www.johnsplaces.com

JOSHUA TREE

The Natural Sisters Café *inexpensive*
Creative dishes are made with organic produce; try the lentil chili, curry rice wrap, and home-made ice cream sandwich dipped in chocolate.
61695 29 Palms Hwy, 92252; 760 366 3600; open 7am–7pm daily

Royal Siam Restaurant *inexpensive*
Family-run Thai restaurant serving curry dishes and other Thai staples. Bargain-priced weekend buffets.
61599 29 Palms Hwy, 92252; 760 366 2923; open 11:30am–8:30pm Wed–Mon

**VISITING JOSHUA TREE
NATIONAL PARK**

Tourist Information
Joshua Tree Visitor Center *6554 Park
Blvd, Joshua Tree, 92256; 760 366 1855*

Oasis Visitor Center *74485 National
Park Dr, Twentynine Palms, 92277;
760 367 5500; www.nps.gov/jotr*

Parking
The campsites and visitor centers have
parking spaces, and parking areas are
located along the paved roads.

Hiking
Wear a sunhat and sunscreen, and carry
a gallon (3.5 liter) of water per person
per day. Flash floods are a danger, so
avoid drainage areas during and after
rains. Watch out for rattlesnakes and
give them a wide berth. Note that
cellphone coverage is poor.

WHERE TO STAY

TWENTYNINE PALMS

Harmony Motel *inexpensive*
Four individually styled rooms and a
cabin around a pool.
*71161 29 Palms Hwy, 92277; 760 367
3351; www.harmonymotel.com*

The Desert Lily *moderate*
This peaceful B&B has five eclectic
cabins with quirky decor. Gourmet
breakfasts are served.
*8523 Star Ln, 92252; 760 366 4676;
www.thedesertlily.com*

29 Palms Inn *moderate*
Charming, rustic cottages, plus a pool
and an excellent restaurant.
*73950 Inn Ave, 92277; 760 367 3505;
www.29palmsinn.com*

Roughley Manor *expensive*
Two suites with fireplaces, five cottages,
and a two-room farmhouse are on offer
at this pet-friendly, non-smoking B&B.
*74744 Joe Davis Dr, 92277; 760 367
3238; www.roughleymanor.com*

---

⑥ Joshua Tree National Park
San Bernardino County; 92277
Serenity, stunning scenery, and diverse
habitats characterize this national
park, which protects two distinct
realms – the Mojave Desert above
3,280 ft (1,000 m) elevation, and the
lower Colorado Desert, spanning
1,240 sq miles (3,212 sq km). It is
named for the Joshua trees *(see p204)*
that grow here in abundance. Park
Boulevard climbs from West Entrance
Station to **Hidden Valley**, where
massive boulder formations glow gold
at sunset; the valley can be explored
on a short, easy loop trail. The park has
10 campgrounds, all with pit toilets,
picnic tables, and fire rings; very few
have water. Backcountry camping
requires registering at any one of the
13 registration boards across the park.

Reserve a ranger-led, two-hour
guided walking tour *(760 367 5555;
Oct–May: 10am & 1pm daily)* of **Keys
Ranch**, a relic homestead where
entrepreneurial pioneers Bill and
Frances Keys raised five children,
defying the desert's harshness during
their six decades here; the ranch
house, workshop, well, and other
structures still stand amid rusty old
cars, trucks, and mining equipment.

Nearby **Barker Dam** is good for
spotting wildlife around the reservoir.
From here, follow the signs to **Keys
View**, a lookout providing a panorama
of the Coachella Valley; the San
Andreas Fault is clearly visible far
below. Return to Park Boulevard and
continue east to **Skull Rock**, named
for its resemblance to a human skull.
Follow Park Boulevard north and exit
the park via the North Entrance
Station. On the outskirts of

Twentynine Palms, explore the short,
trails at **Oasis de Mara**, first settled by
Native Americans and now home to
park headquarters and the Oasis
Visitor Center.

🚐 *Continue north on Utah Trail for
Twentynine Palms and park roadside.*

⑦ Twentynine Palms
San Bernardino County; 92277
Originally a small way-stop for
wagons on the Utah Trail and today a
good stop-off when exploring the
national park, Twentynine Palms
combines yesteryear "Old West"
architecture with a lively modern
cultural scene. The **29 Palms Art
Gallery** *(74055 Cottonwood Dr, 92277;
760 367 7819; open noon–3pm Wed–Sun)*
has changing exhibits. Stop at the
Chamber of Commerce *(73484 29
Palms Hwy, 92277; 760 367 3445)* to pick
up a self-guided tour map of the
Oasis of Murals *(www.oasisofmurals.
com)* – 24 murals that chronicle the
area's history and culture. Local history
buffs maintain the **Old Schoolhouse
Museum** *(www.29palmshistorical.com)*,
with photographs and memorabilia
from yesteryear, including a 1920s bus.

Reenter the national park by
returning south on Utah Trail, and
after 5 miles (8 km) turn onto Pinto
Basin Road. Stop at **Cholla Cactus
Garden** to stroll amid the "jumping
cholla" – but do not touch any as the

Above left Visitors in the Cholla Cactus Garden,
Joshua Tree National Park **Below** Boulders by
Park Boulevard, Joshua Tree National Park

spines can cause severe pain. Passing the **Ocotillo Patch**, a grove of spindly ocotillo cactus, the road then snakes down to **Cottonwood Spring**, an oasis reached by a short trail from the Cottonwood Visitor Center. An *arrastra* (a primitive gold processing mill) can be seen here, and the **Lost Palms Oasis Trail** leads 8 mile (13 km) to the park's largest fan palm oasis.

🚗 *Continue south and turn east onto I-10. Follow signs to Chiriaco Summit.*

⑧ Chiriaco Summit
Riverside County; 92201
During World War II, a 18,000 sq mile (46,620 sq km) swath of desert became the US First Army's Desert Training Center, commanded by Major General George S. Patton and headquartered at Camp Young – now Chiriaco Summit. The **George Patton Memorial Museum** *(www.general pattonmuseum.com)* commemorates Patton and the Desert Training Center and thrills military history enthusiasts with its vast display of exhibits from World War II and other major conflicts of the 20th and 21st centuries. A highlight is the Big Map, a massive 3-D scale model of the Mojave Desert. The various military tanks on display include a World War II Sherman. It is a good idea to fill up with gas, water, and snacks at Chiriaco Summit, as there are no gas stations or services until Vidal Junction (87 miles/140 km east from here).

🚗 *Return to I-10 eastbound and after 20 miles (32 km) exit at Desert Center and take SR 177 north to Hwy 62 (32.5 miles/52 km). Continue 23.5 miles (38 km) east towards Rice.*

⑨ Desert Roads
San Bernardino County
SR 177 and Highway 62 sweep across a vast desert plain shimmering with heat-waves. Magnificent in its austere beauty, the lonesome route delivers vistas of distant sand dunes and dry lake beds against a backdrop of mauve-gray mountains. Highway 62 (Aqueduct Road) parallels the 242-mile (389-km) **Colorado Aqueduct**, which channels water from Lake Havasu to Riverside County; and the **Arizona and California Railroad**, upon whose embankment passers-by over the past century

have spelled their names with rust-colored volcanic rocks.

🚗 *Continue east on Hwy 62 to Earp (33.7 miles/54 km). Cross the junction onto Parker Dam Rd and follow signs for Parker Dam (15.5 miles/25 km).*

⑩ Parker Dam
San Bernardino County; 92267
From Earp, Parker Dam Road parallels the Colorado River. It is a thrill to snake up through the red-rock canyon, with the river on the right below. Known as **The Parker Strip**, this stupendously scenic byway is lined with resorts, RV parks, and marinas luring vacationers for river tubing, water-skiing, and fishing. Cresting a rise, the graceful **Parker Dam** comes into view. Pull over for photographs, as vehicles are not allowed to stop above the dam, which was completed in 1938. Spanning the Colorado River between the borders of Arizona and California, it is the deepest dam in the world, but only 85 ft (26 m) of the 320-ft (98-m) tall structure is visible above the waterline. It holds **Lake Havasu**, a reservoir stretching 45 miles (72 km) along the Colorado Canyon, and a paradise for watersports. Its banks are lined with wildlife refuges that are havens for birds and draw hordes of birders.

🚗 *Cross the dam and descend to the junction with AZ 95. Note that traffic is only permitted across the dam 5am–11pm daily. Turn left and follow signs for Lake Havasu City (23 miles/37 km). Follow AZ 95 to London Bridge Rd; turn left to park by the visitor center.*

Above left One of the paintings at the Oasis of Murals, Twentynine Palms **Above** The Parker Strip at dusk, Parker Dam

---

EAT AND DRINK

TWENTYNINE PALMS

Carousel Café *inexpensive*
Small café-diner with filling omelets and pancakes.
72317 29 Palms Hwy, 92277; 760 367 3736; open 6am–9pm daily; www.29palmsinn.com

The Rib Company *moderate*
This Wild West-themed restaurant serves pulled pork sandwiches, ribs, sirloins, and more exotic meats such as alligator and kangaroo.
72183 29 Palms Hwy, 92252; 760 367 1663; closed breakfast; www.theribco.com

Bistro Twentynine *expensive*
This elegant restaurant serves fresh seafood, filet mignon, and home-made desserts. Beers on tap.
73527 29 Palms Hwy, 92277; 760 361 2229; open 4–9pm Mon–Thu, noon–10pm Fri & Sat, noon–8pm Sun; www.bistrotwentynine.com

AROUND CHIRIACO SUMMIT

Desert Center Café *inexpensive*
Not much has changed at this diner since Major General Patton and his troops ate sandwiches and burgers here. The milkshakes are worth the stop.
44321 Ragsdale Rd, Desert Center, 92239; 760 227 3231; open 7am–7pm daily

---

Eat and Drink: inexpensive under $25; moderate $25–50; expensive over $50

Above The original London Bridge straddling Lake Havasu, Lake Havasu City

VISITING LAKE HAVASU CITY

Tourist Information
420 English Village, 86403; 928 855 5255; open 9am–5pm daily

Convention & Visitors Bureau *314 London Bridge Rd, 86403; 928 453 3444; www.golakehavasu.com*

Parking
Public street parking on London Bridge Rd and free public parking (24 hrs) on the south side of McCulloch Blvd, west of London Bridge.

WHERE TO STAY

LAKE HAVASU CITY

The Heat Hotel *moderate*
This chic, contemporary-themed hotel has an unbeatable location next to London Bridge. Spacious rooms with excellent amenities and balconies with views over Bridgewater Channel.
1420 N McCulloch Blvd, 86403; 888 898 4328; www.heathotel.com

London Bridge Resort *moderate*
Despite its crude mock-Tudor exterior and public areas, rooms here are elegant. It has a disco and gets lively during Spring Break.
1477 Queens Bay, 86403; 928 855 0888; www.londonbridgeresort.com

NEEDLES

Fenders River Road Resort *inexpensive*
A friendly and attentive family run this restored motel beside the Colorado River. Its simple yet cozy cabins recall the better days of Historic Route 66.
3396 Needles Hwy, 92363; 760 326 3423

AROUND MOJAVE NATIONAL PRESERVE

Wills Fargo Motel *inexpensive*
An inviting Moroccan-theme lounge, and spacious, clean rooms.
72252 Baker Blvd, Baker, 92309; 760 733 4477

⑪ Lake Havasu City
Mohave County; 86403

Begun as a rest camp for World War II soldiers, this city on the east bank of Lake Havasu sprung to life as a resort in the 1960s, when millionaire businessman Robert P. McCulloch initiated a planned community and later erected London Bridge, which he bought from the City of London in 1968. Today a year-round center for fishing and watersports, Lake Havasu City gets thronged with college students during Spring Break (Mar–Apr). It is also the setting for boat regattas, powerboat races, and the International Jet-Ski World Finals.

A two-hour walking tour

Park across from the **visitor center** *(open 9am–5pm daily)* ① and stroll through the **English Village** ②, with red telephone booths and faux Tudor buildings. Pass under the graceful arches of London Bridge and along Bridgewater Channel, and turn left onto Queens Bay and left again to enter **London Bridge Resort** ③. The Gold State Coach in the lobby is an exact-scale replica of the horse-drawn carriage used in every English coronation since 1712.

Exit the lobby and turn left through the hotel parking lot, then cross McCulloch Boulevard to admire a **bronze statue** ④ of Robert P. McCulloch and city planner C.V. Wood. Head west across **London Bridge** ⑤, noting the original detailing such as the cast-iron lamp standards. The bridge was first erected over London's River Thames in 1831, but was dismantled in 1968 and shipped brick by brick to be reassembled at Lake Havasu after being purchased by McCulloch. On its west side, descend the steps and walk south along the Bridgewater Channel to **London Bridge Beach** ⑥, a green space with sand lots. Return to McCulloch Boulevard. If up for a longer, 1-hour walk, follow McCulloch Boulevard west as it loops past functioning scale replicas of US

Dragon statue at English Village

lighthouses, before coming back to the same junction. Back at McCulloch Boulevard, cross London Bridge, then descend the stairs to **Freedom Bridge Foundation Memorial Walkway** *(www.havasufreedombridge.com)* ⑦, a series of memorials and plaques laid out along Bridgewater Channel honoring local servicemen and recalling key moments in America's formative history. Continue to **Windsor State Park** ⑧, where the Mojave Sunset Trail leads past a small beach and nature reserve to the **Arroyo-Camino Interpretive Garden** ⑨, showing local flora and fauna. Retrace the route along the trail and walkway to return to the parking.

🚗 *Exit Lake Havasu City on AZ 95 north to I-40 (19 miles/30 km). Take I-40 west, cross the Colorado River to reenter California, and continue to Needles (21 miles/34 km). Follow E Broadway St into town.*

⑫ Needles

San Bernardino County; 92363
Named for the jagged spires that rise from the desert to the south of town, Needles clings to its 19th-century heritage as a stop on the Santa Fe Railroad and, later, a service center on Historic Route 66. Check out the old wagon and Native American petroglyphs on a tiny plaza at Broadway and Palm Way.

🚗 *Take Broadway west to rejoin I-40. Follow Historic Route 66 signs, exiting onto SR 95. Turn left onto Route 66 and continue via Goffs to Fenner. Rejoin I-40 and take the next exit, on Essex Rd, for Hole-in-the-Wall (35 miles/56 km); veer right at Black Canyon Rd.*

⑬ Hole-in-the-Wall

San Bernardino County
This region of dramatic volcanic formations is named for its rhyolite cliffs and spires riddled with holes and hollows caused by erosion. Trails that begin at the visitor center *(760 252 6104)* wind among volcanic pinnacles and canyons. The Rings Trail, for experienced hikers, leads through a narrow slot canyon and involves scrambling over boulders. There is a campsite surrounded by sculpted cliffs at 4,400 ft (1,341 m) , and rangers offer interpretive walks (Oct–May).

🚗 *Return along Essex Rd, pass under I-40, and drive to Historic Route 66. Turn right for Amboy (37.5 miles/60 km).*

⑭ Amboy

San Bernardino County; 92304
Once a major town on Route 66 and the Santa Fe Railroad, this ghost town is worth a stop for a soda at the landmark **Roy's Motel & Café**; its atomic-age neon sign has featured in many Hollywood films. Stop to photograph the "Route 66" stencils on the road. The **Amboy Crater National**

Natural Landmark, a volcanic cone 2 miles (3 km) southwest of town, rises over **Bristol Dry Lake**, where salt is extracted in evaporation pans.

🚗 *Retrace Historic Route 66 east to Kelbaker Rd and turn left for Mojave National Preserve (11 miles/17 km).*

⑮ Mojave National Preserve

San Bernardino County; 92309
This massive national park enshrines a mosaic of volcanic cinder cones, lava flows, sand dunes, Joshua tree forests, and dry lake beds. Many of its striking formations can be seen from Kelbaker Road, which snakes up through **Granite Pass** then descends to the **Kelso Dunes** that rise to over 700 ft (200 m); a 3-mile (5-km) round-trip hike to the peak rewards with stunning views. Farther along Kelbaker Road, **Kelso Depot Visitor Center** has superb displays on local ecology and Native American culture. Farther north, 32 volcanic cones surrounded by a gently sloping sea of hardened lava make up the **Cinder Cones National Natural Landmark**. High ground clearance 4WD vehicles can drive along Aiken Road to a hollow lava tube. Kelbaker Road leads to the small town of Baker, with a gas station and amenities.

Left Cacti punctuating the landscape near Hole-in-the-Wall **Below** Route 66 stencils on Historic Route 66, Amboy

VISITING MOJAVE NATIONAL PRESERVE

Tourist Information
Kelso Depot Visitor Center
Kelbaker Rd, 92309; 760 252 6108; open 9am–5pm daily

EAT AND DRINK

LAKE HAVASU CITY

Barley Bros. *moderate*
This casual restaurant and brewpub serves pastas, pizzas, rotisserie chicken, and Jamaican BBQ salmon.
1425 N McCulloch Blvd, 86403; 928 505 7837; open 10am–10pm Mon–Thu, 10am–11pm Fri–Sun; www.barleybrothers.com

AMBOY

Roy's Motel & Café *inexpensive*
This legendary Route 66 diner is more museum than functioning café, but it still offers burgers, snacks, and sodas.
Rt 66, 92304; 760 733 1066; open 7am–8pm daily

MOJAVE NATIONAL PRESERVE

The Beanery *inexpensive*
A restored historic diner serving salads, sandwiches, plus root beer floats.
Kelso Depot Visitor Center, Kelbaker Rd, Kelso, 92309; 760 252 6165; open 9am–5pm daily

DAY TRIP OPTIONS
This route is easy to divide into themed day trips.

A geologist's dream
Explore the dramatic rock formations at Joshua Tree National Park ❻, and then head to Twentynine Palms ❼ to admire the Oasis of Murals. Unwind with a meal or coffee.

Park Blvd connects Joshua Tree National Park to Twentynine Palms.

Making a splash!
Parker Dam ❿ and Lake Havasu City ⓫, offer endless choices for fishing, boating, and more watersports.

Parker Dam Rd connects with AZ 95, which leads to Lake Havasu City.

Road to nostalgia
Take the iconic Historic Route 66 to Amboy ⓮ and get a snap clicked in front of the famous Roy's Motel & Café. Continue to Mojave National Preserve ⓯ to hike among sand dunes and volcanic craters.

Take Historic Route 66 east to Kelbaker for the preserve.

Eat and Drink: inexpensive under $25; moderate $25–50; expensive over $50

Desert Lows to Mountain Highs

Palm Springs to Idyllwild

Highlights

- **The haunt of the rich and famous**
  Admire Hollywood celebrity homes and relax retro-style at Palm Springs

- **All creatures big and small**
  Look at mountain lions, bighorn sheep, and other desert critters at the Living Desert in Palm Desert

- **Desertscapes**
  Explore the palm-studded canyons and Indian petroglyphs at the Anza-Borrego Desert State Park

- **Call of the wild**
  Cool off amid the pines while hiking the trails of Mount San Jacinto State Wilderness from Idyllwild

The Borrego Palm Canyon Trail cutting through Anza-Borrego Desert State Park

Desert Lows to Mountain Highs

Palm Springs, with its stylish Modernist homes, natural hot-spring spas, a world-class museum, and eclectic boutique hotels, has served as a favorite getaway for Hollywood celebrities for decades. From here, the scenic palm-lined Highway 111 snakes through the Coachella Valley, with its lush golf resorts and vast date groves. The route then skirts the Salton Sea, a vast man-made lake good for birding, before passing through the dramatic landscapes of Anza-Borrego Desert State Park, laced with canyon oases offering excellent hiking. The drive finally continues up into the refreshingly cool, pine-clad San Jacinto Mountains and the idyllic artists' retreat of Idyllwild.

Above Hikers in Palm Canyon, Indian Canyons, *see p215*

ACTIVITIES

Ride the iconic Palm Springs Aerial Tram to admire the views and hike in Mount San Jacinto State Wilderness

Get to know the desert wildlife up close and personal at the Living Desert in Palm Desert

Sample the dates at Shields Date Garden and stock up on a dozen varieties in Indio

Discover a wilderness paradise in the rugged canyons of Anza-Borrego Desert State Park

Swap the car for a horse in Idyllwild and explore the pine forests of the San Jacinto Mountains

KEY

— Drive route

Above The well-paved SR 22 passing through a rocky section of Anza-Borrego Desert State Park, *see p216*

0 kilometers   10

0 miles   10

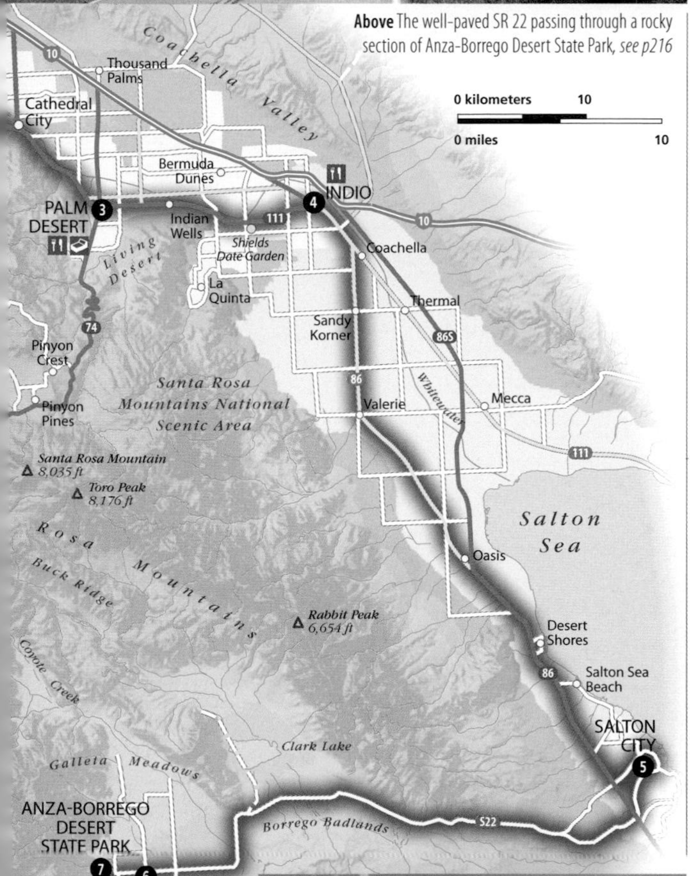

Above Barrel cactus in Anza-Borrego Desert State Park, *see p216*

PLAN YOUR DRIVE

Start/finish: Palm Springs to Idyllwild.

Number of days: 3 days, allowing a full day to explore Anza-Borrego Desert State Park.

Distance: 242 miles (389 km).

Road conditions: Well-paved and signposted, but steep terrain and winding roads in Anza-Borrego Desert State Park and Santa Rosa & Jacinto Mountains National Monument, which can be snowbound in winter.

When to go: The winter months are temperate, although higher elevations are prone to occasional snow. Feb and Mar, when desert wildflowers bloom, are comfortable. Summer months are extremely hot in the desert, but the climate higher up is agreeable.

Main market days: Palm Springs: Thu pm. **Borrego Springs:** Nov–Jun: Fri am.

Opening times: Shops and galleries tend to open 9am–5pm Mon–Sat; some stay open longer, and on Sun. Museums usually open 10am–5pm daily but hours vary and some close on Mon and during summer months.

Shopping: Look out for collectible retro furnishings in Palm Springs, and collector art and haute couture fashion on El Paseo, Palm Desert.

Major festivals: Palm Springs: Palm Springs International Film Festival, Jan. **Palm Desert:** The Art of Food & Wine Festival, Mar. **Indio:** Southwest Arts Festival, Jan. **Borrego Springs:** Springs Days Desert Festival, Oct. **Idyllwild:** Jazz in the Pines, Aug.

DAY TRIP OPTIONS

Those interested in **art** and **architecture** will find a treasure trove of Modernist buildings in **Palm Springs**, which also has the Palm Springs Art Museum. **Outdoor lovers** can enjoy the natural glory of **Anza-Borrego Desert State Park** and **Mount San Jacinto State Wilderness**, which can be explored by biking, hiking, or horseback. For full details, *see p217*.

Right Sign for Palm Desert's El Paseo boulevard **Far right** Tall palm trees, Palm Springs

❶ Palm Springs
Riverside County; 92262

Once synonymous with Hollywood hedonism, this chic resort town at the west end of the Coachella Valley has been reinvigorated with trendy spa resorts and boutique hotels beneath mountains that glisten with snow in winter. Before setting out on the drive, take a stroll past Palm Springs' fabulous Modernist public buildings and the impressive homes of the rich and famous.

VISITING PALM SPRINGS

Tourist Information
2901 N Palm Canyon Dr, 92262; 760 778 8418; open 9am–5pm daily; www.palm-springs.com

Parking
In the Palm Springs Art Museum parking lot, or the public parking lot on N Museum Dr.

WHERE TO STAY

PALM SPRINGS

Casa Cody *moderate*
A relaxing retreat built in hacienda adobe style, Casa Cody is just steps from downtown Palm Springs' main boulevard. It offers charmingly furnished cottages open to orchard gardens, as well as a heated outdoor pool.
175 S Cahuilla Rd, 92262; 760 320 9346; www.casacody.com

Del Marcos Hotel *moderate*
Evoking the 1950s, this quirky hotel is fitted with period furnishings. Rooms surround a sundeck, where martinis are served poolside.
225 W Baristo Rd, 92262; 1 800 676 1214; www.delmarcoshotel.com

Viceroy Palm Springs *expensive*
Popular with Hollywood celebrities, this Regency-style hotel has deluxe rooms, three swimming pools, and a terrific spa. Service is faultless and the bar gets lively.
415 S Belardo Rd, 92262; 760 320 4117; www.viceroypalmsprings.com

PALM DESERT

Mojave Resort *moderate*
A small high-tech boutique hotel, Mojave Resort has stylish retro-themed furnishings in desert colors. It has a courtyard pool and a whirlpool bath. Non-smoking.
73721 Shadow Mountain Dr, 92260; 1 800 391 1104; www.resortmojave.com

A three-hour walking tour
Start at the **Palm Springs Art Museum** ① *(www.psmuseum.org)*, which displays fine contemporary art, and then follow N Belardo Road north to **The Cloisters** ②, the Spanish Colonial-style former home of entertainer Liberace. Follow W Alejo Road west to N Patencio Road and turn right onto W Merito Place, passing the **former home of Sir**

Laurence Olivier ③ *(401)*, the British actor. Continue along N Mission Road and turn left onto W Hermosa Place – the Spanish estate on the left is the **former home of Elizabeth Taylor** ④ *(417)*; opposite, the **former home of Dinah Shore** ⑤ *(432)* is considered an exemplar of 1950s Desert Modernist design. At the end of W Hermosa, turn left then right to reach N Via Monte Vista. Turn right and walk gently uphill to crooner **Dean Martin's former house** ⑥ *(1123)*. Return via N Via Monte Vista to W Alejo Road. Turn right onto Palm Canyon Drive. At W Tahquitz Canyon Way, a bronze **statue of Lucille Ball** ⑦, the actress and comedienne, sits on a bench outside the Coffee Bean café. Continue south past the historic **Plaza Theatre** ⑧, with the **Walk of Stars** ⑨ underfoot honoring famous people associated with the city. At **Village Green Heritage Plaza** ⑩ visit the tiny Agua Caliente Cultural Museum to learn about local Native American culture. At Ramon Road, admire the dramatic Modernist facade of the **Washington Mutual Bank** ⑪, while the iconic **Bank of America** ⑫, one block south, recalls French architect Le Corbusier's chapel at Ronchamp, France. Return to Ramon Road and walk west one block, turn right onto

Map labels:
- ⑥ Dean Martin's Former House
- Former Home of Dinah Shore ⑤
- Former Home of Elizabeth Taylor ④
- ③ Former Home of Sir Laurence Olivier
- ② The Cloisters
- Palm Springs Art Museum ①
- Statue of Lucille Ball ⑦
- Plaza Theatre ⑧
- Walk of Stars ⑨
- Village Green Heritage Plaza ⑩
- Del Marcos Hotel ⑬
- Washington Mutual Bank ⑪
- Bank of America ⑫
- 0 meters 400
- 0 yards 400
- E TACHEVAH DR
- E ANDREAS RD
- E ALEJO ROAD
- E AMADO RD
- E ANDREAS ROAD
- E TAHQUITZ CANYON WAY
- E ARENAS RD
- W BARISTO RD
- E RAMONA RD

S Belardo Road to the **Del Marcos Hotel** ⑬, an angular Modernist classic built in 1947. Return to the car.

For some scenery, visitors can take the Palm Springs Aerial Tram *(www.pstramway.com)* to the San Jacinto Mountain Wilderness *(see p217)*.

🚗 *Follow W Tahquitz Canyon Way and turn onto Palm Canyon Drive (SR 111). Stay right on S Palm Canyon Dr at the split where SR 111 turns east, and continue to the Indian Canyons.*

② Indian Canyons
Riverside County, 92262

Slicing into the base of the San Jacinto Mountains, the three Indian Canyons *(closed Jul–Sep: Mon–Thu)* are laced with 30 miles (48 km) of trails that wind through groves of California fan palms fed by natural springs. The canyons are owned by the Agua Caliente Band of Indians, whose ancestors carved petroglyphs etched on rocks in **Andreas Canyon**, while **Palm Canyon** has the largest palm grove in North America. Shady and cool, the canyons offer a good chance for hikers to spot mule deer, rabbits, and even bighorn sheep on the craggy canyon slopes – **Murray Canyon** is recommended for wildlife viewing amid its oases of sycamores, cottonwoods, and willows.

🚗 *Take S Palm Canyon Rd north and turn right onto SR 111 (E Palm Canyon Dr) for Palm Desert (12 miles/19 km). Park on El Paseo.*

③ Palm Desert
Riverside County; 92260

The most upscale of the Desert Resort communities, Palm Desert is the Coachella Valley's main center for arts – the McCallum Theater for the Performing Arts hosts performances by international stars. Lined with upscale boutiques and art galleries, **El Paseo** boulevard is studded with 18 contemporary sculptures. Stroll the **Civic Center Sculpture Walk** *(Fred Waring Dr & San Pablo Ave)* to admire its avant-garde sculptures. On the south side of town, the **Living Desert** *(www.livingdesert.org)* is a huge wilderness zoo, home to bighorn sheep, mountain lions, and other creatures that inhabit deserts and savannas around the world.

🚗 *Continue east on SR 111 to Indio.*

④ Indio
Riverside County; 92201

This working-class town has been largely shaped by its sizable Mexican population, many of whom work in the date palm groves that extend for miles south of town. The story of date production is explained at **Shields Date Garden** *(www.shieldsdategarden.com)*. A store sells 12 kinds of dates, including gift boxes, and drinking a date shake at the 1950s counter is *de rigueur*.

The historic Old Town is graced by seven **Indio Murals** tracing the city's past. Guided walks led by museum docents can be arranged *(www.indiochamber.org)*.

🚗 *Continue east on SR 111, then turn right on SR 86 (Harrison St) for Salton City (34 miles/55 km).*

The Humble Date

Date palms were introduced to California by the Spanish around 1765 and cultivated in the Coachella Valley by the early 1900s. Today, more than a dozen varieties of dates are grown in about 5,000 acres (2,000 ha) of groves. The palm needs lots of ground water and a hot, dry climate to fruit. Commercial date gardens typically have one pollen-producing male tree per 50 fruit-bearing females, which can produce 150 lbs (68 kg) of fruit annually for about 70 years.

Above Palm-studded Palm Canyon, Indian Canyons **Below left** Date palms lining an irrigated field, Indio

EAT AND DRINK

PALM SPRINGS

Rick's *inexpensive*
This Cuban-American diner serves *ropa vieja* (a shredded meat dish), with omelets, pancakes, and fruit, and *huevos rancheros* (eggs on a tortilla) all-day breakfasts. Salmon salads and hot plates, tuna melts, and meatloaf sandwiches for lunch.
1973 N Palm Canyon Dr, 92262; 760 416 0090; open 6am–3pm daily; www.ricksrestaurant.biz

Johannes *expensive*
Sophisticated ambience, great service, and creative fusion fare. Try the roasted beets with goat's cheese, the wild mushroom soup, or Weiner Schnitzel with creamed cucumber.
196 S Indian Canyon Dr, 92262; 760 778 0017; closed Mon; www.johannesrestaurants.com

PALM DESERT

Castelli's *expensive*
This Italian restaurant serves pasta, superb seafood, and a 10-ounce (275 g) filet mignon with marsala wine sauce.
73098 SR 111, 92260; 760 773 3365; open Jun–Aug: 5:30–10pm Wed–Sat, Sep–May: 5:30–10pm daily; www.castellis.cc

INDIO

The Café at Shield's *inexpensive*
This courtyard café serves omelet and pancake breakfasts, plus *huevos rancheros* with cactus and Peruvian beans. Leave room for a date shake.
80225 SR 111, 92201; 760 775 0902; open 7am–2:30pm daily; www.shieldsdategarden.com

Above One of the many trails in Mount San Jacinto State Wilderness

VISITING ANZA BORREGO

Tourist Information
Borrego Springs Chamber of Commerce & Visitor Center *786 Palm Canyon Dr, 92004; 760 767 5555; www.borregospringschamber.com*

WHERE TO STAY

BORREGO SPRINGS

The Palms Hotel *moderate*
A Modernist hotel with comfy rooms overlooking a pool and two spacious bungalows with fireplaces. It has two restaurants.
2220 Hoberg Rd, 92004; 760 767 7788; www.thepalmsatindianhead.com

Borrego Valley Inn
moderate-expensive
This romantic hotel is themed like a rustic adobe *pueblo* and rooms are elegantly furnished in Southwestern desert style.
405 Palm Canyon Dr, 92004; 1 800 333 5810; www.borregovalleyinn.com

IDYLLWILD

Quiet Creek Inn *moderate*
Exuding cozy charm, this lodge has six duplex cabins with fireplaces in a woodsy setting. Amenities include Wi-Fi, cable TV, and DVD players.
26345 Delano Dr, 92549; 951 659 6110; www.quietcreekinn.com

⑤ Salton City
Imperial County; 92275
Half a century ago, **Salton Sea** *(www.saltonsea.ca.gov)* was a watersports resort drawing hordes of tourists to Salton City. Today, visitors come to this decrepit town to spot more than 400 bird species, such as snow geese, cormorants, and blue-footed boobies, that feast in California's largest (and most saline) lake – created accidentally in 1905 when a levee of the Imperial Canal washed out and for two years the Colorado River waters poured into the below-sea-level basin.

🚗 *Turn south off SR 86 at Salton City and turn right on S 22 and continue 28 miles (45 km) to Borrego Springs.*

⑥ Borrego Springs
San Diego County; 92004
Surrounded by Anza-Borrego Desert State Park, this slow-paced resort town thrives on seasonal tourist traffic, including golfers served by three courses. A magnet for artists, its main boulevard – Palm Canyon Drive – is lined with galleries. Life-size metal sculptures of prehistoric creatures such as mammoths, sabre-toothed cats, and giant ground sloths, plus historical figures such as Spanish expeditionary Juan Bautista de Anza stand amid the cactus and creosote bushes at **Galleta Meadows** *(www.galletameadows.com)*.

Sculpture of a gomphotherium, Galleta Meadows

🚗 *Take Palm Canyon Dr west to the Anza Borrego Desert State Park visitor center.*

⑦ Anza-Borrego Desert State Park
San Diego County; 92004
The largest state park in California tempts with a chance to head out on foot, bike, or horse to experience the desert close up. Etched with scenic canyons and buttes, it is renowned for its spring wildflowers. Spade-foot toads and desert pupfish can be seen when pools fill with winter rains, while bighorn sheep can be spotted amid the craggy canyons. Stop at the **visitor center** *(200 Palm Canyon Dr, Borrego Springs; 760 767 4205; www.parks.ca.gov/)* to look at exhibits on desert ecology. From here, the popular **Borrego Palm Canyon Trail** leads to a palm oasis, and **Hellhole Canyon Trail** leads uphill to **Maidenhair Falls**. More than two dozen other trails throughout the park range from easy to challenging; pick up a trail guide before setting out. The Anza-Borrego Foundation *(www.theabf.org)* offers educational hikes plus campfire programs. South of Borrego Springs, signs along SR 78 point the way to ancient Native American sites in the **Indian Hill** area. The County Road S2 leads to **Box Canyon**, an unmarked, rugged hike, and to lush **Bow Willow Canyon**, a former village site. Look out for rock-art pictographs and *morteros* – hollows for grinding seeds. Toward the east, the **Borrego Badlands** offer spectacular scenery.

🚗 *Exit Borrego Springs west on S 22, continue on San Felipe Rd and then turn right on SR 79 to Warner Springs (28 miles/45 km from Borrego Springs).*

Above Desert landscape at the entrance to Anza-Borrego Desert State Park

⑧ Warner Springs
San Diego County; 92086
On the old Butterfield Overland Mail stagecoach route, this small community nestles in a vale beneath the Cuyamaca Mountains. The windswept valley is a popular venue for gliding – **Sky Sailing** *(www.skysailing.com)* arranges trips. The **Warner Springs Ranch**, which includes the 1849 adobe home of pioneer frontiersman Kit Carson, is a renowned spa retreat that offers horseback riding, golfing, and spa treatments at its hot mineral springs.

Farther along, call in at **Shadow Mountain Vineyard** *(34680 SR 79; 760 782 0778; www.shadowmountain vineyards.com)* to taste premium local wines. The **Oak Grove Butterfield Stage Station** nearby is well preserved.

🚗 *Take SR 79 north to Aguanga (20 miles/32 km), then SR 371 right to SR 74 (20.5 miles/33 km). Turn left to Mountain Center (12.5 miles/20 km), then turn right on SR 243 for Idyllwild.*

⑨ Idyllwild
Riverside County; 92549
Deep in a ponderosa pine forest, this alpine resort is popular in summer with visitors escaping the desert heat for hiking, horseback riding, and rock climbing – **Tahquitz Rock** and **Suicide Rock** are famous climbing venues. Idyllwild is home to many bohemian artists and has a lively cultural scene. Book hotels months ahead for the annual Jazz in the Pines Festival (Aug).

From town, Deer Springs Trail and Devils Slide Trail lead to the **Mount San Jacinto State Wilderness**, part of the 272,000 acre (110,884 ha) Santa Rosa & San Jacinto Mountains National Monument. The latter trail connects with the **Pacific Crest Trail**

(www.pcta.org), extending from Mexico to Canada. However, most visitors access the wilderness from Palm Springs via the Palm Springs Aerial Tram *(see p215)*, which offers a 10-minute ride aboard a rotating tramcar. From the Tramway Mountain Station (8,516 ft/2,596 m), an easy loop trail through **Long Valley** has nature signs. More adventurous hikers can ascend a trail to the summit of the 10,834-ft (3,302-m) high **Mt San Jacinto**, reached from both the tram and Idyllwild. In winter, it is a great for snow-shoeing and cross-country skiing.

Above California fan palms at the start of Palm Canyon Trail, Anza-Borrego Desert State Park **Below left** Snow in spring, Mount San Jacinto State Wilderness

VISITING MOUNT SAN JACINTO STATE WILDERNESS

Tourist Information
25905 SR 243, Idyllwild, 92549; 951 659 2607; open daily; www.parks.ca.gov/

EAT AND DRINK

BORREGO SPRINGS

The Krazy Coyote *moderate*
This restaurant in The Palms Hotel has an eclectic menu ranging from sashimi to rack of lamb and filet mignon. The adjoining Red Ocotillo serves comfort food and has a palm-shaded patio. *2220 Hoberg Rd, 92004; 760 767 7788; open 5–8:15pm Mon–Thu, 5–8:45pm Fri & Sat; www.thepalmsatindianhead.com*

IDYLLWILD

Café Aroma *inexpensive*
A hub for local bohemians serving eggs Benedict and pancakes, squash casserole, garlic bisque, and polenta pie. Live jazz and poetry readings. *54750 N Circle Dr, 92549; 951 659 5212; open 7am–9pm Mon–Thu, 7am–10pm Fri & Sat; www.cafearoma.org*

DAY TRIP OPTIONS
This drive can be divided into three distinct day trips that cater to specialized interests.

Cultured Coachella
Tour the museums, Modernist buildings, and murals of Palm Springs ❶, Palm Desert ❸, and Indio ❹.

All the sights are accessed directly off

SR 111, which begins as Palm Canyon Dr in Palm Springs.

Desert delights
Be sure to pack hiking shoes to explore Anza-Borrego Desert State Park ❼, where dozens of trails begin near Borrego Springs ❻.

From Palm Springs, take SR 111 to SR 86, then SR 22 west to Borrego Springs.

Mountain highs
Nature lovers can head to Mount San Jacinto State Wilderness, which can be accessed from Idyllwild ❾, or Palm Springs ❶ via the Palm Springs Aerial Tram.

From Palm Springs, take SR 111 west to I-10, then SR 234 south from Banning to reach Idyllwild.

- Stockton
- San Jose
- Monterey
- Fresno
CALIFORNIA
- Bakersfield
Santa Barbara •
Los Angeles
• San Bernardino
• San Diego

Edge of the World

Redlands to Cajon Junction

Highlights

- **A citrusy tale**
  Explore charming Redlands, once the largest producer of navel oranges in the world

- **Forest in the sky**
  Hike amid Douglas firs in the San Bernardino National Forest, home to Southern California's highest peak

- **Birding pleasures**
  Look out for bald eagles, herons, and pelicans at Big Bear Lake

- **Fun on the lake**
  Enjoy a ride on Lake Arrowhead aboard the *Lake Arrowhead Queen* paddle steamer

A fruit-laden orange grove and towering date trees along a road in Redlands

Edge of the World

The Rim of the World Scenic Byway traverses the border of the San Bernardino Mountains from San Gorgonio Pass to Cajon Pass, passing through some of the most pristine natural areas in Southern California. The drive skirts sparkling lakes and connects the lowlands to the alpine resort towns of Big Bear City and Lake Arrowhead. Warm summer days are perfect for hiking, biking, or rowing a boat around Crestline's Lake Gregory in the pine-scented air. In winter, the mountains clad in snow draw skiers to Big Bear's acclaimed slopes. The gateway town of Redlands is one of the prettiest in Southern California, with tree-shaded streets lined with Victorian mansions.

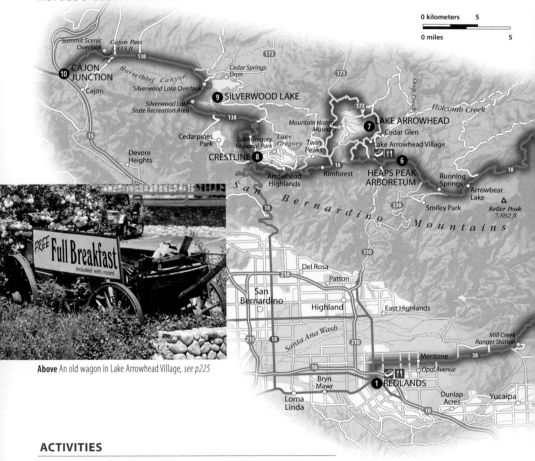

Above An old wagon in Lake Arrowhead Village, *see p225*

ACTIVITIES

Stroll the streets of Redlands and absorb its mellow urban ambience

Hike in San Bernardino National Forest and take in the scent of pine trees and the fresh mountain air

Ride the Scenic Sky Chair lift to the top of Snow Summit near Big Bear Lake

Walk the Sequoia Trail at Heaps Peak Arboretum to admire the wildflowers and other alpine flora

Fish for trout and spot bald eagles at Silverwood Lake

KEY

 Drive route

Above Wildflowers growing along the shore of Silverwood Lake, *see p225*

Doble

18

Baldwin Lake
Ecological Reserve

Bertha Peak
8,201 ft △

4 BALDWIN LAKE

Fawnskin

38

Big Bear
Discovery Center

Baldwin Lake
Stables

BIG BEAR LAKE **5**

Big Bear
Solar Observatory

Big Bear
City

Woodlands

Boulder Bay

18

Big Bear
Lake

Moonridge

38

Big Bear
Dam

Snow Summit
Ski Resort

ONYX
SUMMIT

Snow Summit
8,200 ft △

3

White Mt. Peak
14,246 ft △

Seven
Oaks

Sugarloaf Mountain
9,952 ft △

Santa Ana

Barton Flats
Visitor Center

38

Angelus
Oaks

2

SAN BERNARDINO
NATIONAL FOREST

Anderson Peak
10,840 ft △

Dry
Lake

San Bernardino
Peak △
10,649 ft

*San Gorgonio
Wilderness*

San Gorgonio
11,502 ft △

Thurman Flats

Mountain
Home Village

Mill Creek Canyon

Forest Falls

Oak
Glen

Above Rim of the World Scenic Byway snaking through the
San Bernardino Mountains

PLAN YOUR DRIVE

Start/finish: Redlands to Cajon
Junction.

Number of days: 2–3 days, allowing a
full day for skiing at Big Bear in winter.
Negotiating the winding mountain
roads may take longer than expected.

Distance: 135 miles (217 km).

Road conditions: The mountain
roads have steep inclines and
switchback bends. The route can be
snowbound in winter, when snow
chains may be needed. The road
around Crestline is often shrouded in
fog; drive with the headlights on.
Roads are well signed, but follow the
directions carefully, as there are many
minor roads in the mountains.

When to go: The San Bernardino
Mountains are popular year round –
summer is warm with clear weather
and winter offers excellent skiing.
Come prepared for very cold weather
and possible snow storms in winter.

Main market days: Redlands: 6–9pm
Thu. Big Bear City: 8:30am–1pm Tue.
Lake Arrowhead: summer: 5–8pm Fri.

Opening times: Shops open 9am–5pm
Mon–Sat, but many stay open later in
summer. Ski resorts open 9am–
4:30pm in winter, and often stay open
into May, depending on snow levels.

Shopping: Look out for carved tree
trunks in Big Bear Lake.

Major festivals: Redlands:
Shakespeare Festival, May;
Summer Music Festival, Jun; Redlands
Spring Festival, Sep. Big Bear Lake:
JazzTrax Summer Festival, Jun;
International Film Festival, Sep. Lake
Arrowhead: Film Festival, Apr; Art &
Wine Festival, Jun.

DAY TRIP OPTIONS

Those who enjoy the **outdoors** are in
their element around the mountain
lakes, and **shoppers** can browse for
custom wood carvings in **Big Bear
Lake**, and for clothing and accessories
at **Lake Arrowhead**. **Redlands** will
appeal to **history lovers**. For full
details, *see p225*.

Above Old bell at Asistencia Misión de San Gabriel, Redlands **Below** A lone Jeffrey Pine in San Bernardino National Forest

VISITING REDLANDS

Tourist Information
Chamber of Commerce *1 E Redlands Blvd, 92373; 909 793 2546*

Parking
Most downtown streets are unmetered but have a 2-hour time limit. For longer stays, use the lots on Redlands Blvd & 6th St.

WHERE TO STAY

REDLANDS

Ayres Hotel *moderate*
A modern hotel in typical California Mission-style, it has 107 deluxe rooms with furnishings inspired by old-world Spain, yet with modern amenities, including kitchenettes. It is set beside the I-10 freeway.
1015 W Colton Ave, 92374; 909 335 9024; www.ayreshotels.com

Where to Stay: inexpensive under $100; moderate $100–200; expensive over $200

❶ Redlands

San Bernardino County; 92373

This sprawling city has a charming small-town feel, enhanced by eclectic Victorian mansions built with the wealth generated from the orange groves that were Redland's major industry in the 19th century. The well-preserved historic downtown is a delight to walk. There are also several other attractions that can be visited by car, such as the 1830 Asistencia Misión de San Gabriel and the San Bernardino County Museum, tracing the area's history and natural history.

A two-hour walking tour

Park on Redlands Boulevard and walk to the **Chamber of Commerce** ① *(1 E Redlands Blvd; 909 793 2546)*, which has a tourist bureau, and walk north one block to admire the **Santa Fe Depot** ② *(Orange St & Oriental Ave)*, an 1888 train station with a Grecian portico and columns. Return along Orange Street, cross Redlands Boulevard, and turn left on State Street, a tree-lined boulevard with charming buildings; note the huge clock outside **Smith's Jewellers** ③ *(110 E State St)*, and the **murals** ④ on 6th Street. Turn right on 6th Street and right on Citrus Avenue, then left on Cajon Street. Look out for the Romanesque **City Hall** ⑤ *(Cajon St & E Citrsus Ave)*, built as a Depression-era project. It is slated to house the Redlands Museum *(www.redlands historicalmuseum.org)*. Turn right onto Vine Street for the redbrick **Smiley Library** ⑥ *(125 W Vine St; 909 798 7565; www.akspl.org)*. Built in 1898 in flamboyant Moorish Mission style, its interior features oak carvings of gargoyles and griffins. The triangular park out front is pinned by the **Smiley Memorial** ⑦ *(Eureka St & Vine St)*, dedicated to 19th-century benefactors Albert and Alfred Smiley. Walk one block north along Eureka Street to Brookside Avenue, where the 1933 **Post Office** ⑧ *(201 Brookside Ave)* is exemplary of Spanish Revival architecture. Admire the ornate ironwork, old brass postal boxes, and Post Office Museum, in the former postmaster's office. The 1962 Modernist-style **City of Redlands Safety**

Hall ⑨ is across the street. Next, walk west on Brookside Avenue and turn left on Grant Street. After 110 yards (100 m), walk through the **Redlands Bowl** ⑩ *(www.redlandsbowl.org)*, an open-air Classical amphitheater that hosts the annual Shakespeare Festival. Back on Eureka Street, stop at the **Lincoln Memorial Shrine** ⑪ *(www.lincolnshrine.org)*, the only museum west of the Mississippi River dedicated to the study of Abraham Lincoln and the American Civil War. Its fascinating exhibits include Civil War firearms and uniforms. Exit the memorial onto 4th Street and walk south one block; turn left on W Olive Avenue. The redbrick Gothic **First Congregational Church** ⑫ *(2 W Olive Ave)*, completed in 1899, stands on the northwest corner. Turn left onto Cajon Street to return to the car.
🚗 *Exit Redlands north on Orange St. Turn right on E Lugonia Ave. Fill up with gas at Wabash Ave or Opal Ave and continue on SR 38 (later Mill Creek Rd) for the Mill Creek Ranger Station.*

② San Bernardino National Forest

San Bernardino County; 92408
Delineated in 1907, this 1,236 sq-mile (3,200 sq-km) pristine wilderness rises from shaded canyons to 11,502 ft (3,506 m) on top of Mt San Gorgonio. Stop at **Mill Creek Ranger Station** *(34701 Mill Creek Rd, Mentone, 92359; 909 382 2882)*, against a scenic backdrop on the chaparral-covered lower slopes of the San Bernardino Mountains. From here the road rises through the Santa Ana River Valley via **Angelus Oaks**, with views over Thurman Flats, which has trails through California's largest alder grove; bring binoculars to spot rare birds, mule deer, and black bears along the rivercourse. The road then begins to switchback uphill, offering stunning vistas down the mountain. Stop after 7 miles (12 km) at **Barton Flats Visitor Center** *(909 794 4861; summer only)*, the main gateway to the trails and campgrounds of the San Gorgonio Wilderness, which tempts with placid lakes, alpine meadows, and granite peaks. An Adventure Pass for hiking and camping can be obtained at ranger stations and various outlets.
🚗 *Continue north on SR 38 to Onyx Summit.*

③ Onyx Summit

San Bernardino County
A roadside marker 30.2 miles (48.6 km) north of Mill Creek Ranger Station denotes Onyx Summit, which at 8,443 ft (2,573 m) is the highest point of the climb, as well as the highest highway pass in Southern California. The approach to the summit offers sensational views of Mt San Gorgonio, glistening with snow well into summer. Look out for bighorn sheep, deer, and eagles. From the summit, the road begins to descend to Big Bear Basin.
🚗 *Continue north on SR 38 to the T-junction. Turn right onto Shay Rd to circle Baldwin Lake. Keep left at the junction with N Shore Dr; park roadside.*

④ Baldwin Lake

San Bernardino County; 92314
Set in a treeless plain, this alkaline T-shaped lake is located at the northeast end of Big Bear Valley. It often dries up in the summer and ices over in winter, when bald eagles flock and can be seen roosting on top of bare pines. Isolation, pebble-strewn clay soils, and harsh conditions have created a plant community found nowhere else on earth. The lake is surrounded by wetlands, chaparral, and seasonal meadows that flare up in spring, when endemic plants such as slender-petaled mustard, buckwheat, and paintbrush blossom after the snow melts away. The **Baldwin Lake Ecological Reserve** on the north side of the lake has a self-guided interpretive trail, which offers the chance to spot coyotes, deer, the occasional mountain lion, screech owls, red-tailed hawks, and kestrels. **Baldwin Lake Stables** *(www.baldwinlakestables.com)* offers horseback rides, and kids can ride ponies, and stroke llamas, goats, and other farm animals.
🚗 *Continue west along N Shore Dr for Big Bear Lake.*

Sign, San Bernardino National Forest

> Pinnacles
> **TRAILHEAD**
> SAN BERNARDINO
> *National Forest*

VISITING SAN BERNARDINO NATIONAL FOREST

Tourist Information
USDA Forest Service *909 382 2600; www.fs.usda.gov/sbnf*

VISITING BALDWIN LAKE

Tourist Information
North Shore Dr & Holcomb Valley Rd; 909 484 0167; open Apr–Jul: 10am–2pm Sat

EAT AND DRINK

REDLANDS

Café Royal *inexpensive*
A coffee shop in the heart of historic downtown, it serves gourmet coffees and teas, plus panini sandwiches, salads, and pastries. Free Wi-Fi.
101 Cajon St, 92373; 909 335 6787; open 6am–9pm Mon–Fri, 7am–10pm Sat & Sun

Joe Greensleeves *moderate*
Try the clams and mussels in white wine sauce, then a classic New York steak or salmon with champagne and caper cream sauce at this elegant yet casual surf-and-turf restaurant.
220 N Orange St, 92373; 909 792 6969; open 11am–2:30pm & 5–9pm Mon–Fri, 5–9pm Sat; www.joegreensleeves restaurant.com

Wild Rocket *moderate*
This fun and friendly establishment whips up dishes big on flavor. Go for the Kobe beef sliders and do not miss out on the incredible selection of beers, many from local breweries.
345 W Pearl St 140, 92374; 909 798 6300; open 5pm–midnight Mon–Thu, 5pm–2am Fri, 10am–2pm Sat & Sun

Eat and Drink: inexpensive under $25; moderate $25–50; expensive over $50

Above Canoeing at Boulder Bay, Big Bear Lake
Below Big Bear Solar Observatory

VISITING BIG BEAR LAKE

Tourist Information
630 Bartlett Rd, Big Bear Lake, 92315;
909 866 7000; www.bigbear.com

VISITING LAKE ARROWHEAD

Tourist Information
J Putnam Henck Visitor Center
28200 SR 189, Lake Arrowhead Village,
92352; 909 337 3715;
www.lakearrowhead.net

WHERE TO STAY

AROUND BIG BEAR LAKE
Windy Point Inn *moderate*
Val and Kent Kessler are gracious hosts
at this lakeside B&B with fabulous
views through vast picture windows.
Spacious guestrooms have fireplaces
and balconies; some have in-room
whirlpool tubs.
39015 N Shore Dr, Fawnskin, 92333; 909
866 2746; www.windypointinn.com

LAKE ARROWHEAD
Lake Arrowhead Resort & Spa
expensive
A deluxe lakeside lodge with 162
rooms and 11 suites, all sumptuously
furnished. It has a full-service spa and
an elegant restaurant looking out over
the lake.
27984 Hwy 189, 92352; 909 336 1511;
www.laresort.com

⑤ Big Bear Lake
San Bernardino County; 92315
This popular resort area lures visitors
for watersports, hiking, and biking
during the summer, and is
transformed into the region's largest
ski resort in winter. The lake draws
waterfowl in winter, and great blue
herons and American white pelicans
can be seen year round. On its north
shore, the **Big Bear Discovery Center**
(www.sbnfa.org) has exhibits on local
ecology and information on outdoor
recreation. Guided tours to see bald
eagles are offered in winter, as are
spring flower walks. Nearby, the **Big
Bear Solar Observatory** *(www.bbso.
njit.edu)*, the world's largest solar
telescope, rises over the lake at the
end of a pier. Continue west as the
road snakes along the shore to the
quaint hamlet of **Fawnskin**, an alpine
village with old Western antique
stores, saloons, and Fawn Park, which
has a stuffed grizzly bear and other
life-size "Old West" figures.
Backtrack along North Shore Drive
and turn right onto Stanfield Cutoff to
cross the lake; then turn left onto Big
Bear Boulevard to reach Big Bear City.
Here, the **Big Bear Valley Museum**
*(Greenway Dr; 909 585 8100; open May–
Oct: 10am–4pm Wed, Sat & Sun)* has a
trove of antiques and artifacts
including a collection of early skis
and sleds, restored wagons, and even
an old hearse. In summer, **Snow
Summit Ski Resort** on the south
shore, transforms one of its lifts into
the Scenic Sky Chair. Take it for a
15-minute ride to the summit at
8,200 ft (2,499 m) for hiking or
mountain biking; bikes can be rented
on site. SR 18 leads west along the

Bald Eagles
The San Bernardino Mountains
support the largest wintering bald
eagle population in Southern
California. The eagles arrive in
November and depart by June.
They usually move between
Arrowhead, Big Bear, and
Silverwood lakes. The birds
are easily seen perched on the
tallest trees near open water or
skimming the water for fish.

south shore to the exquisite **Boulder
Bay**, made more scenic by boulders
that stud the lake. Continue to **Big
Bear Dam**, where SR 18 and SR 38 join.
Westward, the Rim of the World
Scenic Byway winds up to **Lakeview
Point**; stop to admire the views of the
lake and San Gorgonio Wilderness.
🚗 *From the dam, continue left on SR
18 via Running Springs to Heaps Peak
Arboretum (17.5 miles/28 km).*

⑥ Heaps Peak Arboretum
San Bernardino County; 92352
Learn about the flora of the San
Bernardino National Forest at the
Heaps Peak Arboretum *(www.
heapspeakarboretum.com)*, west of
Running Springs. An Adventure Pass,
available at ranger stations around
the National Forest must be
displayed on the car windshield. The
self-guided Sequoia Trail loop leads
through dense forest of Arizona
cypress, quaking aspen, black oak,
and white fir. Stop at the footbridges
over a seasonal creek to spot gray
fox, mule deer, and other mammals.
The trail passes through a grove of
giant sequoias planted in 1930.
🚗 *Continue west on SR 18 to the
junction with SR 173. Turn right for
Lake Arrowhead.*

⑦ Lake Arrowhead
San Bernardino County; 92352
This scenic mountain resort is
centered on a private lake, and while
the public has limited access to the
waters, it is possible to journey across
the crystal-clear waters on the *Lake
Arrowhead Queen* paddlewheel boat
(www.lakearrowheadqueen.com), which
offers narrated tours. **McKenzie
Water Ski School** *(www.mckenziewaters
kischool.com)* provides water-skiing,
including lessons, for all ages. Step
back in time at the **Mountain History**

Museum *(909 336 6666; www.rimofthe worldhistory.com)*, with exhibits on early Native American cultures and the area's history as a center for logging and as an escape for Hollywood stars. **Lake Arrowhead Village** *(28200 Hwy 189)*, on the south shore, has dozens of shops and discount outlets, and **Cedar Glen**, in the hills to the lake's southeast, has several antique stores.

🚗 *Circle the lake on SR 173; turn left onto N Grass Valley Rd. Take a left at junction with SR 189 and continue to Daley Canyon Rd, turn right to return to SR 18. Continue to junction with SR 138 and turn right for Crestline.*

⑧ Crestline
San Bernardino County; 92325
A labyrinth of lanes, this sprawling community at 4,800 ft (1,463 m) is often shrouded in fog rising from the Los Angeles Basin, and at least 20°F (7°C) cooler than down the mountain. Consider a short side trip to **Lake Gregory Regional Park**, which boasts a jade-colored lake. Rent paddleboats and rowboats, or get a thrill from waterslides.

🚗 *Continue on SR 138 for 10.5 miles (17 km) to Silverwood Lake.*

⑨ Silverwood Lake
San Bernardino County
Formed in 1971 by the construction of Cedar Springs Dam, this lake at 3,350 ft (1,067 m) and the park *(www. parks.ca.gov/)* that surrounds it form a major recreational area. Thirteen miles (20 km) of hiking and biking trails offer a chance to see California mule deer, black bear, and beavers along the Mojave River. The lake attracts Canada geese and other waterfowl, and in winter, bald eagles glide silently over the lake; guided eagle-spotting tours are offered Feb–Jun. The south shore has two swimming beaches and a marina with boat rentals. The best view of the lake is from the Silverwood Lake Overlook.

🚗 *Continue west on SR 138, which climbs to Silverwood Lake Overlook before descending through Horsethief Canyon to Cajon Junction.*

⑩ Cajon Junction
San Bernardino County; 92371
Descendng from the San Bernardino Mountain, the route straightens and flattens out through **Horsethief Canyon**, so named because Ute Native Americans used it to move stolen horses in the 1800s. Now in the Mojave Desert, witness the pine forests give way to cactus and Joshua trees. At the valley's western end, SR 138 weaves downhill through badlands to Cajon Junction, where it meets the I-15 freeway, which climbs through Cajon Pass and connects Las Vegas to San Bernardino and Los Angeles. Stop at the **Summit Scenic Overlook**, about 600 yards (660 m) west of Cleghorn Road, for a superb view over the canyon and a dramatic bend in the Burlington Northern Santa Fe Railroad immediately below.

Above Approaching Cajon Junction on SR 138
Below left Views over Silverwood Lake

EAT AND DRINK

BIG BEAR LAKE
Big Bear Mountain Brewery *moderate*
This brew-pub serves dishes such as home-made chili and hot beef dip sandwiches to accompany its six hearty pilsners, ales, and stouts.
40260 Big Bear Blvd, 92315; 909 866 2337; open 11:30am–8:30pm Mon–Fri, 11am–10pm Sat & Sun; www.mountainbrewery.com

Hacienda Grill *moderate*
This no-frills Mexican restaurant serves consistently tasty and satisfying food.
41787 Big Bear Blvd, 92315; 909 866 8667; open 11am–9pm Sun–Thu, 11am–10pm Fri & Sat; www.haciendagrill.net

LAKE ARROWHEAD
Belgian Waffle Works *inexpensive*
This dockside restaurant offers waffles, sandwiches, and burgers.
28200 Hwy 189 # E150, 92352; 909 337 5222; open summer: 8am–5pm Mon–Thu, 8am–8pm Fri & Sat, 8am–6pm Sun; winter: 8am–4pm Mon–Thu, 8am–5pm Fri–Sun; www.belgianwaffle.com

---

DAY TRIP OPTIONS
This route can be broken up into day trips serving different interests.

A day in Redlands
Visit the mid 19th-century Asistencia Misión de San Gabriel *(26930 Barton Rd; open 10am–3pm Tue–Sat)*, and stop by the French château-style Kimberly Crest House *(1325 Prospect Dr; www.kimberlycrest.org)*, which overlooks tiered Italianate gardens.

End with a stroll around downtown Redlands ①.

From the Asistencia head east on Barton Rd, and turn right onto Terracina Blvd. Turn left on W Cypress Ave, right on S Center St, and left on W Highland Ave for Kimberly Crest. Exit on Cajon St and head north for downtown.

Outdoors and shopping
Hike or bike the trails around Big Bear Lake ⑤ and pick up log carvings of bears or eagles at custom workshops at the namesake city. Alternatively, enjoy watersports on Lake Arrowhead ⑦ and then shop for discount clothing at factory outlets in Lake Arrowhead Village.

Big Bear Lake is on SR 38, then return on North shore Dr and SR 18 for the city. SR 18 leads to Lake Arrowhead and Lake Arrowhead Village.

Surf Country
La Jolla to Avalon

Highlights

- **Lofty La Jolla**
  Stroll the town's hilly shorefront lanes lined with quaint cottages and gorgeous mansions

- **Maritime marvels**
  Be amazed by the sea creatures at the Scripps Institute of Oceanography's Birch Aquarium

- **Hang ten**
  Ride the waves at San Clemente, one of California's finest surfing spots

- **Chill on Catalina**
  Take the high-speed ferry to Catalina Island to relax at the resort town of Avalon

Expertly surfing the waves of the Pacific at San Clemente

Surf Country

Paralleled virtually the entire way by the scenic Pacific coast highway, the coast north of San Diego offers a visual treat of seemingly endless white-sand beaches framed by craggy cliffs. The beach culture is sophisticated, and the surf scene is laid-back yet intense. This drive begins in La Jolla, an exclusive resort and university town, and the setting for a world-class aquarium and underwater marine reserve. Farther ahead, there are coastal wildlife sanctuaries, lively beach towns, two 18th-century Spanish missions, LEGOLAND®, and the thrill of horse races at Del Mar Racetrack. The route ends at the harbor town of Dana Point, from where high-speed ferries to Catalina Island offer a chance to spot dolphins and whales.

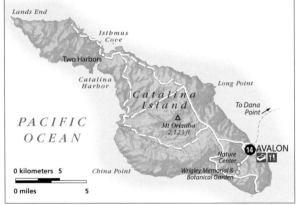

0 kilometers 5

0 miles 5

*Avalon
30 miles (50 km)*

KEY

Drive route

Above Boats moored at Avalon's harbor, Catalina Island, *see pp234–5*

ACTIVITIES

Shop the ritzy fashion stores and boutiques in La Jolla

Enjoy a nature hike along the coast in Torrey Pines State Reserve

Shoot down water slides at LEGOLAND® near Carlsbad

Swap the car for a surfboard and learn to hang ten at any of the surfing beaches

Look out for dolphins on the ferry ride to Catalina Island

Don a wetsuit and scuba tanks and take the plunge at Avalon for some of California's best diving

Above Waves lapping the sands at La Jolla Cove, La Jolla, *see p230*

PLAN YOUR DRIVE

Start/finish: La Jolla to Avalon.

Number of days: 2–3 days, allowing for at least one full day on Catalina Island.

Distance: 77 miles (124 km).

Road conditions: Mostly well-maintained major highways, but La Jolla's city streets are deteriorated, with broken, uneven paving.

When to go: Spring and fall are the best time, when the weather is sunny and warm; fall offers the best surfing.

Main market days: La Jolla: 9am–1pm Sun. Del Mar: 1–4pm Sat. Carlsbad: 1–5pm Wed & Sat.

Opening times: The missions open 10am–5pm daily. Most museums open 9am–5pm daily, but some close Mon, with shorter hours in winter. Shops usually open 10am–6pm Mon–Sat. Restaurants typically open 11am–10pm daily.

Major festivals: La Jolla: Festival of the Arts, Jun; Art & Wine Festival, Oct. Del Mar: San Diego County Fair, Jun & Jul. Solana Beach: Fiesta del Sol (music), Jun. Carlsbad: Music Festival, Sep. Catalina Island: Jazztrax, Oct.

DAY TRIP OPTIONS

This tour can be easily treated as a series of day trips. **Beach lovers** can combine the sands of **La Jolla**, **Torrey Pines**, and **Oceanside**. **History buffs** can explore the missions at **San Luis Rey** and **San Juan Capistrano**. Leave the road for a boat trip to **Avalon** on Catalina Island. For full details, *see p235*.

Above Birch Aquarium at the Scripps Institute of Oceanography, La Jolla

VISITING LA JOLLA

Tourist Information
7966 Herschel Ave; 619 236 1212; open 11am–4pm daily; www.lajollabythesea.com

Parking
Parking is at a premium, especially on weekends. Street parking is free, but spaces are very difficult to find. A one-hour limit applies to shorefront streets.

WHERE TO STAY

LA JOLLA

Marriott La Jolla *moderate*
This high-rise offers elegant rooms with such amenities as flat-screen TVs. *4240 La Jolla Village Dr, 92037; 858 587 1414; www.marriott.com*

Bed & Breakfast Inn at La Jolla *expensive*
Each of the 15 rooms here is distinct and elegant. Thoughtful extras include fresh flowers, comfy robes, and slippers. *7753 Draper Ave, 92037; 888 988 8481; www.innlajolla.com*

Hotel La Jolla *expensive*
The chic hotel is a 15-minute walk from La Jolla Shores beach and offers contemporary styling in its rooms. *7955 La Jolla Shores Dr, 92037; 858 459 0261; www.hotellajolla.com*

La Valencia Hotel *expensive*
This elegant Spanish Colonial themed charmer has hosted celebrities since 1926. Located above La Jolla Cove, it has 3 restaurants, a landscaped pool, plus 112 luxurious guest rooms. *1132 Prospect St, 92037; 858 454 0771; www.lavalencia.com*

❶ La Jolla

San Diego County; 92037

One of the most exclusive towns in California, La Jolla – pronounced "la hoya" – occupies woody hillsides that rise over cliffs and coves. Its sinuous lanes are lined with multi-million dollar mansions that afford some of the most sublime coastal vistas in the state. Called "the Monte Carlo of California," La Jolla has a Mediterranean-like setting that combines with natural beauty and a cosmopolitan lifestyle to draw film stars and the ultra-rich from around the globe.

At the downtown heart of La Jolla is The Village, where most restaurants, fashion boutiques, jewelers, art galleries, and other businesses are located along Prospect Street and Girard Avenue, the Village's main drags. Don't miss the **Museum of Contemporary Art San Diego** *(www.mcasd.org)*, occupying the 1915 former residence of philanthropist Ellen Browning Scripps. It has a prime ocean-view location above **La Jolla Cove**, where sea lions bask on the rocks. The museum's collection of 4,000 artworks dating from 1950s onwards includes a body of Pop Art, plus a sculpture garden.

La Jolla Shores, the main beach, unfurls to the north of The Village. The sweeping shoreline is popular with surfers and is a launch point for kayakers. It borders the **La Jolla Underwater Park Ecological Reserve**, drawing scuba divers to explore rocky reefs, kelp beds, and underwater canyons. Overlooking the beach, the Scripps Institute of Oceanography hosts the **Birch Aquarium** *(www.aquarium.ucsd.edu)*, with live exhibits representing 60 distinct marine habitats, including "Shark Reef" and coral displays. The Institute is part of the **University of California**, San Diego: the cliff-top campus is renowned for its distinctive Modern and Postmodern buildings and landscaped grounds dotted with artworks from the Stuart Collection of Sculpture. Free tours are offered *(2pm Sun by reservation)*.

🚗 *Exit La Jolla north via La Jolla Shores Dr to N Torrey Pines Rd (S 21); continue to the parking lots at Torrey Pines State Reserve.*

❷ Torrey Pines State Reserve

San Diego County; 92037

This majestic wilderness of cliffs and rugged ravines overlooking the sea is named for the Torrey Pine, a rare and endangered tree species that now grows wild only along this stretch of coastline. Spanning 2,000 acres (810 ha), the park *(www.parks.ca.gov/)* also protects one of the last salt marshes in Southern California, and an inland freshwater lagoon that draws migrating seabirds and waterfowl. Trails wind past wind-sculpted pines and along raised bluffs to overlooks

Below Lookout point above the picturesque La Jolla Cove at La Jolla

above sandstone cliffs. In winter, look out for California gray whales passing close to shore on their yearly migration. Fall and winter are also good times to spot California quail gathered in coveys, while wildflowers burst into bloom in spring. The visitor center, in a pueblo-style structure, has interpretive displays, plus guided nature walks on weekends and holidays. Picnicking is not permitted.

🚗 *Continue north on S 21/Hwy 101 to Del Mar; 15th St has free parking.*

Fishy Business

Every spring, California grunions wash ashore to spawn on the beaches of San Diego and Orange counties. This silvery fish species is endemic to Southern California and Baja California, in Mexico. The fish arrive two to six nights after a full moon night during high tide. Females bury their tails in the sand and lay eggs, while males wrap themselves around the females and release sperm. The eggs hatch with the next high tide, when the young grunions are washed out to sea.

❸ Del Mar

San Diego County; 92014

A beach town associated with surfing, Del Mar is the first beach mentioned in the Beach Boys hit "Surfin' USA" (1963). Its swath of golden sand sweeps north to the mouth of the San Dieguito River. **Del Mar Racetrack** *(www.dmtc. com)* is one of California's top horse-racing venues in mid-summer, and setting for the annual 3-week long San Diego County Fair.

🚗 *Continue on S 21/Hwy 101, following the Camino Del Mar sign for Solana Beach.*

Magic Carpet Ride statue, Cardiff-by-the-Sea

❹ Solana Beach

San Diego County; 92075

Beyond Del Mar, the seaside town of Solana Beach sprawls on top of coastal cliffs. Turn left onto Plaza Street for **Fletcher Cove Beach Park** in a tiny cove offering the town's only beach access via car. Cedros Avenue is lined with art galleries and boutiques. Immediately north of

town, S 21 (also called South Coast Highway 101 here) sweeps downs to Cardiff State Beach, with the wetlands of San Elijo Lagoon to the east.

🚗 *Continue along S21/Hwy 101 for Cardiff-by-the-Sea.*

❺ Cardiff-by-the-Sea

San Diego County; 92007

Named for the Welsh city, Cardiff is another beach town with top-rated surf. Cardiff Reef and Pipes are favorites among surfers for their smooth and consistent wave shape; a flat rock reef exposed at low tide is good for tide-pooling. The sands of **Cardiff State Beach** and **San Elijo State Beach** come and go with the whims of tides. Stop outside the San Elijo State Beach campground to see *Magic Carpet Ride*, or *The Cardiff Kook*, a sculpture of a surfer by Matthew Antichevich. Turn right on Chesterfield Drive, then right onto San Elijo Avenue for **San Elijo Lagoon Ecological Reserve** *(www.sanelijo.org)*. The visitor center has superb displays on the ecology of this wetland, accessible via 7 miles (12 km) of trails. The observation deck offers views of salt and freshwater marshes.

🚗 *Return to S 21/Hwy 101 and continue north to Encinitas; park at S 21/ Hwy 101 & 1st St.*

Above left Dramatic scenery at La Jolla Cove, La Jolla **Top** Show jumping at the famous Del Mar Racetrack **Above** Wild and untamed landscape of Torrey Pines State Reserve

EAT AND DRINK

LA JOLLA

The Cottage *moderate*
Start the day with eggs Benedict or granola with fruit and yogurt at this casual restaurant with patio dining. The health-conscious menu ranges from shrimp and crab salad and mushroom-stuffed ravioli to meatloaf. *7702 Fay Ave, 92037; 858 454 8409; open Jun–Aug: 7:30am–9pm daily, Sep–May: closed for dinner; www.cottagelajolla.com*

George's at the Cove *expensive*
This three-story restaurant has three venues and appeals with its trendy ambience. California Modern serves fusion dishes crafted from seasonal ingredients. The rooftop Ocean Terrace offers a California bistro menu, such as crispy calamari and Asian-style chicken wings. George's Bar has picture windows and is known for its cocktails. *1250 Prospect St, 92037; 858 454 4244; open 11am–4pm & 5:30–10pm Mon–Thu, 11am–4pm & 5–10pm Fri–Sun; www.georgesatthecove.com*

CARDIFF-BY-THE-SEA

The Beach House *moderate*
Beachfront surf-and-turf dining with a world-class sunset view. *2530 Hwy 101, 92007; 760 753 1321; open 11am–2:30pm Mon–Fri, 9am–2:30pm Sat & Sun, 4:30–10pm daily; www.thebeachhouse.com*

VISITING CARSLBAD

Tourist Information
*400 Carlsbad Village Dr; 1 800 227
5722; www.visitcarlsbad.com*

VISITING OCEANSIDE

Tourist Information
California Welcome Center *928
N Coast Hwy; 1 800 350 7873;
www.visitcwc.com/Oceanside*

WHERE TO STAY

CARLSBAD

Pelican Cove Inn *moderate*
This charming New England-style B&B
offers 10 individually styled rooms
with fireplaces and antiques.
*320 Walnut Ave, 92008; 760 434 5995;
www.pelican-cove.com*

Beach Terrace Inn *expensive*
The rooms at this chic beachfront
hotel have flat-screen TVs, iPod docks,
and free Wi-Fi. A glass-enclosed patio
and pool, and complimentary breakfast.
*2775 Ocean St, 92008; 760 729 5951;
www.beachterraceinn.com*

Carlsbad Inn Beach Resort *expensive*
Contemporary decor prevails at this
family-friendly beachfront hotel with a
pool, Mexican restaurant, and patio fire
pits. Many rooms have full kitchens.
*3075 Carlsbad Blvd, 92008; 760 434
7020; www.carlsbadinn.com*

SAN CLEMENTE

Casa Tropicana *moderate*
Gracious, fun-loving hosts at this
B&B with eight stylish rooms, all with
luxury bedding and plenty of
amenities. Pet friendly.
*610 Avenida Victoria, 92672; 949 492
1234; www.casatropicana.com*

Above right Landscaped grounds of the
San Diego Botanical Gardens, Encinitas
Below The pier at San Clemente

6 Encinitas
San Diego County; 92023
Rated by *Surfer Magazine* as one of
best surf towns in the US, tiny
Encinitas epitomizes Southern
California beach culture with its surf
shops, funky art galleries, and New
Age religious centers. Surfers flock to
hang ten at Swami's, a
point break named for
Swami Paramahansa
Yogananda, whose **Self-
Realization Fellowship
Temple** *(939 2nd St)* stands
nearby. After viewing the
beach action, turn right
onto Encinitas Boulevard
and follow the signs for
**San Diego Botanical
Gardens** *(www.SDBGarden.org)*, which
are home to 37 acres (15 ha) of plants
from all over the world, including the
nation's largest bamboo collection.
There is an interactive kids' garden too.
Encinitas is separated from
Carlsbad, to the north, by the
Batiquitos Lagoon *(www.batiquitos
foundation.org)*, a coastal wetland
where avocets, curlews, and herons
are among the 185 species of birds
that can be spotted while hiking a
2-mile (3-km) long nature trail.
🚗 *Return to S 21/Hwy 101 and drive
9 miles (15 km) north via Leucadia for
Carlsbad. Grand Ave has free parking.*

**Flowering cactus
in Encinitas**

7 Carlsbad
San Diego County; 92008
This wealthy and beautiful coastal
town was founded and named in the
1880s after the famous Czech spa
town and evolved as a spa resort
based on its mineral waters. The
deluxe resort hotels here include La
Costa Resort & Spa and the Park Hyatt

Aviara. For a history lesson, stop at
Magee Park *(258 Beech Ave)*, where
19th-century buildings include the
craftsman-style Magee House. In
spring, **The Flower Fields** at Carlsbad
Ranch *(www.theflowerfields.com)*
explode in Technicolor bloom; the
commercial flower farm can be visited
Mar–May. Nearby,
LEGOLAND® *(www.legoland.
com)* is a must-visit if
traveling with kids. This
theme park has dozens of
rides and attractions, many
made from LEGO® bricks.
🚗 *Continue north along
S 21/Hwy 101 to
Oceanside. Turn left
onto Mission Ave and
park in the lots at Rotary Park.*

8 Oceanside
San Diego County; 92049
Also a quintessential beach town,
Oceanside is renowned for its
passion for surfing, its ruler-straight
beach, and the **Oceanside Pier**, the
longest wooden pier in western US
(1,954 ft/596 m). Surfers can be seen
testing their skills at The Jetties. After
strolling the pier, walk inland two
blocks on Pier View Way pedestrian
walkway to the **Oceanside Surf
Museum** *(www.surfmuseum.org)* to
check out its collection of surfboards
dating back to the 1920s, plus
rotating exhibits on surf culture.
Three blocks east, the **Oceanside
Museum of Art** *(www.oma-online.org)*
presents five contemporary art
exhibits annually. It is housed in
adjacent Modernist buildings.
🚗 *Return along Mission Ave; keep
straight for Mission San Luis Rey,
which has free parking.*

Where to Stay: inexpensive under $100; moderate $100–200; expensive over $200

⑨ Mission San Luis Rey

San Diego County; 92057

This National Historic Landmark was founded in 1798, although the current church – adorned with a wooden dome – dates from 1811. This was the largest of the California missions, and at its peak housed almost 3,000 Luiseño Native American converts, who worked here. Following a brief period of secularization, the mission has functioned as a working Franciscan mission since 1895. The visitor center *(www.sanluisrey.org)* has a museum. Note the weathered graves in the cemetery, and crypts that house the remains of many of the friars who served here.

🚌 *Return to S 21 (N Coast Hwy) and follow the signs for I-5 N. Take the San Diego Freeway toward San Clemente. Exit on Basilone Rd (18 miles/29 km north of Oceanside) and turn left over the freeway on Old Hwy 101 for San Onofre State Beach; exit on Beach Club Rd for public parking.*

⑩ San Onofre State Beach

Orange County; 92672

Unfurling along 3 miles (5 km) of cliff-backed shore, this beach *(www. parks.ca.gov/)* is a favorite with surfers and is renowned for one of the West Coast's premier surfing spots – **Trestles**. Rugged trails cut into the sandstone bluffs provide beach access and opportunities for hiking the scenic canyons. There are campgrounds here as well.

🚌 *Return to Basilone Rd and turn left for San Diego Freeway. Continue north to the S El Camino Real exit; turn right then immediately left on El Camino Real. After 2 miles (3 km) it passes under the freeway; turn left*

onto Algodon Ave, left onto Monterey Ave, and left onto Madrid Ave. Drive to Del Mar Beach, with parking lots.

⑪ San Clemente

Orange County; 92672

This hillside town is officially nicknamed "Spanish Village by the Sea" for its Mediterranean-style housing, much of it dating from the 1920s. A maze of streets meanders up from **Del Mar Beach**. Set in an exquisite cove, the sands are a hive of activity. Walk the wooden **San Clemente Pier** – a great location for fishing and watching surfers. Perched on a bluff overseeing Del Mar Beach, the **Casa Romantica Cultural Center & Gardens** *(www.casaromantica.org)* occupies the former home of San Clemente founder Ole Hanson. Now a museum and event center, it has beautiful gardens and historic exhibits.

🚌 *Exit the beach via Avenida del Mar, which returns to N El Camino Real. Turn left and drive north to Doheny State Beach, where the road swings east as Camino Capistrano. Continue to San Juan Capistrano. Park in the lot at Camino Capistrano & Verdugo St.*

EAT AND DRINK

ENCINITAS

Savory *moderate*
A classy yet casual restaurant with a seasonal menu of European-Californian fusion dishes, and a huge wine list. It serves afternoon tea with scones. Live music on Sun evening.
267 N El Camino Real, 92024; 760 634 5556; open lunch & dinner Tue–Fri, dinner Sat & Sun; www.savorycasualfare.com

CARLSBAD

Al's Cafe in the Village *inexpensive*
Popular with locals, this diner has vinyl stools at the counter, and umbrella-shaded patio tables. Serves omelets, pancakes, and waffles for breakfasts. Try the liver and onions or meatloaf with mashed potatoes for lunch.
795 Carlsbad Village Dr, 92008; 760 729 5448

Bellefleur *moderate*
This airy, contemporary restaurant is acclaimed for its surf-and-turf dishes such as crab cakes, crispy salmon strips, filet mignon, and roasted rack of lamb.
5610 Paseo del Norte, 92008; 760 603 1919; open 11am–10pm Mon–Sat, 10am–9pm Sun; www.bellefleur.com

OCEANSIDE

101 Café *moderate*
Classic American dishes served in this casual café popular with the surfing crowd. Start the day with corned beef hash and eggs. Try the burger for lunch and fish 'n' chips for dinner. All-day breakfast served.
631 S Coast Hwy, 92054; 760 722 5220; open 7am–2pm daily; www.101cafe.net

Above left The cemetery at Mission San Luis Rey **Above right** View of a stretch of Encinitas's popular beach **Left** The shady cloister at Mission San Luis Rey

Right The restored Mission San Juan Capistrano, San Juan Capistrano **Below** Cloister at the Mission San Juan Capistrano

VISITING CATALINA ISLAND

Tourist Information
Catalina Island Chamber of Commerce
Green Pleasure Pier; 310 510 1520;
www.catalinachamber.com

Catalina Island Conservancy *310 510 1445; www.catalinaconservancy.org*

WHERE TO STAY

DANA POINT

Blue Lantern Inn *expensive*
Overlooking the harbor, this B&B offers spa treatments plus bicycles for its guests. Sophisticated decor with state-of-the-art amenities.
34343 Street of the Blue Lantern, 92629; 1 800 950 1236;
www.bluelanterninn.com

AVALON

Hermosa Hotel *inexpensive*
This family-run, pet-friendly hotel is a pleasant budget option, with simply appointed rooms.
131 Metropole St, 90704; 310 510 1010;
www.hermosahotel.com

The Inn on Mt Ada *expensive*
A gracious plantation-style inn on top of Mt Ada, this former millionaire's mansion offers sensational harbor and/or ocean views from all six individually furnished bedrooms.
398 Wrigley Rd, 90704; 310 510 2030;
www.innonmtada.com

Pavilion Hotel *expensive*
A beautiful seafront hotel with flat-screen TVs, iPads, and MP3 players. Rooms surround a courtyard garden with fire pit and an open-air lounge.
513 Crescent Ave, 94704; 310 510 2500;
www.VisitCatalinaIsland.com

⑫ San Juan Capistrano

Orange County; 92675

This town evolved around the **Mission San Juan Capistrano** *(www.missionsjc. com)*, founded in 1776. Although its Greco-Roman style Great Stone Church was toppled by an earthquake in 1812, the mission's restored cloisters and living quarters are furnished as they were 200 years ago. The Serra Chapel, built in 1782, is the oldest building in California that is still in use.

From the parking lot, take Camino Capistrano to Del Obispo Street; turn right to the **Los Rios Historic District**, comprising 31 buildings, including three adobe homes built in 1794. Stroll down historic Rios Street to the **O'Neill Museum** *(31831 Los Rios St; 949 493 8444; open 9am–noon & 1–4pm Tue–Fri, noon–3pm Sat & Sun)*, which retells the history of San Juan Capistrano; and the **Capistrano Depot**, the 1894 Spanish-colonial train station, now the setting for Sarducci's restaurant.

🚗 *Exit town west on Del Obispo St for Dana Harbor Dr. Turn left at Golden Lantern for Dana Wharf.*

⑬ Dana Point

Orange County; 92624

With a heritage closely linked to the sea, this upscale town is named after 19th-century adventurer and author, Richard Henry Dana, Jr., who wrote about the area in *Two Years Before the Mast* (1840). The huge harbor berths 2,500 boats and is a departure point for sport-fishing and whale-watching tours. The **Ocean Education Center** *(www.ocean-institute.org)* offers trips aboard two tall-masted ships – *Pilgrim* and *Spirit of Dana Point* – and the *Sea Explorer* research vessel. A public trail system links **Doheny State Beach** and **Salt Creek Beach Park**, separated by Dana Point headlands.

🚢 *The Catalina Express (1 800 481 3470; www.catalinaexpress.com) ferries passengers from Dana Wharf to Catalina Island in 90 minutes; reserve in advance. Parking in the short-term wharf lot is limited to 4 hours; use this to purchase the ferry ticket. A parking pass for the long-term lot is issued after checking in for the ferry.*

⑭ Avalon

Los Angeles County; 90704

The largest of the eight Channel Islands, Catalina Island is 22 miles (35 km) off the Californian coast. This pristine, mountainous island is home to such endemic species as the island fox, bald eagles, and even bison, and draws a large number of hikers and mountain bikers (by permit only). Scuba diving, sport-fishing, and whale-watching are other popular activities on offer. Avalon, its only city, was developed in the 1920s by chewing gum magnate William Wrigley, Jr., who purchased the isle in 1919. Occupying a sheltered valley and cove, it is a popular weekend and vacation getaway and a delight to explore.

A two-hour walking tour

Start at the **ferry terminal** ① and follow the harborside path along Pebbly Beach Road to the junction with Lower Terrace Road, where the life-size bronze *Old Ben* statue ② commemorates a sea lion that frequented the Avalon shorefront from 1898 to 1920. Turn right and follow Crescent Avenue along **South Beach ③** to **Green Pleasure Pier ④**. Walk the pier, keeping a sharp eye for sea lions in the harbor and pelicans begging for fish tidbits on the boardwalk. Pick up a map at the **Catalina Island Chamber of Commerce ⑤**. Now back on Crescent Avenue, continue past **Middle Beach ⑥** two blocks to Whittley Avenue, where a red-brick **fountain ⑦** inlaid with arty mosaics forms a tiny traffic circle. Beyond, pass under the Via Casino archway and follow the **Casino Walkway ⑧**, which is lined with exquisite ceramic murals depicting scenes from the island's culture, history, and flora and fauna. The white clapboard building overhanging the harbor is the **Catalina Yacht Club ⑨**, founded in

1924; its faux lighthouse is topped by a weathervane shaped like a galleon. The 330-ft (300-m) long causeway leads to **Avalon Casino ⑩**. Dominating the harbor, this iconic circular building is a masterpiece of Art Deco design from 1929, and a striking reminder of Catalina's illustrious past. Standing 12 stories tall, it features a lavish ballroom and movie theater. Be sure to visit the **Catalina Island Museum ⑪**, tucked on the south side of the casino, which traces the island's history. Now retrace the route along the waterfront to Sumner Avenue. Turn right and follow Sumner Avenue to the junction with Tremont Street; to the left and ahead is Avalon Canyon Road, which passes the **Pointe Catalina Island Golf Course ⑫** as it slopes gradually uphill 1 mile (1.5 km) to the Catalina Island Conservancy's **Nature Center ⑬** (310 510 0954; open summer: 10am–4pm daily, winter: closed Thu). It has excellent exhibits on local ecology. Continue uphill 0.5 mile (0.8 km) to **Wrigley Memorial & Botanical Garden ⑭** (310 510 2595; open 8am–5pm daily), which showcases plants from around the world. The centerpiece is the memorial of quarried local stone, erected in 1934. Return to Avalon; on weekends and holidays it is possible to take the Avalon Trolley (310 510 0025; $2 one way; www. catalinatransportation services.com).

Above The landmark Art Deco Avalon Casino overlooking the sea

WHERE TO EAT

SAN JUAN CAPISTRANO

Sarducci's *moderate*
Try the signature lamb Wellington or panko-encrusted halibut, and leave room for raspberry cheesecake or fried bread pudding at this atmospheric restaurant.
26701 Verdugo St, 92675; 949 493 9593; open 8am–9pm Sun–Thu, 8am–10pm Fri & Sat; www.capistranodepot.com

AVALON

Avalon Grille *moderate*
This beachfront restaurant with patio dining serves buffalo burgers, roasted chicken, delicious risotto, and mussels in a chorizo, leek, and white wine broth.
423 Crescent Ave, 90704; 310 510 7494; open 11:30am–3pm & 5–10pm daily

CC Gallagher *moderate*
An all-in-one eclectic store, art gallery, café, and sushi bar, this bohemian venue serves Japanese dishes, clam chowder, and fresh-baked treats.
523 Crescent Ave, 90704; 310 510 1278; open 7am–11:30pm daily; www.ccgallagher.com

Map

CHIMES TOWER
ROAD
⑩ **Avalon Casino**
⑪ **Catalina Island Museum**
Catalina Yacht Club ⑨
Avalon Bay
⑧ **Casino Walkway**
Ferry Terminal ①
Middle Beach
Fountain ⑦ ⑥
Green Pleasure Pier ④
South Beach
Catalina Island Chamber of Commerce ⑤ ③
PEBBLY BEACH RD
②
Old Ben Statue
CRESCENT AVE
AVENUE
METROPOLE AVE
MARILLA AVENUE
WHITTLEY AVENUE
VIEDEROLD AVE
CAM. DEL MONTE
OLIVE LN
BEACON ST
CLARESSA AVE
DESCANSO AVE
CATALINA AVE
AVENUE
SUMNER AVE
LOWER TERRACE RD
UPPER TER RD
WRIGLEY
MIDDLE TER RD
WRIGLEY ROAD
COUNTRY CLUB DR
TREMONT AVE
Nature Center ⑬
1 mile (1.5 km)
Pointe Catalina Island Golf Course ⑫
Wrigley Memorial & Botanical Garden ⑭
1.5 mile (2.5 km)
0 meters 400
0 yards 400

DAY TRIP OPTIONS

Following a single coast highway, this route is broken into two clearly delineated sections by the Marine Corps Base Camp Pendleton.

A passion for waves

There is no dearth of great spots to tackle the surf or simply watch the wave action. Be sure to stop at Del Mar ❸, Pipes at Cardiff-by-the-Sea ❺, Swami's in Encinitas ❻, and the surf museum at Oceanside ❽.

All these sights lie along or just off the Pacific coast highway, north of San Diego.

Travel back in time

The Mission San Luis Rey ❾ and Mission San Juan Capistrano ⑫ are must-sees for those interested in California's early history.

To reach Mission San Luis Rey, turn east onto Mission Ave in Oceanside. From Oceanside, I-5 and the coast highway runs north to Capistrano Beach where

it swings inland and becomes Camino Capistrano, which leads to Mission San Juan Capistrano.

Ditch the car

If tired of driving, some whale-watching or a sea voyage at Dana Point ⑬ provides a change of pace. Or take a ferry ride to Catalina Island and its resort town, Avalon ⑭.

Dana Wharf is signed off Dana Point Harbor Dr, which connects to the Pacific coast highway in Dana Point.

Eat and Drink: inexpensive under $25; moderate $25–50; expensive over $50

Scenic San Diego

Gaslamp Quarter to Balboa Park

Highlights

- **Old amid the new**
  Roam the Gaslamp Quarter –
  a historic jewel with trendy
  restaurants and boutiques

- **A pointed view**
  Visit the Old Point Loma Lighthouse
  at Cabrillo National Monument, and
  admire the view over San Diego Bay

- **The way things were**
  Wander through Old Town San
  Diego to get a feel for life as it was
  almost two centuries ago

- **Wildlife from A to Z**
  Be amazed by animals from aardvarks
  to zebras at the San Diego Zoo

Well-preserved houses in the Old Town San
Diego settlement

Scenic San Diego

Founded in 1769, San Diego has grown to be California's second largest city. Charming historic quarters merge into cosmopolitan contemporary districts in this coastal city, which boasts an agreeable Mediterranean climate and a beautiful setting on a natural deep-water harbor protected by the Cabrillo headland and sweeping Coronado peninsula. This drive winds through a medley of residential districts and weaves together many key attractions, from San Diego's lively downtown Gaslamp Quarter and Little Italy districts to the San Diego Zoo, the SeaWorld marine park, and world-class museums concentrated in Balboa Park.

Above Alcazar Gardens in front of Museum of Man in Balboa Park, *see p243*

ACTIVITIES

Absorb naval history at USS *Midway* and the Maritime Museum of San Diego

Savor the Italian flavor in the former fishing community of Little Italy

Hike the cliffside trails at Cabrillo National Monument and look out for passing whales

Hang out with the hippies at Ocean Beach

Commune with sea lions, orcas and other marine creatures at the SeaWorld aquarium

Explore the world-famous San Diego Zoo and other attractions of Balboa Park

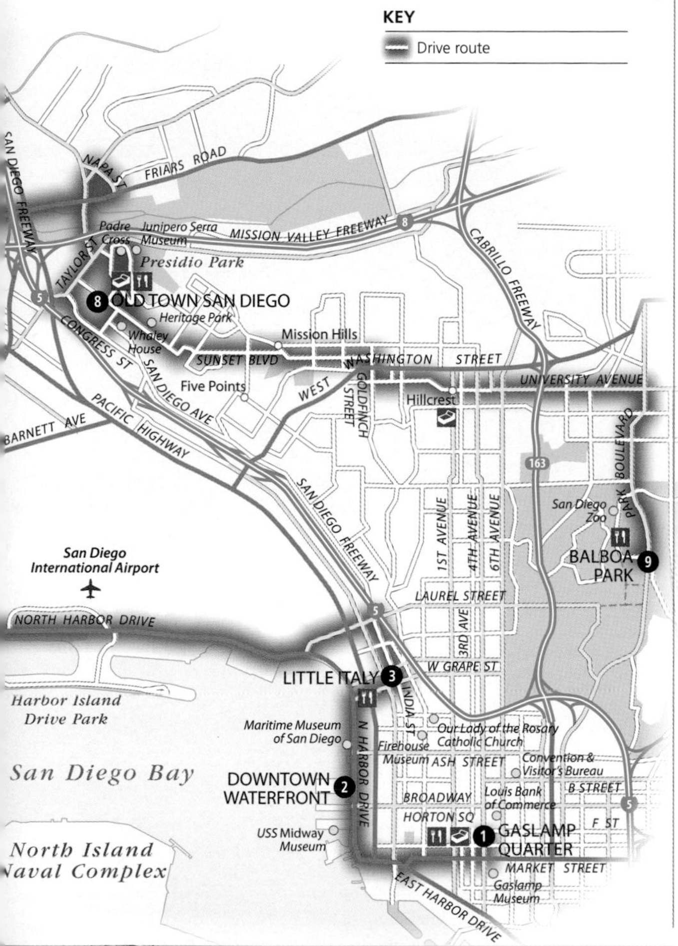

KEY

━━ Drive route

San Diego Freeway

NA PA ST
FRIARS ROAD

Padre Junipero Serra
Taylor St Cross Museum
MISSION VALLEY FREEWAY 8
CABRILLO FREEWAY

Presidio Park

5
8 **OLD TOWN SAN DIEGO**
Heritage Park
Whaley Mission Hills
House WASHINGTON STREET
SUNSET BLVD UNIVERSITY AVENUE
Five Points WEST Hillcrest
BARNETT AVE PACIFIC HIGHWAY GOLDFINCH STREET
163
SAN DIEGO AVE PARK BOULEVARD
San Diego
Zoo
San Diego
International Airport 1ST AVENUE
4TH AVENUE
6TH AVENUE **BALBOA 9**
NORTH HARBOR DRIVE **PARK**
LAUREL STREET

SAN DIEGO FREEWAY
5
3RD AVE
Harbor Island W GRAPE ST
Drive Park **LITTLE ITALY 3**
INDIA ST
Maritime Museum
of San Diego Our Lady of the Rosary
N HARBOR DRIVE Firehouse Catholic Church
DOWNTOWN Museum ASH STREET Convention &
WATERFRONT 2 BROADWAY Visitor's Bureau
Louis Bank B STREET
of Commerce
HORTON SQ F ST
San Diego Bay USS Midway **GASLAMP**
Museum **1 QUARTER**
North Island MARKET STREET
Naval Complex Gaslamp
EAST HARBOR DRIVE Museum

Above Historic vessels at the Maritime Museum of San Diego, *see p240*

PLAN YOUR DRIVE

Start/finish: Gaslamp Quarter to Balboa Park.

Number of days: 1–2 days, allowing a full day to explore Balboa Park's museum and the San Diego Zoo.

Distance: 29 miles (46 km).

Road conditions: Roads are mostly in good condition, but frequent roadworks downtown can cause confusing diversions. Major thoroughfares are subject to heavy traffic during rush hour.

When to go: San Diego has an agreeable Mediterranean climate, with mild, sunny weather year round. Early spring months offer the best weather. March is a time for celebration, with two major festivals.

Main market days: Horton Square Farmers' Market (11am–3pm Thu); Little Italy Mercato (9am–1:30pm Sat); Asian Bazaar, 3rd Ave & J St, Gaslamp Quarter (9am–1pm Sun).

Opening times: Most museums open 10am–5pm Tue–Sun. Shop hours vary, but most open 9am–5pm Mon–Sat.

Major festivals: Mardi Gras (Mar); St. Patrick's Day Parade (Mar); Old Town Cinco de Mayo (May); Wings Over Gillespie Air Show (Jun).

DAY TRIP OPTIONS

This tour is easy to break into segments that appeal to specific interests. Those interested in **history** can combine the **Gaslamp Quarter** with **Cabrillo National Monument** and **Old Town San Diego**. Families with **kids**, and **wildlife lovers**, shouldn't miss **SeaWorld** and **San Diego Zoo**; and the museums of **Balboa Park** can keep **museum-goers** enthralled for hours. For full details, *see p243*.

VISITING GASLAMP QUARTER

Tourist Information
Gaslamp Quarter Association *614 5th Ave, 92101; 619 233 5227; www.gaslamp.org*

Parking
Metered spaces are available on city streets (2-hour limit). It is possible to walk from the Gaslamp Quarter to the USS *Midway* Museum and the Maritime Museum of San Diego.

VISITING LITTLE ITALY

Tourist Information
Convention & Visitor's Bureau *750 B St, Suite 1500, 92101; 619 232 3101*

Download a walking map from the Little Italy Association website *www.littleitalysd.com*

WHERE TO STAY

GASLAMP QUARTER

Keating Hotel *expensive*
A chic luxury boutique hotel occupying a 1890s building in the Gaslamp Quarter, its interior design is by Italian car stylist Pininfarina and features lavish use of Ferrari red. *432 F St, 92101; 619 814 5700; www.thekeating.com*

Above right Arch at the entrance of the historic Gaslamp Quarter **Below** *Star of India* at the Maritime Museum of San Diego

① Gaslamp Quarter
San Diego County; 92101
This National Historic District, immediately southeast of the official downtown, comprises 16 blocks of grand Victorian buildings dating back to the city's boom years of the late 19th century. Once notorious for gambling dens, brothels, and bars, it has now been renovated to form the lively cultural heart of San Diego. Crowds of diners and bar patrons spill onto the sidewalks at night, when the streets are illuminated by cast-iron gaslamps. Look out for the **Louis Bank of Commerce** (*835 5th Ave*), built of granite in 1888; and the Florentine-Italianate style **Old City Hall** (*664 5th Ave*). A must see, the **Gaslamp Museum** (*www.gaslamp quarter.org*) occupies the city's oldest wooden structure – the William Heath Davis House.
🚗 *Head west along Market St and merge north onto Harbor Dr. Turn left onto Navy Pier, which has parking.*

② Downtown Waterfront
San Diego County; 92101
Allow up to two hours to explore the **USS *Midway* Museum** (*www.midway. org*). This mammoth decommissioned aircraft carrier was the longest-serving such vessel of the 20th century (1945–92). Admission includes a self-guided audio tour in which visitors explore this floating city at sea. Almost 30 restored aircraft from World War II to Operation Desert Storm are on display, including the SBD Dauntless dive-bomber, F-4 Phantom, and a Vietnam War-era Huey gunship; many have climb-aboard cockpits. Now walk along the harborfront to the nearby **Maritime Museum of San**

Diego (*www.sdmaritime.org*), boasting one of the world's finest collections of historic ships. Highlights include the *Star of India*, a barque built in 1863, the HMS *Surprise* – a replica of a Nelson-era Royal Navy frigate, and a Soviet submarine designed to track US and NATO warships.
🚗 *Continue north on N Harbor Dr. Turn right at W Grape St, then left onto India St for Little Italy, which has metered parking.*

③ Little Italy
San Diego County; 92101
The heart of San Diego's Italian quarter extends along India Street for five blocks to north and south of Grape Street. Established in the 1920s, it evolved as the hub of the world's tuna fishing and canning industry, when over 6,000 Italian families lived here. Today the area is a bohemian enclave of art studios, cafés, boutiques, and Italian restaurants. Wall murals depicting how this immigrant community is historically tied to the bay include *I Pescatori*, or The Fishermen, on the wall of the Convention & Visitor's Bureau. A One-Mile Walk starts on Union & W Ash Streets and is marked by granite plaques. Don't miss the Greco-Roman-style **Our Lady of the Rosary Catholic Church** (*Date St & State St*), and the **Firehouse Museum** (*1572 Columbia St; open 10am–2pm Thu & Fri, 10am–4pm Sat & Sun*), in the former Fire Station Number 6.
🚗 *Exit Little Italy along India St. Turn left onto Laurel St, which merges into N Harbor Dr. Follow it to the junction with Rosecrans St. Turn left onto Shelter Island Dr and continue to the end of Shoreline Park; free curbside parking.*

4 Shelter Island
San Diego County; 92101

Developed in the 1950s from a former sandbank, this long, narrow island offers a fabulous view across the harbor to downtown San Diego, and is home to the landscaped **Shoreline Park**, hotels, restaurants, and marinas. Stop by **Tunaman's Memorial**, dedicated to the tuna fishermen who were once an important part of the area's economy. Every September, the island's YachtFest features mock battles between replicas of historic ships from the Maritime Museum of San Diego.

🚗 *Return along Shelter Island Dr and turn left on Scott St, then right onto Talbot St and follow the 'Scenic Route' signs. Turn left on Catalina Blvd and follow it to enter the Cabrillo National Monument. Park at the visitor center.*

Quintessential "Navy Town"
San Diego has had a unique partnership with the US Navy since 1846, when the Navy seized the city during the American-Mexican War. The city's harbor has been the West Coast's major port for military ships ever since. It hosts the Pacific Fleet – the largest naval fleet in the world– and numerous Navy and naval air station bases. Warships, from aircraft carriers to submarines, are a part of the San Diego Bay skyline.

---

5 Cabrillo National Monument
San Diego County

In June, 1542, Spanish conquistador Juan Rodríguez Cabrillo departed from Navidad, Mexico, to explore the Pacific Coast. On September 28, he anchored his flagship, the *San Salvador*, on Point Loma's east shore and became the first European to set foot on what is now California. The visitor center (*www.nps.gov/*) has superb displays on his expedition, Native American culture, and local ecology; educational films are screened every hour. Outside, the **Cabrillo Statue** offers views over San Diego and the harbor; interpretive signs identify the various warships, helicopters, and warplanes en route to and from their bases. Be sure to visit the **Old Point Loma Lighthouse**, a short walk south. Dating from 1855,

it was decommissioned in 1891 as it was often shrouded by fog. The lighthouse keepers' quarters are furnished as they were in the 1800s.

To the east, the steep Bayside Trail leads to the bay through a rare remnant scrub habitat. Accessible by car along Cabrillo Road, the rocky intertidal area on the west side of the park can be explored from coastal trails.

Twentieth-century military structures are scattered across Cabrillo, and many monuments commemorate World War II battles. The **Army Radio Station** houses exhibits that interpret the coastal defense history. More than 91,000 naval personnel are buried at **Fort Rosecrans National Cemetery** (*open 8am–4:30pm Mon–Fri, 9:30am–5pm Sat & Sun*), where granite headstones on grassy slopes overlook the Pacific Ocean.

🚗 *Return along Catalina Blvd and turn left on Hill St. Turn right on Cordova St (later Sunset Cliffs Blvd) and follow to Ocean Beach. Turn left on Newport Ave and park in the lot by the beach at Abbott St.*

6 Ocean Beach
San Diego County; 92107

This offbeat beachfront locality popular with students and surfers was once known as San Diego's Haight-Ashbury, after San Francisco's famous hippy district. Newport Avenue is lined with tattoo and piercing shops, funky coffee shops, and surf stores. Walk the **Ocean Beach Municipal Pier**, at the south end of the beach, and watch for the "O.B. air force," a large population of feral parrots.

🚗 *Turn right onto Abbott St. Turn right onto W Point Loma Blvd, then left on Sunset Cliffs Blvd. Follow signs for SeaWorld via W Mission Bay Dr.*

Above Restored interiors of the keepers' quarters, Old Point Loma Lighthouse
Below Popular Ocean Beach

EAT AND DRINK

GASLAMP QUARTER

Bare Back Grill *inexpensive*
A fun, casual California grill known for its all-organic menu, including burgers. The New Zealand owners serve beer and wine from "down under".
624 E St, 92101; 619 237 9990; open 11am–midnight Sun–Wed, 11–1am Thu–Sat; www.barebackgrill.com

Blue Point *moderate*
This award-winning oyster bar and seafood restaurant has a health-conscious menu featuring pan-seared scallops, and seared white tuna with plum tomatoes, olive purée, and sautéed spinach. Leave room for crème brûlée or banana cream pie.
565 5th Ave, 92101; 619 233 6623; open 5–10pm Sun–Thu, 5–11pm Fri & Sat; www.bluepointsd.com

LITTLE ITALY

Mona Lisa *moderate*
Run by the Brunetto family since 1956, this restaurant has a genuine Italian deli selling hams, cheeses, olives, and sandwiches to go. Its sit down menu includes all the expected favorites, from pastas to pizzas.
2061 India St, 92101; 619 234 4893; open 11am–9:30pm Mon–Thu, 11am–10:30pm Fri & Sat, noon–9:30pm Sun; www.monalisalittleitaly.com

Above Whale show, SeaWorld **Below right** Nursery in Fiesta de Reyes, Old Town San Diego **Bottom** Botanical Gardens, Balboa Park

VISITING BALBOA PARK

Tourist Information
House of Hospitality *1549 El Prado, 92101; 619 239 0512; open 9:30am–4:30pm daily; www.balboapark.org*

A Stay-for-the-Day Pass *($35 for entry into any 5 museums)* can be picked up at any of the museums.

WHERE TO STAY

OLD TOWN SAN DIEGO

Cosmopolitan Hotel *moderate*
This 10-room B&B has antiques and staff are dressed in period costume. *2660 Calhoun St, 92110; 619 297 1869; www.oldtowncosmopolitan.com*

AROUND OLD TOWN SAN DIEGO

Hillcrest House B&B *moderate*
Five individually themed rooms with luxurious linens, plush robes, and Wi-Fi. *3845 Front St, Hillcrest, 92101; 619 990 2441; www.hillcresthousebandb.com*

⑦ SeaWorld
San Diego County; 92109
Spanning 150 acres (60 ha) of Mission Bay, this marine zoological park *(www.seaworld.com/sandiego)* provides a close-up look at ocean creatures such as otters, penguins, polar bears, sea lions, and sharks. Entertainment includes dolphin, killer whale, and sea lion shows, and an aquatic adventure park. Be sure to take the Bayside Skyride gondola across Misson Bay.

🚗 *Exit by the east gate and turn left onto Sea World Dr. Turn onto Friars Rd; at the railroad crossing, turn left onto Napa St. Turn left onto Linda Vista Rd to Taylor St. Turn left onto Congress St for Old Town San Diego, with free street parking.*

⑧ Old Town San Diego
San Diego County; 92110
This park *(www.parks.ca.gov/)* preserves the original San Diego settlement. Over 20 restored buildings from the 1820s, set around Plaza de las Armas, function as museums, shops, and restaurants, while docents are dressed in period costumes. The visitor center, on the plaza's west side, displays a model of the town in 1872. Look out for the **Wells Fargo History Museum**, with an original stagecoach; and the **Seeley Stables Museum**, displaying horse-drawn wagons and carriages, plus a working blacksmith's shop.

Old Town also includes the Mission-style **Immaculate Conception Church** *(2540 San Diego Ave)* and **Whaley House** *(2482 San Diego Ave)*, which functioned as a courthouse. To the northeast,

Heritage Park *(Julian St & Harley Way)* preserves Victorian buildings relocated here from around San Diego. Walk west along Juan Street and turn right on Mason Street to Jackson Street. Cross the street and walk the trail uphill to **Presidio Park**, which occupies the hilltop site of a fort built in 1769 by Spanish *conquistador* Gaspar de Portolá, and where Father Junipero Serra initiated Mission San Diego de Alcalá, before it was moved to its current location *(see p248)*. Abandoned in 1835, the original buildings fell to ruins. The **Padre Cross**, west of the car park, is made of tiles from the ruins. The **Junipero Serra Museum** *(www.sandiegohistory.org/serra_museum.html)* was built in Mission Revival style in 1929.

🚗 *Exit east along Juan St. At the top of the hill, turn left onto Witherby St, then right onto Sunset Blvd. Turn right at Goldfinch St, then left on W University Ave. Turn right onto Park Blvd for Balboa Park. Park in the lot on Village Pl.*

---

⑨ Balboa Park
San Diego County; 92101
Home to 15 major museums plus performance venues, Balboa Park is the largest urban cultural park in the US. Created in 1868, its landscaped grounds and traffic-free promenades are graced by Spanish Colonial pavilions built for the 1915 Panama-California Exposition. The 100-acre (40-ha) San Diego Zoo houses almost 1,000 animal species in enclosures that resemble their natural habitats.

A three-hour walking tour
Start at the **Natural History Museum** ① *(619 232 3821)*, with superb exhibits that trace the evolution of flora and fauna distinct to Southern California, from the dinosaur-era to the current day. Next, walk south across Plaza de

Balboa to the **Reuben H Fleet Science Center** ② *(619 238 1233)* to be fascinated by interactive science exhibits and an IMAX theater. Now walk west along El Prado to the **House of Hospitality** ③; pick up maps, brochures, and take an audio

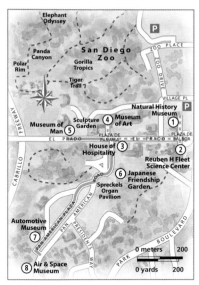

Museum ⑦ *(619 231 2886)* has more than 80 rare, historic autos and motorcycles. Also located at the plaza, the **Air & Space Museum** ⑧ *(619 234 8291)* celebrates aviation history and space exploration with such static exhibits as an actual Apollo 9 Command Module spacecraft, and hands-on exhibits that include a Space Shuttle simulator. Visitors can hop aboard the free tram to Plaza de Panama, from where it is a short walk back to the parking lot.

With so much to see and do, plan on half a day to visit the San Diego Zoo *(2920 Zoo Drive; www.sandiegozoo.org)* if possible. The zoo, 230 yards (200 m) ahead on Zoo Drive, has ample parking space. A map, illustrating 13 separate walks and trails that can be stitched together, is available at the entry. Be sure to visit Elephant Odyssey, Polar Rim, Panda Canyon, Tiger Trail, and Gorilla Tropics.

tour at the visitor center here. Immediately west, cross Plaza de Panama for the **Museum of Art** ④ *(619 232 7931)*, with world-class collections spanning European old masters, Asian art, and contemporary art from throughout the Americas. Walk west 110 yards (100 m) past the Sculpture Garden to the **Museum of Man** ⑤ *(619 239 2001)*. Devoted to anthropology, it has superb exhibits of pre-Columbian cultures as well as on the evolution of man. Return to the plaza and turn right onto Pan American Road to stroll the **Japanese Friendship Garden** ⑥ and admire the Spreckels Organ Pavilion – a performing arts space. Keep right along Pan American Road, which leads to Pan American Plaza, where the not-to-be-missed **Automotive**

Panama-California Expo

Many of Balboa Park's key features are legacies of the 1915 Panama-California Exposition, a World Fair to celebrate the opening of the Panama Canal. It was intended to tout San Diego as a port of call for ships through the canal. The buildings launched the Spanish Colonial Revival-style as California's vernacular architecture. The park's buildings were declared a National Historic Landmark in 1977.

WHERE TO EAT

OLD TOWN SAN DIEGO
La Piñata *moderate*
This Mexican venue claims to be San Diego's oldest restaurant. Try the *carne asada* (roast sirloin with green chili) or *chimichanga* (deep-fried filled burrito). *2836 Juan St, 92110; 619 297 1631; open 11am–9pm Sun–Thu, till 9:30pm Fri & Sat; www.lapinataoldtown.com*

BALBOA PARK
Dinosaur Café *inexpensive*
An airy café in the Natural History Museum, it offers sandwiches, salads, pastries, and gourmet coffees and teas. *1788 El Prado, 92101; 619 255 0317; open 10am–5pm daily*

Albert's *moderate*
Open-air deck dining over a waterfall. Try the roasted chickpea soup with walnut pesto, the slow-roasted pork loin, or the jambalaya gumbo. *2920 Zoo Dr, 92101; 619 685 3200; open 11am–3:30pm daily, 11am–8:30pm daily (summer); www.sandiegozoo.org/zoo/alberts*

Below *Re-creation of a colorful Spanish village, Balboa Park*

DAY TRIP OPTIONS
The area can be divided into day trips that appeal to specific interests.

The way it was
Stitching together visits to the Gaslamp Quarter ❶, the Cabrillo National Monument ❺, and Old Town San Diego ❽ will give history enthusiasts a perspective back through four centuries.

Take N Harbor Dr to Rosecrans St, then Talbot St, and Cabrillo Memorial Dr for

Cabrillo National Monument. Return along Rosecrans St, which leads direct to Old Town San Diego.

If it swings, slithers, or swims...
SeaWorld ❼ and San Diego Zoo in Balboa Park ❾ enthrall all with exhibits of marine and terrestrial creatures from around the globe.

From SeaWorld, take Sea World Dr to Friar Rd, then Napa St to Taylor St. Turn right on Julian St and then take Sunset Blvd to Goldfinch St; turn right. Turn

left on W University Ave, then right onto Park Blvd for Balboa Park.

Museums that wow
For those who enjoy museums, the USS *Midway* Museum and Maritime Museum of San Diego at the Downtown Waterfront ❷, and the various museums of Balboa Park are must-sees.

Follow N Harbor Dr north to W Laurel St. Turn right. Laurel St leads into Balboa Park.

Eat and Drink: inexpensive under $25; moderate $25–50; expensive over $50

Stockton
San Jose
Monterey · Fresno
CALIFORNIA
· Bakersfield
Santa Barbara ·
· San Bernardino
Los Angeles
San Diego

San Diego Backcountry

Mission San Diego de Alcalá to Ramona

Highlights

- **Wonders of the wild**
  Hike the rugged wilderness of Mission Trails Regional Park

- **World-class wine**
  Taste the excellent wines at some of California's lesser-known wineries along Highway 79

- **Starry highs**
  Marvel at the astronomical achievements displayed at the Palomar Observatory Museum

- **Wild safari**
  Hear jungle sounds on a safari at San Diego Zoo Safari Park

The Africa Tram Safari taking visitors on a tour of the San Diego Zoo Safari Park

San Diego Backcountry

This route starts at the oldest Spanish mission in California, set in the mountainous hinterland of San Diego. It then winds through the Volcan Mountain to the quaint resort town of Julian, a former Gold Rush-era settlement, where it is possible to sift for gold and taste locally grown wines. The rural tranquillity reaches a peak at Palomar, the setting for one of the world's most important astronomical observatories. From here, it drops down to verdant plains famous for orchards and the thriving Native American community of Pala. Finally, cut south through Couser Canyon for thrilling wildlife encounters at San Diego Zoo Safari Park, a visit to one of California's most important battle sites, and wine-tasting around Ramona.

Above Indian cemetery, Mission San Antonio de Pala Asistencia, Pala, *see p254*

ACTIVITIES

Spot quail, deer, and rabbits on the Mission Trails Regional Park trail

Learn all about North American gray wolves at the California Wolf Center

Explore the historic gold mines in the hills around Julian, then pan for a lucky strike of gold

Sample and compare the wines at the tasting rooms around Julian and Ramona

Discover the mountain wilderness in Palomar Mountain State Park, with magnificent hikes in pine forest

Go on a wildlife safari and even camp overnight with the animals at San Diego Zoo Safari Park

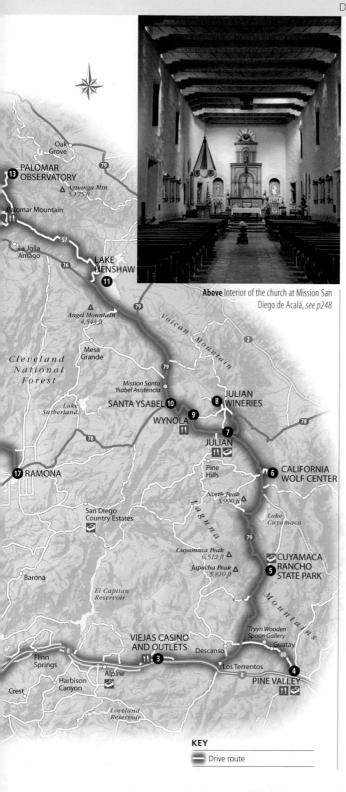

Above Interior of the church at Mission San Diego de Acalá, see p248

PLAN YOUR DRIVE

Start/finish: Mission San Diego de Alcalá to Ramona.

Number of days: 2–3 days.

Distance: 168 miles (276 km).

Road conditions: Roads are well-paved and signposted but the terrain to Julian and the Palomar Observatory is steep, with switchback roads that require caution; these are often snowbound in winter, when snow chains may be mandatory.

When to go: The winter months can be cold in the mountains, while summer months can be extremely hot in the lowlands. Spring and fall are the most comfortable months – wildflowers bloom in spring, while fall is harvest time in the wineries.

Main market days: Wynola: 11am–4pm Sun.

Opening times: Shops tend to open for business 9am–5pm Mon–Sat, some also open on Sun. Museums typically open 10am–5pm and are often closed on Mon.

Shopping: The region is rich in gourmet produce such as grapes, honey, nuts, and local wines. Look out for antiques in Julian and traditional Native American baskets, jewelry, and rugs at Pala.

Major festivals: Julian: Julian Classic Motoring Show, Jul; Palomar Challenge Bike Ride, Jun; Julian Apple Days Festival, Oct.

DAY TRIP OPTIONS

History buffs will find plenty to interest them at the **missions** along the route, while oenophiles can head to one of the **Julian wineries**. **Outdoor enthusiasts** can take to the mountains in **Mission Trails Regional Park**, **Cuyamaca Rancho State Park**, and **Palomar Mountain State Park**. **Animal lovers** will enjoy a visit to the excellent **San Diego Zoo Safari Park**. For full details, see p255.

Right A typical antique store in Guatay, near Pine Valley Far right Displays at the Tryyn Wooden Spoon Gallery, Guatay

VISITING MISSION TRAILS REGIONAL PARK

Tourist Information
Visitor Center *1 Father Junipero Serra Trail, 92119; 619 668 3281; open 9am–5pm daily; www.mtrp.org*

WHERE TO STAY

AROUND VIEJAS CASINO AND OUTLETS

Ayres Inn *moderate*
This mountain lodge is decorated with authentic Western as well as plush leather furnishings. The 99 bedrooms have Queen Anne-style mahogany pieces. It has a heated pool and whirlpool bath.
1251 Tavern Rd, Alpine, 91901; 619 445 5800; www.ayreshotels.com/alpine

PINE VALLEY

Pine Valley Inn *Inexpensive*
A pine-log inn in old Western style adjoining a café. Simple yet cozy rooms with eclectic furnishings are equipped with tiny TVs and kitchenettes, plus free Wi-Fi.
28940 Old Hwy 80, 91692; 619 473 8560; www.pinevalleyinn.com

Below Landscaped grounds of the Mission San Diego de Alcalá

❶ Mission San Diego de Alcalá
San Diego County; 92108

The first Franciscan mission in California, Mission San Diego de Alcalá *(www.missionsandiego.com)* was founded in 1769 and moved to its current location in 1774. It fell into ruins in the 19th century, but has now been restored. This retreat is an oasis of calm amid its modern urban surrounds, within earshot of the crowds at the nearby Qualcomm football stadium. A highlight is the garden, partially shaded by the 42-ft (13-m) tall *campanile* (bell tower) that holds the mission bells. The cloister contains a museum on mission life and is dedicated to Father Luís Jayme, murdered when Native American converts rebelled in 1775 against their coercion. An active parish church, it was named a minor basilica by Pope John Paul II in 1976.

🚗 *Head eastbound on San Diego Mission Rd, turn left at Mission Gorge Rd and continue to Mission Trails Regional Park. Turn left into the Visitor Center, which has parking.*

❷ Mission Trails Regional Park
San Diego County; 92119

This well-developed park protects almost 6,150 acres (2,470 ha) of pristine wilderness on the outskirts of San Diego. Its rugged canyons and mountains are laced with more than 40 miles (64 km) of trails for hikers, bikers, and equestrians. They culminate on top of Cowles Mountain, offering a sensational 360-degree view. The natural stone **Visitor Center** blends in its setting and features impressive interactive exhibits on geology and ecology, as well as local Kumeyaay Native American basketry and pottery. Note the life-size bronze statues of a mountain lion and other creatures in the amphitheater. A 1.5-mile (2.5-km) long interpretive trail loops through chaparral, grassland, and oak woodland, where mule deer, raccoon, and songbirds are easily seen. From the Visitor Center, drive along the one-way Father Junipero Serra Trail, which leads through the heart of the park to the **Old Mission Dam** – a National Historic Landmark and the beginning point for several trails, from easy to challenging. Murray Reservoir, south of Mission Gorge Road, is a lovely setting for a picnic.

🚗 *Exit onto Mission Gorge Rd, which becomes Woodside Ave. Turn right at Maine Ave (Los Coches Rd). Continue to the I-8 freeway (Kumeyaay Hwy), east. After 11.5 miles (18.5 km) take the Willows Rd exit and cross the freeway for the Viejas Indian Reservation, which has free parking.*

Left Part of the Southwestern-style facade of the Viejas Casino and Outlets complex

VISITING VIEJAS CASINO & OUTLETS

Tourist Information
California Welcome Center *5005 Willows Rd Ste 110, Alpine, 91901; 619 445 0180; open 10am–5pm Mon– Sat, 10am–4pm Sun*

EAT AND DRINK

VIEJAS CASINO AND OUTLETS

The Grove Steakhouse *moderate*
This elegant restaurant in the Viejas Casino specializes in steaks but also serves seafood, lamb chops, and occasional specials such as smoked pork with peach chutney glaze, and grilled beer bratwurst with peppers and onions. An impressive wine list.
5000 Willows Rd, Alpine, 91901; 619 445 5400; open 11:30am–4pm & 4:30– 10pm Mon–Fri, 1–10pm Sat, 1–9pm Sun; www.viejas.com

PINE VALLEY

Major's Diner *inexpensive*
A classic 1950s-style diner serving American favorites, such as a biscuits and gravy, chicken nuggets, bacon burgers, plus Julian apple pie and delicious milkshakes.
28870 Old Hwy 80, 91916; 619 473 9969; open 6am–2pm Mon–Wed, 6am–8pm Thu–Sun; www.majorsdiner.com

❸ Viejas Casino and Outlets
San Diego County; 91901

The scenery is simply spectacular as I-8 climbs to over 4,000 ft (1,200 m) amid the undeveloped beauty of the Cleveland Forest, north of the community of Alpine. Located in the heart of a valley full of oak trees and giant boulders, the Viejas Indian Reservation is where the Viejas Band of Kumeyaay Indians operate the El Viejas Casino *(www.viejas.com)* and the VieJas Outlets of more than 60 discount retail stores. Designed in mellow Southwestern style, the complex is centered on a Native American-themed show court with water features; it is a setting for special performances featuring pyrotechnics. The complex also has an ice rink and mini-golf. Pick up maps, brochures, and get information on the region's attractions, hotels, and restaurants at the **California Welcome Center**, on the north side of the show court.

🚗 *Continue east on I-8 to Japatul Valley Rd (SR 79) and turn left. Cross over the freeway and keep straight on SR 79 for, then continue on Old Hwy 80 for Pine Valley.*

❹ Pine Valley
San Diego County; 91962

Historic Route 80 was once a true transcontinental highway, linking San Diego to Savannah, Georgia. The I-8 freeway opened in 1974, stealing the traffic and leaving the communities along old Old Hwy 80 frozen in time. Once such community, the charming hamlet of **Guatay** has dusty antique stores in false-front wooden structures. Drop

> **The Kumeyaay**
> The original inhabitants of San Diego County, the Kumeyaay have lived in this region for more than 10,000 years and met the Spanish when they sailed into San Diego harbor in 1542. In ensuing centuries, they were forced off their ancestral lands. Today, the Kumeyaay are divided into 12 bands on tribal reservations.

in at the **Tryyn Wooden Spoon Gallery** *(27538 Old Hwy 80; 619 473 9030; open 11am–4pm Tue–Sun),* where Brian Chappelow crafts one-of-a-kind kitchenware from precious hardwoods. Three miles (5 km) ahead, the aptly named village of Pine Valley, set amid pines at 3,999 ft (1,219 m), is a great place to stop overnight or for a meal.

🚗 *Return along Old Hwy 80 to the junction with SR 79. Turn right and continue uphill to Cuyamaca Rancho State Park's visitor center.*

Below left Candles at Mission San Diego de Alcalá **Below** *Campanile* with the mission bells at Mission San Diego de Alcalá

Above Visitors riding a pony cart through the streets of Julian

VISITING JULIAN

Tourist Information
Chamber of Commerce *2129 Main St, 92036; 760 765 1857; www.julianca.com*

WHERE TO STAY

CUYAMACA RANCHO STATE PARK

KQ Ranch Resort *inexpensive*
The resort rents trailer cabins, and has place for tents and RVs with hook-ups. There is a heated pool and Jacuzzi.
449 KQ Ranch Rd, 92036; 760 765 2244; www.kqranchresort.com

JULIAN

Eaglenest Bed & Breakfast *moderate*
Four rooms with fireplaces, private hot tubs, and a pool are on offer.
2609 D St, 92036; 760 765 1252; www.eaglenestbnb.com

Julian Gold Rush Hotel *moderate*
A historic landmark with genuine antiques such as a claw-foot bathtub.
2032 Main St, 92036; 760 765 0201; www.julianhotel.com

Orchard Hill Country Inn *expensive*
This lodge offers hand-crafted quilts, antiques, and modern amenities.
2502 Washington St, 92036; 760 765 1700; www.orchardhill.com

⑤ Cuyamaca Rancho State Park
San Diego County; 92036
On the mid-elevation flanks of the Peninsular Range, this pristine world of oak and conifer forest and expansive meadows is punctuated by lakes and sparkling streams. It has campgrounds plus more than 100 miles (160 km) of trails, which reach up to Cuyamaca Peak (6,512 ft/ 1,985 m). The second highest point in San Diego County, it offers breathtaking views over **Lake Cuyamaca** plus the Anza-Borrego Desert State Park *(see p216)* and west toward the Pacific Ocean. The visitor center *(www.parks.ca.gov/)* is set amid pines in an alpine meadow ablaze with wildflowers in spring.

🚗 *Continue north on SR 79 and turn right on KQ Ranch Rd for the California Wolf Center.*

⑥ California Wolf Center
San Diego County; 92036
A truly unique venue, this wildlife education center *(www.california wolfcenter.org)* is one of very few places in the world where packs of wild gray wolves *(Canis lupus)* can be easily seen. The center breeds and studies the free-ranging packs of Alaska gray wolves and endangered Mexican gray wolves – a subspecies once abundant throughout the American Southwest. Various educational tours are offered *(daily, by appointment only)*. Guided tours get visitors up close with a wolf pack, and teach how the center prepares wolves for release to the wild. Note that a reservation is required to visit the center.

🚗 *Continue north on SR 79 to Julian, at the junction with SR 78.*

⑦ Julian
San Diego County; 92036
This mountain town dates back to mining boom days of the 1870s after gold was discovered here in 1869. Many of the original buildings still stand and have been restored as quaint B&Bs, antique stores, restaurants, and gift stores. Apple orchards grow nearby, and people flock for the fall Apple Days festival in October. The town, which occupies a lush meadow between Volcan Mountain and the Cuyamacas, is often snowbound in winter. In any season, it is a delight to walk the streets and soak up the pioneer atmosphere.

A two-hour walking tour
Park on Main Street and stop at the tiny, centenary **Town Hall** ①, which doubles as the town's visitor center. After picking up a map and brochures, turn left onto Washington Street and walk downhill one block to the **Julian Pioneer Museum** ② *(2811 Washington St)*. Nicknamed Julian's Little Attic, this little space is cluttered with sepia-toned photos and other charming mementos of Julian's past, including mining equipment, an original buggy and sleigh, as well as Native American artifacts. Originally a brewery, the building later served as a blacksmith's shop.

Head back to Main Street and turn left. At A Street, turn left for the **Pioneer Cemetery** ③ *(www.juliancemetery.org)*, where long-deceased miners and other pioneers lie beneath weathered graves that date back to the 1870s. Back on Main Street, walk east past the **Levi-Marks Stores** ④ *(2134 Main St)*, the

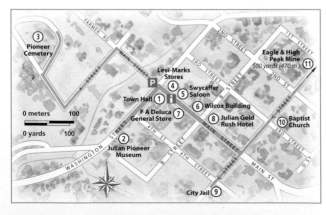

Where to Stay: inexpensive under $100; moderate $100–200; expensive over $200

oldest brick building in town, dating from 1886. Standing next door is the former **Swycaffer Saloon** ⑤, a butcher shop, and the **Wilcox Building** ⑥. The latter was built with hewn beams and served as the former post office and stage coach stop. Across the street, the old **F A Deluca General Store** ⑦ (*2117 Main St*) is now Jack's Market. Cross B Street for the **Julian Gold Rush Hotel** ⑧ (*2032 Main St*), which has functioned as an inn since the 1890s, when it was the Hotel Robinson, owned by an African-American couple, Albert and Margaret Robinson.

Turn right onto C Street and walk one block south to view the two-cell **city jail** ⑨ dating from 1914, on the southeast corner of 4th Street. Return along C Street and continue uphill 220 yards (200 m) past the **Baptist Church** ⑩. At the T-junction on top of the hill, turn right and follow the signs for the

The '69 Gold Rush

In 1869, A. E. "Fred" Coleman, a cattleman and former slave, saw a glint of gold in the bed of Coleman Creek, just west of Julian. Soon, others went seeking the source of the streambed flakes. On February 22, 1870, the first hard rock "lode" was found, leading to San Diego County's first and only gold rush. Hundreds of gold-seekers arrived, giving birth to the town of Julian. The gold was mined out within a decade, but many families stayed and turned to farming.

Eagle & High Peak Mine ⑪ (*760 765 0036*), where it is possible to venture inside an original gold mine on a guided tour. Return to the car.

On Sunday afternoons in summer, the Julian Doves & Desperados (*760 765 1857; 1pm, 2pm & 3pm*) re-enactment group stage historic comedy skits, including shoot-outs on the street.

🚗 *Leave town westbound on Main St and take SR 78. Turn right on Wynola Rd for the Julian Wineries.*

⑧ Julian Wineries
San Diego County
The relatively cool climate of the Volcan Mountain foothills, northwest of Julian, combines with a south-facing, sun-kissed aspect to favor the production of pinot grigio and pinot noir grapes. Vineyards are interspersed with apple orchards that frame several boutique wineries with tasting rooms open to visitors. Look out for the **Blue Door Winery** (*www.thebluedoorwinery.com*) in an orchard and park-like setting. Also worth checking out, **Menghini Winery** (*www.menghiniwinery.com*) hosts live music events plus the Julian Classic Motoring Show, in May, and an annual grape stomp in September.

🚗 *Return to SR 79 and continue north to Wynola; park roadside.*

EAT AND DRINK

JULIAN

Mom's Pie House *inexpensive*
This cozy pine-log restaurant is renowned for its delicious pies and other baked goods. It also serves a soup of the day, flaky crust chicken potpie, and sandwiches.
2119 Main St, 92036; 760 765 2472; open 8am–5pm Mon–Fri, 8am–6pm Sat & Sun; www.momspiesjulian.com

The Julian Grille *moderate*
A cozy cottage with lacy draperies and a warm hearth provides a welcome setting for enjoying hearty omelets, salads, charbroiled burgers, and grilled meats. Leave room for baked Brie with apples and pecans. Dine in the outside patio on sunny days.
2224 Main St, 92036; 760 765 0173; open 11am–9pm Tue–Sun, 11am–4pm Mon

Julian Tea & Cottage Arts *moderate*
Afternoon English tea is served daily in a charming turn-of-the-19th century former home, along with finger sandwiches, plus scones with whipped cream, home-made jam, and dessert.
2124 3rd St, 92036; 760 765 0832; www.juliantea.com; reserve ahead

Above left Julian Pioneer Museum **Below left** Equipment at the Menghini Winery, Julian **Below** Facade of the historic Julian Gold Rush Hotel **Bottom** Cuyamaca Rancho State Park

Eat and Drink: inexpensive under $25; moderate $25–50; expensive over $50

Above Dome of the renowned Palomar Observatory

WHERE TO STAY

AROUND PALOMAR MOUNTAIN STATE PARK

Lazy H Ranch *inexpensive*
Converted from a working ranch, this lodge is set in vast landscaped grounds and has comfy, modestly furnished rooms, plus a pool.
16787 SR 76, Rincon, 92061; 760 742 3669; www.lazyhranchresort.com

Below Indian burial ground at the Mission Santa Ysabel Asistencia, Santa Ysabel
Below right A small lake amid thick forest, Palomar Mountain State Park

⑨ Wynola
San Diego County; 92036
This small hamlet, 3 miles (5 km) west of Julian, packs a punch in terms of places of interest to visit. A cluster of wine-tasting rooms stands roadside, tempting passersby to stop and sample local wines. If traveling with a designated driver, consider stopping at the **Country Cellars** *(www.countrycellars.com)* or **Orfila Winery** *(760 765 0102; open 10am–5pm Fri–Tue)*. Both are in the **Wynola Farms Marketplace** *(www.wynolafarms.com)*, a collection of intriguing shops that range from the Julian Apple Company to Kozy Korner Quilts. If keen to sample some traditional apple cider, make sure to visit the **Julian Hard Cider** *(www.julianhardcider.biz)*. Nearby, the **Wynola Junction** mall *(www.wynolajunction.com)*, in a historic fruit-packing shed, hosts more than 30 antique dealers. Stop to

pan for gold at **Julian Mining** *(www.julianminingcompany.com)*.
🚗 *Continue west on SR 79 as it slopes downhill to Santa Ysabel.*

⑩ Santa Ysabel
San Diego County; 92070
This easily overlooked, tiny T-junction hamlet is set in an expansive meadow surrounded by mountains. Turn right at the junction, where the smell of cinnamon and fresh-baked pies draws all and sundry to call at the **Julian Pie Company** *(www.julianpie.com)* for a slice of apple pie.
Continue on SR 79 (1.5 miles/2 km) to **Mission Santa Ysabel Asistencia**, a beautiful chapel built in 1924 on the site of a Spanish *asistencia* – a sub-mission of Mission San Diego de Alcalá, founded on September 20, 1818. Nothing is left of the original adobe, but the current site includes a small historical museum *(9am–4:45pm daily)*.
🚗 *Continue along SR 79 to SR 76 and turn left. Take the E Grade Rd (SR 7) and turn right for Lake Henshaw.*

⑪ Lake Henshaw
San Diego County
This large lake is surrounded by wide, open meadows and a pine-clad mountain. The reservoir was created in 1923 when the San Luis Rey River was dammed to provide water storage for northern San Diego County. A large fish population draws anglers to cast for crappie, catfish, and bass. After being flooded, the valley also became an

increasingly attractive hunting ground for raptors, which feed on fish and the waterfowl and wildlife drawn to the lake. Stop at the hillside viewpoint, which has interpretive signs and an incredible view over the lake and valley.

🚗 *Continue climbing into the Palomar Mountain on SR 7, being cautious on the switchback bends. Turn left onto State Park Rd for Palomar Mountain State Park, which has parking.*

⑫ Palomar Mountain State Park

San Diego County; 92060

This long, winding road rewards drivers with fabulous views down the mountain, and a pristine forested wilderness waiting to be explored. Palomar Mountain State Park *(www.parks.ca.gov/)* offers a pleasantly cool escape from the lowland heat for hikers who make their way through forests of Douglas fir, black oak, and incense cedar at an average elevation of 5,000 ft (1,524 m). The trails lead to seasonal camps used by Luiseños Native Americans, who called the mountain *Wavamai* till the Spaniards changed the name to Palomar or "Place of Pigeons" ; well-worn bedrock mortars can be seen. Mule deer, chipmunk, squirrel, gray fox, and coyote are frequently seen during hikes, and hikers need to be alert for mountain lions. It is possible to fish for trout in Doane pond (with a license), and Doane Valley Campground – one of two in

the park – accommodates RVs and trailer campervans.

🚗 *Return along State Park Rd and turn left on Canfield Rd (County Hwy S6), which becomes S Grade Rd and leads uphill to the Palomar Observatory parking lot.*

⑬ Palomar Observatory

San Diego County; 92060

Operated by the California Institute of Technology, this astronomical observatory *(www.astro.caltech.edu/palomar)* outside Palomar Mountain State Park stands at an elevation of 6,100 ft (1,859 m) on the summit of the namesake mountain. The huge white dome containing the five telescopes currently in use was completed in 1948. Visitors can view the mammoth computer-controlled 16.7-ft (5.1-m) Hale Telescope – the latest, largest, and most sophisticated of the observatory's telescopes – from a glass-enclosed terrace, which has historical exhibits. The telescope was the world's largest from 1948 to 1993 and has attained many remarkable firsts, including the discovery of quasars and the first direct evidence of stars in distant galaxies. The astronomical discoveries made here are described in a separate museum building.

🚗 *Return down Canfield Rd to the junction with SR 7. Turn right onto Palomar Mountain Rd (SR 6) – drive with extreme caution on the steep inclines and switchback bends. The road merges into SR 76 and continues west to Pala (14 miles/22.5 km).*

Above Grounds of the Mission Santa Ysabel Asistencia, Santa Ysabel **Below left** At the Palomar Observatory

---

WHERE TO EAT

WYNOLA

Jeremy's on the Hill *moderate*
Chef Jeremy Manley uses fresh organically grown produce at this California bistro, serving such fusion dishes as pan-seared Colorado lamb with smoked Cheddar polenta, sautéed spinach and crispy onion. Live piano music Fri & Sat.
4357 Julian Rd, 92036; 760 765 1587; open 11am–8pm Sun–Thu, 11am–9pm Fri & Sat; www.jeremysonthehill.com

PALOMAR MOUNTAIN STATE PARK

Mother's Kitchen & Restaurant *inexpensive*
This homey restaurant at the gateway to both Palomar Mountain State Park and the observatory serves soups, salads, and home-made chili, lasagne, and baked goodies.
Junction of SR 6 & SR 7, 92060; 760 742 4233; open 11am–4pm Mon–Fri, 8:30am–5pm Sat & Sun; www.motherskitchenpalomar.com

Right Fertile fields along the drive to Valley Center, south of Pala **Below far right** Lorikeet at San Diego Zoo Safari Park **Below right** Plaque at San Pasqual Battlefield

VISITING RAMONA

Tourist Information
Ramona Valley Vineyard Association
www.ramonavalleyvineyards.org

WHERE TO STAY

PALA

Pala Casino Spa Resort *moderate*
A mega-resort hotel with 507 rooms, it combines contemporary styling with state-of-the-art amenities. The resort has a pool and spa, and a major entertainment center.
35008 Pala Temecula Rd, 92059; 1 877 725 2766; www.palacasino.com

AROUND RAMONA

Riviera Oaks Resort *moderate*
A good family option, this hotel has one- and two-bedroom villas surrounded by landscaped grounds and rock-strewn mountains. Facilities include two swimming pools, a racquet court, spa, plus bicycles and horseback riding.
25382 Pappas Rd, San Diego County Estates, 92065; 760 788 7711; www.rivieraoaks.net

Below Mission San Antonio de Pala Assistencia, Pala

⑭ Pala
San Diego County; 92059
This small community is the heart of the Pala Indian Reservation, a sovereign nation of the federally recognized Pala Native America tribe. Once poor, and dispossessed in the 19th century of their traditional land farther east, the Pala now operate the **Pala Casino Resort and Spa** *(www.palacasino.com)*, one of the largest casinos and resort hotels in Southern California. On the east side of town, **Mission San Antonio de Pala Asistencia** was founded in 1816 as an *asistencia* or sub-mission to Mission San Luis Rey de Francia. It is unique among the Franciscan missions in California for having a freestanding bell tower. Step inside to admire the chapel interior decorated with wall paintings by Native American neophytes.

Pala was known for its mineral resources, especially pink tourmaline, which is still mined here. Reserve a tour and pan for tourmaline at the **Oceanview Mine** *(760 489 1566; www.digforgems.com)*. The town is also a good place to stop for an overnight stay or for a meal.
🚗 *Depart Pala westbound on SR 76.*

Turn left on Couser Canyon Rd to Lilac Rd; turn right. Keep left at the T-junction with W Lilac Rd and continue to Valley Center Rd (SR 6); turn right. Continue straight to Bear Valley Parkway; turn left and continue to San Pasqual Valley Rd. Turn left for San Diego Zoo Safari Park, which has ample parking.

⑮ San Diego Zoo Safari Park
San Diego County; 92027
A must-visit for anyone touring San Diego County, this park *(www. sdzsafaripark.org)* hosts more than 3,000 animals of over 400 species. These are housed in natural environments representing several distinct habitats in an area spanning 1,800 acres (730 ha). Massive rhino, antelope, ostrich, and herd of elephants, Cape buffalo, and giraffe are among the creatures that roam open-range enclosures. Visitors can also see Western lowland gorillas, Sumatran tigers, and Przewalski's horses – the last truly wild horse. Choose from a range of safari options, including a Behind-the-Scenes Safari on an electric cart, and the opportunity of touring by Segway. Do not miss

the Frequent Flyers live show featuring real birds in flight, and stop by the Veterinary Medical Clinic, where it is possible to watch animals being treated.

🚫 *Exit the park and continue east on SR 78 to San Pasqual Battlefield State Historic Park, with free parking.*

Above Rose garden in front of the Guy B. Woodward Museum, Ramona

16 San Pasqual Battlefield State Historic Park

San Diego County; 92027
Set on a hillside, the San Pasqual Battlefield State Historic Park *(www. parks.ca.gov/)* honors US soldiers and *Californios* (the Mexican inhabitants of California prior to the US takeover) who fought a battle here on December 6, 1846, during the Mexican-American War, when US forces tried to seize California and Mexican forces fought to defend it. Although it was the bloodiest battle in the conflict, neither side was victorious. Short trails offer a sweeping view of the San Pasqual Valley, and the visitor center displays excellent historic artifacts. Living history programs are offered by volunteers in period costume *(open Oct–Jun: first Sun every month).*

🚗 *Continue east on San Pasqual Valley Rd 10 miles (16 km) to Ramona.*

17 Ramona

San Diego County; 92065
The historic town of Ramona is located in the Santa Maria Valley, an AVA (American Viticulture Area) with several wineries and wine-tasting rooms open to visit. In town, call in at the award-winning

Pamo Valley Winery *(www. pamovalleywinery.com)* to taste its fine syrah, cabernet sauvignon, and merlots. Venture along the convoluted lanes outside town to visit boutique wineries west of town, such as **Eagles Nest Winery** *(www.eaglesnestwinery.com)* and, nearby, **Woof 'n Rose Winery** *(www.woofnrose.com).*

Among Ramona's many antique stores is the **Guy B. Woodward Museum** *(open 1–4pm Thu–Sun, by appointment Mon–Wed; www. woodwardmuseum.org)*, with dusty historic artifacts of early Western culture including a large collection of women's clothing, displayed in an early adobe structure – the Verlaque House – as well as a blacksmith's shop and 19th-century doctor's office.

WHERE TO EAT

PALA
Sushi Sake *moderate*
A Japanese restaurant with a sushi bar, it serves delicious sushi, sashimi, teriyaki, and other traditional Japanese dishes.
11154 SR 76, 92059; 1 877 946 7252; open 5–11pm Mon–Thu, 11–2am Fri & Sat, 11am–11pm Sun; www.palacasino.com

---

DAY TRIP OPTIONS

This drive can be broken into three day trip options that appeal to a range of interests.

A bit of everything

Visit the church of Mission San Diego de Alcalá ❶, before heading to the rugged canyons of Mission Trails Regional Park ❷ for some bird-watching. Then continue to Cuyamaca Rancho State Park ❺ to enjoy a picnic in its alpine meadows.

From Mission San Diego, take San Diego Mission Rd east; turn left at

Mission Gorge Rd for Mission Trails Regional Park.

Wine, history, and fresh air

A visit to one of the excellent Julian Wineries ❽ is a good idea if traveling with a designated driver. Next retrace the steps of the Spanish padres at the historic Mission Santa Ysabel Asistencia, in Santa Ysabel ❿. Then hike amid the thick pine forests of Palomar Mountain State Park ⓬ – remember to carry a picnic basket.

From Julian follow SR 78 west to Santa

Ysabel, then SR 79 north for Mission Santa Ysabel Asistencia. Turn west onto SR 76 then right onto SR 7 (E Grade Rd) to reach Palomar.

In the jungle, the mighty jungle...

Consider spending a day meeting the animals at San Diego Zoo Safari Park ⓯, which can be explored by cart, safari trucks, and Segways.

San Diego Zoo Safari Park is most easily accessed off I-15 at Escondido: take the San Pacqual Valley Hwy (SR 78) east to the park.

Eat and Drink: inexpensive under $25; moderate $25–50; expensive over $50

General Index

Page numbers in **bold** refer to main entries

Acknowledgments

Dorling Kindersley would like to thank the many people whose help and assistance contributed to the preparation of this book.

Contributors
Christopher P. Baker – the Lowell Thomas Award 2008 'Travel Journalist of the Year' – has authored more than 20 guidebooks, including DK's *Eyewitness Top 10* guides to Cuba, Puerto Rico, and California's Wine Country.

Lee Foster is a veteran, award-winning travel writer/photographer who delights in covering California from his base in Berkeley. His travel journalism has won eight Lowell Thomas Awards over the years.

Fact checker
Lisa Cope

Proofreader
Aruna Ghose

Indexer
Helen Peters

Cartography
Cartographic Production
John Plumer, JP Map Graphics

Source Data
Base mapping derived from US Geological Survey, National Geospatial Program

Design and Editorial
Publisher Vivien Antwi

List Manager Christine Stroyan

Senior Managing Art Editor Mabel Chan

Senior Cartographic Editor Casper Morris, Stuart James

Project Art Editor Shahid Mahmood

Senior Editors Michelle Crane, Georgina Palffy

Editor Vicki Allen

Picture Researcher Ellen Root

Senior DTP Designer Jason Little

Special Assistance
Christopher P. Baker, Andres F. Puma, Dr. Vanessa R. Sheldon, Robert D. Ecker, Lisa Cope, Carolyn Patten, Robert Cooper

Photography
Christopher P. Baker, Lee Foster, Robert Holmes

Additional Photography
Dave King; Neil Lukas; Peter Peevers; Neil Setchfield; Tony Souter; Chris Stowers

Photography Permissions
The Ahwahnee, Yosemite Valley; Alderbrook Manor; Boonville's Mercantile Stores; Cyrus in Healdsburg; Empire Mine State Historic Park; Ferndale Museum Di volorio resseque; Grandma's House Restaurant; Historic Knight Foundry; Indian Grinding Rock State Historic Park; Keepers Quarters, Old Point Loma Lighthouse; Laws Railroad Museum and Historic Village; Mission San Diego de Acala; Menghini Winery; Murphy's Historic Hotel; Murphy's Gold Country; Railtown 1897 State Historic Park; Sutter's Mill, Marshall Gold Discovery State Historic Park; Scripps Institute of Oceanography; Tryyn Spoon Gallery.

Works of art have been reproduced with the kind permission of the following copyright holders:

Rock Balancing Act © Bill Dan 34c; *Saint Francis* © Beniamino Benvenuto Bufano/ Robert Mondavi Winery 57tr; *Three Ages of Woman* © John Fisher 76c; *Andy's Auto Supply* wall mural © Kenna Allen 117tc; *Temperance* wall mural © Vicki Andersen 137br; *Claude Chana monument* © with kind permission of The Management, Auburn City 157tr; *Hospital Rock red drawings* © NPS Photo 177tr; *Old Guest House Museum* wall mural; © T.Scott Sayre 195tl; *Oasis of Mara* wall mural © Michael Collins 205tl; *Spirit of the Desert* wall mural © Cory Ench 207 tl; *San Bernardino Police Department* wall mural © Christine Curry Coates 223tl; *The Cardiff Kook Sculpture* © www.the cardiffkook.org 231b.

Picture Credits
The publisher would like to thank the following for their kind permission to reproduce their photographs:

Key: a-above; b-below/bottom; c-centre; f-far; l-left; r-right; t-top

akg-images: historic-maps 26–7. **Alamy Images**: Ambient Images Inc 226–7; Anthony Dunn 84–5; Eagle Visions Photography / Craig Lovell 110–11; Ei Katsumata - FLP 94–5; Dennis Frates 52–3; JTB Media Creation, Inc. 236–7; Robert Harding Picture Library Ltd / Michael DeFreitas 142–3; Witold Skrypczak 102–103, 154–5; William Symington 122–3. **Amtrak**: 11bl. **Courtesy California State Parks**, 2011: 147br. **Corbis**: Kevin Burke 218–19, Ted Streshinsky 9br, Rudy Sulgan 2–3. **Getty Images**: Lonely Planet Images / Stephen Saks 152–3. **Greyhound Lines, Inc.**: 10tr. **Masterfile**: F. Lukasseck 162–3. **San Diego Zoo Global**: Ken Bohn 244–5. **San Francisco Travel Association**: Alain McLaughlin 10bl, 10br.

Cover Picture Credits
Front Cover: **4Corners**: SIME / Giovanni Simeone; Back: **Lee Foster**: Lee Foster cr; **Robert Holmes Photography**: Robert Holmes cl, c; Spine: **4Corners**: SIME / Giovanni Simeone t

All other images © Dorling Kindersley

For further information see: www.dkimages.com

Road Signs

REGULATORY SIGNS

No left turn

No right turn

No U-turn

Compulsory stop

Slow down

No parking

Do not enter

Wrong way

Two way left turn

Bus carpool lane ahead

Three tracks

Divided highway

Do not block intersection

Do not pass

Emergency parking only

Left only

Keep right

Left turn yield on green

No turn on red

No parking any time

One way

No turns

Slower traffic keep right

Speed limit

Do not stop on tracks

Right lane must turn right

Two turn

Yield to uphill traffic

Bike lane

Two way traffic ahead